Festa Paschalia

Festa Paschalia

A History of the
Holy Week Liturgy in the Roman Rite

Philip J. Goddard

Gracewing

First published in 2011

Gracewing
2 Southern Avenue
Leominster
Herefordshire HR6 0QF

ISBN 978 0 85244 764 2

Typeset by Action Publishing Technology Ltd,
Gloucester GL1 5SR

For Daphne
Coniugi optimae

CONTENTS

Scriptural quotations are from the *Jerusalem Bible*, London, Darton, Longman and Todd, 1974.

English text of Philo of Alexandria, the *Epistula Apostolorum*, the *Didascalia*, Melito of Sardis (*Peri tou Pascha*), Hippolytus (*Apostolic Tradition*), Dionysius of Alexandria (*Letter to Basilides*), Tertullian (*On Prayer, On Fasting* and *On Baptism*), Eusebius (*Ecclesiastical History*), *The Gospel of the Hebrews*, Athanasius (*First Festal Letter*), Constantine (*Letter to the Churches*) and Canon 1 of the Council of Arles are taken from R. Cantalamessa, *Easter in the Early Church*, trans. by J. M. Quigley, SJ (Collegeville, MN: Liturgical Press, 1993).

ABBREVIATIONS

CC	*Corpus Christianorum*
CUP	Cambridge University Press
DAER	*De Antiquis Ecclesiae Ritibus* Liber IV (E. Martène, Antwerp, 1737)
Eph. Lit.	*Ephemerides Liturgicae*
HBS	Henry Bradshaw Society
HE	*Historia Ecclesiae*
HS	*Hebdomada Sancta* (H. A. P. Schmidt, Rome: Herder, 1956–7)
MC	*Mystagogical Catecheses* of St Cyril of Jerusalem
MRR	*The Mass of the Roman Rite* (J. A. Jungmann, Dublin: Four Courts Press, 1955)
OEL	*Ordo Ecclesiae Lateranensis*
OHS	*Ordo Hebdomadae Sanctae Instauratus* (A. Bugnini and C. Braga, in *Ephemerides Liturgicae* LXX, 1956)
OR	*Ordo Romanus*
ORM	*Ordines Romani du Haut Moyen Age* (M. Andrieu, Louvain, 1948–61)
OUP	Oxford University Press
PE	*Peregrinatio Egeriae*
PG	*Patrologia Graeca*
PL	*Patrologia Latina*
PRG	Romano-German Pontifical
PRM	'Le Pontifical Romain du Moyen Age' (M. Andrieu, *Studi e Testi*, 86–89, (Vatican, 1938–41)

SC   *Sacrosanctum Concilium de Sacra Liturgia*, Second Vatican Council (English translation: London: Catholic Truth Society, 1967)

SCR   Sacra Congregatio Rituum (Sacred Congregation of Rites)

CHAPTER 1

THE EARLY CENTURIES

The Annual Celebration of the Pasch

In the Gospels according to Matthew, Mark and Luke, which together form what we know as the Synoptic Gospels, Christ is arrested in the Garden of Gethsemane on the fifteenth day of the Jewish month of Nisan, after eating, together with his disciples, the Passover meal, the annual supper commemorating the liberation of the Jews under the leadership of Moses from their servitude to the Egyptians. Brought successively before the Jewish High Priest Caiphas and the Roman governor Pontius Pilate, he is condemned to death and crucified on the following afternoon. In the Gospel according to John, the arrest takes place on the fourteenth day of Nisan, and he is crucified at the time of the slaughter of the lambs which are to be cooked and eaten at the Passover.[1]

The question as to which of these chronologies is historically correct has occupied much scholarly time and attention. The majority view is that the Synoptic Gospels follow the historic chronology while John follows a theological one, emphasizing the analogy between the slaughter of the Passover lambs and the sacrifice of Christ, the Paschal Lamb of the New Testament, putting an end to the sacrifices of the Old Law and at the same time inaugurating the single redemptive sacrifice of the New. It is impossible to settle the historical question one way or the other. The difference, however, was to give rise to a serious and long-running dispute over the correct time to celebrate the Pasch in the early church.

The significance of the name 'Passover' ('Pesach' in Hebrew,

'Pascha' in Greek and Latin) is found in Exodus 12:24–7 where Moses, addressing the people of Israel, says to them, 'You must keep these rules as an ordinance for all time for you and your children. When you enter the land that Yahweh is giving you, as he promised, you must keep to this ritual. And when your children ask you, "What does this ritual mean?" you will tell them, "It is the sacrifice of the Passover in honour of Yahweh who passed over the houses of the sons of Israel in Egypt, and struck Egypt but spared our houses"'.[2] Later generations of Jews were to attach secondary significances to the word, namely the crossing of the Red Sea and the liberation of the soul from slavery to its passions to the freedom of life in God. Thus Philo, a member of the Jewish community in Alexandria during the first half of the first century AD, says, 'After the new moon comes the fourth feast, called the Crossing-Feast, which the Hebrews in their native tongue call Pascha', and 'This is the real meaning of the Pascha of the soul: the crossing over from every passion and all the realm of sense … to the realm of mind and of God'.[3] These secondary meanings were adopted by the early Christian community, who saw in the Old Testament Passover an image both of the passage of Christ from death to life in his Resurrection, and of the liberation of man from slavery to sin to new life in Christ, and they coupled these interpretations with the figure of Christ as the paschal lamb, sacrificed for our sins, which features so prominently in St John's Gospel. A mere twenty years or so after the Death and Resurrection of Christ, St Paul is telling his readers in Corinth that 'Christ our Passover has been sacrificed; let us celebrate the feast, then, by getting rid of all the old yeast of evil and wickedness, having only the unleavened bread of sincerity and truth' (1 Cor. 5:7–8).

There is no certain reference in the New Testament to any annual commemoration of the Passion, Death and Resurrection of Christ, and this is understandable given that the first Christians were anticipating his return and the establishment of his Kingdom at an early date. The disciples naturally followed the command to 'Do this in memory of me' by celebrating the Eucharist, particularly on the first day of the week, the Lord's Day. In the same letter to the Corinthians, written some time between the years 55 and 57, St Paul tells them that every time they celebrate the Eucharist they proclaim the death of the Lord

(1 Cor. 11:26). The first day of the week was chosen as the day for the Eucharist because it was the day on which Christ, by rising from the dead, had inaugurated the new era, as against the Jewish Sabbath, the day on which God had, by completing the work of creation, inaugurated the old, though it is extremely probable that the earliest Christians, as devout and observant Jews, continued to observe the Sabbath as well (cf. Acts 3:1).[4] The selection of Sunday as the day for the Eucharistic assembly seems, from the same letter of St Paul (1 Cor. 16:2), as well as from the Acts of the Apostles (20:7), to have been made no later than twenty years or so after the Resurrection, and indeed the weekly Eucharist may well have been celebrated on Sunday from the very beginning.[5] By the time the Book of Revelation came to be written, towards the end of the first century, 'the Lord's Day' had become a normal expression for Sunday among Christians.[6] So on every Sunday of every week without interruption, down to the present day, the Church has proclaimed the Passion, Death and Resurrection of the Lord. It is difficult to find any other events in history that are so well attested.

Paul's language in 1 Corinthians (coupled with the fact that, as we learn from 16:8, the letter was sent at about the time of Passover) has led some authorities to believe that it was written specifically in connection with an annual celebration of the Christian Pasch in Corinth at the time. This is possible but perhaps it stretches the evidence too far.[7] What it does demonstrate, however, is that the Passover and the sacrificial death of Christ were associated with one another from the very beginning. As God saved his people from slavery to the Egyptians by the crossing of the Red Sea, so he has saved them from sin and death by the sacrifice of his only Son.

Some scholars, notably M. H. Shepherd and F. L. Cross, have seen in individual books of the New Testament a reflection of the Easter Vigil liturgy of the first century. Shepherd also saw in the reference in Mark's Gospel (9:15) to fasting in the absence of the Bridegroom, and in the time sequence of his Passion narrative (13:35 and 15:25–33), an indication of a Paschal celebration in mid-first-century Rome consisting in a fast followed by an all-night vigil and an all-day watch.[8] The views of these authors have not, however, found general favour. But the fact that the date of Easter was fixed by reference to the Jewish lunar calendar and not by reference to the Roman solar one indicates that its observation began, in the eastern part of the Roman Empire at least, during the brief period when Jewish Christians predominated numerically over Gentile ones, and certainly, therefore, well before the end of the first century.

At whatever date the annual Paschal celebration began, it seems to have consisted in a fast followed by an all-night vigil. The first secure evidence that we have for an annual commemoration is the so-called *Epistula Apostolorum*. This apocryphal document, which purports to be a letter from the eleven apostles to the Christian churches, belongs to the second century, though at precisely what point in that century it came to be written is uncertain. It seems to have been composed in either Syria or Egypt. In it we read that Christ is supposed to have said,

> After I have gone to the Father you are to remember my death. Now when the Pascha comes, then one of you will be thrown into prison for my name's sake, and he will be in grief and anxiety that you celebrate Pascha while he is in prison ... he will grieve that he does not celebrate the Pascha with you. Thereupon I will send ... the angel Gabriel, and the gates of the prison will open, and he will come out and come to you; he will spend a night of watching with you and stay with you until the cock crows. But when you have completed the memorial that is for me, and my Agape, he will again be thrown into prison ...

This is not, of course, any sort of evidence for what Christ actually said or commanded, but it is good evidence that in the East during the second century there was an annual celebration of the Pasch consisting in an all-night vigil concluding at dawn with the Eucharist. There is, however, no indication on what day of the week this celebration took place, and whether it was fixed or variable.

Further evidence as to the nature of the celebration comes from the *Didascalia Apostolorum*, a church order written in Syria in the first few decades of the third century. In Chapter 5 we read,

> make a beginning when your brethren who are of the People [i.e. the Jews] keep the Pascha ... Therefore you shall fast in the days of the Pascha from the tenth, which is the second day of the week, and you shall sustain yourselves with bread and salt and water only, at

the ninth hour, until the fifth day of the week. But on the Friday and on the Sabbath fast wholly and taste nothing. You shall come together and watch and keep vigil all the night with prayers and intercessions, and with reading of the Prophets, and with the gospel and with psalms, with fear and trembling and with earnest supplication, until the third hour in the night after the Sabbath, and then break your fasts ... Especially incumbent on you therefore is the fast of the Friday and of the Sabbath; and likewise the vigil and watching of the Sabbath, and the reading of the Scriptures, and psalms, and prayer and intercession for them that have sinned, and the expectation and hope of the resurrection of our Lord Jesus, until the third hour in the night after the Sabbath. And then offer your oblations; and thereafter eat and make good cheer, and rejoice and be glad, because that the earnest of our resurrection, Christ, is risen ... Wherever, then, the fourteenth of the Pascha falls, so keep it; for neither the month nor the day squares with the same season every year, but is variable.

A number of important conclusions can be drawn from this passage. First, the Christian Pasch is celebrated at the same time as the Jewish Passover, though this can only have been approximate since the Jewish feast does not fall on the same day of the week every year, whereas the Christian Easter is always celebrated on the first day of the week. Secondly, the fast, in Syria at least, has been extended to last from Monday of the week before Easter until Saturday; the concept of a full week of commemoration is already beginning to take shape. Thirdly, there is a total fast lasting two days, from Friday (equivalent to the fourteenth day of Nisan) to Saturday (the fifteenth day); the Johannine chronology, according to which Christ died on the Day of Preparation, is followed. Fourthly, the nature of the vigil on the night of Saturday-Sunday is described in some detail; it consists of prayers, readings and psalms, and ends at around 3 a.m. on Sunday morning, with the celebration of the Eucharist ('then offer your oblations').

In some places at least the vigil included not only prayers, readings and psalms but also a sermon, and at least one of these, by Melito, Bishop of Sardis in western Asia Minor, has survived. This sermon was probably delivered between about 160 and 170 (though this date has been challenged).[9] What is clear from the text of this sermon is that the vigil was a celebration of the whole mystery of redemption, including the Incarnation, the Passion, Crucifixion and Resurrection. There is no notion of celebrating these as separate events; the whole character of Melito's address is eschatological rather than strictly historical. The sermon begins, 'The Scripture from the Hebrew Exodus has been read and the words of the mystery have been plainly stated, how the sheep is sacrificed, how the people is saved, and how Pharaoh is scourged through the mystery'. Evidently therefore one of the readings was the description of the Passover from Exodus 12, a passage which has remained a feature of the vigil readings in diverse liturgies throughout the two succeeding millennia.

So far our evidence for an annual commemoration of the Christian Pasch has come from the East. Around the year 200 it is also attested for Africa, in the treatise 'On Prayer' by Tertullian where, at the end of a passage in which he discusses the kiss of peace, he adds, 'on Good Friday [*die Paschae*] when the fasting is a general and, as it were, a public religious observation, we rightly omit the kiss of peace'. And in his 'On Fasting', written after he had converted to Montanism, he says, 'They [i.e. his orthodox opponents] think that the gospel prescribes for fasting the days during which the Bridegroom is taken away, and that these are the only legitimate days of Christian fasting' (cf. Matt. 9:15). Further on in the same treatise he tells us that he and his fellow Montanists never fast on a Saturday 'except at Easter'.

That attendance at the Easter Vigil was universal, even quasi-obligatory on Christians, appears from another work of Tertullian, 'To his Wife', in which he advises Christian women not to marry pagans, since a pagan husband is likely to take exception to her attending an all-night vigil.[10] At the time of Tertullian, therefore, around the beginning of the third century, the observance of Easter in Africa paralleled that in the East, namely a general fast for two days, Friday and Saturday, followed by an all-night vigil on Saturday-Sunday, and this observance was, if not strictly obligatory under pain of sin, at least something which no Christian would ever, without good reason, consider omitting.

There is no documentary evidence for the date at which the Christian Pasch began to be celebrated as an annual feast at Rome itself. The earliest evidence that we have is contained in a passage from the *Ecclesiastical History* of Eusebius (written between 303 and 323) concerning a dispute which flared up around the year

195 between Pope Victor and the bishops of Asia Minor concerning the correct date on which to celebrate Easter. The latter, who followed the Johannine chronology of the Passion, were accustomed to celebrate it on the fourteenth day of Nisan, which they held to be the day of the Crucifixion, regardless of the day of the week on which this fell. From this custom they became known as 'Quartodecimans', from the Latin word for fourteen. In other parts of the East, notably in Alexandria, and universally in the West, it was celebrated on a Sunday, the day of the Resurrection, regardless of the calendar date of the Sunday in question (though different churches had different ways of determining the right Sunday). Various synods and episcopal conferences had resolved that Sunday was the only proper day on which to celebrate the Resurrection, but the Asian bishops refused to fall into line with their colleagues in the rest of the Christian world, pleading the antiquity and authority of their own custom. Eventually Pope Victor lost patience and excommunicated them. At this point a number of other bishops, who felt that Victor had acted too hastily, intervened, in particular Irenaeus, then Bishop of Lyons. He wrote a letter to Victor, quoted by Eusebius, in which he pleaded with him for restraint. In the course of that letter he mentioned the visit of St Polycarp, Bishop of Smyrna, to Rome in the time of Pope Anicetus some thirty or forty years earlier. Anicetus had tried to persuade Polycarp to change the Asian custom, but Polycarp had declined, on the grounds that the custom went back to the time of St John, whom Polycarp had known as a young man. They had accordingly agreed to differ. At that time, Irenaeus says, the differences on this question between Rome and Asia Minor were greater than they were at the present time, yet even so there had been no recriminations, 'while the whole Church, both observants and non-observants, remained at peace'.

It is not clear exactly what is meant by 'observants and non-observants', or exactly why the difference between Rome and Asia Minor should have been greater in the time of Anicetus and Polycarp than it was at the time of Victor. Some authorities have concluded that at the earlier time there was no annual celebration of Easter at Rome at all, and that such a celebration began at some point during the period between Popes Anicetus and Victor. The difference between celebrating the Pasch and not celebrating it is clearly greater than any difference as to the date on which such a celebration should fall.[11] Others regard it as unlikely that Rome should have taken so long to follow a custom that had become virtually universal everywhere else, in addition to which Eusebius also tells us that the reason for Polycarp's visit to Rome was 'some controversy about the day for the Pascha'.[12] If this is right then 'observants' and 'non-observants' will mean those who observe the fourteenth Nisan as the correct date and those who do not, respectively. In this case we cannot tell to what Irenaeus was referring when he says that the difference between Rome and Asia at the time of Anicetus and Polycarp was greater than in his own day. In the absence of further evidence there is no way in which this problem can be satisfactorily resolved.

At any rate, for Hippolytus of Rome, writing about the year 215, the Paschal fast was of such importance that if for some good reason it could not be kept at the proper time, it should be kept immediately after the fifty days of Easter were over: 'if a person was at sea or in some necessity and did not know the day, when he will have found it out, let him make up the fast after the Pentecost'.[13]

It was popularly believed that the second coming of Christ would occur at the time of the Paschal Vigil. In the apocryphal *Gospel of the Hebrews*, dating from the first half of the second century, we read 'wise men are of the opinion that the day of judgement will come in the time of the Pascha, inasmuch as Christ rose on that day so that the saints in turn might rise on it'.[14] The tradition is also mentioned by Lactantius and St Jerome in the fourth century; the latter warns against dismissing the faithful before midnight on the grounds that only once this hour is past can one be certain that the parousia will not occur on that very night.[15]

The Extension of the Paschal Fast

The length of the fast seems to have varied, though, as the passage from the *Didascalia* quoted above shows, there was a tendency to extend what seems to have been the original two-day fast. St Irenaeus, in his letter to Pope Victor concerning the dispute between the latter and the bishops of Asia Minor, says 'some think it necessary to fast one day, others two, others even more days; and others measure their day as lasting forty hours, day and night. And such variation in the observance did not begin in our time but much earlier, in our forefathers' time'. The rather curious reference to a day 'lasting forty hours, day and night' appears to relate to the interval between the Crucifixion, which began about midday on Good Friday, to the Resurrection, understood as having occurred at about dawn on Sunday.

Variations in the length of the fast evidently persisted, as we learn from a letter from Dionysius, Bishop of Alexandria, written about the year 250.[16] His correspondent, Basilides, Bishop of the Pentapolis, had asked his advice on how to deal with these variations. Dionysius advises prudence: 'you ask me to set an exact limit and a definite hour, which is both difficult and risky ... one ought to start the feast and the gladness after the time of our Lord's resurrection, up till then humbling our souls with fastings'. This creates a problem however, as the Evangelists do not tell us at what hour Christ arose. Dionysius thinks that those who break their fast before midnight deserve censure, and those who persevere until 'the fourth watch' (between about 3 and 6 a.m.) deserve praise. Those who end the fast between these times should not be blamed, especially since not everyone will have started the fast at the same time; some will have remained without food until cockcrow on each of the six preceding days, others on two, three or four of those days, and others on none of them. Someone who has fasted on only Friday and Saturday and then claims credit for continuing his fast until dawn on Sunday should not be compared with someone who began his fast earlier. At Alexandria, therefore, the obligatory two-day fast could be extended for up to six days, evidently at the choice of the individual.

It is apparent from the letter of Irenaeus to Pope Victor, from the *Didascalia Apostolorum*, and from the letter of Dionysius of Alexandria to Basilides, all written between about 195 and 250, that there was a growing tendency, both in the East and in the West, to extend the original two-day fast ('the days during which the Bridegroom is taken away') backwards in time. This tendency is rationalized in the *Didascalia* (chapter 21), which propounds a curious chronology of the Passion at variance with that of the Gospels.[17] On Monday Judas agrees to betray Christ. The Passover supper takes place on Tuesday evening. Christ is brought before Caiphas on Wednesday and before Pilate on Thursday, with the Crucifixion taking place, as in the Gospels, on Friday. The purpose of this odd chronology is evidently to harmonize the events of the Passion with the six-day fast which was practised in Syria at the time the *Didascalia* was written. There is, of course, no historical justification for this chronology, and it does not seem to have had much currency outside Syria. But Hippolytus of Rome, in section 36 of his *Apostolic Tradition*, links specific hours of the day to specific events of the Passion.[18] Christ is condemned at cockcrow and crucified at the third hour. The darkness over the whole earth takes place at the sixth hour. At the ninth hour his side is pierced with the lance and he descends into hell. Hippolytus also calls the period from cockcrow to the sixth hour (approximately noon) the first day of the Passion, that from the sixth to the ninth hour the first night, the period from the ninth hour to sunset the second day of the Passion, and that from sunset to cockcrow (when the Resurrection takes place) the second night. In both of these works (the *Didascalia* and the *Apostolic Tradition*) we can already see around the year 200 the tendencies which were to lead eventually to the observance of the whole of the week preceding Easter as a week of particular holiness and significance.

Wednesdays and Fridays of every week seem to have been fast days from a very early time, since the *Didache*, probably written before the end of the first century, urges the faithful to fast on these days, on the grounds that Mondays and Thursdays were the days on which 'the hypocrites' (whoever these may have been) were accustomed to fast. Although the Eucharist was not celebrated on either Wednesday or Friday, the twice-weekly fast was accompanied by a service of psalms, readings and intercessions, known as a *Synaxis Didactica*. The readings culminated in a Gospel passage, and according to the earliest surviving Roman evangeliary, the Gospel texts for the Wednesday and Friday of the week before Easter comprised the passion narratives according to St Luke and St John respectively.[19] The evangeliary in question dates only from the seventh century but, as we shall see later, there is good reason to believe that these passion narratives were read from at least the early part of the fourth century. By the time the so-called *Apostolic Constitutions* came to be composed in Syria in the second half of the fourth century, the Wednesday fast was being linked to the betrayal of Christ by Judas, and the Friday fast to his crucifixion. These events would, of course, have been remembered with particular poignancy in the week in which they actually took place, and the Wednesday and Friday of this week ('Spy Wednesday' and 'Good Friday' as we have come to know them) would therefore have acquired a particular significance.

The propensity to rationalize existing practices can be seen once again in the letter of Pope Innocent I (402–417) to Bishop Decentius of Gubbio, where he explains that the absence of any liturgical celebration on the Friday and Saturday before Easter is 'no doubt' due to the fast which the apostles observed on those days, owing to their grief and their fear of the Jews. No such fast is mentioned in any of the canonical Gospels, but Innocent invokes one to provide an explanation of current practice.[20]

Baptism and the Vigil

In his letter to the Colossians (Col. 2:12), written between the years 61 and 63, St Paul links the death and resurrection of Christ with the sacrament of baptism, the conferring of which was to become intimately associated with the Easter Vigil, 'You have been buried with him, when you were baptised; and by baptism, too, you have been raised up with him through your belief in the power of God who raised him from the dead'. And in his first letter to the Corinthians (1 Cor. 10:1–5), written as we have seen some six or seven years earlier, he links baptism with the passage of the Red Sea, regarded then as now as an Old Testament type of Christ's Death and Resurrection as well as of the passage of the Christian from the death of sin to life in Christ. We do not, however, know exactly when the Paschal Vigil became recognized as the occasion par excellence for the administration of the sacrament. The *Didache* (section 7), whose date is much disputed but which may have been composed towards the end of the first century, contains a brief baptismal rite, and St Justin in his *Apologia* (I. 61), written in Rome in the middle of the second century, includes a somewhat longer rite for baptism, but neither of these is linked in any way with the Easter Vigil, though in Justin's case baptism is followed immediately by participation in the Eucharist, which became a standard practice for those baptized at the Vigil. The *Didascalia Apostolorum*, from Syria in the early third century, gives us, as we have seen, a fairly detailed account of the vigil but it does not mention baptism as something which takes place on that occasion, though in a later chapter it prescribes rules for the administration of the sacrament. However Tertullian in Africa, writing at about the same time as the *Didascalia*, states unequivocally in his treatise *On Baptism* that

> The Pascha affords a more [than usually] solemn day for baptism since the passion of the Lord, in which we are baptised, was accomplished [then] … After this, the Pentecost is an extremely happy period for conferring baptisms, because the Lord's resurrection was celebrated among the disciples and the grace of the Holy Spirit was inaugurated and the hope in the Lord's coming indicated … For that matter, every day is the Lord's [Day]; every hour and every day is suitable for baptism.

So the most appropriate time for baptism, in Tertullian's view, is at Easter itself, followed by any time within the fifty days following but, failing that, the sacrament may be administered on any day of the year.

From references in the same author's *De Corona* (III.1–3) and *De Baptismo* (VII–VIII and XX) we can piece together an outline of the baptismal rite of the African Church in Tertullian's time. Those desiring baptism must prepare for it by frequent prayer, fasting and watching, and they must confess the sins which they have committed in their past life. Before entering the water, they must, in the presence of the bishop, formally renounce the devil, his works and his angels. They are then immersed three times in the water, on emerging from which they receive a drink of milk and honey mixed. After being anointed with the oil of chrism, they are confirmed by the laying on of hands and the invocation of the Holy Spirit.

In Chapters 16 to 23 of his *Apostolic Tradition*, written about 215 AD, Hippolytus of Rome describes not only the rite for the administration of baptism in that city, similar to that described by Tertullian but in much greater detail, but also the preparation which the candidates (referred to here for the first time as 'catechumens') had to undergo before they could receive the sacrament, as well as giving an account of the first Mass and Communion which followed.[21] First, the catechumens are questioned as to their motives in wanting baptism. Then they are told that if they follow certain specified occupations they must give them up since they are not compatible with the Christian faith. Those who survive these preliminaries must then undergo instruction for a period of three years; they are told that if, during this time, they are put to death for the sake of the faith to which they aspire, they will have received baptism of blood. The catechumenate involves the practice of good works as well as the receipt of instruction and is accompanied by daily exorcisms. Finally, the catechumens attend a ceremony in which they formally receive the Gospel, after which they must fast on the Friday and Saturday, and receive a final exorcism, in which the bishop breathes on their faces and makes the sign of the cross on their ears and nose. He then bids them rise and keep watch throughout the night, while they listen to readings and are given further instructions. Baptism takes place at cockcrow; any children are baptized first, then the men and finally the women. Those who are to be baptized take off their clothes and the women unbind their hair and remove any jewellery which they might be wearing.[22] Each catechumen as he or she comes forward is required to formally renounce Satan, and is then anointed with 'the oil of exorcism' and baptized.

The baptismal formula is tripartite; the catechumen is first asked, 'Do you believe in God the Father Almighty?' and replies 'I do believe', following which he or she is immersed in a font of running water. There follow two further questions:

> Do you believe in Jesus Christ, the Son of God, who was born of the Holy Spirit and the Virgin Mary, crucified in the time of Pontius Pilate, died, rose again on the third day from the dead, ascended into heaven, is seated at the right hand of the Father, and will come again to judge the living and the dead? [and] Do you believe in the Holy Spirit, in the Holy Church, and in the resurrection of the body?

After each of these questions, and the reply 'I do believe', the catechumen is immersed again in the water of the font. Finally he or she is anointed with 'the oil of thanksgiving'.

When all the catechumens have been baptized, the bishop says a prayer over them, asking that those who have been found worthy of receiving baptism should be made worthy also of receiving the Holy Spirit, and then proceeds to confirm them individually, by laying hands on them, invoking the Holy Spirit, anointing them and signing them on the forehead. Baptism can be performed either by the bishop or by a priest, assisted by a deacon, but confirmation is given only by the bishop. After all the catechumens have been baptized and confirmed, they give each other the kiss of peace, and then take part for the first time in the celebration of the Eucharist. Communion is given to them in both kinds, and at the same time each receives a drink of water and of milk and honey mixed together, the water signifying purification, and the milk and honey the promised land.

Although the baptismal rite described in such detail by Hippolytus is clearly intended to take place at a vigil, he does not specifically mention the Paschal Vigil in this context. The rite could in theory take place at any vigil. However, in his contemporary *Commentary on Daniel* (I. 16), Hippolytus, like Tertullian, expresses the view that Easter is the most opportune time for baptism. There can therefore be little doubt that the rite which he describes was in use in Rome at the Easter Vigil from at least the beginning of the third century, and probably for some time before that. Presumably while the catechumens are being baptized and confirmed the remainder of the Christian community are taking part in the vigil of prayers, psalms and readings in a different, though not too far distant place, since the newly baptized evidently join them for the celebration of the Easter Eucharist, at which they make their first communion. Whether there were other vigils during the year, at some or any of which baptisms could take place, is a question which cannot be positively decided on present evidence, but the fact that Hippolytus does not specifically link the rite to the Paschal Vigil suggests that there may well have been.

So close did the association between baptism and Easter become in the West that as late as the end of the sixth century we find the Council of Macon (585) forbidding Christians to have their children baptized outside Easter, except in the case of serious illness or approaching death (Canon 3), and the Synod of Auxerre (c.578) forbidding it altogether at any other time, except for the dying (Canon 18).[23]

The administration of baptism in a place detached from but adjacent to the place where the vigil was being observed is confirmed by the discovery at Dura-Europus in Mesopotamia of a house, three rooms of which had been converted, around the year 240, into a small church and a separate baptistery. The latter incorporated a rectangular font let into the floor, covered by a canopy, and with contemporary frescoes of scenes from the Old and New Testaments, including the Good Shepherd and the Women at the Sepulchre.[24] Constantine, after issuing his edict of toleration, erected the Lateran baptistery outside his basilica of St John, which survives to this day, with its magnificent (though somewhat later) mosaics and octagonal font. He also built a separate baptistery in the complex of ecclesiastical buildings which he erected in Jerusalem over the site of the Crucifixion and Resurrection.[25] Slightly later, from the middle of the fourth century, is the baptistery at Nocera, and from the middle of the fifth century the two baptisteries at Ravenna, one Arian and the other Catholic. Later, as the numbers of baptisms increased enormously, baptism by immersion gave way to baptism by affusion and the baptism of adults dwindled to vanishing point. Most baptisms took place outside Easter and the separate baptistery was replaced almost everywhere by a font in the nave of the church.[26] But in Italy (and occasionally elsewhere, for example at Poitiers) the custom of erecting separate baptisteries continued well into the Middle Ages. There are especially splendid surviving examples at Cremona (1167), Parma (1196–1270), Pisa (1153–1278) and Florence (1290).

Lent

The tendency to extend the pre-Paschal fast brings us to the question of the origin of Lent.[27] The Lenten fast appears to originate in the final period of preparation by the catechumens for their baptism at the Paschal Vigil, an exercise in which zealous individuals among the already baptized came increasingly to participate.[28] The earliest direct evidence for a Lenten fast incumbent on all comes from Alexandria. It was the custom for the patriarch there to issue an annual letter to the faithful (known as the festal letter), in the course of which he announced the date on which Easter would be celebrated that year. In the first of his festal letters, written in the year 329, the Patriarch Athanasius says,

> We shall begin the holy fast on the fifth of Pharmuthi and immediately join to it those six holy and magnificent days which symbolise the creation of this world. We shall terminate the fast on the tenth

of the same month, on the Holy Sabbath of the week, and the Holy
Sunday will dawn on us on the eleventh of the month.

In 329, therefore, there is at Alexandria a six-day fast beginning on
Monday and ending on Saturday. However, in his second festal
letter the following year Athanasius announces the date for the
commencement of a fast beginning on 9 March, with Easter falling
on 19 April. The total duration of this fast is therefore forty days,
plus the traditional two days immediately before Easter, though
because Saturdays (except the final Saturday) and Sundays were
excluded, there were just thirty-one days of actual fasting.

This is the first reference to a fast of forty days as a specific
preparation for Easter. However, Origen mentions a forty-day
fast, not tied to any particular period during the year.[29] A fast of
this length therefore appears to have existed in Egypt in the first
half of the third century. A forty-day fast in expiation of the sin of
apostasy under persecution is also enjoined in a canon of the
Patriarch Peter of Alexandria in 305, but this too is not linked in
any way to Easter.[30] In a letter to Serapion, Bishop of Thmuis,
written from Rome in 340, Athanasius berates the people of Egypt
for their slackness in observing the Lenten fast, which he says is
dutifully observed everywhere else.[31] Ten years is not long
enough, in the circumstances of the ancient world, for a custom
which had begun in Alexandria to be adopted by all the churches.
Either Athanasius is exaggerating for rhetorical effect, or a forty-
day fast, designed specifically as a preparation for Easter, began
elsewhere at some date in the first quarter of the fourth century,
and was adopted at Alexandria in 330, and generally by 340.

It is uncertain when Rome adopted this practice, and whether
Lent at Rome originally lasted forty days or was for a shorter
period. Socrates of Constantinople, in his *Ecclesiastical History*,
written around the year 440, tells us that in Rome there was in his
day a continuous fast lasting three weeks before Easter, with the
exception of Saturdays and Sundays.[32] He is wrong in both particulars. Unlike eastern Christians, the Romans always fasted on
Saturdays in Lent, and both St Jerome, in his letter to Marcella of
384, and Pope Siricius, in his to Himerius of 385, mention a forty-
day fast in Rome at that time.[33] It is possible however that Lent at
Rome began earlier in the fourth century as a three-week fast
which was later extended to six weeks. We would then have to

assume that Athanasius' statement concerning the universality of the forty-day fast in 340 is an exaggeration. This may seem unlikely, seeing that Athanasius was in Rome at the time. However, the fact that what is now the fifth Sunday in Lent (or Passion Sunday, as it later came to be known) was for a long time referred to by the curious name of 'Dominica in mediana' ('the Sunday in the middle') may suggest that Lent in Rome originally began either on what is now the fourth Sunday, or perhaps on the Friday before, which would give a three-week Lent, ending on Holy Thursday, plus the two ancient fast days on Friday and Saturday of Holy Week.[34] If so, it would account for Socrates' curious mistake, which is otherwise inexplicable.

At this time it appears that the non-eucharistic synaxes on Wednesdays and Fridays were the only services held on weekdays in Rome. This was still the case outside Holy Week in the mid-sixth century, when the Lectionary of St Victor of Capua, dating to 545/6, has readings only for the Wednesdays and Fridays of Lent down to Palm Sunday.[35] Mondays seem to have been the first days to have been added, since the Tract *Domine non secundum* is found in the old Roman liturgy[36] on the Mondays, Wednesdays and Fridays of each week in Lent. Saturdays and Tuesdays followed, with Thursdays being added last of all, by Gregory II in the early eighth century.[37]

In the old Roman liturgy the Mass formulae actually fall into two distinct 'halves'. Down to the Wednesday before the fourth Sunday in Lent most of the Gospel readings are taken from St Matthew. The main exceptions are the Thursday Masses but, as we have seen, there were no Masses on the Thursdays of Lent before the eighth century, so the Gospels for these days are intrusive.[38] The theme of the Masses in this part of Lent also concentrates heavily on fasting and repentance. However, beginning with the following Friday (the day on which Lent at Rome may have originally begun), down to the Passion on Good Friday, the Gospels are taken from St John. The only exceptions are the Thursday Gospels, for the reason previously given, and those of Tuesday and Wednesday in Holy Week. Tuesday is not a genuine exception, since in the oldest Roman evangeliaries the Gospel for this day is likewise from St John, the Passion according to St Mark having been substituted for it at a later date. The Passion according to St Luke on the other hand appears always to have been read on the Wednesday of Holy Week, since it formed the Gospel reading at the *Synaxis Didactica* held on that day, and it must predate the selection of the readings on the other days. The Friday before the fourth Sunday is also the day on which the theme of the Lenten Masses broadens. Though fasting is not forgotten (especially in the Collects), the cleansing waters of baptism now also figure in the liturgy.[39]

Whether or not it was preceded by a three-week Lent, the six-week Lent at Rome originally commenced not on Ash Wednesday but on the following Sunday.[40] St Leo the Great (440–461) calls this day the *initium* and the *caput* of Lent.[41] The old Roman liturgy also bears witness to this. The Secret prayer from the Mass of that day begins 'With solemn rite we offer sacrifice at the opening of Lent...' (*Sacrificium quadragesimalis initii solemniter immolamus ...*), the Gospel is taken from St Matthew's account of Christ's forty-day fast in the desert, and Psalm 90 is sung in full as the Tract for the day, an indication of the great antiquity of the Mass formula for this day. Since, however, there was no fasting on Sundays, the actual fast days during the six-week Lent totalled only thirty-six. This was still the position at the end of the sixth century, as we learn from St Gregory himself.[42] But a further four days, starting from the present Ash Wednesday, were later added to bring the total up to forty. This change must have occurred during the seventh century, since in the Old Gelasian Sacramentary, the only surviving manuscript of which dates from about 740, Lent begins on Ash Wednesday, as it has done ever since in the West.[43]

The Date of Easter

The Quartodecimans of Asia Minor celebrated the Pasch on the fourteenth of the Jewish month of Nisan (the first month of the year), the day on which they believed the Crucifixion had taken place, according to the Johannine chronology which they followed. Thus the *Didascalia Apostolorum* lays down that, 'Wherever, then, the fourteenth of the Pascha falls, so keep it; for neither the month nor the day squares with the same season every year, but is variable'. The Jewish calendar, however, was a lunar one and its year was accordingly shorter than that of the solar Julian calendar which prevailed in the rest of the Roman empire. It was necessary to insert an extracalendary month from time to time to bring the two calendars into line. The time for inserting this extracalendary month was determined by the Rabbinical authorities, at least prior to the destruction of the Jerusalem temple in 70 AD; after this it seems to have been regulated according to a nineteen-year cycle, with an extra month added approximately every three years. The Quartodecimans were accordingly dependent on the Jewish authorities for the date on which they celebrated the annual Pasch. This was seen as an unsatisfactory state of affairs in any case, but as time went by the vagaries of the lunar calendar could sometimes mean that the fourteenth Nisan fell before the vernal equinox, the earliest date on which most Christians thought it proper to celebrate Easter, and occasionally there were even two such dates in the same solar year. Thus in Constantine's letter to the churches, written after the conclusion of the Council of Nicaea in 325, we read

> it was decided by common accord that it would be well for everyone everywhere to celebrate on the same day ... it seemed unsuitable that we should celebrate that holy festival according to the custom of the Jews ... they celebrate the Pascha twice in the same year. Why should we follow them, when it is acknowledged that they are afflicted with frightful error?[44]

To the natural disinclination among Christians to celebrate the feast twice in the same year there was evidently added by this time a strong streak of anti-Judaism.

In the Asian version of the Julian calendar, the fourteenth day of the first month in spring was the equivalent of our 6 April. The Montanist sect, which originated in Asia Minor in the second half of the second century, adopted this day as a fixed date for the observation of the Paschal festival, in order to avoid the difficulties involved in following the Jewish lunar calendar, and the Quartodecimans may at some stage have done so as well. Other groups of eastern Christians, however, celebrated the Pasch on the day of the Resurrection rather than that of the Crucifixion, but they differed as to the day in question. The church at Antioch, and other groups such as the Audians of the fourth century, clung to the lunar calendar, observing the Pasch on the Sunday following the fourteenth Nisan. Yet others who followed the solar calendar regarded 25 March rather than 6 April as the date of the Crucifixion, and celebrated Easter on the following Sunday.[45]

The majority of the churches in both East and West celebrated the Pasch on the Lord's Day, the day of the Resurrection. Anatolius, Bishop of Laodicea in Syria, in his treatise *De ratione paschali*, written about the year 270, observes that

> all the bishops of Asia up to the present, who have accepted without question the rule by irreproachable authority, namely of John, who leant on our Lord's bosom (cf. John 13:23) and who was no doubt the imbiber of spiritual teachings, celebrated the Pasch without question every year whenever it was luna 14 and when the lamb was sacrificed among the Jews, once the equinox was over, not assenting to the authority of certain men, that is of Peter and Paul, and their successors, who taught all the churches in which they sowed the spiritual seeds of the Gospel, that the feast of our Lord's resurrection could only be celebrated on Sunday.[46]

But even among the churches which celebrated the Pasch on Sunday there was considerable variation as to the proper Sunday on which to do so. The church at Antioch, for example, was one of those which simply celebrated it on the Sunday following the Jewish Passover, a custom open to the difficulties that its calculation depended on the Jewish authorities and that it could occur before the vernal equinox. Anatolius agreed with those who believed that it was wrong to celebrate the Pasch before the equinox, commenting

> in this concordance of the sun and the moon, the Pasch is not to be offered up, because as long as they are discovered in this combination, the power of darkness is not overcome, and as long as equality between light and dark prevails and is not diminished by the light, it is shown that Pasch is not to be offered. And therefore it is enjoined that the Pasch be offered after the vernal equinox.[47]

The churches in Alexandria and Rome, as distinct from Antioch, observed the Pasch on the Sunday following the first full moon after the equinox, regardless of when the Jewish Passover fell, but even here, notwithstanding the agreement in principle, the day could vary owing to the use of different systems of calculation: Alexandria used a nineteen-year cycle (the cycle favoured by Anatolius), but Rome followed an eighty-four-year cycle, and the Alexandrians regarded the equinox as falling on 22 March, the

Romans on 25 March. Canon 1 of the First Council of Arles, held in 314, expressed the desire that the Pasch should be celebrated 'on the same day and at the same season everywhere in the whole world' and requested Pope Silvester to notify all the bishops of the world of their decision, and the Council of Nicaea determined to put an end to the variant practices obtaining in some parts of the East.[48] It was easier however to issue decrees than to achieve actual harmonization among the various churches. According to St Ambrose, Easter in the year 377 was celebrated in Gaul on 21 March, in Italy on 18 April and in Alexandria on 25 April.[49] Harmonization throughout the West was not finally achieved until the ninth century, and between West and East it has not been achieved to this day.

The Triduum

There is no question in these early centuries of separating the various historical events of Holy Week into their disparate historical parts and celebrating them individually on different days. The Pasch was a unitary celebration of all the events by means of which our redemption was procured. Its emphasis was eschatological and not, or at least not primarily, historical.

The word 'Triduum' is first found in the Gospels of St Matthew and St Mark, in connection with the false evidence given against Christ, in his trial before Caiphas, that he had undertaken to destroy the temple and rebuild it within three days.[50] The witnesses were clearly referring to the incident recorded in the Gospel of St John (2:18–22), where, in response to a request for a sign, Christ replies 'Destroy this sanctuary, and in three days I will raise it up', prophesying, John tells us, his own death and resurrection.

The first instance of the use of the word in the post-apostolic period appears to be in a letter written in 386 by St Ambrose, in which he refers to 'the sacred triduum ... in the course of which He suffered, was buried and rose again'.[51] The triduum in question is evidently one beginning in the afternoon of Good Friday and ending in the early morning of Easter Sunday. St Augustine uses the term a few years later in exactly the same sense in his letter to Januarius where he refers to 'the most holy triduum of Him who was crucified, buried and raised again'.[52]

When the notion of three separate feasts, one celebrating the institution of the Eucharist, one the Passion and one the Resurrection emerged at a later date, the term 'Triduum' shifted its meaning slightly to the three days from Holy Thursday to Holy Saturday inclusive.[53] Eventually, in the period of liturgical reform following the Second Vatican Council, the Triduum was formally defined as the period commencing with the evening Mass of Maundy Thursday and ending with Vespers of Easter Day.[54]

Notes

[1]   The Jewish day extended from dusk to dusk. The 14th day of Nisan (the day of Preparation) therefore began on Wednesday evening in the Synoptic chronology and on Thursday evening in the Johannine. The 15th day of Nisan (the day of Passover) began on Thursday evening in the Synoptic chronology and on Friday evening in the Johannine. Confusingly, however, some authors, more familiar with either the Greek system, in which the day begins at dawn, or the Roman, in which it begins at midnight, use 14 and 15 Nisan to refer to the whole of Thursday and Friday (or Friday and Saturday), respectively.

[2]   Scriptural quotations are from the *Jerusalem Bible* (London: Darton, Longman and Todd, 1974).

[3]   English text of Philo of Alexandria, the *Epistula Apostolorum*, the *Didascalia*, Melito of Sardis (*Peri tou Pascha*), Hippolytus (*Apostolic Tradition*), Dionysius of Alexandria (*Letter to Basilides*), Tertullian (*On Prayer*, *On Fasting* and *On Baptism*), Eusebius (*Ecclesiastical History*), *The Gospel of the Hebrews*, Athanasius (*First Festal Letter*), Constantine (*Letter to the Churches*) and Canon 1 of the Council of Arles are taken from R. Cantalamessa, *Easter in the Early Church* (Collegeville, Minnesota: Liturgical Press, 1993).

[4]   For continued observance of the Sabbath by the first Christians see T. J. Talley, *The Origins of the Liturgical Year* (New York: Pueblo Books, 1986), pp. 14–15 and M. H. Shepherd, *The Paschal Liturgy and the Apocalypse* (London: Lutterworth, 1960), p. 31.

[5]   Observance of Sunday as the Lord's Day in apostolic times: see contribution by Richard Swinburne in *The Resurrection* (OUP, 1997), pp. 207–12.

[6]   Rev. 1:10.

[7]   The evidence from 1 Cor. for a supposed annual feast is discussed *in extenso* by K. Gerlach, *The Antenicene Pascha* (Leuven: Peeters, 1998), pp. 32–7.

[8]   M. H. Shepherd, op. cit. pp. 34–5; F. L. Cross, *1 Peter: a Paschal Liturgy* (London: Mowbray, 1954).

[9]   For the date see S. G. Hall, *Melito of Sardis: on Pascha and Fragments* (OUP, 1979), pp. xi–xxii, and A. Stewart-Sykes, *The Lamb's High Feast* (Leiden: Brill, 1998), pp. 1–2. Gerlach, (op. cit., p. 73) believes in a later date for Melito, though he gives no reasons for his view.

10 Tertullian's advice not to marry a pagan: 'To his Wife' 2,4,2. For the evidence from Tertullian see A. A. McArthur, *The Evolution of the Christian Year* (London: SCM Press, 1953), pp. 90–91.
11 Martimort believes that there was no annual celebration of the Pasch at Rome until the second half of the second century, though he does not state any reason for this conclusion (A. G. Martimort, *The Church at Prayer; An Introduction to the Liturgy* (Collegeville, Minnesota: Liturgical Press, 1987), Vol. IV, p. 33). Cantalamessa on the other hand believes that there was (op. cit., Introduction, pp. 10–11).
12 Eusebius' statement that Polycarp visited Rome in connection with the controversy regarding the date of the Pasch is in his *Ecclesiastical History* 4, 14, 1.
13 Cantalamessa, op. cit., 44.
14 Cantalamessa, op. cit., 13.
15 Lactantius, *Divine Institutes* 7, 19, 3; Jerome, *Commentary on the Gospel of Matthew*, 4. Texts in Cantalamessa, op. cit., nos. 103 and 113.
16 Migne, *Patrologia Graeca* 10, 1275. See McArthur, op. cit., pp. 93–4.
17 Chronology of the Passion in *Didascalia*, chapter 21: see Gerlach, op. cit., pp. 215–16, McArthur, op. cit., pp. 92–3.
18 Hippolytus' chronology of the Passion: see J. G. Davies, *Holy Week: a Short History* (Richmond, VA: John Knox Press, 1963), pp. 21–2.
19 Earliest Roman evangeliary: *Evangeliorum Capitulare Romanum* A, of about 650 (Würzburg: Universitätsbibliothek, Mp. th. f.62). H. A. P Schmidt, *Hebdomada Sancta* (Rome: Herder, 1956–7), pp. 458–9.
20 Letter of Innocent I to Decentius of Gubbio: 'Nam utique constat, Apostolos biduo isto in moerore fuisse, et propter metum Iudaeorum se occuluisse. Quod utique non dubium est, in tantum eos ieiunasse biduo memorato, ut traditio Ecclesiae habeat, isto biduo sacramenta penitus non celebrari' (*PL* 20, 555–556).
21 There is an English translation of Hippolytus' *Apostolic Tradition* paragraphs 16 to 23 in L. Deiss, *Early Sources of the Liturgy* (London: G. Chapman, 1967), pp. 50–63. See also McArthur, op. cit., pp. 87–8.
22 Nudity was commonplace in the public baths and the baptismal candidates would not have been embarrassed by it. However in Syria (*Didascalia Apostolorum*, chapter 16) the male and female candidates were segregated, and it is possible that this obtained in Rome at the time of Hippolytus also, though he does not say so.
23 Council of Macon: CC (Concilia Gallicana) CXLVIII, vol. A, p. 240; Synod of Auxerre: ibid., p. 267.
24 The *Excavations at Dura-Europos*, (New Haven: Dura-Europos Publications, 1967), Final Report VIII, part II.
25 The baptistery is mentioned in the so-called 'Itinerary of the Bordeaux Pilgrim'. The Latin text of this work can be found in *Itineraria Romana* Vol. I (ed. O. Cuntz, Teubner, 1929), pp. 86–102. The relevant portions of the work are translated in J. Wilkinson, *Egeria's Travels*, 3rd ed., (Warminster: Aris and Phillips, 1999), pp. 22–34, (reference to the baptistery, p. 31). Cf. also Cyril of Jerusalem, *Mystagogical Catecheses* I.2.

26 In the early centuries baptism by affusion, though regarded as valid, was administered only in emergency (Eusebius, *Ecclesiastical History* 6.43).

27 The origins of Lent are treated extensively in Talley, op. cit., pp. 164–203. See also McArthur, op. cit., pp. 115–39.

28 'Lent in the form we know does not originate as an historical commemoration of our Lord's fast in the wilderness or even as a preparation for Holy Week and Easter, but as a private initiative of the devout laity in taking it upon themselves to share the solemn preparation of the catechumens for the sacraments of baptism and confirmation. It was the fact that these were normally conferred at the paschal vigil which in the end made of Lent a preparation for Easter.' (Dom Gregory Dix, *The Shape of the Liturgy* (London: A. & C. Black, 1945), p. 356. Cf. also R. Greenacre and J. Haselock, *The Sacrament of Easter* (Gracewing, 1995), pp. 8–9.

29 Origen, Tenth Homily on Leviticus (X.2): Talley, op. cit., p. 192.

30 Peter of Alexandria's canons: Talley, op. cit., p. 190–1.

31 Letter of Athanasius to Serapion of Thmuis: *PG* 26, 1412: Talley, op. cit., p. 170.

32 Socrates: 'οι μεν γαρ 'εν Ρωμη τρεις προ του Πασχα 'εβδομαδας πλην Σαββατου και Κυριακης συνημμενας νηστευουσιν (*Historia Ecclesiastica* V.22).

33 Jerome, Ep. XLI.3; Siricius ad Himerium Episcopum (*PL* 13, 1134): Talley, op. cit., p. 166.

34 Talley, op. cit., p. 167.

35 Lectionary of St Victor of Capua: H. Thurston, *Lent and Holy Week* (London: Longmans Green, 1904), p. 153, Schmidt, HS, pp. 470–1.

36 By 'the old Roman liturgy' I mean the Romano-Gallican liturgy in general use in the West down to 1969, after which it was replaced by the new Roman liturgy of Paul VI. Many of the archaic features which had survived in the old Roman liturgy, particularly during Lent and Holy Week, were eliminated in the new liturgy.

37 Extension of services to other weekdays of Lent: Thurston, op. cit., pp. 153–4. The only surviving manuscript of the Gelasian Sacramentary, which dates to about 740, has no Masses for the Thursdays of Lent. In the case of the Thursday in the third week of Lent, no complete Lenten Mass was in fact ever provided, the celebrant's prayers for this day being borrowed from a Mass for the feast of SS Cosmas and Damian, the dedicatees of the stational church.

38 A similar system is observable in the Communion verses of the weekdays in Lent, which start on Ash Wednesday with a verse from Psalm 1, and continue in order throughout the psalter, omitting all the Thursdays, until they end with Psalm 26 on the Saturday of Passion Week.

39 See Dix, op. cit., p. 355. The Mass for the Friday of the third week in Lent in the old Roman rite, at which point the Gospel readings from St Matthew give way to those from St John, is particularly rich in baptismal texts.

40 Beginning of Lent on first Sunday: see G. G. Willis, *A History of Early Roman Liturgy* (Henry Bradshaw Society, 1994), pp. 62–3 and J. A. Jungmann, *Public Worship* (London: Challenor, 1957), p. 182.

41 Sermo XXXIX Cap. III (*PL* 54, 264). See Willis, op. cit., p. 87.

42 Sixteenth Homily on the Gospels: 'A praesenti etenim die usque ad paschalis sollemnitatis gaudia sex hebdomadae veniunt, quarum videlicet dies quadraginta et duo fiunt. Ex quibus dum sex dies dominici ab abstinentia subtrahuntur, non plus in absentia quam triginta et sex dies remanent'. (*Corpus Christianorum* Series Latina CXLI (Turnhout, 1999), pp. 113–14).

43 Rome, Vatican Library, Reg. lat. 316.

44 The text of the letter appears in Eusebius' *Life of Constantine* 3, 17–20. The letter was probably composed by Eusebius himself; some authorities in fact believe that it was not written until after the Emperor's death.

45 Talley, op. cit., pp. 7–10. For the Audians see Epiphanius, *Panarion*, 9.2–3, 10. 1–6 (text in Cantalamessa, op. cit., texts 64 and 65). The notion that 25 March or 6 April was the date of the Crucifixion seems to have governed the celebration of the Nativity on either 25 December or 6 January, following the commonly held belief that Christ's earthly life began and ended on the same date.

46 *De ratione paschali*, 7. Translation taken from D. P. McCarthy and A. Breen, *The ante-Nicene Christian Pasch, De ratione paschali, The Paschal tract of Anatolius, bishop of Laodicea* (Dublin: Four Courts Press, 2003). The authenticity of this treatise, long regarded as a later forgery, is vigorously defended by the authors.

47 *De ratione paschali*, 3.

48 Cantalamessa, op. cit., texts 104 (Council of Arles) and 53 (Council of Nicaea). See also Ambrose, Ep.XXIII 1 (*PL* 16, 1026–7), for the Council of Nicaea.

49 Ambrose Ep. XXIII 14 (*PL* 16, 1030–1).

50 'Possum destruere templum Dei, et post triduum reaedificare illud' (Matt. 26:61). Cf. also Mark 14:58. The original Greek in both passages is 'διὰ τριων 'ημερων'.

51 'triduum sacrum ... intra quod triduum et passus est et quievit et resurrexit' (Ep. XXIII 13 [*PL* 16, 1030]). See also Martimort, op. cit., vol. IV, p. 39.

52 'sacratissimum triduum crucifixi, sepulti, suscitati' (Ep. ad Januarium, *PL* 33, 215). See McArthur, op. cit., pp. 112–13.

53 Abelard, for example, writes 'sic praesens triduum in lucto ducere, ut risum tribuas paschalis gratiae' (*In Parasceve Domini*, III Nocturn), where the day of the Resurrection is evidently not included in the triduum, seen here exclusively as a time of mourning.

54 General Norms for the Liturgical Year and the Calendar (1969), para. 19; Letter of the Congregation for Divine Worship (1988), para. 27. (English translation published under the title *Celebrating Easter* by the Catholic Truth Society, London, 1988.)

CHAPTER 2

HOLY WEEK IN JERUSALEM AT THE TIME OF ST CYRIL

Historical Background

In the year 70, during the first Jewish revolt against Roman rule, a Roman army under the command of the future emperor Titus recaptured Jerusalem and in the subsequent sack most of the city was destroyed.[1] The destruction included the Temple whose treasures were carried off to Rome to embellish the triumphal procession of Titus, scenes from which can be seen to this day carved in relief on his triumphal arch in the Roman Forum.[2] Most of the inhabitants who had survived the siege and sack were either dispersed or enslaved. One section of the city was converted into a fortress for the Tenth Legion; the rest of the defences were demolished, except for part of the great Temple platform, the complete destruction of which evidently proved too laborious an undertaking, and which still survives.[3]

In 130, sixty years later, the emperor Hadrian visited Judaea and decided to refound Jerusalem as a Roman colonia, under the name of Aelia Capitolina, with a temple dedicated to Jupiter on the site of the former Jewish Temple.[4] His intention may well have been a factor in igniting the second Jewish revolt, which broke out in 132 and lasted until 135. Following its suppression Hadrian went ahead with his plans and Aelia Capitolina was duly built, complete with its temple of Jupiter, in what is now the northern part of the old walled city, between the Jaffa Gate and the Temple Mount.[5] Jews were strictly prohibited from entering the new city.[6] As a result, the succession of bishops of Jerusalem's Christian community, which had hitherto consisted entirely of ethnic Jews, from the Apostle James onwards, devolved from that time forwards on Gentile Christians only.[7]

The traditional site of the hill of Golgotha had been outside the city wall at the time of the Crucifixion, a fact to which all the Gospels attest and which has been confirmed by archaeological investigation.[8] Shortly afterwards, between 41 and 44 in fact, it was included in an extension to the city carried out by Herod Agrippa. It remained inside the city when the latter was refounded by Hadrian. The summit of the hill, however, including the nearby rock tomb venerated as that in which the body of Christ was laid after his death, was levelled by the dumping of earth and, according to Eusebius' *Life of Constantine*, written about 338, a temple to Venus was constructed on top of this artificial platform.[9] St Jerome, writing some sixty years later (Ep. 58.3), tells us that Hadrian erected a statue of Jupiter on the site of the tomb of Christ, and one of Venus on the site of the Crucifixion. His account is generally supposed to be at variance with that of Eusebius but it is not necessarily so. In any event, after the demolition of this temple (and the statues, if they existed) by Constantine in 326, excavations were undertaken to rediscover the tomb of Christ, buried under the former structures. These excavations, described by Eusebius in graphic detail, were triumphantly successful.[10]

Over the newly-cleared site Constantine proceeded to erect a great complex of buildings, which was dedicated in 335. The tomb was enclosed within a small quasi-circular shrine, which itself was surrounded by a great rotunda whose roof rested on a circle of columns; this building was popularly known as the Anastasis.[11] To its immediate east it opened on to a colonnaded courtyard, in the south-east corner of which stood the old summit of Golgotha, the site of the Crucifixion. Further east again was a large triple-aisled basilica, known as the Martyrion, approached from the main north-south street of the city via an imposing atrium.[12] There was a separate baptistery, whose location has not yet been identified.[13] The whole complex survived until 1009, when it was comprehensively destroyed under orders of the Muslim Caliph al-Hakim. The Anastasis itself was rebuilt a few years later, on its original foundations and roughly according to its former plan, and at the same time extended eastwards into what had been the courtyard, to form the present Church of the Holy Sepulchre.[14] The Martyrion was never rebuilt.

Constantine also erected two buildings on the Mount of Olives. The larger of the two, a church know as the Eleona ('of olives'), was believed to cover the spot where Christ taught his apostles about the end of the world (Matt. 24:3–25:46). Constantine's church has long since vanished but has now been replaced by a church built in the nineteenth century. The second was a small circular colonnade, which at first seems to have been venerated as the site of the Transfiguration, but later was associated with the Ascension. No trace of it survives, but its site is presently marked by the beautiful little octagonal church, now a mosque, erected by the Crusaders. In the fourth century it was known as the Imbomon (meaning probably 'on the hillock').[15]

The *Peregrinatio Egeriae*

Egeria's home was at the far end of the Mediterranean from Jerusalem, possibly somewhere on the Atlantic coast of the Iberian Peninsula. She spent three years, probably from 381 to 384, in Jerusalem on an extended pilgrimage, and wrote an account of her time there and her visits to other places in the same area, most of which account has survived.[16] It was written for the benefit of her compatriots who, together with herself, were probably, from the manner in which she addresses them, members of a religious order. For example, she begins her description of the liturgical practices of the Jerusalem Church, 'Loving sisters, I am sure it will interest you to know about the daily services they have in the holy places, and I must tell you about them'.[17] She would no doubt have been extremely surprised had she known that it would be of at least equal interest to readers in the twenty-first century.

Egeria is not the only fourth-century pilgrim who has left an account of her visit. Some fifty years earlier, in 333 to be exact, a pilgrim from the Bordeaux area who had visited Palestine wrote a detailed narrative of his (or her, since the sex of the pilgrim is unclear) journey. But, although the account is of great topographical interest, there is little about the liturgy and nothing about any Holy Week ceremonies, since the pilgrim was not in Jerusalem at the relevant time.[18] Egeria on the other hand was present in the

city for the whole of Holy Week, and has left us a detailed description of the liturgy as it was celebrated during the episcopate of St
Cyril, who was bishop of Jerusalem from about 349 to 387. It must
have been an extremely exhausting experience for all those who
took part, especially since most of them would have been fasting
all week.

Sunday

On the Sunday before Easter, the day on which the Great Week
('*septimana maior*'), as Egeria tells us it was known in Jerusalem,[19]
began, the people 'do everything as usual at the Anastasis and the
Cross from cockcrow to daybreak, and then as usual assemble in
the Great Church known as the Martyrion' where the normal
service takes place.[20] What this means, Egeria tells us elsewhere,
is that at cockcrow, in the presence of the bishop, three responsorial psalms and three prayers are said, ending with a general
prayer for all the faithful, after which an incensation of the shrine
takes place and the bishop reads the Gospel of the Resurrection;
everyone then goes across the courtyard to the site of the
Crucifixion, singing in procession, and there is a further psalm
and prayer, followed by a blessing from the bishop. The clergy
then return to the Anastasis to sing further psalms and antiphons,
with prayers, while the people are dismissed and most of them go
back home for a short rest. At daybreak they assemble again in the
Martyrion, where there is a synaxis, including sermons from any
priest present who wishes to preach, ending with a sermon from
the bishop.[21] This lasts until the fourth or fifth hour (approximately ten or eleven o'clock in our reckoning), and then the
archdeacon instructs everyone to return there at the ninth hour
(three o'clock) on every day of the coming week, except today,
when they should assemble at the Eleona Church at the seventh
hour.[22] After this the people go singing again in procession to the
Anastasis. The faithful (but not the catechumens) enter the
building and the bishop celebrates the Eucharist. This ends with
another blessing from the bishop, and the people are dismissed, at
about eleven or twelve o'clock.[23] After the Eucharist in the
Anastasis everyone goes home to eat a quick lunch, so as to be
ready in the Eleona Church at the appointed hour.[24]

At about our one o'clock, therefore, they reassemble on the Mount of Olives, where they sing hymns and antiphons and listen to readings, suitable to the day and place, for a space of two hours. At the ninth hour (three o'clock) they proceed, singing more hymns, from the Eleona church to the Imbomon, where there are further hymns, antiphons, readings and prayers. At the beginning of the eleventh hour (five o'clock), the Gospel about the children who ran to meet Christ with palm branches, singing 'Blessed is He who comes in the name of the Lord', is read (Matt. 21:8–9). Then all the people descend the Mount of Olives, carrying branches of palm or olive, singing hymns and antiphons, and repeating, 'Blessed is He who comes in the name of the Lord', before the bishop, 'in the very way the people did when once they went down the hill with the Lord'. The procession ends at the Anastasis, where they celebrate the service called the Lucernare.[25] This involves the lighting of lamps and candles from the flame kept burning in the shrine, accompanied by hymns, psalms and antiphons. A deacon then reads a prayer for named individuals; after each name a boys' choir sings 'Kyrie eleison' (very loudly, Egeria says). The bishop says a general prayer for everyone, and then gives a general blessing, first to the catechumens, who stand with bowed heads, and afterwards to the faithful, who also bow their heads to receive it. Then each person present receives an individual blessing.[26] After a final prayer at the site of the Crucifixion, the people are dismissed and return home.[27]

Monday to Wednesday

On the following day, and likewise on Tuesday and Wednesday, 'they do the same as in the rest of Lent, from cockcrow till morning, at nine o'clock, and at midday'.[28] These three services take place in the Anastasis and consist again of hymns, psalms, antiphons and prayers; the bishop is present at the second and third service, each of which ends with his blessing the people present individually.[29] At the ninth hour, as instructed by the Archdeacon the day before, they reassemble in the Martyrion, where there are further hymns, antiphons and prayers, as well as readings appropriate to the day and the place. This goes on for some four hours, and about seven o'clock in the evening the service of Lucernare is held, as on the previous day, except that it takes place in the Martyrion, with the blessing and dismissal in the Anastasis.[30]

That is all for Monday, but on Tuesday and Wednesday there is more to come. On Tuesday, after the dismissal in the Anastasis following the Lucernare, the people go up the Mount of Olives to the Eleona church, where the bishop reads the eschatological discourse from St Matthew's Gospel (Matt. 24:1–26:2). After a prayer, he blesses the catechumens and the faithful separately, and everyone goes home 'very late indeed', as one can well imagine.[31]

On Wednesday, following the dismissal in the Martyrion, the people go to the Anastasis where a priest, in the presence of the bishop, reads the Gospel passage recounting the betrayal by Judas Iscariot (Matt. 26:3–16). While this reading is taking place 'the people groan and lament ... in a way that would make you weep to hear them'. The service ends, as on the previous evening, with a prayer followed by a separate blessing of the catechumens and faithful.[32]

Thursday

On Thursday, the morning services are the same as on the three previous days. In the afternoon, however, the people reassemble in the Martyrion earlier, at the eighth hour (two o'clock) to be precise, for a celebration of the Eucharist. This lasts until the tenth hour, and at the conclusion the deacon bids the people assemble again in the Eleona church at seven o'clock. Then they go to a place which Egeria describes as 'Behind the Cross', and which may be either a chapel in the south aisle of the Martyrion or a separate building, and the Eucharist is celebrated again, by the bishop himself this time, and everyone receives Communion. It is the only day in the year, Egeria tells us, when the Eucharist is celebrated in this par-ticular place. When it is over, they go to the Anastasis, where a prayer is said, followed by the usual blessing of the catechumens and faithful, and the dismissal, as on the three previous evenings. A quick meal at home is taken, and then, as instructed, the people reassemble at the Eleona church, where, for the next four or five hours, they occupy themselves with hymns and antiphons suitable to the place and day, interspersed with readings and prayers. At about midnight they leave the Eleona church and go up to the Imbomon, where the hymns, antiphons, readings and prayers continue until cockcrow on Friday morning.[33]

Friday

At cockcrow the bishop, clergy and people leave the Imbomon and go to a place described as 'where the Lord prayed', by which Egeria seems to mean what we know as the Garden of Gethsemane. The Gospel recounting the Agony in the Garden (Matt. 26:1–46) is read. After this everyone, 'including the smallest children', go singing with hundreds of lighted candles to 'Gethsemane', meaning the place where Christ was arrested, where they listen to the relevant Gospel passage (Matt. 26:47–56). The reading is accompanied by 'groaning and lamenting and weeping' on the part of the people, so loud that it can be heard in the city across the valley. Then all return, singing, to Jerusalem, which they reach just as it is starting to get light, and proceed through the city to the site of Golgotha, where the trial of Christ before Pilate (John 18:28–19:16) is read. The bishop then exhorts the people not to flag in their efforts, since God will reward them out of all proportion to their labours, after which he dismisses them for a short rest, telling them to return about the second hour (eight o'clock), so that they can venerate the Wood of the Cross (incredibly, some people, instead of taking this good advice and going straight home for a rest, apparently go to Mount Sion first to pray at the traditional site of the Flagellation). At the hour appointed by the bishop they return to Golgotha, to the place where the second Eucharist was celebrated the previous day, where the bishop, flanked by two deacons, takes his seat before a table on which is placed the relic of the Cross, securely held by the deacons (in case, Egeria tells us, someone should try to steal it). All the people, catechumens as well as faithful, venerate the relic one by one, touching it first with their forehead, then with their eyes, and then kissing it. They proceed to venerate two other relics held by the deacons, the ring of Solomon and the horn with which the kings of Judaea were anointed. After everyone has venerated the Cross and the other relics, which takes until about midday, they go into the courtyard between the Anastasis and the

Martyrion, and from the sixth to the ninth hour they listen to
scriptural readings appropriate to the day. The air is filled with
the sound of weeping, as the people meditate on the sufferings
Christ endured for us. At the ninth hour, the passage from St John
recounting Christ's death on the Cross (John 19:17–37) is read;
there follows a prayer and the dismissal. That is not, however, the
end. Instead of going back home, they return to the Martyrion,
where they attend an afternoon service similar to that on the
previous days of Holy Week. Then they go to the Anastasis and
listen to the Gospel about the Entombment (Matt. 27:57–61). This
is followed as usual by a prayer, the separate blessing of the catechumens and the faithful, and the dismissal. Only then can they
return home. However, those young and fit enough keep a second
night's vigil, together with the clergy. Most of the people spend at
least part of the night in this way.[34]

Saturday

On Saturday the usual services are held at nine o'clock and
midday. From three o'clock onwards the preparations for the
Easter Vigil begin. Disappointingly from our point of view Egeria
tells us hardly anything about this vigil, on the grounds that it was
not much different from the one at home. There is one additional
ceremony; after the baptisms have taken place, the bishop leads the
newly baptized into the Anastasis, where a hymn is sung and he
says a prayer for them. They then join the faithful in the Martyrion,
where the vigil is being observed 'in the usual way'. After they
have done 'all the things to which we are accustomed', the bishop
celebrates the Eucharist, on completion of which they go singing
across the courtyard to the Anastasis, where the Gospel account of
the Resurrection is read (John 19:38–20:18), and a second Eucharist
is celebrated. The vigil ends at the same time as at home, though
Egeria does not tell us what time this is.[35]

The Armenian Lectionary

While the *Peregrinatio Egeriae* gives us a fascinating and detailed
account of the Holy Week ceremonies in Jerusalem in the second
half of the fourth century, it is defective in some respects. In

particular, although Egeria refers frequently to hymns, psalms, antiphons and readings, she never, with the exception of a few Gospel passages, tells us what they were. Fortunately, we possess an old lectionary, written for the use of the Armenian community in Jerusalem, which goes a long way to supplying this deficiency. It has survived in three manuscripts, ranging from around the turn of the fifth century to about 440, and it is therefore closely contemporary to Egeria's pilgrimage.[36] There are some differences between the three manuscripts, but for our purposes they are not material. The general impression created by the lectionary is that there has been no really significant change in the services in the interim, though they seem to be somewhat shorter than those prevalent in Egeria's time.

The lectionary prescribes for the morning service on the Sunday before Easter (which the lectionary calls 'the day of the Palms') Psalm 98, a reading from Ephesians 1:3–10, Psalm 90, and a Gospel reading from Matthew 21:1–11 (the account of Christ's triumphal entry into Jerusalem). It goes on, 'On the same day at the ninth hour they go forth to the Mount of Olives with palm branches, and there they pray and sing psalms until the tenth hour. And after that they go down into the holy Anastasis, chanting Ps. 118'. This is the psalm which contains the verse 'It was the stone rejected by the builders that became the keystone. This was the Lord's doing and it is wonderful to see', which St Matthew says was applied by Christ to himself.[37] The antiphon given in the lectionary is, not surprisingly, taken from verse 26, 'Blessed is He who comes in the name of the Lord', which Egeria tells us was repeated over and over in the course of the procession. The lectionary does not mention the preliminary service at the Eleona church; otherwise the times and location correspond exactly with those given by Egeria.

For Tuesday in Holy Week the lectionary confirms the evening service at the Eleona church and the Gospel from St Matthew of the eschatological discourse, though since Egeria's day the timing of the service has been advanced to the tenth hour (about 4 p.m.), perhaps to allow the people to return home earlier in view of the strenuous exercises which they will be undertaking over the next few days.[38] The lectionary also supplies the other scriptural readings at the service: the story of Noah (Genesis 6:9–9:17), Proverbs 9:1–11, Isaiah 40:9–17, and Psalm 25.

For Wednesday the lectionary confirms the afternoon service in the Martyrion, with readings from Genesis. 18:1–19:30 (the story of Sodom and Gomorrah), Proverbs 1:10–19, Zechariah 11:11–14 (the thirty pieces of silver), and Psalm 41. It also records the move to the Anastasis 'after the psalm' for the reading of the Gospel from Matthew 26:3–16.

Thursday is described as the day 'of the old Zatik [i.e. Passover], as touching which Jesus said to his disciples, With desire have I desired to eat with you this Zatik. They assemble at the seventh hour in the holy shrine of the city'. The readings are from Genesis 22:1–18 (the sacrifice of Isaac), Isaiah 61:1–6, Acts 1:15–26 (the election of Matthias to replace Judas), and Psalm 55 (the theme of which is betrayal by a friend). Then the catechumens are dismissed, and after further readings, Psalm 23 (the Good Shepherd), 1 Corinthians 11:23–32 (the institution of the Holy Eucharist) and Matthew 26:20–39 (the Last Supper and the Agony in the Garden), two Eucharists are celebrated, as described by Egeria, one 'in the holy shrine', and the other 'before the holy cross'.[39] This second Eucharist is followed by a procession to Sion, which appears to be a recent development since it is not mentioned by Egeria, where further readings take place, including St Mark's account of the Last Supper (Mark 14:12–26, 'and in the same hour they go forth to the Mount of Olives, and perform the evening service of worship. And they join with the same the Vigil'. For this vigil the lectionary prescribes fifteen psalms, sung in five groups of three, with a prayer after the end of each group. After the last prayer Christ's discourse at the Last Supper is read (John 13:16–18:1). The people then visit in turn the Imbomon, 'the room of the disciples'[40] and 'the holy Mount of Olives in Gethsemane'; appropriate Gospel readings are prescribed for each locality.

After the visit to Gethsemane the procession back to the city takes place, but on the way the lectionary prescribes an additional visit to the Court of the High Priest and the Place of Peter's Repentance, where Matthew 26:57–27:2 (the trial before Caiphas and Peter's denial) is read.[41] Egeria's narrative implies that the procession in her time went directly from Gethsemane to Golgotha, which means that after crossing the brook Kedron it would have entered the city through St Stephen's Gate and followed what is now known as the Via Dolorosa. However, the

traditional site of the house of Caiphas lies outside the walled city
to the south-west, which involves a more circuitous route, going
first south and then west, and entering the city through the Sion
Gate. The procession ends at Golgotha with the reading of John
18:2–27 (Christ before Caiphas), followed, at dawn, by John
18:28–19:16 (Christ before Pilate). The lectionary continues, 'At
dawn on the Friday the holy wood of the cross is set before holy
Golgotha, and the congregation adore until the ninth hour. The
adoration is completed, and at the sixth hour they assemble in
holy Golgotha'. There are eight psalms, eight Old Testament and
eight New Testament readings, each accompanied by a prayer,
said kneeling, and four Gospel readings. This agrees well with
Egeria's narrative, where the adoration of the Cross ends at
midday (the sixth hour) and is followed by three hours of psalms,
prayers and readings. As one would expect, the four Gospel
readings are the narratives of the Crucifixion in each of the four
evangelists. The psalms prescribed include Psalm 22, beginning
'My God, my God why have you deserted me', quoted by Christ
on the Cross, and always seen by Christians as a prophecy of the
Crucifixion; the readings include the third and fourth songs of the
Servant of Yahweh (Isaiah 50:4–9 and 52:13–53:12) and the apocalyptic poem on the vengeance of Yahweh (Isaiah 63:1–6).[42] All this
takes place in the open courtyard between the Anastasis and the
Martyrion. Then the people enter the Martyrion 'at the tenth hour'
to hear further readings, ending with Psalm 22 once more. They
then go to the Anastasis, as described by Egeria, to hear
Matthew's account of the Entombment (Matt. 27:57–61).

For the Easter Vigil the lectionary prescribes that 'At eventide
on the Sabbath day they light a torch in the holy Anastasis. First
the bishop repeats Psalm 113. And then the bishop lights three
candles, and after him the deacons, and then the whole congregation. And then after that they go up into the church, and begin the
vigil of the holy Zatik, and read twelve lessons. And with each of
them they sing psalms'.[43] The readings are preceded by Psalm
117, with the antiphon 'This is the day which the Lord has made,
let us exult and rejoice in it', and before each reading there is a
prayer, recited kneeling.[44] Between each verse of the sixth reading
(Isaiah 60:1–13) the people sing 'Behold there is come the king of
glory of light, illumining all creatures'. The final reading is Daniel
3:1–90, which includes the song of Azariah in the furnace and the

song of the three young men. After the words 'do not withdraw your favour from us' (verse 35) the people sing 'The incorruptible holy Trinity has beamed forth on us from incorruptible light. And do thou work propitiatory mercy, for thee alone do we know to be our saviour'. At the beginning of the song of the three young men, after the words 'all three in unison began to sing, glorifying and blessing God, there in the furnace, in these words' (verse 51) they add 'The ram of Isaac has been exchanged. Christ is become unto us for salvation', and between each verse of the hymn is sung 'Praise and exalt him for ever'. During the singing of this hymn the bishop and clergy enter the church with the newly baptized. When it is over Psalm 65 is sung, followed by a reading from St Paul, 1 Corinthians 15:1–11, Psalm 30 with Alleluia, and finally, as the Gospel, the Resurrection narrative from St Matthew 28:1–20. The bishop then celebrates the Eucharist, at the end of which the people are dismissed. But the bishop immediately goes to the Anastasis and celebrates a second Eucharist, at which the Gospel of the Entombment and Resurrection from St John 19:38–20:18 is read.

Such was the Easter Vigil as observed not only in Jerusalem but, as Egeria tells us, also in her remote home at the far end of the Mediterranean, and, as we may reasonably conclude, throughout the Christian world in the fourth century.

St Cyril

St Cyril was born around 315 AD and became bishop of Jerusalem about the year 349, in succession to Maximus. His nineteen Catecheses, or set of instructions in the Christian faith to catechumens preparing for baptism at the Easter Vigil, have survived, together with a set of five sermons (the so-called 'Mystagogical Catecheses') delivered to the newly baptized during Easter Week (there seem to have originally been six, as one would expect). He died in 386, two years after Egeria's visit.

There are two pertinent questions which we can properly ask. First, to what extent were the Holy Week ceremonies described in such detail by Egeria and in the Armenian Lectionary the work of St Cyril (other than the Easter Vigil of course)? Secondly, what more can we learn about the Jerusalem Holy Week liturgy from his extant writings?

The origin of these services must fall between the dedication by Constantine of the relevant buildings in and around which the liturgy is centred, and the visit of Egeria, in other words between 335 and 384. For the first thirteen or so years of this period the church in Jerusalem was ruled by Bishop Maximus, who was succeeded by Cyril about 348/349.[45] Cyril delivered his nineteen pre-baptismal catecheses, the text of which has survived, at the site of the Crucifixion,[46] either just before or just after he became bishop,[47] and it appears from the text of the last one that it was delivered towards the end of Holy Week itself.[48] By the time of Egeria the instruction of the catechumens had been completed by the beginning of Holy Week. It appears that this change took place in order to accommodate the very time-consuming services described by Egeria.[49] If so, their institution must be the work of Cyril. It has been suggested that because Epiphanius of Salamis, writing about 377, does not mention any of the elaborate Holy Week services in Jerusalem, they cannot have existed at that time.[50] However, in the passage in question he was commenting only on the nature of the fast, and would not necessarily have mentioned something which was not relevant to that. Egeria gives the impression that the Holy Week services in which she participated between 381 and 384 were well established; if this impression is accurate, their institution probably belongs to the earlier part of Cyril's episcopate rather than to the later.

In his lectures delivered to the newly baptized during Easter week, known as the 'Mystagogical Catecheses', St Cyril explains the significance of the rites which they had undergone during the Easter Vigil, and in so doing gives us a detailed description of the rite of baptism and confirmation in fourth-century Jerusalem, information that is not contained in the pages of either the *Peregrinatio Egeriae* or the Armenian Lectionary.[51] After entering the outer hall of the baptistery, the catechumens, facing towards the west (thought of as the region of the devil), stretch out their hands and formally renounce Satan, saying, 'I renounce you, Satan, and all your works, and all your pomp, and all your worship'.[52] After this they turn towards the east, the region of light, and pronounce the formula, 'I believe in the Father and in the Son and in the Holy Spirit, and in one baptism of repentance'.[53] They then enter the baptistery itself and remove their clothes,[54] after which they are anointed all over with holy oil, to signify that they have become companions of Jesus Christ, Who is the true olive tree.[55] They are then conducted ('just as Christ was taken from the cross to the tomb which stands before you') to the baptismal pool, by the side of which each is asked in turn whether he or she believes in the name of the Father and of the Son and of the Holy Spirit. After replying in the affirmative, baptism takes place by triple immersion, compared by St Cyril to the three days which Christ spent in the tomb.[56] Confirmation then follows; the candidate is anointed on the forehead, on the ears, on the nostrils and on the breast, each anointing being given a symbolic meaning. Finally, wearing their white garments, they are led by the bishop, as Egeria tells us, into the Anastasis, whence after a hymn and a prayer they join the congregation in the Martyrion for the Easter Eucharist.

The order of the Eucharist proper is given by St Cyril in his fifth 'Mystagogical Catechesis'. The celebrant washes his hands and the kiss of peace is exchanged ('a sign that our souls are united and all grudges banished'). Then comes the Dialogue, in the form which we know it today,[57] the Preface, Sanctus and Epiklesis. 'After the completion of the spiritual sacrifice', prayers are said for the Church and for the living, followed by a commemoration of the saints and prayers for the dead, 'for we believe that great benefit will result for the souls for whom prayer is offered when the holy and most awesome sacrifice lies on the altar'.[58] After the Lord's Prayer comes the communion rite and the final thanksgiving.

Appendix

It has been suggested[59] that the blessing of palms and the procession on the Sunday before Easter began not at Jerusalem but elsewhere, and was adopted in Jerusalem at the instigation of pilgrims who were accustomed to celebrating it at home. The reason given is that the Gospel of St Matthew was the only one in use in the liturgy of the Jerusalem church, and in this Gospel there is no chronological link between the entry of Christ into Jerusalem and the Passion, as there is in that of St John, where we are told explicitly that only five days elapsed between the entry into Jerusalem and the Passover (John 12:1 and 12).

It is true that in the Gospel of St Luke we learn that following the entry into Jerusalem 'He taught in the Temple every day'

(19:47) and 'In the daytime he would be in the Temple teaching, but would spend the night on the hill called the Mount of Olives. And from early morning the people would gather round him in the Temple to listen to him' (21:37). This certainly suggests, if it does not prove, that the Synoptic chronology of the events between the entry into Jerusalem and the Crucifixion was longer than the Johannine, by at least several days. However, the passages quoted from St Luke do not occur in St Matthew, and to anyone unacquainted with the former the narrative of St Matthew would appear to fit into a shorter timeframe. Following his entry into Jerusalem, Christ goes to the temple, where he expels the money changers, an action which arouses the wrath of the chief priests and the scribes (Matt. 21:1–16). He retires to Bethany that evening, returning to Jerusalem the next morning (21:17–18). There he teaches in the Temple by means of parables. The chief priests and the scribes, realizing that his parables relate to them, wish to arrest him but are deterred for fear of the crowds (21: 45–46). The Pharisees go away in order to work out how to trap him in his teaching (22:15). A confrontation with their disciples and with the Sadducees follows on the same day (22:16–46). Having failed in their attempt, they go away, whereupon Christ denounces the scribes and the Pharisees for their hypocrisy (23:1–36). After this 'Jesus left the Temple' and retired to the Mount of Olives (24:1–3). There, in answer to a request from the disciples, he tells them about the end of the world (24:4–46). We are then told that 'Jesus had now finished all he wanted to say, and he told his disciples, "It will be Passover, as you know, in two days' time, and the Son of Man will be handed over to be crucified"' (26:1–2). Meanwhile, the chief priests and the elders of the people hold a meeting in the house of the high priest, where they plot to arrest him and have him put to death (26:3–5). Christ himself sups at Bethany, in the house of Simon the leper (26:6–13), while Judas goes to the chief priests and arranges to betray him (26:14–16). The narrative of the preparation and consumption of the Passover supper follows (26:17–29).

The chronology of these events can therefore be plausibly reconstructed as follows:

Sunday: Entry into Jerusalem and expulsion of the money changers.

Monday:	Teaching in the Temple and confrontation with the scribes and Pharisees.
Tuesday:	Eschatological discourse on the Mount of Olives. Meeting of the priests and elders.
Wednesday:	Christ at Bethany. Judas arranges to betray him.
Thursday:	Preparations for the Passover supper, which takes place in the evening.

A possible objection to this reconstruction might be that in Matthew 26:55 Christ is reported as saying, 'I sat teaching in the Temple day after day and you never laid hands on me'. The phrase translated here as 'day after day' is 'καθ' 'ημεραν'. This is indeed its usual meaning and, bearing in mind the chronology found in Luke, there is no reason to suppose that in the Synoptic tradition it originally meant anything else. However, the phrase is sometimes found with the meaning 'by day'. Christ could therefore be understood as saying, in effect, 'Why did you not arrest me openly in the Temple by day, rather than secretly in the garden by night?' Interpreted in this way, as it could well have been in fourth-century Jerusalem, the saying is perfectly compatible with the Temple teaching having occupied only a single day.

There seems to be no good reason, therefore, to doubt that the commemoration of Christ's entry into Jerusalem with a blessing of palms and a procession, together with the commemorations of the other events of the Passion, originated in Jerusalem.

Notes

[1] The siege and sack of Jerusalem are described in Josephus, *Jewish Wars* V 1–13 and VI 1–10.
[2] Destruction of the Temple: ibid. VII 1; Triumph of Titus, ibid. VII 4. 3–6.
[3] Camp of Tenth Legion: ibid. VII 1. 2.
[4] Dio Cassius, Roman History 69.12. Mentioned also by St Paulinus of Nola, Ep. 31 ad Severum (*PL* 61, 326–7).
[5] For the topography of Aelia see K. Kenyon, *Digging up Jerusalem* (London: Ernest Benn, 1974), pp. 257–64, and M. Biddle, *The Tomb of Christ* (Stroud: Sutton, 1999), pp. 54–69.
[6] Exclusion of Jews from Aelia: Eusebius *HE* 3.6.
[7] Bishops of Jerusalem from James until the second Jewish revolt (fifteen in all): Eusebius *HE* 3.5 and 10.12.
[8] Confirmation that Golgotha was outside the city before 41 AD: Kenyon, op. cit., pp. 226–34.

9   Temple to Venus on the summit of Golgotha: Eusebius *Vita Constantini* 3.26–7. Eusebius does not say when this temple was built.

10   Discovery of the buried tomb of Christ: Eusebius, ibid., 3.28.

11   The Anastasis itself, as distinct from the shrine, seems in fact not to have been built until after the death of Constantine. See E. J. Yarnold, *Cyril of Jerusalem* (Abingdon: Routledge, 2000), pp. 15–17. For the appearance of the first shrine, see Biddle, op. cit., p. 69 and Fig. 64.

12   Building of the Anastasis and Martyrion: Eusebius, ibid., 3.29, 33–40. For a general account of Constantine's buildings in Jerusalem see Wilkinson, op. cit., pp. 12–22.

13   See Chapter 1, note 25.

14   Rebuilding of the Holy Sepulchre: Biddle, op. cit., pp. 74–81.

15   Eleona Church and the Imbomon: Itinerary of the Bordeaux Pilgrim (where the Imbomon is associated with the Transfiguration), Wilkinson, ibid., p. 32; *Peregrinatio Egeriae* 30.3, 35.2–3 (association of the Eleona with the teaching of Christ), 35.4, 43.5 (association of the Imbomon with the Ascension), Wilkinson, ibid., pp. 151, 153–4, 160.

16   For the date of Egeria's pilgrimage see Wilkinson, ibid., pp. 169–71. This work includes (pp. 107–64) an English translation of all the surviving parts of Egeria's account, from which the quotations in this chapter are taken. Latin text in *Corpus Inscriptionum Christianorum*, Vol. 175 (Turnhout, 1953ff.).

17   *PE* 24.1.

18   See note 13 above.

19   This name for Holy Week is common throughout the East. See for example St John Chrysostom: 'Καὶ γὰρ 'εν ταυτῃ τῃ 'εβδομαδα τῃ μεγαλῃ 'η χρονια του διαβολου κατελυθη τυραννις, 'ο θανατος 'εσβεσθη ... 'η 'αμαρτια 'ανηρεθη, 'η καταρα κατελυθη, 'ο παραδεισος 'ανεωχθη ... Δια τουτο μεγαλη καλειται 'εβδομας' (*Homilia Habita in Magnam* Hebdomadam 1, [*PG* 55, 520]).

20   *PE* 30.1.

21   *PE* 24.8–25.2.

22   *PE* 30.1–3.

23   *PE* 24.2–4.

24   *PE* 30.3.

25   *PE* 31.1–4.

26   *PE* 24.4–7.

27   *PE* 31.4.

28   *PE* 32.1.

29   *PE* 27.4, 24.1–3.

30   *PE* 32.1–2.

31   *PE* 24.33.

32   *PE* 34.

33   *PE* 35 1–4.

34   *PE* 36.1–37.9.

35   *PE* 38.1–2.

36   For particulars of the manuscripts in question see E. Yarnold, op. cit., p. 49, Wilkinson, op. cit., pp. 175–94, Talley op. cit., p. 38. The lectionary was first published in English translation by F. C. Conybeare, *Rituale Armenorum*

(OUP, 1905), but at that time only one manuscript (that in Paris) was known. Quotations are from Conybeare, op. cit., pp. 520–23.

37   Matt. 21:42, Lk. 20:17. In the new Roman rite it is sung at the Easter Vigil as part of the 'Gospel acclamation'.

38   See above for Egeria's comment that on this day the people do not return home until 'very late indeed'.

39   Egeria says this second Eucharist was celebrated 'behind the Cross' ('*post Crucem*'). There is no doubt however that Egeria and the lectionary are referring to the same ceremony.

40   It is not clear what locality is meant, perhaps the cave below the Eleona church, but Egeria has a visit at this point to 'the place where the Lord prayed', which seems to mean the Garden of Gethsemane. The remaining locations mentioned in the lectionary agree very well with Egeria's account.

41   The Paris manuscript of the Armenian Lectionary locates the reading of St Matthew's narrative of the trial before Caiphas and St Peter's denial of Christ at Golgotha itself, with a subsequent visit 'to the palace of the Judge', where St John's account of the trial before Pilate is read. According to the Itinerary of the Bordeaux Pilgrim, Pilate's Praetorium, where the trial and condemnation of Christ took place, was situated in a valley to the right hand side of Golgotha (Wilkinson, op. cit., p. 31). The description is too vague to enable us to locate the site with any degree of confidence. It seems likely in any event that a visit to the Praetorium would have taken place before the procession's arrival at Golgotha, not after. The same manuscript prescribes St Luke's account of the journey to Calvary (Luke 23:24–31) during the final stage of the procession between the Praetorium and Golgotha. See Conybeare, op. cit., p. 522 and Wilkinson, op. cit., p. 186.

42   The fourth song of the Servant of Yahweh and the apocalyptic poem on the vengeance of Yahweh were read on Wednesday of Holy Week in the old Roman rite. This practice goes back at least to the oldest known lectionary of the Roman rite, the *Comes* of Würzburg of the seventh century, and probably much further than that. In the new rite the third song is read on Wednesday and the fourth on Good Friday. The apocalyptic poem has been dropped altogether from the reformed liturgy, thus ending a tradition which went back at least 1600 years.

43   Conybeare, op. cit., p. 523

44   For the lessons read at the vigil in Jerusalem see the table in the Appendix I to Chapter 9.

45   The date is given by Jerome (Chronicles) as the eleventh year of the reign of the sons of Constantine, who succeeded their father on his death in 337, (*PL* 27, 683).

46   *Catecheses* iv. 10; xvi. 4.

47   In *Catechesis* vi. 20, Cyril says that the heresy of Mani arose seventy years earlier, during the reign of the Emperor Probus. Probus ruled from 276 to 282 AD.

48   *Catechesis* xviii. 17, 32.

49   *PE* 46.4: 'there are three hours of teaching a day for seven weeks. But in the eighth, known as the Great Week, there is no time for them to have their

teaching if they are to carry out all the services I have described'. See McArthur, op. cit., pp. 107–8, 111–12.

50 By Davies, op. cit., pp. 35–6. The relevant passage is in Epiphanius, *Expositio Fidei* 22. (*PG* 42, 825–8).

51 *MC* I. 2–9,11; II. 3–4; III. 4; IV. 8. English translations of passages from the *Mystagogical Catecheses* are taken from Yarnold, op. cit.

52 *MC* I. 4–8 ('αποτασσομαι σοι σατανα, και πασι τοις 'εργοις σου, και παση τη πομπη σου, και παση τη λατρεια σου).

53 *MC* I. 9 (πιστευω 'εις τον πατερα και 'εις τον 'υιον και 'εις το 'αγιον πνευμα και 'εις 'εν βαπτισμα μετανοιας).

54 The nakedness of the baptismal candidates is compared by Cyril to the nakedness of Christ on the Cross, as well as to the putting off of the old man and a return to the innocence of Paradise (*MC* II. 2).

55 *MC* II. 3–4. This pre-baptismal anointing is also found in the *Apostolic Tradition* of Hippolytus (21.10).

56 *MC* III. 4, IV.8.

57 'Lift up your hearts'. 'We have lifted them up to the Lord'. 'Let us give thanks to the Lord'. 'It is right and fitting'.

58 On the question of whether the Eucharistic Prayer in the Jerusalem Liturgy of St Cyril's time contained an Institution Narrative and Anamnesis, see Yarnold, op. cit., pp. 41–2.

59 By Talley, op. cit., pp. 39–44.

CHAPTER 3

SOURCES FOR THE HOLY WEEK LITURGY IN MEDIEVAL WESTERN EUROPE

Historical Background[1]

Liturgical books of the Roman rite began to penetrate the Merovingian kingdom of Gaul during the seventh century, where they had a profound and steadily increasing influence on the local Gallican liturgy. This steady Romanization of the liturgy received strong political support, particularly as the power of the Merovingian kings declined and that of the hereditary 'mayors of the palace' increased throughout the seventh and eighth centuries. After the death of Charles Martel in 741, his sons Carloman and Pepin recalled St Boniface to France with the task of reforming the Frankish church, which had fallen into decay partly as the result of the Muslim ravages, checked though not ended by Charles Martel at the Battle of Poitiers in 732, and partly from the practice of the Merovingian kings of giving ecclesiastical offices to their relations and supporters, some of them illiterate laymen who in turn conveyed church lands to their illegitimate children. Under Boniface synods were held, which provided for the creation of new sees and the appointment of new bishops, the filling of vacant sees, the deposition of unsatisfactory clergy, the restoration of discipline and a system of annual councils. Pope Zacharias urged Boniface to uphold the Roman rite in the Frankish kingdom,[2] and at the Council of Cloveshoe in 747 the Frankish bishops prescribed the use of the Roman rite for the celebration of Mass, the administration of baptism and the singing of the chant, and the use of the Roman martyrology for the feasts of the saints.[3]

In the same year Carloman retired to a monastery and Pepin became the sole ruler of the kingdom. He determined to seize the kingship for himself, and secured the approval of Zacharias for the deposition of the last Merovingian king, whose power had by now become purely nominal, in his own favour. Pepin was an enthusiastic Romanizer. In 753 his agent, Bishop Chrodegang of Metz, who was Pepin's chief instrument in the Romanization of the Gallican liturgy, and who introduced into his own diocese the Roman concept of stational Masses, visited Rome and persuaded Pope Stephen II to return with him. Stephen's visit, during which he anointed Pepin and his two sons, Charles and Carloman, at St Denis as Kings of the Franks, lasted from 753 to 755. This long papal visit enabled the local clergy to familiarize themselves with the nobility and dignity of the Roman rite, and the beauty of its chant, compared to their own diverse and chaotic practices, and thus supplied a powerful incentive towards the adoption of the former.[4] In return for Stephen's support, Pepin invaded northern Italy and defeated the pope's enemy, King Aistulf of the Lombards, at Pavia in 755.

Pepin died in 768, and his kingdom was divided between his two sons. After the death of his brother Carloman in 771, Charles, known to history as Charlemagne, became sole ruler. In 773 he invaded Italy to rescue Pope Adrian I from Desiderius, King of the Lombards, who had invaded part of the papal dominions, and in the following year visited Rome, where he received the title 'King of the Franks and Lombards and Patrician of the Romans' from the pope. He continued his father's policy of Romanizing the liturgy. But the universal adoption of the Roman rite was severely hampered by a great shortage of suitable books. In a general admonition dated 23 March 789, Charles complains of the poor quality of the liturgical books in general use, and urges that the task of copying such books be undertaken by older men, who should exercise the greatest care in their work.[5] At about the same time he requested Pope Adrian I to send him a model sacramentary of the Roman rite. In reply Adrian sent him one which he described as '*immixtum*' (i.e. a pure sacramentary of the papal rite, untainted by external elements). It has become known to history as the *Hadrianum*. Charlemagne employed Alcuin of York, who was at his court from 782 onwards, to supplement this sacramentary by adding Masses for the ordinary Sundays of the year and non-papal feast days, drawing on both Roman and Gallican sources. The result was a hybrid Romano-Gallican liturgy, which eventually replaced the local rites throughout the Frankish kingdom.

In the course of the tenth century the possession of the papacy became a matter of strife between rival Roman families and the Holy Roman Emperors, and bloody battles were fought in the streets of Rome between the adherents of the various factions. In consequence the chair of Peter fell into the hands of a succession of men of little merit or worth. The effects on the Roman liturgy were disastrous. Liturgical books fell into disrepair and were not replaced, because the papal scriptoria had ceased to function. The papal liturgy itself ceased to be celebrated, and the ancient rite was adulterated by liturgical books brought into Rome from outside.

But towards the end of the tenth century copies of a Romano-German Pontifical, the prototype of which had been produced in the scriptorium of the abbey of St Alban at Mainz some half a century earlier, reached Rome, as well as other Italian and European cities. This pontifical contained the texts and rubrics of the hybrid Romano-Gallican liturgy, which had evolved in the Frankish kingdom during the eighth and ninth centuries. It was this liturgy that was now adopted in Rome, in place of the city's ancient liturgy which had fallen into desuetude. The Emperor Henry II finally succeeded in gaining control of the situation in Rome, and in the year 1046 his nominee, Suidger, Bishop of Bamberg, was elected pope as Clement II. He was followed by a series of popes of German origin, like himself. Under their rule the use of the Romano-Gallican liturgy was securely established in the Eternal City. The Romano-German Pontifical became the source for the Roman pontificals of the twelfth century, and through them of the liturgy of the Western church down to the post-Vatican II reforms.[6]

Liturgical Books

The missal, containing both the ordinary of the Mass and the proper texts for every Sunday, feast day and feria throughout the year, with which all Catholic faithful were familiar down to the mid-twentieth century, was a relatively late medieval development. In the early part of the Middle Ages the texts and rubrics required by each person or group of persons involved in the celebration of the liturgy were found in separate books. The sacramentary contained the prayers proper to the celebrant himself (Collect, Secret, Preface and Postcommunion) for each day, as well as the Canon of the Mass and rubrics to guide the priest in its celebration. They also included other texts and rubrics required from time to time by priests or bishops, such as ordination rites and miscellaneous blessings. The lectionary or epistolary indicated the non-Gospel texts from the Old or New Testaments which were to be chanted on each Sunday or feast day by the lector or subdeacon,[7] and the evangeliary the Gospel passages chanted by the deacon; sometimes these were combined into a single book, known as a *comes*. The choirmaster was provided with an antiphonal, containing the proper texts to be sung by the choir (Introit, Gradual, Alleluia or Tract, Offertory verse, and Communion verse). The texts of the Gradual and Alleluia or Tract were sometimes also collected in a separate book, known as the *graduale*. These books began to make their appearance from the sixth century; before that, the celebrant's prayers for each day were contained in separate booklets, known as *libelli*, and the relevant scriptural passages would have been taken from a copy of the complete Bible.

Most of the earliest liturgical books known to us survive in the form of manuscripts written in the scriptoria of Frankish monasteries in the eighth, ninth and early tenth centuries. They were produced as part of the intensive effort on the part of both the civil and the ecclesiastical authorities to Romanize the liturgy of the Frankish kingdom. To the same source and the same period belong, notwithstanding their name, the *Ordines Romani*, which were for the most part composed as instructions to the local clergy in the correct manner of celebrating the Mass and the Divine Office according to the Roman rite.

As time went by, the need was felt for a single book containing all the prayers and rubrics required for the celebration of the liturgy and the administration of the sacraments and the various rites, such as ordination and the consecration of churches, appropriate to a bishop. Thus was born the pontifical, which makes its first, rather rudimentary, appearance in the eighth century with the Pontifical of Egbert, from England.[8] Others followed, but the first pontifical to reach Rome, as described above, was the so-called Romano-German Pontifical. Soon afterwards the missal began to make its appearance, a book containing all the texts and rubrics required for the celebration of Mass on each day of the year, but omitting the rite of administration of the sacraments and those functions reserved solely to a bishop.[9]

The Old Gelasian Sacramentary

This sacramentary (also referred to as the 'Gelasian of the Seventh Century') survives in a single manuscript, now in the Vatican Library,[10] but written either at St Denis or at Chelles, near Paris. It constitutes a collection of celebrant's prayers with corresponding rubrics for all sacramental rites, in three books. The surviving manuscript can be dated to before the middle of the eighth century (it does not include the Masses for the Thursdays in Lent, which were introduced by Gregory II c.740). The text of the Canon itself has been updated by reference to Gregory the Great's revisions of about 595, but many of the votive Masses in Book III, which have clauses for insertion in the Canon, ignore the Gregorian addition ('Diesque nostros ... grege numerari') to the *Hanc igitur*. Even at first glance, therefore, it clearly draws on material much earlier than the date of the surviving manuscript. However, although the name of Pope Gelasius has been connected with it since very early times,[11] modern scholarship has discounted any actual connection with Gelasius.[12]

The three books are: the *Temporale*, containing the liturgical formularies for the Christmas and Easter cycles, as well as ordination rites for major and minor orders; the *Sanctorale*, containing Masses for the feasts of Our Lady and the saints, and for the Sundays of Advent and the Ember days; and a Supplementary containing a list of Masses for ordinary Sundays, a series of blessings 'super populum', the text of the Canon and votive Masses for various occasions as well as Masses for the dead.

The nature and origin of the prototype of the Gelasian Sacramentary has been a matter of considerable scholarly dispute,[13] but it has generally been agreed that the rites and prayers which it contains are, as the sacramentary itself proclaims, Roman.[14] However, the prototype has been amended to make it suitable for use in the Frankish kingdom, for example, a Gallican rite of ordination for minor orders has been added, and Gallican names have been substituted for Roman ones, such as *Contestatio* (for the Roman Preface) and *Secreta* (for the Roman *Super Oblata*). The *Francorum imperium* is mentioned in the *Orationes Sollemnes* of Good Friday, and Frankish saints are included in the commemoration of saints in the Canon.

At one time it was thought that the Gelasian Sacramentary represented the Roman rite at an early stage in its development, before the reform initiated by Gregory the Great gave rise to the production of the Gregorian Sacramentary. However, as H. A. P. Schmidt pointed out, if this were so, the liturgy of Rome would not so much have been revised by St Gregory as almost entirely rewritten by him. In a lengthy, detailed and masterly analysis of this sacramentary,[15] Antoine Chavasse has established that the prototype of the Old Gelasian was actually derived from an old Roman presbyteral (i.e. non-papal) sacramentary, which itself had been put together from a collection of *libelli*, and carefully edited. The collection and editing was done by Roman priests for use in the Roman *tituli*, or local churches of the city, before the end of the sixth century. No manuscript of it survives, but its existence can be inferred from the profound influence it has exercised over the compilation of the Old Gelasian, as well as over the papal Gregorian sacramentary and the sacramentaries of the Gallican rite. The differences between the presbyteral liturgy and the papal liturgy of the Lateran are marked, particularly as regards the cere-monies of Holy Week but also in the *Sanctorale*, where the feasts include the celebration of vigils and octaves which the papal liturgy ignores. When celebrating in the Roman *tituli* on the stational days, the pope used his papal sacramentary, the Gregorian, and the priests attached to the *tituli*, when celebrating on their own, used their presbyteral sacramentary.[16] There existed in the city and environs of Rome, therefore, two liturgies, distinct though closely related.

During the seventh and eighth centuries the Gregorian Sacramentary gradually established itself in the titular churches also, either replacing the presbyteral sacramentary entirely or giving rise to a hybrid liturgy. At about the same time Masses for saints' days from other parts of Italy, and even prayers peculiar to Roman monasteries, were incorporated into the presbyteral sacramentary. During the seventh century the latter, incorporating the additions already made to it, penetrated Gaul, where it influenced the local Gallican liturgy. What we know as the 'Old Gelasian' represents a sacramentary of this type adapted for Frankish liturgical purposes, and modified by the incorporation of Gregorian elements (notably the Canon).

The Gregorian Sacramentary

The traditional ascription of the compilation of the first papal sacramentary to St Gregory the Great[17] (who died in 604) is now widely regarded as incorrect, though it does appear to incorporate a significant number of prayers composed by him, and dates from no later than the first half of the seventh century.[18] The earliest surviving manuscript was written at the behest of Bishop Hildoard of Cambrai in 811/2 (*Sacramentum Gregorianum Cameracense*).[19]

It was a copy of this sacramentary which Adrian I sent to Charlemagne, at his request, some time between 784 and 791. The original of this so-called *Hadrianum* has not survived but there is no doubt that it was virtually identical to the Cambrai manuscript, which was written only some twenty to twenty-five years later. Since the *Hadrianum* was a papal feast-day and stational sacramentary only, it did not contain any formularies for the remaining days of the year. In particular, of ordinary Sundays only those of Advent appear; there are none for the Christmas, Epiphany, Easter or Pentecost seasons. Alcuin was therefore employed by Charlemagne to supplement it for the needs of the Frankish church. The supplement (known as the *Hucusque*, from its first word) draws on Frankish Gelasian sources.[20] It contains the Sunday Masses missing from the *Hadrianum*, the common of saints and votive Masses, ending with a series of prefaces and episcopal blessings. There are four Masses for the Advent Sundays, two after Christmas, three before and six during Lent, five after Easter and twenty-four after Pentecost. This scheme became standard throughout the West (and remained so until 1969). The *Hucusque* was originally kept separate from the *Hadrianum* but was later fused with it in the tenth to the eleventh centuries. The resulting sacramentary replaced the older Gelasian books only gradually (for example, a

Pontifical of Poitiers from about 900 provides for the lessons at the Easter Vigil to be either 'secundum Gelasium' or 'secundum Gregorium').[21]

A significant number of Gregorian sacramentaries, tracing their origin to the *Hadrianum*, are known from various parts of Europe; they include the Sacramentary of Leofric,[22] the Sacramentary of St Eligius[23] and the Missal of Robert of Jumièges,[24] dating from the tenth to eleventh centuries.

The Eighth-Century Gelasians

The penetration of the Frankish kingdom by Roman liturgical books gave rise to a series of hybrid sacramentaries, combining in various degrees elements of the Gregorian and Gelasian rites with Gallican elements. They are known as the 'Eighth Century Gelasians' or 'Frankish Gelasians'. The most important of these are the Sacramentary of Angoulême, originating in that city between 768 and 781;[25] the Sacramentary of Gellone, from the end of the eighth century and very similar to that of Angoulême;[26] the Sacramentary of Autun, also from the end of the eighth century;[27] the Sacramentary of Rheinau, of about 800;[28] and the Sacramentary of St Gall, from the first half of the ninth century.[29] These are all basically Gregorian sacramentaries which have been expanded to varying degrees with elements taken from the Gelasian tradition and local Gallican rites. They betray the fact that they are later than the Old Gelasian, *inter alia*, by their inclusion of Masses for the Thursdays of Lent.

Into a somewhat different category comes the so-called Sacramentary of Padua.[30] This seems to have been derived, around the year 680, from a Gregorian sacramentary, adapted by incorporating from the presbyteral sacramentary the Sunday Masses missing from the Gregorian and Masses for feasts, particularly the Marian feasts of the Assumption, Annunciation and Nativity, instituted in the seventh century. This adaptation appears to have taken place in Rome itself. It found its way to Gaul about the beginning of the eighth century. The compilers of the Frankish Gelasian sacramentaries appear to have taken the Gregorian content of their sacramentaries from the Paduan rather than from the *Hadrianum*.[31]

Later sacramentaries in the mixed Gregorian-Gelasian tradition include the Sacramentary of Fulda[32] and the Sacramentary of Ross[33] from the late tenth and eleventh century respectively.

The *Ordines Romani*

The ordines which contain material relevant to the study of the Holy Week liturgy are:[34]

Ordines XIIIA and XIIIB

These ordines date from the first half and the end of the eighth century respectively. They contain *inter alia* a list of the readings at Tenebrae on each day of the Triduum.

Ordines XV-XVI

These two ordines, which are both from the same hand, were composed shortly before the year 787. *Ordo* XV is concerned with the liturgy celebrated in ordinary churches and *Ordo* XVI with that appropriate to Benedictine monasteries.[35] They were both written with the purpose of promoting liturgical unity and substituting the Roman rite in place of rival traditions, as the author himself tells us in the closing paragraphs of *Ordo* XV.

Ordo XVII

Almost all the elements of this ordo are taken from *Ordo* XV or *Ordo* XVI. The title is identical to that of the latter (with the substitution of 'Breviarium' for 'Instructio'). The date is 790–800, the author a Frankish monk who, like the author of *Ordo* XV and *Ordo* XVI, was keen to promote liturgical unity and the use of the Roman rite.

Ordo XXIII

This ordo appears to be an unofficial account by a liturgically-minded Frankish monk, possibly from the region of Einsiedeln in modern Switzerland, of the papal ceremonies of the Triduum which he had witnessed in the course of a visit to Rome. The date seems to be eighth century, possibly the first half.

Ordo XXIV

This is an account, written by a Frankish monk some time during the second half of the eighth century, of the rites celebrated in

Rome from Wednesday to Saturday of Holy Week. Although it does not specifically mention the pope or the papal entourage, nor the Roman basilicas by name, the chants and prayers are those of the Roman antiphonaries and sacramentaries, and it refers to the 'pontifex' and clergy who on Wednesday and Thursday celebrate the liturgy at the altar in the principal church (*ecclesia maiore*). The Good Friday liturgy is stated to be celebrated in a different church within the city (as indeed it was), by the pontifex or by his designated representative, together with all the priests and clergy of the city and suburbs. The writer is describing either the papal ceremonies themselves, or possibly those ceremonies as adapted for celebration in the parish churches of the city.

Ordo XXV

This ordo dates from the opening years of the ninth century, and comprises a very brief description of the rites accompanying the blessing of the paschal candle in the parish churches of the city and suburbs of Rome (there was no such blessing in the papal rite).

Ordo XXVI

This ordo appears to be contemporary to *Ordo* XXIV. It is found in the same four manuscripts as *Ordo* XXIV and may indeed have been composed by the same person. It includes a description of the rites surrounding the kindling of new fire on each day of the Triduum and the extinction of lights during the night office of Tenebrae, in the churches of suburban Rome, as well as an account of the manufacture and distribution of the wax images known as 'Agnus Deis'.

Ordo XXVII

This is in two distinct parts, of different origin. The first part is almost entirely an amalgam of *Ordo* XXIV and *Ordo* XXVI, with which the ordo is approximately contemporary. The second part contains the Easter vespers which the pope celebrated at the Lateran, surrounded by the bishops of the suburban dioceses and the priests of the titular churches.

Ordo XXVIII

The author of this ordo, which dates from around 800, describes it in his title as for the period from the Sunday before Palm Sunday to the octave of Easter.[36] Most of the material is taken from *Ordo* XXVII, which in turn is dependent on *Ordines* XXIV and XXVI, though material from other ordines is also employed.

Ordo XXIX

The purpose of this ordo was to adapt the liturgy of the Triduum contained in *Ordo* XXVII to the requirements of a monastic community. One of the two surviving manuscripts in which it is found was written at the monastery of Corbie, in Picardy, and the ordo may well have been composed there, in the second half of the ninth century.

Ordo XXXA

This appears to have been written for a community of monks or canons regular, during the eighth century. It is concerned with the rites for Holy Week and Easter Week, commencing with Tenebrae of Holy Thursday and ending with the Saturday after Easter.

Ordo XXXB

A description of the papal rites celebrated in Rome from Tenebrae of Holy Thursday to the Saturday of Easter Week. The author, a Frankish monk, was evidently not personally familiar with the ceremonies which he describes, but has put together his account by drawing on material from several other *Ordines Romani*. It belongs to the end of the eighth century.

Ordo XXXI

This ordo was probably composed in north or north-east France in the second half of the ninth century. It covers the period from Palm Sunday to the octave of Easter, as celebrated in Rome according to the papal liturgy. As in the case of *Ordo* XXXB, it has been compiled by using material taken from several other ordines, notably *Ordo* XXVIII.

Ordo XXXII

Like *Ordo* XXIX this ordo may well have been composed at Corbie, the source of one of the two extant manuscripts which contain it. It is a description of the rites celebrated in a cathedral during the Triduum, according to the Roman rite, and belongs to the closing years of the ninth century.

Ordo XXXIII

This very short ordo survives in only a single manuscript of the eleventh century, and both its date and place of composition are unknown. It relates to the ceremonies of the Triduum according to the Roman rite.

Antiphonals

Five antiphonals relating to the period from around 750 to 900 survive, the Antiphonal of Mont Blandin (c.750–800), the Antiphonal of Rheinau (c.800), the Antiphonal of Senlis (c.880), the Antiphonal of Corbie (c.900) and the Antiphonal of Compiègne (end of the ninth century). These contain the texts to be sung by the choir throughout the year. To these may be added the Gradual of Monza (beginning of the ninth century), from Lombardy, which contains the texts of the Gradual and Tract or Alleluia sung between the Epistle and Gospel.[37]

The Romano-German Pontifical

It would be difficult to overestimate the importance of this pontifical in the history and development of the liturgy of the Western church. Composed in the scriptorium of the monastery of St Alban at Mainz around the middle of the tenth century, it soon spread rapidly throughout the Empire and even beyond its frontiers, in the course of the next two centuries. The liturgy which it contains represents the cross-fertilization of the imported Roman liturgy and the native Gallo-Frankish traditions which had been taking place over a period of some two and a half centuries. It was copied over and over again and survives today in some three dozen manuscripts, from Germany, France, Italy, England, Austria, Switzerland and Poland.[38] It reached Rome towards the end of the tenth century, and was immediately adopted for use in the Roman churches and basilicas, almost completely replacing the liturgy hitherto celebrated in the city and its environs.

Later Pontificals

The Romano-German Pontifical, apart from its unwieldy size which made its copying a lengthy and laborious process and its use in ordinary cathedrals and churches difficult, also contained details of ceremonies and texts which were foreign to the Roman rite, while omitting others belonging to the Roman liturgical tradition which had managed to survive the upheavals of the tenth century. In the course of the eleventh and twelfth centuries, therefore, further pontificals appeared, all of them offshoots of the Romano-German Pontifical, but adapted for use both in Rome and elsewhere, by pruning the latter book of rubrics and texts which were inappropriate to the Roman rite and adding others that were traditional to Rome or to the churches for which the new pontificals were intended.[39] These books achieved a very wide diffusion, owing to a number of factors, especially the emergence of the papacy as victorious in the struggle for supremacy with the empire for the leadership of Christian Europe, in consequence of which Christianity now looked to Rome as its definitive centre, where resided its head who, as the heir to the prerogatives of St Peter, was superior to every earthly power. Thanks to their more frequent contacts with the Holy See, the bishops and priests of different countries could learn about the books used in Rome and have copies made for use in their own dioceses and parishes.[40] A version of this pontifical even reached Syria in the wake of the Crusades.[41]

These books are known today collectively as the Pontifical of the Twelfth Century. But at the beginning of the thirteenth century, probably during the reign of Innocent III, an edition of the pontifical was produced specifically for use in the papal liturgy itself. This pontifical, known as the Pontifical of the Roman Curia, survives in a large number of copies, and in three versions: an original short one, a later longer one, created by the incorporation, during the later thirteenth century, of additional material from the Ordinary of the Papal Chaplains, and an intermediate one, created by the insertion of some of the additional material from the text of the longer version into that of the shorter one.[42]

Finally, during the years 1292 to 1295, Durandus, Bishop of Mende in Gévaudan, composed a new pontifical, with the object of producing a book for the universal use of the Latin Church.[43] Durandus achieved his objective, since his book scored an immediate and lasting success, in particular with the papal court at Avignon, where material from it was used to supplement the Pontifical of the Roman Curia, thus giving rise to hybrid pontificals. For a while both the Pontifical of the Roman Curia and that of Durandus, together with the various hybrid versions to which they had given rise, all circulated simultaneously. But it was the Pontifical of Durandus which eventually supplanted all others, and formed the basis for the first printed edition of 1485, and via this for the Tridentine Pontifical of 1595. The result was that the Holy Week ceremonies as described by Durandus remained in force, with little or no alterations, until the reform of 1955.

Monastic Customaries

The monastic customaries, or *consuetudines*, contain rules for the celebration of the liturgy in monastic houses, and are therefore of use in reconstructing the liturgy of Holy Week as celebrated in monastic communities. Examples of these customaries include the *Regularis Concordia* of St Dunstan, a code of monastic observance for England adopted by the Synod of Winchester during the episcopate of St Ethelwold (963–984),[44] the *Disciplina Farfensis et Monasterii Sancti Pauli Romae*, containing details of the ceremonies performed in the monastery of Farfa and that of St Paul outside the walls of Rome around the year 1040,[45] the *Consuetudines* of Cluny, from about 1060[46] and the *Decreta* of Lanfranc, Archbishop of Canterbury from 1070 to 1089.[47]

The Later *Ordines Romani*

Unlike the earlier *Ordines Romani*, these later ones, seven in all, were actually composed in Rome, during the course of the twelfth to fourteenth centuries. They were the work of the masters of ceremonies at the Lateran, and their purpose was to provide a comprehensive rubric to the ceremonies conducted in the papal chapel.[48] In conjunction with the Pontifical, which contained the required texts, they would have presented a complete guide to the performance of the rites in question.

Evangeliaries and Lectionaries

The evangeliary and lectionary began life as notes in the margin or the text of the scriptures, sometimes with an additional chronological list according to the ecclesiastical calendar, as an indication to the reader which passages were to be read on which days. An example of this type, the *Lectionum Capitulare et Notae Capuenses*,[49] comes from the region of Capua, near Naples, and is dated to just before the middle of the sixth century. At a somewhat later stage true evangeliaries and lectionaries, comprising lists of the relevant passages in separate books, make their appearance. The oldest known evangeliary of the Roman church is the *Evangeliorum Capitulare Romanum* of about 645.[50] It was twice revised around the middle of the eighth century. Other important early medieval evangeliaries include the Evangeliary of St Cuthbert, surviving in two manuscripts written in Lindisfarne around 700[51] but actually reproducing an original Neapolitan evangeliary of the mid-seventh century, and the Evangeliary of Salzburg, from the ninth century.[52]

Early lectionaries include the Lectionary of Würzburg, belonging to the seventh-eighth century,[53] the Lectionary of Corbie, of 772–780[54] and the Lectionary of Alcuin from 781–783.[55] Examples of books containing both non-Gospel and Gospel readings are the *Comes* of Murbach, from the end of the eighth century,[56] and the *Comes* Theotinchi, of about the same date.[57]

The Franciscan Missal

The Franciscan Missal originated in the demand of members of the newly-founded Franciscan Order (whose rule received papal approval in 1223) to be able to celebrate Mass every day. This was at a time when the habit of private celebration was growing and it was becoming accepted that every ordained priest had the right, if not the duty, to say Mass every day, whether there was any congregation present or not. The Franciscans were an itinerant order, and they found the wide diversity of the liturgies celebrated in the places through which they passed in the course of their travels confusing. They decided therefore to adopt, as a standard for their Order, the liturgy of the papal court. The first Franciscan missal was produced around 1241. It was shortly followed by a second edition under the direction of Haymo of Faversham, the fourth Minister General of the Order, who drew up an independent set of rubrics for both the office and the Mass. A further revision was undertaken by St Bonaventure, who became the sixth Minister General in 1257. As a result of the itinerant nature of the Order, their missal became widely diffused and was instrumental in disseminating the knowledge of the papal liturgy throughout Europe in the course of the thirteenth and fourteenth centuries.[58]

Medieval Commentators

A considerable amount of information about the medieval Holy Week liturgy can be gleaned from the pages of commentators who often describe the ceremonies in detail, frequently with the purpose of explaining the rites concerned in allegorical terms. The principal such commentators are Amalarius of Metz (c.780–850); Rabanus Maurus, Abbot of Fulda and Archbishop of Metz (c.776–856); John of Avranches, Archbishop of Rouen from 1067 to 1079; Rupert, Abbot of Deutz, near Cologne (c.1075–1129); Honorius of Autun (died c.1151); John Beleth, Rector of the University of Paris (died c.1190); Sicardus, Bishop of Cremona (1160–1215); and Durandus, Bishop of Mende in Lozère (c.1230–1296). To these may be added an anonymous treatise known as the *De divinis officiis*, once attributed to Alcuin of York but now known, on internal evidence, to date from the tenth to eleventh century, and commonly referred to as Pseudo-Alcuin.

Notes

[1]   This historical sketch is based principally on the preliminary chapter to M. Andrieu, *Les Ordines Romani du Haut Moyen Age*, Vol. 2 (Louvain, 1948), with additional material from *The Shorter Cambridge Medieval History* and *The Oxford Illustrated History of Medieval Europe*, ed. George Holmes (OUP, 1990).

[2]   Regulam catholicae traditionis suscepisti, frater amantissime; sic omnibus praedica, omnesque doce, sicut a sancta Romana, cui Deo auctore

deservimus, accepisti Ecclesia. (Ep. xiii, Zachariae papae ad Bonifacium episcopum, *PL* 89, 952).

3 Ut uno eodemque modo Dominicae dispensationis in carne sacrosanctae festivitates, in omnibus ad eas rite competentibus rebus, id est in baptismi officio, in missarum celebratione, in cantilenae modo celebrentur, iuxta exemplar videlicet quod scriptum de romana habemus ecclesia. Itemque ut per gyrum totius anni natalicia sanctorum uno eodem die, iuxta martyrologium eiusdem romanae ecclesiae ... venerentur. (Canon 13, A.W. Haddan and W. Stubbs, *Councils and Ecclesiastical Documents Relating to Great Britain and Ireland*, Vol. III (OUP, 1871), p. 367.

4 Cantilenae vero perfectiorem scientiam, quam pene tota Francia diligit, Stephanus papa, cum ad Pippinum, patrem Caroli magni imperatoris, in Franciam pro iustitia sancti Petri a Langobardis expetenda venisset, per suos clericos, praesente eodem Pippino, invexit, indeque usus eius longe lateque convaluit (Walafrid Strabo, *Liber de exordiis et incrementis quarundam in observationibus ecclesiasticis rerum*, c.26 [ed. A. Knoepfler, Munich, 1890, p. 84]).

5 Psalmas, notas, cantus, compotum, grammaticam per singula monasteria vel episcopia et libros catholicos bene emendate; quia saepe, dum bene aliqui Deum rogare cupiunt, sed per inemendatos libros male rogant. Et pueros vestros non sinite eos vel legendo vel scribendo corrumpere; et si opus est evangelium, psalterium et missale scribere, perfectae aetatis homines scribant cum omni diligentia. (Charlemagne, *Admonitio generalis* 72 MGH leg. Sect. II 1.60.2).

6 See Andrieu, 'Le Pontifical Romain au Moyen-Age', (*Studi e Testi*, 86–89, Vatican, 1938–41) Vol. I, pp. 3–12.

7 In the post-Vatican II reforms the ancient order of the subdeacon, who still performed an important role in the High Mass of the old Roman rite, including the chanting of the Epistle, was abolished. Non-Gospel scriptural readings are now normally read by a layman. The custom of chanting them, which went back to the synagogue practice of apostolic times, has virtually disappeared.

8 Paris BN lat. 10575. Modern edition by W. Greenwell, *The Pontifical of Egbert, Archbishop of York*, Surtees Society 27 (Durham, 1853). The texts appropriate to Holy Week may also be found in Schmidt, *HS*, pp. 552–6.

9 Confusingly, the term 'missal' is sometimes applied to books that are not true missals at all, but sacramentaries, such as the Missal of Leofric and the Missal of Bobbio.

10 Vatican Regina lat. 316. The standard modern edition of the Old Gelasian Sacramentary is L. C. Mohlberg, in *Rerum Ecclesiasticarum Documenta*, Series Major Fontes iv (Rome: Herder, 1960).

11 Walafrid of Strabo, Abbot of Reichenau, writing around the year 840, tells us that Pope Gelasius made a compilation of prayers, some composed by himself and some by others, which were adopted in Gaul and were still in use there in his day (*De Rebus Ecclesiasticis* XXII [*PL* 114, 946]).

12 See B. Capelle in 'Messes du pape s. Gélase, dans le sacramentaire léonien', *Revue Bénédictine* LVI (1945–46), pp. 12–41, and A. Chavasse in 'Messes du

pape Vigile, dans le sacramentaire léonien', *Ephemerides Liturgicae*, LXIV, pp. 161–213.

13 W. H. Frere, in *Studies in Early Roman Liturgy*, Alcuin Club 28 (1930) Vol. 1, pp. 35ff, argued that the prototype was a sacramentary of the Roman Church, which was adapted first for use in suburban Rome and the neighbourhood of Capua and then, after a copy of this book had crossed the Alps, adapted again for use in the Frankish kingdom. H. A. P. Schmidt (*HS*, pp. 346–8), on the other hand, while not disputing that it was of Roman origin, argued that it was compiled in Gaul from the many Roman *libelli* (individual Mass formulae) which had come to Gaul during the second half of the sixth century, and was expanded by the addition of Gallican material, to produce a true sacramentary.

14 'liber Sacramentorum Romanae aecclesiae ordinis anni circuli'.

15 A. Chavasse, *Le Sacramentaire Gélasien*, (Bibl. de Théologie, Série IV, Tournai, 1958), Vol. 1. Chavasse's conclusions are briefly summarized in T. Klauser, *A Short History of the Western Liturgy*, 2nd ed. (OUP, 1979), pp. 55–8.

16 On a stational day the pope celebrated the Eucharist in the basilica or titulus designated for that day, the priests of the city concelebrating with him. Each priest then returned to his own church and celebrated a second Eucharist. See Chavasse, op. cit., pp. 78–9. Although this practice was long since obsolete, the name of the church in which the pope celebrated on each stational day was still printed in Roman missals down to the post-Vatican II liturgical reforms.

17 The heading to the oldest surviving manuscript of the sacramentary proclaims the book to be 'Liber Sacramentorum de circulo anni expositum a S. Gregorio Papa Romano edito ex authentico libro bibliothecae cubiculi scriptum'.

18 For the elements probably composed by Gregory himself see Henry Ashworth, OSB, 'Liturgical Prayers of St Gregory', in *Traditio* (Fordham, 1959).

19 Cambrai, cod. 164. Other important early mss include *Ottobonianus* (Vat. Ottob. lat. 313) written for the cathedral of Paris in the third quarter of the ninth century and *Reginensis* (Vat. Reg. lat. 337) written in Gaul, possibly at Lyon, in 867–872. Modern editions of all three by H. A. Wilson, *The Gregorian Sacramentary under Charles the Great, Edited from Three MSS of the Ninth Century*, HBS, Vol. XLIX (London, 1915).

20 Its attribution to Alcuin (originally in the eleventh century *De Ecclesiasticis Observationibus*) has been doubted by some scholars, in favour of Benedict of Aniane.

21 Si vero lectiones secundum Gelasium recitandae fuerint, post benedictionem cerei antequam legatur prima lectio: *In principio creavit Deus*, dicitur a sacerdote oratio haec: *Deus qui divitias misericordiae tuae*. Quod si secundum Gregorium, non dicitur haec oratio, sed post benedictionem cerei, statim prima lectio recitatur, non pronuntiante lectore titulum lectionis, quod et in ceteris observandum sive secundum Gelasium, sive secundum Gregorium legantur. (Martene, *De Antiquis Ecclesiae Ritibus* (Antwerp, 1737), Lib. III, cap. XXIV (col. 434).

22 Oxford Bod. ms Bodl 579. Modern edition by F. E. Warren, *The Leofric Missal* (OUP, 1883).

23 Paris BN lat. 12051. No modern edition exists, but the full text is in *PL 78*, 25–240. Texts appropriate to Holy Week in Schmidt, *HS*, pp. 437–45.

24 Rouen, Bibliothèque Municipale, Y6. Modern edition by H. A. Wilson, *The Missal of Robert of Jumièges*, HBS 11 (London, 1896). Texts appropriate to Holy Week in Schmidt, *HS*, pp. 446–50.

25 Paris, BN lat. 816. Modern edition in Volume CLIX C of the *Corpus Christianorum*, Series Latina (Turnhout, 1987).

26 Paris, BN lat. 12048. Modern edition in Volume CLIX A of the *Corpus Christianorum*, Series Latina.

27 Berlin, Staatsbibliothek Phillips 1667. Modern edition in Volume CLIX B of the *Corpus Christianorum*, Series Latina.

28 Zurich, Zentralbibliothek, Hds. Rh 40. Modern edition A. Haenggi-A. Schönherr, *Sacramentarium Rhenaugiense* (Fribourg, 1970).

29 St Gall, Stiftsbibliothek, Cod. 348. Modern edition K. Mohlberg, *Das fränkische Sacramentarium Gelasianum in alamannischer Ueberlieferung* (Münster, 1939).

30 Padua, Biblioteca Capitolare D 47. The surviving manuscript belongs to the beginning of the ninth century. Modern edition K. Mohlberg and A. Baumstark, *Die älteste erreichbare Gestalt des Liber Sacramentorum anni circuli der Römischen Kirche* (Münster, 1927).

31 See Chavasse, op. cit., pp. 552–68.

32 Göttingen, University Library, Cod. theol. 231. Modern edition by G. Richter and A. Schönfelder, *Sacramentarium Fuldense saeculi X der K. Universi-tätsbibliothek zu Göttingen* (Fulda, 1912). Texts relating to Holy Week in Schmidt, *HS*, pp. 420–6.

33 Vatican, Ross. lat. 204. Modern edition by J. Brinktrine, *Sacramentarium Rossianum, Cod. Lat. 204* (Freiburg, 1930). Texts appropriate to Holy Week in Schmidt, *HS*, pp. 429–32.

34 The full texts of these ordines may be found in Andrieu, *ORM* Vol. 3, on which the brief summaries which follow are based.

35 *OR XV* is entitled 'Capitulare ecclesiastici ordinis, qualiter a sancta atque apostolica romana ecclesia celebratur', and *OR XVI* 'Instruccio ecclesiastici ordinis qualiter in coenubiis fideliter domino servientes tam juxta auctori-tatem catholice atque apostolice romane ecclesie quam iuxta dispositione et regulam sancti Benedicti missarum solemniis vel nataliciis sanctorum seu et officiis divinis anni circoli die noctuque auxiliante domino debeant celebrare'.

36 'Incipit ordo a dominica mediana usque in octabas paschae'.

37 All six published in R. Hesbert, *Antiphonale Missarum Sextuplex d'après le Graduel de Monza et les antiphonaires de Rheinau, du Mont-Blandin, de Compiègne, de Corbie et de Senlis.* (Brussels, 1935). Texts relating to Holy Week in Schmidt, *HS*, pp. 480–98.

38 Complete list in Andrieu, *ORM* Vol. 2, pp. 497–8. For an account of the origin and distribution of this pontifical see pp. 495–511 of the same work. See also Andrieu, *PRM* Vol. I, pp. 3–8.

39   For text and commentary see Andrieu, PRM Vol. I.
40   Andrieu, PRM Vol. I, pp. 16–17.
41   In the shape of the so-called Pontifical of Apamea. See Andrieu, PRM Vol. I, pp. 102–10.
42   For text and commentary see Andrieu, PRM Vol. II.
43   For text and commentary see Andrieu, PRM Vol. III.
44   *PL* 137, 490–5.
45   *PL* 150, 1197–1204. The abbey of Farfa is in the Sabina area, about 30 miles north of Rome.
46   *PL* 149, 657–64.
47   *PL* 150, 455–68.
48   There is a problem with the numbering of the two sets of *Ordines Romani*. For the earlier ordines Andrieu employed upper case Roman numerals. Unfortunately these had also been used for five of the later ordines, first published by J. Mabillon in Musaeum Italicum (Paris, 1689) and later by Migne in *PL* Vol. 78, and the two sets of numbers overlap. I have followed Andrieu in using upper case Roman numerals for the earlier ordines, and have used lower case Roman numerals for the later ones. Two of the later ordines, the *Ordo Albini* and the *Ordo Ecclesiae Lateranensis*, were not published either by Mabillon or by Migne, but may be found in P. Fabre and L. Duchesne, *Le Liber Censuum de l'Eglise Romaine* (Paris, 1910) and in L. Fischer, *Bernhardi Cardinalis et Lateranensis Ecclesiae Prioris Ordo Officiorum Ecclesiae Lateranensis* (Munich and Freising, 1916) respectively.
49   Fulda, Landesbibliothek 1. The section for Holy Week is to be found in Schmidt, HS, pp. 470–1.
50   Surviving in four manuscripts, of which the oldest is that in the library of the University of Würzburg (Mp. th. fol. 62), written around 700. For the date of composition see Chavasse, op. cit., p. 552. It is usually known by the Greek letter Π, to distinguish it from its two later revisions, Λ of about 740 and Σ of about 755. Schmidt designates them as *Evangeliorum Capitulare Romanum* A, B and C respectively (*HS*, pp. 308–9). See Th. Klauser, *Das römische Capitulare evangeliorum* (Münster, 1935). The sections for Holy Week can be found in Schmidt, *HS*, pp. 458–60.
51   British Museum, Cotton Nero D IV and Cod. Regio I B VII. Holy Week section in Schmidt, *HS*, pp. 471–2.
52   Salzburg, Benediktinerstift St Peter, A VIII 33. Section for Holy Week in Schmidt, *HS*, pp. 466–7.
53   Würzburg, University Library, Mp. th. fol. 62. See G. Morin, 'Le plus ancien comes ou lectionnaire de l'église Romaine', *Revue Bénédictine* XXVII (1910), pp. 41–74. Section for Holy Week in Schmidt, *HS*, pp. 457–8.
54   St Petersburg. Cod. Q.V. I.16. See W. Frere, *Studies in Early Roman Liturgy*, III. The Roman Epistle-Lectionary, Alcuin Club 32 (London, 1935). Section for Holy Week in Schmidt, *HS*, pp. 462–3.
55   Cambrai, Bibl. Capitulaire 553 and Paris BN lat. 9452. Modern edition by A. Wilmart, OSB, 'Le lectionnaire d'Alcuin', *Ephemerides Liturgicae* LI (1937), pp. 136–97. Holy Week section in Schmidt, *HS*, pp. 463–4.
56   Besançon, Bibl. Municipale, 184. See A. Wilmart, OSB, 'Le comes de

Murbach', *Revue Bénédictine* XXX (1913), pp. 25–69, 124–32. Section for Holy Week in Schmidt, *HS*, p. 464.

57   Beauvais, Bibl. Capitulaire. Text in *PL* 30, 487–532. Section for Holy Week in Schmidt, *HS*, pp. 465–6.

58   See J. H. Walker, 'Early Franciscan Influence on Thirteenth Century Roman Liturgy', in Subornost, Series 3 no. 19 (1956); also J. A. Jungmann, *The Mass of the Roman Rite*, Vol. I (Dublin: Four Courts Press, 1955), p. 101. There is no modern edition of the Franciscan Missal.

CHAPTER 4

PALM SUNDAY

In Chapter 2, we saw how the Holy Week celebrations in late fourth-century Jerusalem included a procession during the afternoon of the Sunday before Easter (called 'the Day of the Palms' in the Armenian Lectionary) from the Mount of Olives to the church of the Holy Sepulchre, in which the people carried palms in imitation of the crowds who greeted Christ on his triumphal entry into Jerusalem. We also saw how information concerning the rites celebrated in Jerusalem at that time was relayed by pilgrims such as Egeria and the Bordeaux Pilgrim to their compatriots in other parts of the Christian world. There must have been many Egerias whose accounts have not survived the ravages of time, and many others too who never committed their experiences to writing, but who recounted them by word of mouth to their fellow members of local churches when they arrived back home from their pilgrimage.

It is not surprising, therefore, to find that the ceremonies associated in Jerusalem with Palm Sunday were soon being imitated throughout the East.[1] We do not know, however, exactly when the churches of western Europe began to follow them. There is a gap of over two hundred years between Egeria's account and the first reference to 'the Day of the Palms' in the West. This occurs in the *Liber Etymologiarum* of St Isidore of Seville, written about the year 620.[2] Isidore refers to the day as the *Dies Palmarum* and tells us that it was so called because a multitude of people on that day had gone out to meet Christ with palm branches crying, 'Hosanna, blessed is He who comes in the name of the Lord, the King of Israel'. He goes on to say that it was also commonly known as *Capitilavium*, because it was the day on which the heads of the children who were to be baptized were washed for the first time since the beginning of Lent, so that they would be clean for their baptism, and that it was on this day that the ceremony known as the *traditio symboli*, the disclosure of the Creed to the catechumens, was performed.[3]

At Jerusalem in St Cyril's time the disclosure and exposition of the Creed (the *traditio symboli* and *explanatio symboli*) took place over a period of two weeks, the sixth and seventh weeks of the eight-week Jerusalem Lent.[4] The candidates were expected to learn it by heart and repeat it back (the *redditio symboli*) on the Saturday of the seventh week. In Gaul and Spain, however, (but not in Rome) the *traditio* took place on Palm Sunday, as decreed by the Council of Agde in 506.[5] Besides St Isidore of Seville, it is also mentioned by St Ildefonsus, Archbishop of Toledo from 657, who says of it,

> This creed which the *competentes* receive on the day of anointing [Palm Sunday], either on their own account if they are adults or through the medium of guardians if they are children, should be recited and repeated back to the priest on Holy Thursday, so that, having thus proved their faith, they may approach the coming sacrament of the Lord's Resurrection through the holy fount of baptism.[6]

The learned Rabanus Maurus, Abbot of Fulda and, from 847, Archbishop of Mainz, a one time pupil of Alcuin, also tells us that the day was known as *Capitilavium*, and attests the practice of the *traditio symboli* on this day.[7]

By the early eighth century the day was already known in England as 'Palm Sunday', being referred to as such by St Bede in his twenty-third homily.[8] His approximate contemporary, St Aldhelm, Bishop of Sherborne, calls the day the *sacrosancta palmarum solemnitas*, and refers to the singing of *Benedictus qui venit in nomine Domini* and *Hosanna*.[9] The Old Gelasian Sacramentary of the same period from France calls it *Dominica in Palmis de Passione Domini*,[10] a title which combines both Gallican and Roman concepts of the day, as does the Sacramentary of Angoulême, of about 780,[11] and, in a somewhat different way, the Sacramentary of Gellone, of around 800.[12] All five of our earliest antiphonals, from between about 750 and 900, refer to it simply as 'Palm Sunday', as does the Gradual of Monza.[13] The name *Pascha florum* or *Pascha floridum* is also sometimes found, deriving from the widespread custom of using flowers either together with palms or instead of them when they were not available.[14]

In the earliest surviving manuscript of the Gregorian Sacramentary, written in France at the beginning of the ninth century, but believed to be a faithful copy of one sent to Charlemagne from Pope Adrian, the day is called *Die Dominica in Palmas ad sanctum Iohannem in Lateranis*, notwithstanding that there is no blessing of palms or procession in the Roman rite at this date, the liturgy of the day in Rome centring instead on the reading of the Passion according to St Matthew. On the other hand, the various editions of the *Evangeliorum Capitulare Romanum*, which date from the middle of the seventh to that of the eighth century, merely refer to it as the sixth Sunday in Lent.[15]

Other early names for the day, based on the desire or preparation for baptism, are known, such as the *Pascha petitum* and the *Pascha competentium*.[16] The Bobbio Missal, a Gallican sacramentary from Piedmont datable to the seventh or eighth century, calls it, in rather eccentric Latin, *In Symbolum ad Aures Apercionis ad Elictus* ('of the Creed and the opening of the ears of the chosen ones').[17]

Yet another name for the day is *Dies indulgentiae* or *Dominica indulgentiae* ('the day of pardon' or 'the Sunday of pardon'). This is the name given to it, for example, in both the *Comes* of Würzburg and the *Comes* of Murbach, as well as in the Evangeliary of St Cuthbert.[18] The name appears to originate in the late Roman custom whereby the Emperor granted prisoners fourteen days clemency, from the Sunday before to the Sunday after Easter, to enable them to take part in the ceremonies of Holy Week and Easter Week.[19]

Most of the above names for the day figure in the lengthy heading to the Palm Sunday rite of the Romano-German Pontifical, which reads 'The Sunday of Pardon, which is known by various names, that is to say the Day of Palms or Flowers and Branches, Hosanna, the Longed for Pasch or that of the Co-seekers and the Washing of Heads; station at Saint John Lateran'.[20]

The Blessing of Palms

We do not know how long before the time of St Isidore the celebration of Palm Sunday in Spain began; in fact, we cannot be totally certain that the day was marked by any special celebration involving palms even in his time, since he merely mentions the name and tells us nothing about the liturgy of the day. However, the Jerusalem ceremonies were known about in Spain by the end of the fourth century at the latest (Egeria herself was probably Spanish), and it is improbable that the local church merely talked about it for some two hundred years or more before proceeding to imitate it. It seems likely, therefore, that the observation of Palm Sunday, in Spain at least, began during the fifth century. There may well have been a blessing and procession of palms, but in the absence of any relevant evidence no details are known.[21]

The first references we have to a blessing of palms come from the Bobbio Missal, from Northern Italy, and the Mozarabic Oracional Visigotico, from Spain. Both of these belong to the seventh or eighth century, but unfortunately they cannot be more closely dated than this.[22] The Bobbio blessing is headed 'Benedictio Palmae et Olivae super Altario' ('Blessing of the Palm and the Olive upon the Altar'). It asks that the olive branches and palms 'may be blessed with a perpetual blessing' in order that the people may take them to their homes, to act as a protection against illness and the designs of their enemies, 'so that all nations may know that Thy name is glorious for ever and ever'.[23] There are two blessings in the *Oracional Visigotico*, headed 'Die dominico in Ramos palmarum benedictio' and 'Die dominico in Ramos palmarum ad benedictionem palmarum'. Notwithstanding the latter heading, the texts, which are in a tripartite form character-istic of the Mozarabic and Gallican liturgies, suggest rather a blessing of the people than of the palms which they are carrying:

> Bless, O Lord, Thy people, who desire to see this mystery. Amen. So that they who carry palm branches, may deserve to see Thee in the kingdom of heaven. Amen. May they also deserve to see with the utmost joy the resurrection day of Him whom they proclaim with shouts of 'Hosanna'. Amen.[24]

The earliest reasonably datable blessing involving palms is in the Pontifical of Egbert of York which appears to belong to the middle of the eighth century.[25] It survives in a copy made in France.[26] Like the blessing in the *Oracional Visigothico*, it is in tripartite form and is a blessing of the people rather than of the palms themselves. It asks God to grant that 'just as you have come zealously to Him with branches of palm and other trees, so after death you may appear worthy of the palm of victory and the fruit of good works'.[27] There is no reference to taking the palms home or to any procession.

Slightly later than the blessing in the Pontifical of Egbert come three blessings, two from Languedoc and the other from Central Europe. The first two come from the Sacramentary of Gellone, written during the last decade of the eighth century.[28] They are both real blessings of the palms themselves; in the second God is asked to sanctify them

> so that those who receive them may be filled with Thy grace in all things, and obtain the remedy of salvation, and, as they rejoice in the solemnity of this day, so wouldst Thou fill their homes with Thy blessing, and keep their bodies and minds clean from all pollution.[29]

The third comes from the almost contemporary Sacramentary of Prague;[30] after referring to the Old Testament prototypes of Noah and Jacob, it goes on 'we beseech Thee, almighty God, to bless these branches of olive, which Thy servants are about to receive in their hands, coming to meet Thee with blessings and cries of "Blessed is He who comes in the name of the Lord, the King of Israel"'.[31]

From the middle of the following century we have a blessing of palms in one manuscript of the Gregorian Sacramentary, written for use in the Cathedral of Paris.[32] Since the blessing is not found in other manuscripts of this sacramentary, in particular in the copy of the *Hadrianum* made at Cambrai in 811–812, it is certain that it is a Frankish addition to the original.

> O God whose son came down to earth from heaven for the salvation of the human race, and as the hour of His passion approached willed to enter Jerusalem on an ass and be praised and hailed as king by the crowds, deign to bless these palms and branches of other trees, so that all those who are carrying them may be so filled with the gift of Thy blessing that in this world they may overcome the temptations of the ancient enemy, and in the world to come may be worthy to appear before Thee with the palm of victory and the fruit of good works.

The closing words of this blessing ('et in futuro cum palma victoriae et fructu bonorum operum tibi valeant apparere') mirror those of the blessing found in the Pontifical of Egbert some hundred years previously, though the blessing is now specifically one of the palms themselves.

It is noteworthy that there was a procession of palms in the Jerusalem liturgy but no antecedent blessing; at least, if there was, Egeria does not mention it. In the early medieval western rites, however, there is a blessing of palms but no mention of any procession. These rites also show some differences from one another. In the Bobbio rite the emphasis is on the taking home of the blessed palms to act as a safeguard against natural disasters and human enemies; in the *Oracional Visigotico*, as in the Pontifical of Egbert, the blessing is more one of the people, who we are told are carrying branches of palm or other trees, and proclaiming Christ's entry into Jerusalem with shouts of 'Hosanna'. We do not know if any of these blessings was followed by a procession; the fact that none is mentioned is not conclusive. The pre-1955 Roman rite included no less than six prayers of blessing of the palms, and none of them makes any reference to the procession which took place immediately afterwards. The evidence from the seventh and eighth centuries is in fact simply too meagre to enable us to tell for sure whether there was a procession or not at that time.

The Procession

The earliest certain evidence that we have for a procession of palms comes from the Frankish kingdom and belongs to the early ninth century. There is a famous story that the processional hymn *Gloria Laus et Honor*, which is still in use today, was composed by Theodulph, Bishop of Orleans, in the year 818 while he was imprisoned at Angers for his involvement in a conspiracy against the emperor, Louis the Pious, son of Charlemagne. The story goes that he sang his newly-composed hymn when he heard the Palm Sunday procession, with the emperor in attendance, go past the window of his cell, and that Louis was so impressed that he ordered his immediate release and reinstatement. There is no reason to doubt the attribution of the hymn to Theodulph,[33] and it was certainly composed at Angers, as the many references to the topography of the city in its original thirty-nine verses indicate,[34] though the elements of the story regarding the circumstances of its composition are probably apocryphal.[35] What seems to be certain is that at Angers in the early ninth century, and almost certainly throughout the Frankish kingdom at the time, there was a procession with palms, or with whatever foliage was locally available to represent them, in honour of Christ's entry into Jerusalem, for which Theodulph composed his famous hymn. The text of the hymn indicates that the procession began separately in the various parish churches of the surrounding area and then converged on the cathedral in the centre of the city, praying and singing hymns all the while. Theodulph's hymn is written in 'heroic couplets', alternating non-rhyming hexameters and pentameters, a verse form which went back to classical antiquity and was already becoming obsolete by the ninth century.

Amalarius of Metz, writing about the year 830, tells us that it is customary to carry palms around the churches and cry 'Hosanna' in memory of Christ's triumphal entry into Jerusalem.[36] A procession in ninth-century Spain is also envisaged by the Mozarabic *Liber Ordinum*, which refers to a preliminary assembly of the faithful in one church where the palms are blessed, followed by a procession to another where Mass is celebrated.[37] But the first full account of a rite encompassing both the blessing and procession to be found in any liturgical book comes from the Romano-German Pontifical, composed in Mainz around the middle of the tenth century. In this document it is already highly developed, though unfortunately we cannot trace the steps by which this development came about. Since it is both the first surviving comprehensive account of the blessing and procession of palms on Palm Sunday, and the principal source for that liturgy as celebrated in the Roman rite down to the middle of the twentieth century, it is worth describing in some detail.

After the singing of Terce and a litany, branches of palm, olive or other trees are laid out, and a priest blesses salt and water and mixes them together. A cantor begins the Introit *Osanna filio David*, after which the priest says the Collect *Deus quem diligere et amare iustitia est*, followed by a reading from Exodus 15:27–16:10. Two paraphonistae then sing the Tract *Collegerunt pontifices et pharisaei* from John 11:47–50, 53. When they have finished the deacon reads the Gospel of Christ's triumphal entry into Jerusalem, either from Matthew 21:1–9 or from Mark 11:1–10 (some manuscripts prescribe one and some the other). The Gospel may be followed by a sermon from the bishop, should he feel so inclined. After the Gospel, or the sermon, as the case may be, the palms are first exorcized and then blessed. Nine prayers of blessing are provided. Some of these are clearly intended as alternatives, depending on the type of branches to be blessed: olives and palms together, olives alone, olives with branches of other trees, or palms together with branches of other trees. Some of the blessings however are simply headed 'Alia', the meaning of which is not free from ambiguity; it is not clear whether they are intended as alternative blessings or additional ones. One of these prayers is identical to that found as a Frankish addition in the *Codex Ottobonianus* of the Gregorian Sacramentary, except that the phrase 'those who are carrying them' is replaced by 'those who are about to carry them', since they have not yet been distributed, and another is the first of the two blessings which we have already met in the Sacramentary of Gellone. There then follows a lengthy prayer cast in the form of a preface, preceded by the usual dialogue. After recalling Old Testament prototypes, it ends with a petition that 'Thou wouldst save us Thy servants from the mouth of hell and deign to grant us the assistance of Thy grace, so that after living just, devout and holy lives Thou wouldst admit us to the company of Thy saints and Thine elect'.[38] A prayer of blessing is then said over the people, and holy water is sprinkled over the palms, olives or other branches, and they are incensed. Two further prayers, that the palms may sanctify both those places into which they are brought and those who live in them, follow in the manuscripts. These are almost certainly intended as alternatives. Finally the palms are distributed to the people, accompanied by the singing of the antiphon *Ante sex dies sollemnis paschae*. A final prayer follows, and then the procession to the church where Mass is to be celebrated begins.

Along the way, the antiphons *Cum appropinquaret, Cum audisset* and *Turba multa* are sung, with psalm 97, *Cantate domino*. Then a stop is made at a place designated as the Station of the Holy Cross. The clergy and people halt reverently in their proper places, and the child *paraphonistae* begin the antiphon *Fulgentibus palmis*. The schola replies on the people's side with *Occurrunt turbae*. Then the members of the schola on the side of the cross approach it with measured pace and, throwing their cloaks or caps on the ground with every reverence, they prostrate themselves in veneration of the crucifix, while the clergy sing *Pueri Hebraeorum vestimenta prosternebant*. They withdraw and lay boys from the other side, singing *Kyrie eleison* and following the banner which is carried before them, throw their palm branches on the ground at a given signal, and then they too prostrate themselves in veneration of the crucifix, while the clergy sing *Pueri Hebraeorum tollentes ramos olivarum*. They withdraw in their turn and the child paraphonistae sing the first verse of the hymn *Gloria laus et honor* beside the cross, the clergy repeating it. The remaining five verses follow in order, the schola, either looking in the direction of the Gospel book or bowing their heads towards the cross, repeating the first verse between each of the others. At the end of the hymn the schola begins the antiphon *Omnes conlaudent*, followed by Psalm 147 *Lauda Jerusalem*; then all the people throw their flowers or branches down while the clergy sing the antiphon *Cum angelis et pueris*. Afterwards the bishop or priest approaches the cross and, prostrate on the ground, venerates the crucifix with all the people, likewise prostrate, while the clergy sing the antiphon *Scriptum est enim: Percutiam pastorem*. The bishop, rising, says the prayer *Deus qui miro dispositionis ordine*. Then the procession, following the cross and the banners, goes on to the city or the church where Mass is to be celebrated, the clergy singing along the way antiphons or responsories appropriate to the feast, or the hymn *Magnum salutis gaudium*. As they enter the gates of the city all the people sing *Kyrie eleison* and the choirmaster begins the antiphon *Ingrediente domino*. The clergy take up the responsory and the verse *Cumque audissent* with the *Gloria Patri*. If this ends before the procession arrives at the principal church, other antiphons from the Matins of the day are sung to fill the gap. On arrival at the church, a cantor begins the antiphon *Coeperunt omnes turbae*, followed by the *Benedictus*. The procession ends with a short prayer, *Adiuva nos, Deus, salutaris noster*, said by the priest, after which the Mass of the day begins.[39]

The first part of this rite is cast in the form of a *missa sicca* or 'dry mass'. We have an Introit, a Collect, a reading from the Old Testament, a Tract and a Gospel, which may be followed by a sermon. This formula exactly mirrors the first part of the Mass itself, or the Liturgy of the Word, as it is now generally known. In a later version of the rite, found in the Roman Pontifical of the

Twelfth Century, though not in the Romano-German Pontifical, there is also a Preface and Sanctus. It is tempting to speculate that this format reflects the remnants of a Mass celebrated in the church where the palms were blessed, before the procession to the principal church where the Mass of the day took place. There is no actual evidence of this, though in view of the fact that there is to all intents and purposes no detailed evidence at all of the development of the rite prior to its appearance in the Romano-German Pontifical, the possibility cannot be entirely ruled out. It is more likely, however, that it was always a 'dry mass', given that such 'masses' were quite common in the Middle Ages. The form of such a rite is explained by Durandus of Mende; the priest, vested as though for a true Mass, proceeds as usual as far as the Offertory, and no further, except that he may, if he wishes, say the Preface as well.[40] The Preface and Sanctus in the Roman Pontifical, which survived in the Roman rite until the 1955 reform, are in any event an importation; not only are they not found in the Romano-German Pontifical, but the Preface is clearly an adaptation of one for the common of martyrs from the *Missale Gothicum* of around 700.[41] The reason for celebrating a *missa sicca* before the palms were blessed may well have been to provide the liturgy of the day with a series of readings and chants appropriate to Christ's triumphal entry into Jerusalem, in counterpoise to those of the Mass itself, which concentrate on his Passion.[42]

In the rite described in the Romano-German Pontifical the high point of the procession is the veneration of the processional cross. As well as the cross, banners are borne before each section of the crowd (clergy, choir and people), and of course the palms themselves are carried. In the document known as Pseudo-Alcuin, however, which was composed in Gaul about the end of the tenth century, the focal point of the procession is a receptacle containing the Gospel book. The rite itself is a good deal simpler than that of the Romano-German Pontifical. There is no *missa sicca*. First the priest recites a prayer commencing, *Omnipotens sempiterne Deus, qui antequam Filium tuum Dominum nostrum pro nobis mortem perpeti sineres*. Then the palms, and other branches where relevant, are blessed, apparently with a single prayer, *Omnipotens Deus Christe*, not found in the pontifical, and, it would seem, addressed to Christ rather than to God the Father. The blessed palms are distributed and the antiphon *Pueri Hebraeorum* is intoned (the author does not tell us which of the two antiphons beginning with these words he means). The deacons take up the container with the Gospel book ('shouldering with great exultation the sweet yoke of Christ and His light burden', the unknown author comments), and the procession moves off, preceded by incense, candles and holy water. The schola, with banners borne before them, follows 'a long way off'. As they leave the church the antiphon *Cum appropinquaret Dominus* is sung, followed by *Coeperunt omnes, Cum audisset* and *Appropinquante*. At the entrance to the city *Ingrediente Domino* is sung, then *Collegerunt pontifices*. When the procession reaches the principal church, the clergy and people enter the atrium, but the choir remains outside. The antiphon *Occurrerunt* is sung antiphonally between the two groups. Two cantors then begin Theodulph's hymn at the verse *Israel es tu rex* and the schola, bowing towards the Gospel book, reply with the verse *Gloria laus et honor*. The remaining verses (presumably only the first six are meant) are sung in the same manner. The schola then sings the antiphon *Pueri Hebraeorum*, and the procession moves towards the altar, throwing down their palms and singing *Osanna filio David*.[43]

Although the theme of the celebration, the triumphal entry of Christ into Jerusalem, was everywhere the same, there were evidently considerable variations in the rite from place to place. For example, the *missa sicca*, found in the Romano-German Pontifical but not in Pseudo-Alcuin, occurs in a much attenuated form, restricted to a simple reading from Exodus 15:27–16:10 and a Gospel from John 12:12–19, in the English Sarum missals of the fourteenth to sixteenth centuries.[44]

The rite as celebrated in monasteries also differed in detail from that celebrated in cathedrals and parish churches. According to Lanfranc's *Decreta pro Ordine Sancti Benedicti* of about 1070, the ceremony begins after Terce with the blessing of palms, flowers and branches of other trees by the abbot, before the main altar, after which the palms are distributed to the abbot, priors, and the most senior members of the community, and the flowers and branches of other trees to those of lower rank. The two antiphons beginning *Pueri Hebraeorum* are then sung, after which the procession begins. Servants lead with banners, followed by a novice carrying a vessel with holy water, then two others bearing two crosses, then another two with lighted candles, and a further two with lighted thuribles. Then come two subdeacons, carrying two Gospel books. The lay brothers follow, then the boys with their masters, finally the remainder of the community, two by two, with the abbot himself bringing up the rear. Appropriate antiphons are sung, such as *Ante sex dies, Cum appropinquaret, Cum audisset* and *Omnes conlaudant,* and a station is made outside the city, at which a receptacle containing the Blessed Sacrament is venerated, the community lining up on each side of it as though they were in choir, with the boys standing on their own a little apart from them.[45] After *Occurrunt turbae* the antiphon *Hosanna filio David* is sung twice, first by the boys and then by the community. The singers venerate the Sacrament by a genuflection at the beginning and at the end of the antiphon. Another antiphon, *Cum angelis,* is sung twice in the same manner, with the singers making a further genuflection at the end. The Sacrament is then carried through the throng and each person venerates it as it passes with an individual genuflection, while the antiphon *Ave Rex noster* is sung. The procession then returns, in the same order in which it came. At the gates of the city the receptacle containing the Sacrament is again set down and a further station is made, the hymn *Gloria laus et honor* being sung antiphonally in the usual fashion. After it is finished, a cantor begins the antiphon *Ingrediente Domino,* and the procession moves on. A third station is made at the entrance to the monastery, at which *Collegerunt pontifices* is sung. Inside the church there is a fourth station before the crucifix, unveiled for the purpose, accompanied by the singing of *Circumdederunt.* Mass then follows. Everyone holds his palm in his hand until after the Canon, at which point it is formally offered back.[46]

Amongst the Gilbertines, who were founded in the mid-twelfth century and who at the time of the Reformation had around twenty-five houses in England, the blessing and distribution of palms and the beginning of the procession was much the same as that found in Lanfranc's *Decreta,* except that the procession took place in the cloister and the number of antiphons required was accordingly much less. However, a chest containing relics was carried instead of the Sacrament and the processional cross was initially covered. At the first station, the community facing one another as if in choir, antiphons including *Collegerunt* were sung. A second station was made at the entrance to the church, where after the reading of the Gospel a ceremony similar to the veneration of the cross on Good Friday was performed, the cross being unveiled gradually and venerated on bended knee; the antiphon *Ave rex noster* was sung at each stage of the unveiling, three times in all. Then the boys entered the church and, closing the doors behind them, sang the first verse of the *Gloria laus*, which was repeated by those outside; they then proceeded with the remaining verses, those outside responding with *Gloria laus* and *Cui puerile decus* alternately. After a second repeat of the first verse by both groups the prior began *Ingrediente domino*, the doors of the church were opened and, taking up the rest of the antiphon, the procession entered. [47]

The medieval love of the dramatic led to a great elaboration of the procession during the later Middle Ages. The clergy and people would assemble outside the town or city in a high place, representing the Mount of Olives.[48] Christ was represented in various ways: by the Gospel book, as in Pseudo-Alcuin (especially in France), by a great crucifix, veiled and wreathed in green branches (especially in northern Italy), by a figure of Christ on a wooden donkey (especially in the German-speaking countries), which after the end of the procession was exposed for veneration in the church until Maundy Thursday, by a chest full of relics and, in England and Normandy, by the Blessed Sacrament Itself. This last-named custom seems to have been an innovation of Lanfranc, Archbishop of Canterbury from 1070 to 1089, as a riposte to the heresy of Berengarius of Tours, who denied the reality of Christ's presence in the Eucharist.[49] The first mention of the use of a wooden figure of Christ on a donkey, known as the Palmesel, appears to be at Augsburg in the time of St Ulrich, who died in 973.[50]

At the collegiate church in Essen, in the fourteenth century, the procession went first to the church of St Gertrude, where the Palmesel was awaiting it, and then returned with it to the collegiate church. On arrival there, it was met by a priest who hung a silver cross on it, and by one of the bell-ringers carrying holy water and incense. It was then drawn into the centre of the church and three carpets were laid before it. The *Gloria Laus et Honor* was sung, followed by the antiphons *Pueri Hebraeorum vestimenta, Occurrunt turbae, Turba multa, Ave rex noster, Scriptum est enim, Gaude et laetare Jerusalem* and *Ingrediente Domino*, in the course of which prostrations were made before the figure. Finally the Palmesel was moved again to a station before the altar tomb of St Alfred.[51]

Each section of the Palm Sunday procession was preceded by banners, and candles and incense were carried. At Venice, doves were released into the air while a boys' choir sang the *Gloria laus et honor* from the balcony over the west door alternately with the people below, throwing down flowers and garlands at the beginning of each verse.[52] Stations, which varied in number from place to place, were made along the way. At Salisbury there were four, the first at the cross in the churchyard, where the Gospel of Christ's entry into Jerusalem from St Matthew was read, followed by the singing of various antiphons, the second on the south side of the cathedral, where the hymn *Gloria laus et honor* was sung by a boys' choir from an elevated position, the third at the west door, and the fourth before the cross in the cathedral itself. The Sacrament was carried in procession in a hanging pyx, preceded by an unveiled cross and two banners, in a procession that began separately but joined the main procession at the first station.[53] At Wells there is a graphic example of the medieval passion for the dramatic: a singing gallery is concealed behind the row of sculpted angels on the west front of the cathedral, above the entrance, with sound holes through the facade to the outside; when the verses of the *Gloria laus et honor* were sung by choristers stationed in this gallery it must have seemed as if they were being sung by the angels themselves.

The Palm Sunday procession in an ordinary English parish church at the beginning of the sixteenth century is thus described by Thomas Becon:

> In the beginning of the procession the people goeth out having every one a palm in their hand, following the cross, which is covered with a cloth ... that which they bear indeed in their hands is not properly called a palm, for they are the boughs of a sallow tree; but because we have no palms growing in this land, therefore do we bear them instead of palms ... Then they go forth with the cross, until they come unto a certain stead of the churchyard, where they stand still, and in the mean season the priest reads the gospel ... the gospel being done, then goeth the people forth with the cross which is covered, and even straightways not far from them come other people and the priest with the sacrament, which have with

them a cross bare and uncovered, pricked full of green olives and palms ... there come certain children before the naked cross, singing a certain song, which beginneth, *En, Rex venit:* 'Behold, the King cometh' ... After the song of the children, the priest goeth forth with the sacrament and certain people also with the naked cross, until they meet with that cross that is obvelated and covered. They are not so soon met, but the bumbled cross vanish away, and is conveyed from the company straightways. Then all the whole people inclose together with great joy, singing and making melody, triumphantly following the naked cross, bearing in their hande every one a palm: in some places also they bear green herbs in the stead of olives. These things once done, then the people goeth somewhat further into the church-doorward, and there standeth still ... Immediately after, certain children, standing upon an high place right against the people, sing with a loud voice a certain hymn in the praise of our Saviour Jesus Christ, which beginneth, *Gloria laus* ... At the end of every verse the children cast down certain cakes, or breads, with flowers ... these things once done, then goeth the procession forth, until they come to the church door, which, when they come into it, is sparred, and certain children in the church singing. The song being once done, the priest taketh the cross into his hand, and putteth the door from him with it, and so openeth it, and entereth in with all the other people after him ... When they are once entered into the church, whereby heaven is signified, then doth all the people kneel down, and the priest, plucking up the cloth wherewith the crucifix was covered, and making it open to all that are there present, singeth a certain song, the people in the mean season praying and giving thanks unto God. And so endeth the procession. ...[54]

Becon gives us an allegorical explanation of each of these events, in the usual medieval fashion.

The ceremony of knocking at the door with the cross for admission to the church is mentioned in the *Ordo Romanus* xv, of about 1392, as a common practice, not followed in the papal liturgy.[55] It was adopted in the latter only in 1604.[56] The bishop knocked on the door singing *Attollite portas principes vestras et introibit Rex gloriae* to which the singers from behind the door replied *Quis est iste Rex gloriae?* (Psalm 24). This ritual was twice repeated; after the second repetition the bishop replied *Dominus exercituum ipse est Rex gloriae.* The door was then opened and the procession entered.[57] The rite was later simplified; the subdeacon knocked in silence and the door was immediately opened. It was suppressed altogether in the 1955 reform.

The Blessing and Procession of Palms at Rome

There is no reference to any blessing or procession of palms either in the *Ordines Romani* or in the sacramentaries, Gelasian or Gregorian, of the Roman rite. It was not until the end of the tenth century, under the influence of the Romano-German Pontifical, that this ceremony was adopted in the Eternal City. The rite found in the Roman Pontifical of the Twelfth Century is a modified version of the Romano-German rite described above. The people assemble in a designated place, which may be outside the city, singing antiphons and hymns appropriate to the day. The bishop says the Collect *Deus quem diligere.* Then the subdeacon reads the lesson from the Book of Exodus. Either *Collegerunt pontifices* or *In monte Oliveti* is sung, and the deacon reads the Gospel of Christ's entry into Jerusalem. If the bishop wishes he preaches a sermon. The blessing of the palms and flowers then takes place, beginning with an exorcism. Seven prayers of blessing are provided, five of which are identical to blessings in the Romano-German Pontifical, one of them, *Deus qui dispersa congregas et congregata conservas*, being a petition that the palms may sanctify those places into which they are brought and those who live in them. Of the two new blessings one is the Preface *Qui gloriaris in concilio sanctorum*, adapted from the Preface for martyrs in the *Missale Gothicum*. Again it is not wholly clear whether all these blessings are intended to be used or whether some are, at least in origin, merely alternatives. The branches and flowers are sprinkled with holy water, with the antiphon *Asperges me, domine,* and incensed. Then, as prescribed in the Romano-German Pontifical, the prayer *Deus qui filium tuum dominum nostrum* is said and the palms and flowers distributed with the antiphon *Pueri Hebraeorum* and other antiphons suitable to the day. After this another prayer *Omnipotens sempiterne Deus qui Dominum nostrum Iesum Christum die azymorum* is said, and the procession begins with the antiphons *Occurrerunt turbae* and *Turba multa* or others appropriate to the day. There are no stations along the way, but when the procession reaches the gates of the city (or the doors of the church if the blessing and procession have taken place inside the city), two cantors on the inside begin the *Gloria laus*. After the end of each verse the clergy and people on the outside reply with *Gloria laus* again. When the hymn is finished the cantor begins the antiphon *Ingrediente domino* and the procession enters the city or the church, whereupon all the bells are rung and Mass begins.

At the Lateran, the palms are blessed by a cardinal in the chapel of St Silvester within the palace, and then taken to the pope in the Leonine Hall, where he distributes them to the cardinals, after which all proceed through the palace to the Lateran Basilica, singing *Pueri Hebraeorum* and other antiphons. They halt outside the door between the two buildings, which is closed, and the *Gloria laus* is begun by two cantors inside the basilica, then, after two verses, taken up by the cardinals and by the clergy and people outside. When the hymn is finished the doors are opened, the choirmaster intones *Ingrediente domino*, the bells ring out and everyone enters the basilica.[58]

The Roman Pontifical of the Twelfth Century was widely disseminated throughout Europe, and its Palm Sunday rite became gradually standardized throughout the West.[59] The influence of the Franciscan Missal, which followed the liturgy of the papal court, was also of particular importance in this process of standardization. With fairly minimal changes,[60] it entered the first printed Missal of 1474 and the Missal of Pius V of 1571. It was superseded only in the 1955 reform.

The Papal Rite of the Later Middle Ages

Detailed descriptions of the papal rite are contained in the later series of *Ordines Romani*, which were composed by the masters of ceremonies of the Lateran Basilica between the twelfth and four-teenth centuries. According to *Ordo* xiv of about 1350, the junior cardinal priest and all the clergy assemble in the church of St Silvester, within the Lateran Palace, where the branches of palms, olives or other trees are laid out. The cardinal, or a priest, then blesses salt and water, and the antiphon *Hosanna filio David* is sung, followed by *Collegerunt* or *In monte Oliveti*. The palms, etc. are then blessed and distributed, after which they are borne by the clergy and people, singing, to the chapel in the Lateran Palace. The pope then comes out and gives a spray of palms to each cardinal and bishop, and to others if there are enough to go round.

He then throws the palm and olive branches to the people (who presumably are assembled in the courtyard below), except for some (the author does not say who) who receive them from the pope's hand, following which a cantor begins 'the antiphon', after which the Mass begins.

This ceremony seems to have undergone some development by the end of the same century, when *Ordo Romanus* xv was composed. In this ordo the palms are blessed by the junior cardinal priest, if the pope is celebrating the Mass, otherwise by whichever cardinal bishop is celebrating. Following the blessing the pope receives his own palm and then distributes the rest to the clergy in strict order of rank, while *Hosanna filio David* and other antiphons are sung. The procession then forms up, the cross being carried by a subdeacon attended by two candle bearers and a thurifer. Four men of high rank hold a canopy over the pope. When the procession reaches the portico overlooking the great courtyard of the palace, he goes to the window and throws palms down to the people assembled below. On arrival before the door of the chapel, the *Gloria laus et honor* is sung alternately by cantors within and without the chapel. When this hymn, and all the antiphons prescribed in the Roman Missal, are finished, the door is opened and the procession enters. After a short pause for prayer before the altar, the Pope goes to a portico on the right side of the chapel, and scatters more palms to the people outside. The Mass follows.

The Mass

In contrast to the procession, the Mass of the day wears a solemn aspect, concentrating as it does on the forthcoming Passion and Death of Christ. The station is at St John Lateran. The readings from the earliest times down to the 1971 reform comprised a passage from St Paul's Epistle to the Philippians (2:5–11)[61] and the Passion from St Matthew's Gospel (26:1 to 27:66).[62] We know, in fact, that in fifth-century Rome the latter was read on this day, the day on which St Leo the Great (440–461) preached the first of his sermons on the Passion, the second taking place on the following Wednesday.[63] St Augustine tells us that the recital of the Passion narrative must, since Christ shed his blood to wash away our sins, be performed solemnly.[64]

The tone for the Passion is unique in Gregorian chant, because of its dramatic character. The recitation is at three different pitch levels and speeds, low and slow for Christ, high and fast for the crowd and medium for the narrator. The earliest manuscripts (of the ninth and tenth centuries) distinguish only between the words of Christ and the rest of the text by marking the former 't' (for *tarde, trahe* or *tene*) and the latter 'c' (for *celeriter, cito* or *citius*). The letter 's' (for *sursum*) was then added to characterize the parts spoken by the crowd and by protagonists other than Christ. Later a cross was substituted for the letter 't', and the letters 'c' and 's' came to be understood as signifying *chronista* (narrator) and *synagoga* (crowd).[65] The custom of having three deacons read the Passion began in the tenth century, but was not adopted in Rome until towards the end of the Middle Ages.[66] Originally each of the deacons wore a different coloured stole, white for the narrator, red for the crowd and black for Christ, but later all three wore violet.[67] The custom of the crowd's part being sometimes sung polyphonically by the choir began in Italy in the fifteenth century.[68] It was quite commonly sung in plainchant by the congregation even in ordinary churches down to the 1970 reform.[69]

The dialogue between the deacon and people preliminary to the Gospel reading was originally the same as on a normal day, with the substitution of *Passio domini nostri Jesu Christi* for the normal *Initium* or *Sequentia sancti evangelii*.[70] The custom then seems to have developed of omitting the people's response *Gloria tibi Domine*.[71] By the time of the Romano-German Pontifical the *Dominus vobiscum* too was being left out in some places.[72] The evidence from Rome in the first half of the twelfth century is conflicting; the full dialogue is still found in *Ordo Romanus* xi of c.1140–1143,[73] but the *Ordo Ecclesiae Lateranensis* of c.1120 prescribes the omission of *Gloria tibi Domine* and the Roman Pontifical of the Twelfth Century both *Dominus vobiscum* and *Gloria tibi Domine*.[74] It seems therefore that the practice in Rome was in the course of changing. According to the *Missale Lateranense* of c.1230, all the preliminaries, including the blessing of the reader and the procession with lights and incense, as well as the dialogue, are to be omitted, and this became the rule, the reading beginning simply with the words *Passio Domini nostri Jesu Christi secundum Matthaeum*.[75]

The custom of interrupting the narrative at the words *Emisit spiritum* for a few minutes' silent meditation is attributed to Louis the Pious, who had observed it in monastic houses, and introduced it first in his private chapel.[76] It is not found in Rome until the end of the fourteenth century.[77]

In the later Middle Ages it became customary for the final section of the Passion, beginning with the words *Altera autem die*, to be sung in the normal gospel tone by a single deacon, and preceded by the blessing of the reader, as if this section were the proper Gospel of the day. The first references to this custom appear to be in the *Mitrale*, written by Sicardus, Bishop of Cremona, about the year 1210, and in the *Missale Lateranense*, both of which also mention the carrying of incense at this point.[78] The rubric in the first printed missal of 1474 reproduces that of the *Missale Lateranense* exactly. From here it passed into the Missal of Pius V. The latter also prescribes the recitation by the reader of the prayer *Munda cor meum* here.[79] The practice was abolished entirely in the 1955 reform.

The Romano-German Pontifical prescribes that the clergy and people should hold the blessed palms in their hands until the end of Mass.[80] For England, however, the *Regularis Concordia*, from around 970, and the *Decreta pro Ordine S. Benedicti* of Lanfranc, of about a century later, provide that they should be held in the hand until after the Canon, and then presented as an offering to the celebrant.[81] According to *Ordo Romanus* xiii, of the thirteenth century, the pope holds his palm in his hand during the singing of the Passion. *Ordo* xv, from the end of the fourteenth century, contains an elaborate ritual: at the start of the Passion narrative a cardinal deacon standing to the left of the pope is handed a spray of palms by a member of the papal household, which he then passes to the pope, after first kissing the latter's hand. The pope holds the palms throughout the Passion narrative, as do all the cardinals and other prelates. When the Passion is finished the pope hands the palms back to the same cardinal deacon, who gives them back to the man from whom he had received them, whereupon all the prelates give their own palms back to their servants, to be held by them until the end of the Mass.[82]

The Introit, Gradual, Tract, Offertory and Communion verses remained virtually unchanged from the eighth century (at the latest) until the liturgical reforms of the post-Vatican II era.[83] Their theme is the Passion and Death of Christ. As in Holy Week generally, the *Gloria Patri* is omitted from the Introit. The Tract, consisting as it does in almost the whole of Psalm 21, is a particularly good example of the so-called 'Baumstark's Law', that 'primitive conditions are maintained with greater tenacity in the more sacred seasons of the Liturgical Year'.[84] The Secret[85] and Postcommunion prayers were likewise, until 1970, identical to those in the Gregorian Sacramentary of the seventh century. The Collect appears to be a synopsis of a sermon preached by St Leo (440–461), and may well have been composed by him,[86] a consideration which perhaps persuaded the post-Vatican II reformers to retain it. Of the rest of the ancient Palm Sunday Mass, the Epistle, part of the Tract, St Matthew's Passion (the latter alternately with the two other synoptic Passions, in accordance with the three-year cycle of readings initiated by the reform) and the Communion verse remain in the new rite.

Neither the Old Gelasian Sacramentary nor the *Hadrianum* have any Preface for the day. A brief special Preface is found however in Alcuin's supplement to the latter and is copied in some of the Frankish Gelasians as well as later sacramentaries in the Gregorian tradition:[87] 'It is truly right and fitting, just and salutary, that we should always and everywhere give Thee thanks, holy Lord, almighty Father, eternal God, through Christ our Lord, through Whom pardon is granted to us and peace is preached throughout the ages, and teaching is handed down to all believers, so that the holy day which is to come may find us sanctified'.[88] Different Prefaces are found in the Sacramentaries of Prague (*Claritatem tui altaris ingressi*), from the late eighth century, and of Fulda (*Qui se ipsum pro nobis optulit immolandum*), from the late tenth, both in the Gelasian tradition. The theme of the former is Christ the King of the new era, and of the latter the Priesthood of Christ and the Sacrifice of the Cross.[89] But the *Ordo Ecclesiae Lateranensis* of about 1120 prescribes the use of the Preface of the Holy Cross, originally composed for the feast of the Exaltation of the Holy Cross, for all five days from Palm Sunday to Holy Thursday.[90] This rubric was repeated in the first printed missal of 1474, from where it entered the Missal of Pius V, remaining in force until the 1970 reform.

The author of the *Ordo Ecclesiae Lateranensis* tells his readers that they should sing the *Sanctus* with particular fervour today, the day on which the crowds greeted Christ with the acclamation *Benedictus qui venit in nomine domini, Hosanna in excelsis*; 'let every tongue, every age, every rank, every sex and condition sing out *Hosanna in excelsis* to the highest King and cry *Sanctus Sanctus Sanctus* from their hearts'.[91]

Ordo Romanus xiv, written about the year 1350, tells us that it was not previously the custom for the pope to officiate at this Mass, but to say his own Mass early in the morning in his private chapel, after which he took part in the distribution of palms; however, at the time the ordo was composed, he did sometimes celebrate the Mass in the basilica.[92] By the time of *Ordo* xv, around the end of the same century, this had become customary.[93] The earlier *Ordo Ecclesiae Lateranensis* gives two alternative processional rites, one for when the pope officiates at the Mass and the other for when one of the seven bishops celebrates it.[94]

The custom of associating differently coloured vestments with particular feasts began around the start of the thirteenth century.[95] The colour adopted for Palm Sunday at Rome was violet, as Durandus and the later series of *Ordines Romani* attest. Durandus tells us however that some churches used white for the blessing of palms and procession, and according to *Ordo* xiii red was the colour used in the Gallican Church.[96] Violet remained the colour prescribed for the whole of the Palm Sunday liturgy until the 1955 reform, when red was adopted for the blessing and procession, violet being retained for the Mass, an arrangement which corresponded more closely to the character of each part of the liturgy. From 1971 red replaced violet as the colour for the Mass also.

Appendix

Texts of Antiphons sung during the blessing of palms and the procession.

Ante sex dies sollemnis paschae, quando venit Dominus in civitatem Jerosolymam, occurrerunt ei pueri, et in manibus portabant ramos palmarum, et clamabant voce magna dicentes: Hosanna in excelsis. Benedictus qui venisti in multitudine misericordiae tuae. Hosanna in excelsis.*

Six days before the solemn Passover, when the Lord entered the city of Jerusalem, children went to meet him, holding palm branches in their hands, and shouting in a loud voice 'Hosanna in the highest. Blessed are you who have come in the multitude of your mercies. Hosanna in the highest'.

Appropinquante Jesu filio Dei Jerosolymam pueri Hebraeorum dicebant: Osanna Redemptor mundi.

As Jesus the Son of God approached Jerusalem the Hebrew children cried out 'Hosanna, Redeemer of the world'.

Ave rex noster, fili David redemptor mundi, quem prophetae praedixerunt salvatorem domui Israel esse venturum. Te enim ad salutarem victimam Pater misit in mundum, quem expectabant omnes sancti ab origine mundi et nunc. Hosanna filio David, benedictus qui venit in nomine domini, hosanna in excelsis.

Hail to our king, son of David and redeemer of the world, whom the prophets predicted was to come as a saviour to the house of Israel. For the Father sent you into the world as the saving victim whom all the saints were expecting from the beginning of the world until now. Hosanna to the son of David, blessed is he who comes in the name of the Lord, hosanna in the highest.

Coeperunt omnes turbae descendentium gaudentes laudare Deum voce magna super omnibus quas viderant virtutibus, dicentes: Benedictus qui venit rex in nomine Domini. Pax de caelis et gloria in excelsis. (Luke 19:37–8)

As the rejoicing crowds were descending [the Mount of Olives] they all began to praise God at the top of their voices for all the miracles they had seen, crying out 'Blessed is the king who comes in the name of the Lord. Peace from the heavens and glory in the highest'.

Collegerunt pontifices et pharisaei concilium et dixerunt: Quid facimus, quia hic homo multa signa facit? Si dimittimus eum sic, omnes credent in eum, et venient Romani, et tollent nostrum locum et gentem. Unus autem ex illis, Caiphas nomine, cum esset pontifex anni illius, prophetavit dicens: Expedit vobis ut unus moriatur homo pro populo, et non tota gens pereat. Ab illo ergo die cogitaverunt interficere eum, dicentes: Et venient Romani, et tollent nostrum locum et gentem. (John 11:47–50, 53)*

The priests and pharisees came together in council and said 'What can we do, since this man performs many signs? If we let him go, everyone will believe in him, and the Romans will come and take away our land and people.' But one of them, called Caiphas, since he was high priest for that year, prophesied, saying, 'It is expedient for you that one man should die on behalf of the people, so that the whole nation should not perish'. From that day therefore they laid plans to kill him, saying, 'The Romans will come, and take away our land and our people'.

Cum angelis et pueris fideles inveniamur, triumphatori mortis clamantes: Hosanna in excelsis.*

May we be found faithful with the angels and the children, calling out to him who triumphed over death 'Hosanna in the highest'.

Cum appropinquaret Dominus Jerosolymam, misit duos ex discipulis suis, dicens: Ite in castellum quod contra vos est, et invenietis pullum asinae alligatum, super quem nullus hominum sedit; solvite et adducite mihi. Si quis vos interrogaverit, dicite: Opus Domino est. Solventes adduxerunt ad Jesum, et imposuerunt illi vestimenta sua, et sedit super eum; alii expandebant vestimenta sua in via; alii ramos de arboribus sternebant, et qui sequebantur clamabant: Hosanna, benedictus qui venit in nomine Domini, benedictum regnum patris nostri David. Hosanna in excelsis, miserere nobis, fili David. (Matt. 21:1–9, Mark 11:1–10)*

As the Lord was approaching Jerusalem, he sent on two of his disciples, saying 'Go into the village facing you; there you will find a tethered colt that no one has yet ridden. Untie it and bring it to me. If anyone questions you, say "The Lord needs it".' They untied it and brought it to Jesus, and threw their cloaks on its back, and he sat on it. Some spread their cloaks in the road, others strewed branches from trees, and those who followed kept calling out, 'Hosanna, blessed is he who comes in the name of the Lord, blessed the kingdom of our father David. Hosanna in the highest, have mercy on us, son of David'.

Cum audisset populus quia Jesus venit Jerosolymam acceperunt ramos palmarum, et exierunt ei obviam, et clamabant pueri, dicentes: Hic est qui venturus est in salutem populi. Hic est salus nostra et redemptio Israel. Quantus est iste, cui Throni et Dominationes occurrunt! Noli timere, filia Sion; ecce, Rex tuus venit tibi, sedens super pullum asinae, sicut scriptum est. Salve, Rex, fabricator mundi, qui venisti redimere nos. (John 12:12–15) *

When the people heard that Jesus was coming to Jerusalem they took up palm branches and went out to meet him, and the children kept crying out, saying, 'This is He who is to come for the salvation of the people. He is our deliverance, and the redeemer of Israel. How great he is, surrounded by Thrones and Dominions! Be not afraid, daughter of Sion; behold, your king comes to you, seated upon a colt, as it is written. Hail, King, creator of the world, who have come to redeem us'.

Fulgentibus psalmis prosternimur advenienti domino. Huic omnes occurramus cum hymnis et canticis glorificantes et dicentes: Benedictus dominus.

At the coming of the Lord we prostrate ourselves, singing joyful psalms. Let us all go out to meet him with hymns and canticles, exalting him and saying 'Blessed is the Lord'.

Gaude et laetare Jerusalem; ecce rex tuus venit, de quo prophetae praedixerunt, quem angeli adoraverunt, cui Cherubim et Seraphim *Sanctus, Sanctus, Sanctus* proclamant.

Be glad and rejoice, Jerusalem; behold, your king is coming, he whom the prophets foretold and the angels adored, to whom the Cherubim and Seraphim declaim, 'Holy, Holy, Holy'.

Hosanna filio David; benedictus qui venit in nomine Domine. O Rex Israel; Hosanna in excelsis. (John 12:13)*

Hosanna to the son of David, blessed is he who comes in the name of the Lord. O king of Israel, hosanna in the highest.

In monte Oliveti oravit ad Patrem: Pater, si fieri potest, transeat a me calix iste. Spiritus quidem promptus est, caro autem infirma; fiat voluntas tua. Vigilate et orate ut non intretis in tentationem. Spiritus quidem promptus est, caro autem infirma. (Matt. 26:39–41, Mark 14:35–8)*

    On the Mount of Olives he prayed to the Father, 'Father, if it is possible, let this chalice pass from me. The spirit indeed is willing, but the flesh is weak; let thy will be done. Watch and pray, that you do not enter into temptation. The spirit indeed is willing, but the flesh is weak'.

Ingrediente Domino in sanctam civitatem, Hebraeorum pueri resurrectionem vitae pronuntiantes, cum ramis palmarum: Hosanna, clamabant, in excelsis. Cum audisset populus quod Jesus veniret Jerosolymam exierunt obviam ei, cum ramis palmarum: Hosanna, clamabant, in excelsis.*

As the Lord entered the holy city, the Hebrew children, with palm branches, foretelling the resurrection to life, cried, 'Hosanna in the highest'. When the people heard that Jesus was coming to Jerusalem they went out to meet him, with palm branches, crying, 'Hosanna in the highest'.

Occurrunt turbae cum floribus et palmis Redemptori obviam, et victori triumphanti digna dant obsequia. Filium Dei ore gentes praedicant, et in laudem Christi voces tonant per nubila: Hosanna in excelsis.*

The crowds go out to meet the Redeemer with flowers and palms, and pay him homage worthy of a triumphant victor. The people acclaim the Son of God, and in praise of Christ their voices reverberate to the clouds, 'Hosanna in the highest'.

Omnes conlaudent nomen tuum et dicent: Benedictus qui venit in nomine domini.

Let all together praise thy name, saying 'Blessed is he who comes in the name of the Lord'.

Pueri Hebraeorum portantes ramos olivarum obviaverunt Domino, clamantes et dicentes: Hosanna in excelsis.*

The Hebrew children went to meet the Lord, carrying branches and crying out 'Hosanna in the highest'.

Pueri Hebraeorum vestimenta prosternebant in via, et clamabant dicentes: Hosanna filio David, benedictus qui venit in nomine Domini.*

The Hebrew children spread their cloaks in the road, crying out 'Hosanna to the son of David, blessed is he who comes in the name of the Lord'.

Scriptum est enim: Percutiam pastorem et dispergentur oves gregis; postquam autem surrexero, praecedam vos in Galilaeam, ibi me videbitis, dicit Dominus. (Matt. 26:31–2; Mark 14:27–8).

'For the scripture says "I shall strike the shepherd and the sheep of the flock will be scattered", but after my resurrection I shall go before you to Galilee, there you will see me,' says the Lord.

Turba multa quae convenerat ad diem festum clamabat Domino: Benedictus qui venit in nomine Domini. Hosanna in excelsis.*

A large crowd which had come together for the festival cried out to the Lord 'Blessed is he who comes in the name of the Lord. Hosanna in the highest'.

Notes

[1]   A. Baumstark, *Comparative Liturgy* (London: Mowbray, 1958), pp. 148–9; *OHS*, p. 89.

[2]   Isidore, *Etymologiarum* Liber VI cap. xviii, 13–15: 'Dies palmarum ideo dicitur quia in eo Dominus et Salvator noster ... Jerusalem tendens asellum sedisse perhibetur. Tunc gradiens cum ramis palmarum multitudo plebium obviam ei clamaverunt *Osanna, benedictus qui venit in nomine Domini, Rex Israel'* (*PL* 82, 251). See also his *De ecclesiasticis officiis* Lib. I cap. xxviii 1–2: 'In ramis enim palmarum significabatur victoria, qua erat Dominus mortem moriendo superaturus, et trophaeo crucis de diabolo mortis principe triumphaturus' (*PL* 83, 763).

[3]   See also A. Bugnini and C. Braga, 'Ordo Hebdomadae Sanctae Instauratus', in *Ephemerides Liturgicae* LXX, (1956), pp. 86–7. For the practice in different churches see J. W. Tyrer, *Historical Survey of Holy Week*, Alcuin Club Collections 29 (OUP, 1932), pp. 47–8, and *The Study of Liturgy* (London: SPCK, 1978), pp. 132–4.

[4]   *PE* 46.3–5 and St Cyril, *Catecheses* 6–18.

[5]   Canon xiii (*PL* 84, 265).

[6]   Ildefonsus, *De cognitione baptismi* cap. xxxiv: 'Hoc symbolum quod competentes in die unctionis accipiunt, aut per se si maiores aetate sunt aut per ora gestantium si parvuli sunt, quinta feria ante Pascha sacerdoti recitant atque reddunt, ut eorum probata fide merito perveniant ad vicinum resurrectionis

---

* Antiphons which survived in the Roman rite until 1955.

dominicae sacramentum per fontis sacri baptismum' (*PL* 96, 127). For the meaning of 'competentes' see note 16 below.

7   Rabanus, *De clericorum institutione* II cap. xxxv (*PL* 107, 347).

8   Bede, *Homilia XXIII In dominica palmarum* (*PL* 94, 120).

9   Aldhelm, *De laudibus virginitatis* xxx, 'De qua laetantes evangelici consona vocis harmonia psallentes concorditer cecinerunt *Benedictus qui venit in nomine Domini*. Cuius rei regulam nostra quoque mediocritas, authentica veterum auctoritate subnixa, in sacrosancta palmarum solemnitate binis classibus canora voce concrepans, et geminis concentibus *Osanna* persultans, cum iucundae iubilationis melodia concelebrat.' (*PL* 89, 128).

10 Mohlberg, op. cit., n.329.

11 'Dominica VI in Palmas [sic] de Passione Domini' (CC CLIX Vol. C, p. 558).

12 'Dominica VI ad S. Ioannem in Lateranis. In palmis' (CC CLIX Vol. A, p. 565).

13 Schmidt, *HS*, pp. 480, 483, 485, 488, 490 and 495.

14 *OHS*, p. 87. The use of flowers is attested by many authorities, for example Sicardus of Cremona, *Mitrale* Lib.VI cap. x: 'In representatione gloriosae Dominicae receptionis, celebrat hodie cum ramis et floribus ecclesia processionem' (*PL* 213, 293) and John Beleth, *Rationale* xciv: 'Cum autem palmas non habemus, laurum vel buxum, quod perpetuo suo virore virtutes connotent, deportamus, vel flores etiam, qui simili ratione virtutem significant' (*PL* 202, 95).

15 'Ebdomada VI die dominico ad Lateranis' (Schmidt, *HS*, pp. 458–9).

16 Baptismal candidates were commonly known as 'competentes' ('co-seekers'). 'Petitum' means 'desired' or 'longed for'. Both names, 'Pascha petitum' and 'Pascha petentium', are mentioned in a list of the names for the day given in Pseudo-Alcuin, *De Divinis Officiis* xiv: 'Pascha petitum, sive competentium dicitur, quia hodie symbolum competentibus tradebatur ... competentes enim, quasi simul petentes, dicuntur, id est, gratiam Christi petentes' (*PL* 101, 1200). In its present form this document dates from around the end of the tenth century, but incorporates much material from earlier periods. St Ildefonsus in *De cognitione baptismi*, cap. xxx, says that a baptismal candidate 'ex eo quod accepto symbolo iam petit gratiam Dei competens vocatur' (*PL* 96, 124–125). See also J. W. Tyrer, op. cit., pp. 45–6 and *OHS*, pp. 86–7.

17 *Missale Bobbiense*, ed. E. Lowe, HBS, Vol. LVIII, 174. The reference to the opening of the ears of the candidates is to a ceremony found in many baptismal rites whereby the bishop touched their mouths and ears saying to each one 'Ephphata, that is, be opened' (Mark 7:34). It was usually performed on the day of baptism itself.

18 'Dominica indulgentia [sic] ad Lateranis' in the *Comes* of Würzburg, 'Dom. indulgentia [sic] ad Lataranis [sic]' in the *Comes* of Murbach and 'Dominica VI de indulgentia' in the Evangeliary of St Cuthbert (Schmidt, *HS*, pp. 457, 464 and 471).

19 J. A Jungmann, *Public Worship* (London: Challoner, 1957), p. 182. A different explanation for the name, that it derives from the proximity of the reconciliation of the penitents and their admission to the ecclesiastical communion, is suggested in *OHS*, p. 87.

20 'Dominica indulgentiae, quae diversis vocabulis distinguitur, id est dies

palmarum sive florum, atque ramorum, Osanna, pascha petitum sive competentium et capitolavium, statio ad sanctum Iohannem in Lateranis'.
(Andrieu, *ORM* Vol. 5, p. 162).

21 N. M.-D. Boulet, 'Le Dimanche de Rameaux', in *La Maison-Dieu* 41 (1955),
p. 22, argues for a procession in Spain possibly as early as the fifth century.

22 Modern edition of the Bobbio Missal by E. Lowe, HBS, Vols LIII, LVIII and
LXI (London, 1917–1924). It is closely related to the *Missale Gothicum*, a
Gallican sacramentary with signs of Gelasian revision, which probably originated in Burgundy and survives in a manuscript written between 690 and
715 (Vat. Reg. lat. 317; modern edition by H. Bannister, HBS, Vols LII and LIV
(London 1917–1919)). For the blessings in the *Oracional Visigotico* see note 24
below.

23 'hac quoque creaturam arboris olivarum, una cum palmis, que populus pro
tuis laudibus benedicatur benediccione perenni, ut quicumque pie
devocione pro expellendis languoribus sive etiam pro expugnandas omnes
insidias inimici in cunctis habitacionibus suis eas adportaverit aut biberit
[*sic*] ab omne sint inpugnacione inimici securi ut cognuscant omnes gentes
quia nomen tuum gloriosum est super omnia scla sclorum' (Lowe, op. cit.,
558, p. 170.) Spelling and grammar as in original.

24 'Benedic, Domine, populum tuum, qui hunc mysterium videre desiderant.
Amen. Ut qui deportant folias palmarum, te videre mereantur in regno
caelorum. Amen. Et ad quem praeconiis vocibus proclamant hosanna, ipsius
resurrectionis diem mereantur videre cum summa laetitia. Amen'. (CC
CLXII (*Corpus Benedictionum Pontificalium*) Pars I, no. 103. For the text of the
other blessing see ibid., 1301).

25 The *Missale Gothicum* contains a prayer headed 'Benedictio super ramos
palmarum'. It is not however a true blessing at all, but merely the Collect
from the Bobbio Missal for the Palm Sunday Mass under another name (cf.
Bannister, op. cit., 197, and Lowe, op. cit., 190). The change in the nomencla-
ture of the prayer is nevertheless significant.

26 Paris BN lat. 10575. Modern edition by W. Greenwell , *The Pontifical of Egbert,
Archbishop of York, AD 732–766*, Surtees Society 27 (Durham, 1853). Alcuin
was one of Egbert's pupils, and may have brought the original with him
when he came to the court of Charlemagne.

27 'ut sicut ei cum ramis palmarum caeterarumve frondium praesentari
studuistis, ita cum palma victoriae et fructu bonorum operum post obitum
apparere valeatis'.

28 See Chapter 3, note 26. The sacramentary bears the name of William of
Aquitaine, the founder of the abbey at Gellone, in the department of Hérault.

29 'hos quoque ramos et flores palmarum ... tua benedictione sanctifica, ut
quicumque ex eis acceperint tua in omnibus repleantur gratia, et salutis
consequantur medellam; et, sicut per huius diei sollemnitatem laetantur, ita
eorum habitacula tua benedictione repleas, corporaque et animas ab omni
contagione mundas efficias'. For the full text of the blessing see Schmidt, *HS*,
p. 382.

30 Prague, Bibliothek des Metropolitankapitels, Cod. O.32. Modern edition
by A. Dold and L. Eizenhöfer, *Das Prager Sakramentar der Bibliothek*

Metropolitankapitels (Beuron in Hohenzollern, 1944).

[31] 'rogamus te, omnipotens deus, ut benedicas hos ramos olivarum, quos tui famuli in suis manibus sunt suscepturi, venientes in occursum tuum benedicentes et dicentes: Benedictus qui venit in nomine domini, rex Israel'. Full text of the blessing in Schmidt, *HS*, p. 413

[32] *Codex Ottobonianus* (Rome, Vat. Ottob. lat.313). This blessing also appears in the Sacramentary of Fulda, of mixed Frankish Gelasian and Gregorian origin, from about 975 (Schmidt, *HS*, p. 420).

[33] The attribution was first made by Lupus of Ferrières, a younger contemporary of Theodulph, who died around the year 862. Ferrières is a small town about 40 miles from Orleans. See Martène, *DAER* IV, cap. xiii, col. 203.

[34] Full text in Schmidt, *HS*, pp. 656–8.

[35] For a full discussion see Schmidt, *HS*, pp. 653–6. Theodulph's punishment seems to have been exile rather than imprisonment, though he was eventually forgiven and reinstated. The traditional story may be found in Durandus, *Rationale divinorum officiorum* Lib.VI, lxvii, 6, ed. J. Dura (Naples, 1831, p. 502).

[36] Amalarius, *De ecclesiasticis officiis* Lib. I, cap. x: 'In memoriam illius rei nos per ecclesias nostras solemus portare ramos et clamare: *Osanna.*' (*PL* 105, 1008).

[37] The *Liber Ordinum* survives in two manuscripts, one of the ninth century in Madrid, Academia de la Historia (cod. Emilian. 56) and one of the mid-eleventh, in the library of Silos monastery (cod. 3). Modern edition by M. Férotin, *Le Liber Ordinum en usage dans l'Eglise Wisigothique et Mozarabe d'Espagne du cinquième au onzième siècle*, Monumenta Ecclesia Liturgica 5 (Paris, 1904); see p. 193 et seq. Cf. *OHS*, p. 89.

[38] 'Quapropter quaesumus, Domine, clementiam tuam, ut nos famulos tuos … eruas de ore inferni et adiutorium gratiae tuae nobis tribuere digneris, ut iuste et pie sancteque viventes, cum electis et sanctis tuis facias habere consortium.'

[39] PRG cap. xxiii, 1–46 (Andrieu, *ORM* Vol. 5, pp. 162–83).

[40] Durandus, *Rationale* Lib. IV, i. 23 (Dura, pp. 143–4).

[41] Bannister, HBS, Vol. LII, 200, p. 61. Baumstark suggests that the borrowed Preface goes back to the time of the persecutions ('La solemnité des palmes dans l'ancienne et la nouvelle Rome', in *Irenikon* 13 [1936]).

[42] M. Righetti, *Manuale di Storia Liturgica* (Milan: Editrice Ancora, 1955), Vol. II.91, p. 149.

[43] Pseudo-Alcuin, *De divinis officiis* xiv (*PL* 101, 1201–1202).

[44] Modern edition by J. Wickham Legg, *The Sarum Missal* (OUP, 1916, reprinted 1969). There is an English translation of the missal, taken from the printed edition of 1526, by F. E. Warren, *The Sarum Missal in English* (London: A. Moring, 1911).

[45] The carrying of the Blessed Sacrament in the procession was a particular feature of the Palm Sunday liturgy in England. See for example Bishop Pecock, *The Repression of Over-much Blaming of the Clergy* (c.1450), 'in later days and particularly in some churches, the Eucharist is borne forth and the procession meeteth with the Eucharist borne in a chest among relics, and in

many places He is borne in a cup ordained thereto ...' (quoted in Thurston, op. cit., p. 218), and the reminiscences of a parishioner of Long Melford in the late sixteenth century, 'upon Palm Sunday the Blessed Sacrament was carried in procession about the churchyard under a fair canopy borne by four yeomen' (ibid., p. 221). The practice seems to have begun as a result of the controversy between Lanfranc and Berengar of Tours over the nature of Christ's presence in the Eucharist.

[46] Lanfranc, *Decreta* cap. I, iv (*PL* 150, 455–457).

[47] *Ordinale Gilbertinum*, Pembroke College Cambridge ms 226 (first half of fifteenth century). Modern edition by R. M. Wooley in HBS, Vols LIX –LX, (1921–1922); see pp. 16–18. The Gilbertines, an order confined to England, were founded by St Gilbert of Sempringham (c.1083–1189). The first rule of the order dates from 1148. They were unusual in that each of their establishments was distinguished by having parallel houses for men and women.

[48] Durandus, *Rationale* Lib. VI, lxvii, 9 (Dura, p. 503).

[49] Righetti op. cit., Vol. II.90, p. 148, *OHS*, pp. 90–2, Martène, *DAER* IV, cap. XX, cols. 200–201, 208.

[50] There is a well-preserved example of a Palmesel in the medieval galleries of the Victoria and Albert Museum in London.

[51] K. Young, *The Drama of the Medieval Church* (OUP, 1933), Vol. I, pp. 94–8.

[52] *OHS*, p. 93

[53] J. Wickham Legg, op. cit., pp. 92–6, and Warren, op. cit., pp. 216–26. For a fuller account of the Sarum rite procession see Tyrer, op. cit., pp. 57–60.

[54] Quoted from *The Early Works of Thomas Becon*, ed. John Ayre, (Cambridge: Parker Society, 1843). Becon was chaplain to Thomas Cranmer, Archbishop of Canterbury 1533–1553.

[55] 'Dominus papa non percutit cum cruce portam, sicut saeculares consueverunt', (*PL* 78, 1301). The ceremony seems to have originated in medieval religious drama; see Jungmann, *Public Worship*, p. 192.

[56] *OHS*, p. 97, Righetti, op. cit., Vol. II.91, p. 150. The statement by Righetti that the custom appears in the Roman Pontifical of the Twelfth Century appears to be an error.

[57] *OHS*, p. 97.

[58] Roman Pontifical of the Twelfth Century, XXIX. 1–19 (Andrieu, PRM Vol. I pp. 210–14); *OR* xi. 38 (*PL* 78, 1039–1040).

[59] For the factors which governed this dissemination see Chapter 3, pp. 57–8.

[60] The insertion of the long prayer *Deus qui miro dispositionis ordine*, which is found in the Romano-German Pontifical but not in the Roman Pontifical of the Twelfth Century, after *Deus qui dispersa congregas*, and the deletion of the last of the prayers of blessing, *Omnipotens sempiterne Deus, effunde super hos ramos*.

[61] See Schmidt, *HS*, pp. 462–5 for the earliest surviving lectionaries.

[62] Schmidt, *HS*, pp. 458–61. In the 1955 rite however the reading begins at 26:36.

[63] St Leo, Sermo LIV, c.5, 'Sed quia multum est, dilectissimi, ut omnia hodierna sermo percurrat, in quartam feriam, qua lectio Dominicae Passionis iterabitur, residua differantur' (*PL* 54, 322). Cf. Schmidt, *HS*, p. 673; *OHS*, p. 87.

64 Augustine, Sermo CCXVIII, i (*PL* 38, 1084).
65 W. Apel, *Gregorian Chant* (London: Burns and Oates), p. 207; David Hiley, *Western Plainchant. A Handbook* (OUP, 1993), p. 56; *OHS*, pp. 100–1.
66 The *Ordo Officiorum Ecclesiae Lateranensis* of about 1120, ed. L. Fischer (Munich, 1916, p. 44), *OR* xi. 38 of about 1140 (*PL* 78, 1040) and *OR* xv. 60 from the end of the fourteenth century (*PL* 78, 1303–1304) all have the Passion read by a single deacon.
67 Righetti, op. cit., Vol. II.92, pp. 151–2; *OHS*, p. 101.
68 Schmidt, *HS*, p. 683.
69 Since the 1970 reform the custom of singing the Passion has virtually disappeared. It is now usually simply recited in the vernacular.
70 See *OR* XXVIII. 3, from about 800 (Andrieu, *ORM* Vol. 2, p. 391).
71 See *OR* XXXI. 3, from the second half of the ninth century, 'Et omnes a responsione sileant' (Andrieu, *ORM* Vol. 2, p. 491), and John of Avranches, *Lib. de officiis ecclesiasticis*, from about 1060–1070 (*PL* 147, 47–48).
72 'Intermittunt aliqui salutationem in passione, id est *Dominus vobiscum*' (PRG cap. xxiii 47). However, the almost contemporary *Regularis Concordia S. Dunstani* prescribes the omission of *Gloria tibi Domine* but not *Dominus vobiscum* (*PL* 137, 490). Pseudo-Alcuin repeats the wording of the PRG exactly (*PL* 101, 1202).
73 *OR* xi. 38 (*PL* 78, 1039–1040).
74 Fischer, *OEL*, p. 44; Roman Pontifical of the Twelfth Century XXIX. 19 (Andrieu, *PRM* Vol. I, p. 214).
75 Rome, Archivio Lateranense, Cod.65. There is no modern edition. Quoted in Schmidt, *HS*, p. 605. Rubric repeated in *OR* xv. 60 (*PL* 78, 1303), from the fourteenth century.
76 *OHS*, p. 105; Righetti, op. cit., Vol. II.92, p. 52.
77 *OR* xv. 60 (*PL* 78, 1303–1304). According to this ordo the pause should be of about the same length as it takes to say a *Pater Noster*.
78 Sicardus, *Mitrale*, Lib.VI cap. x (*PL* 213, 294). For the *Missale Lateranense* see Schmidt, *HS*, p. 677: 'Pervento autem ad partem illam quae in tono evangelii legitur, benedictio petitur, incensum portatur sicut consuetum est fieri ad evangelium'. Durandus, in the thirteenth century, says that the custom is observed in certain churches, 'In fine tamen, in quibusdam ecclesiis, benedictio petitur, incensum portatur, et sub Evangelii tono legitur' (*Rationale* Lib.VI, lxviii. 7). *OR* xv, of about 1392, prescribes a procession with both lights and incense; the Gospel book is incensed by the deacon who makes the sign of the cross with his thumb upon it and upon himself before proceeding with the rest of the Gospel (*PL* 78, 1303–1304).
79 This prayer, which was introduced into the Mass liturgy in the eleventh century (cf. Jungmann, *MRR* Vol. I, pp. 454–5), was still being recited before the beginning of the Passion in the late fourteenth century, according to *OR* xv. 60 (*PL* 78, 1303–1304).
80 PRG cap. xxiii. 47 (Andrieu, *ORM* Vol. 5, p. 183).
81 *Regularis Concordia*: PL 137, 489–490; Lanfranc, *Decreta* cap. I, iv (*PL* 150, 457).
82 *OR* xv. LX (*PL* 78, 1304).
83 See the Antiphonals of Mont Blandin, Rheinau, Senlis, Corbie and

Compiègne, and the Gradual of Monza. Holy Week sections in Schmidt, *HS*, pp. 480–98.

[84] Baumstark, op. cit., p. 27. The Gradual or Tract originally comprised a large part or even all of a psalm, sung between the scriptural readings of the synaxis. The Tract for the First Sunday in Lent in the old (pre-1969) Roman rite, which consists of almost the whole of Psalm 90, is another example of this law.

[85] Now generally known as the prayer over the gifts (*super oblata*). The name 'Secret' is Gallican.

[86] Schmidt, *HS*, p. 707.

[87] Alcuin's Supplement: *Codex Ottobonianus* (Wilson, HBS, Vol. XLIV, p. 269). Frankish Gelasians: sacramentaries of Gellone, Angoulême and St Gall. Later Gregorian sacramentaries: those of St Eligius and Robert of Jumièges. (Schmidt, *HS*, pp. 392, 382, 406, 437 and 446 respectively).

[88] 'Per quem nobis indulgentia largitur et pax per omne saeculum praedicatur, traditur cunctis credentibus disciplina, ut sanctificatos nos possit dies sanctus venturus excipere'.

[89] For the texts see Schmidt, *HS*, 413 and 420 respectively.

[90] Fischer, *OEL*, p. 44.

[91] 'omnis lingua, omnis etas, omnis ordo, omnis sexus et conditio *Osanna in excelsis* regi altissimo voce et corde clamat *Sanctus Sanctus Sanctus*' (Fischer, *OEL*, p. 44).

[92] 'In hac die non consuevit esse sermo, nec Romani pontifices officiare consueverunt, sed bono mane in capella secreta celebrant Missam suam; eunt tamen et distribuunt palmas, licet aliquando modernis temporibus celebrent' (*OR* xiv. 82 [*PL* 78, 1203–1204]).

[93] 'Modernis autem temporibus est Missa papalis' (*OR* xv. LIII [*PL* 78, 1299]).

[94] Fischer, *OEL*, pp. 42–4.

[95] Jungmann, *MRR* Vol. I, p. 112. The earliest known instance of a formal scheme of colours seems to come from twelfth-century Jerusalem (J. W. Legg, 'An Early Sequence of Liturgical Colours, hitherto but little known, apparently following the Use of the Crusaders' Patriarchal Church in Jerusalem in the Twelfth Century', in *Essays Liturgical and Historical* [SPCK, 1917]).

[96] Durandus, *Rationale Lib.* III. xxviii 9 (Dura, p. 131), *OR* xiii. 21 (*PL* 78, 1117), *OR* xiv. LII (*PL* 78, 1155).

CHAPTER 5

THE INTERMEDIATE DAYS

Monday

Our earliest surviving lectionary of the Roman rite, that of Würzburg,[1] from the eighth century, contains two Old Testament readings for the Mass of this day, Isaiah 50:5–10 and Zachariah 11:12–13:9. The same two readings are prescribed in the Lectionary of Corbie (c.775)[2] and that of Alcuin (c.780).[3] But the *Comes* Theotinchi, of about 800,[4] has only a single reading, the one from Isaiah. This eventually became the norm, surviving in the Mass liturgy of the day until 1970, although the system of two readings evidently continued, at least in some places, for a considerable time.[5]

All three editions of the *Evangeliorum Capitulare Romanum*[6] give John 12:1–36 as the Gospel for the day. This simply continued the series of readings from the Gospel of St John which characterize the Masses of the second half of Lent. However, both the *Comes* of Murbach[7] and the *Comes* Theotinchi have a shorter reading, John 12:1–23, which was subsequently shortened again to verses 1–9 (the account of the Supper at Bethany). The reason for this seems to have been that the second part of the original reading, from verses 10 to 36, was adopted as the Gospel for the Saturday of the fifth week in Lent, the day immediately preceding Palm Sunday, when Masses first began to be celebrated on the Lenten Saturdays.[8] The reading survived the 1970 reform, the only text of the ancient Mass for this day, except for part of the Introit, to do so.

Prior to 1971 the Collect, Secret, Postcommunion and prayer over the people[9] were all identical to the prayers found in the Gregorian Sacramentary of the seventh century, and the Introit,

Gradual, Tract, Offertory and Communion verse were similarly identical to those in the antiphonals of Mont Blandin, Rheinau, Senlis, Corbie and Compiègne and the Gradual of Monza, from the eighth and ninth centuries.

Most of the sacramentaries do not prescribe any special Preface for this day, but those of Fulda, in the Gelasian tradition, and St Eligius and Robert of Jumièges, in the Gregorian, have a separate Preface (*Cuius nos humanitas*) for this, as well as for each of the other days of Holy Week. They first occur in Alcuin's Supplement to the *Hadrianum*. At some date prior to the twelfth century they were replaced by the Preface of the Holy Cross, as in the rest of Holy Week.

The liturgical colour for all three days between Palm Sunday and Holy Thursday is violet.[10] The station for Monday was either at Sta. Prassede (according to the Gregorian Sacramentary) or at SS. Nereus and Achilleus (according to the Frankish Gelasian sacramentaries).

Tuesday

As on Monday, the earliest Roman lectionaries (including this time the *Comes* Theotinchi) give two Old Testament readings for this day, Jeremiah 11:18–20 and Wisdom 2:12–22. Also as on Monday, the second reading eventually disappeared, the reading from Jeremiah surviving on its own until the 1970 reform.

The continuous reading of the Gospel according to St John continued in the earliest Roman evangeliaries with John 13:1–32, the account of the washing of the feet of the disciples after the Last Supper, and the treachery of Judas. The first of these documents, the recension known as Π, dating from around 645, has no Gospel for Holy Thursday, since at this time no synaxis, or Mass of the Catechumens, appears to have been celebrated on that day, the Eucharist beginning simply with the Offertory.[11] But the two later recensions, those known as Λ from about 740 and Σ from around 755, indicate that John 13:1–15, the washing of the feet of the disciples, had been adopted as the Gospel in the synaxis which had by that time been added to the Holy Thursday liturgy. In these two recensions the Gospel for Tuesday is still shown as John 13.:1–32, but the *Comes* of Murbach and the *Comes* Theotinchi both substitute John 12:24–44 for 13:1–32, presumably in order to avoid the same Gospel passage being read on both days. Another solution espoused was to reduce Tuesday's Gospel to the second part of the original reading, namely verses 16–32.[12] Neither solution was entirely satisfactory; the former still left an overlap with the Gospel of the previous Saturday, and the latter reversed the chronological sequence of the narrative. Eventually, from around the year 900, Tuesday's Gospel began to be replaced with the Passion according to St Mark, the only one of the four accounts for which there had hitherto been no place in the liturgy of Holy Week.[13] The various practices surrounding the reading of the Passion which had developed in the course of the Middle Ages, and which were described in Chapter 4, were extended to this day also.[14]

As on Monday, the Collect, Secret, Postcommunion and prayer over the people were, down to 1970, identical to those found in the Gregorian Sacramentary of the seventh century, and the Introit, Gradual, Tract, Offertory and Communion verse were similarly identical to those in the ancient antiphonals. Of the ancient readings and texts however only the Collect survives in the present liturgy.

There is a special Preface (*Cuius salutiferae passionis*) prescribed in the Sacramentaries of Fulda, St Eligius and Robert of Jumièges.

The station for the day was at Sta. Prisca.

Wednesday

Originally the only services held on weekdays in the Roman rite were non-liturgical synaxes (readings from Holy Scripture interspersed with responsories or psalms) on Wednesday and Friday mornings, the two days mentioned in the *Didache* as those on which Christians should fast.[15] The synaxes ended with a homily and a series of prayers for the Church, similar to the *orationes sollemnes* which are still a feature of the Good Friday liturgy. These prayers, also known as the Prayer of the Faithful, were later dropped from the Mass liturgy generally, possibly by St Gelasius (492–496 AD) when he introduced a litany (the so-called *deprecatio Gelasii*) into the Mass after the Introit.[16] They continued to be said, however, at a separate morning assembly on the Wednesday and Friday of Holy Week, another example, it would seem, of the operation of Baumstark's Law. They are mentioned frequently in the *Ordines Romani*,[17] as well as in the Romano-German Pontifical[18] and the Gregorian Sacramentary of St Eligius,[19] both from the tenth century. The assembly began at the third hour (about nine o'clock). First, the prayer *Deus a quo et Iudas*, which is probably attributable to St Leo, was said.[20] Then the pope, or whoever was presiding, announced the intention of the first prayer, *Oremus, dilectissimi, in primis pro Ecclesia sancta Dei*, etc., after which the deacon bade the faithful kneel for a short private prayer, and then to stand, with the words *Flectamus genua ... Levate*, and their private prayers were summed up by the president of the assembly in a Collect. There was no genuflection made, however, at the prayer for the Jews. The ceremony ended with the kissing of the altar. This morning assembly was still being celebrated in Rome, with the pope presiding, at the end of the twelfth century, but thereafter it died out.[21]

The Mass of the day, which was probably introduced in the mid-fifth century,[22] was celebrated in the afternoon, at the eighth or ninth hour (about two or three o'clock). At first it seems to have consisted in the Eucharist (Offertory, Canon and Communion) only, while the existing synaxis continued to be held in the morning. The readings and other scriptural passages however were joined with the Eucharist, in the customary way, at some later stage (perhaps when Gelasius abolished the prayer of the faithful on other days), leaving the *orationes sollemnes* on their own in the morning. Another possibility, perhaps less likely, is that the synaxis was combined with the Mass from the beginning, and the *orationes sollemnes* were separated therefrom and transferred back to the morning at a later date. In any event, the system of readings at the Wednesday Mass, unlike those of Monday and Tuesday, preserved both of the original Old Testament readings, Isaiah 62:11–63:1–7 (the apocalyptic poem on the vengeance of Yahweh), and Isaiah 53:1–12 (the fourth Song of the Suffering Servant).[23] The ancient practice of summoning the people to kneel and pray for a brief period between the first Collect and reading (*Flectamus genua ... Levate*), was retained until 1970, when the ancient system of two readings on this day was abolished. The Gospel was the Passion according to St Luke. All three readings are associated in the earliest surviving lectionaries and evangeliaries with this day.[24]

It is generally believed that at the time of St Leo (440–461) the

Passion according to St Matthew was read at today's synaxis, on the strength of the statement in his sermon, preached on Palm Sunday, that on Wednesday 'the reading of the Lord's Passion will be repeated'.[25] However, since St Leo merely speaks of a repetition of the Passion narrative and not to any specific evangelist's version, he could just as easily be referring to the Passion according to St Luke, and this would in fact be more consistent with the principal theme of St Leo's Wednesday sermon, which is the story of the two thieves from the latter Gospel.[26]

One curious feature of the Mass of this day is that until the ninth century at the earliest it did not contain any *Kyrie eleison*, the Collect following immediately upon the Introit.[27] The reason for this probably stems from the fact that the *Kyrie eleison* originated as part of the *deprecatio Gelasii*, which as we have seen was substituted for the prayer of the faithful towards the end of the fifth century. Since the latter continued on Wednesday of Holy Week, there would have been no *deprecatio Gelasii* in the Mass of this day, and consequently no *Kyrie*.

Of the remaining texts of the Mass, the Introit, Gradual, Tract, Offertory and Communion verse were, until 1970, those prescribed for this day in the earliest antiphonals. The Tract, with its five full verses from Psalm 101, was, like the Tract on Palm Sunday, an indication of the antiquity of the Mass.[28] The Collect, Postcommunion and prayer over the people were from the Gregorian tradition, though the Secret, exceptionally, was taken from the Gelasian. It was probably preferred because it refers specifically to the Crucifixion, whereas the Gregorian Secret for the day is expressed in merely general terms. All the ancient readings and texts of the Mass, with the exception of the Introit (in part), Collect and Secret, together with all the surviving indications of its antiquity, were swept away in the ruthless post-Vatican II modernization of the rite.

As on the two previous days, there is a special Preface (*Qui innocens pro impiis voluit pati*) prescribed in the Sacramentaries of Fulda, St Eligius and Robert of Jumièges. The eighth century Sacramentary of Angoulême has a unique Preface for the day (*Qui ut dilectam tibi*), found only in this source.[29]

The station was at the basilica of St Mary Major, an indication of the importance attached to Wednesday of Holy Week as compared with the two preceding days. It was the custom at

Rome in the later Middle Ages for the pope, after Mass on this day, to grant a special indulgence to pilgrims present in the city.[30]

Although all three of these days ranked only as simple feasts, the scriptural readings at Mass displayed, before the reform of 1970, a gradual escalation towards the Triduum which was not the less effective for being at least partly an accident of liturgical history. On Monday we heard a prophecy from Isaiah and the Gospel of the Supper at Bethany. On Tuesday there was a prophecy from Jeremiah and the Passion narrative according to St Mark, followed on Wednesday, the most important of the days, by two quite lengthy prophecies from Isaiah and the Passion according to St Luke. This gradual build up to the Triduum was suppressed by the 1970 reform which eliminated the second Old Testament reading on Wednesday and substituted Gospel readings from John 13 and Matthew 26 (out of chronological order) in place of the two Passion narratives.

Appendix

Allegorical Interpretation of the Ceremonies relating to the Passion Readings

Sane Passionem lecturus benedictionem non petit, quia in illa describitur esse sublatus qui auctor est benedictionis, unde non est a quo petatur. Legitur quoque sine luminaribus, quia ille morte extinctus nuntiatur qui, secundum Ioannem, lux est mundi, et ut repraesentatur quia eius discipuli tunc quasi extincti sunt, quibus ipse vivens dixerat: *Vos estis lux mundi.* Non fertur etiam incensum, ad notandum quod tunc fervor devotionis vel orationis, qui per incensum designatur, in Apostolis tepuit, vel potius quasi extinctus fuit. Legitur etiam sine salutatione, sive sine *Dominus vobiscum*, in detestationem salutationis Iudae; et sine responsione, non enim respondetur *Gloria tibi Domine*, qui in ipsa exprimitur quod Christus fuit a suis separatus per mortem corporaliter et spiritualiter, qui metu mortis eo derelicto fugerant, et nulla gloria sibi erat. Non legitur etiam tota sub tono Evangelii, sed cantus verborum Christi dulcius moderantur, ad notandum quod dulcius verba Christi in ipsius ore resonabant, quam in ore cuiuslibet Evangelistae referentis, cuius verba in tono Evangelii proferuntur. Verba vero impiissimorum Iudaeorum clamose et cum asperitate vocis, ad designandum quod ipsi Christo aspere loquebantur. In fine tamen, in quibusdam ecclesiis, benedictio petitur, incensum portatur, et sub Evangelii tono legitur, quia finita est iam narratio Passionis, et ex tunc omnia verba sunt Evangelistae narrantis quae post Christi mortem usque ad resurrectionem contigerunt. In aliis tamen ecclesiis finis Passionis, quae ad sepulturam pertinet, in tono legitur doloroso, ut planctus mulierum de Passione Christi lamentantium designetur.

Durandus, *Rationale divinorum officiorum* Lib. VI, lxviii. 5–7.

The reader of the Passion manifestly does not ask for a blessing, since the source of blessing is described therein as having been taken away, so that there is no one from whom it may be sought. And it is read without lights, because the death of him who, according to John, is the light of the world, is proclaimed therein, and to indicate that the disciples, whom he had called the light of the world while he was alive, have been as it were put out. And incense is not carried, in order to make it clear that at that time the fervour of devotion and of prayer, which is signified by incense, grew tepid in the Apostles, or rather became virtually extinct. It is also read without a greeting, that is without *Dominus vobiscum*, in repugnance at the greeting of Judas, and without a response, since there is no *Gloria tibi Domine*, in order to denote that Christ was separated, both bodily and spiritually, by death from his own, who from fear of death had left him and fled, and that there was no glory remaining in him. And it is not all read in a gospel tone, since the chant for the words of Christ is changed into a more mellifluous one, to indicate that the words of Christ resonated more mellifluously in his mouth than in the mouth of any of the Evangelists, whose words are pronounced in the gospel tone. But the words of the impious Jews are sung loudly and in a harsh tone of voice, to signify that they used to speak harshly to Christ. At the end, however, in some churches a blessing is sought, incense is carried, and a gospel tone is used for the reading, since the Passion narrative is finished, and from then on all the words are those of the Evangelist telling what happened after the death of Christ until his Resurrection. In other churches however the end of the Passion, which concerns the burial, is read in a sorrowful tone, to represent the lamentation of the women mourning the Passion of Christ.

Notes

¹ See Chapter 3, note 53.
² See Chapter 3, note 54.
³ See Chapter 3, note 55.
⁴ See Chapter 3, note 57.
⁵ Writing around 1290, Durandus says, 'In quibusdam ecclesiis in hac et in tertiis feriis dicuntur duae lectiones in missa' (*Rationale* Lib. VI. lxviii 2 [Dura, p. 505]). He attributes the two readings to the fact that the Passion of Christ was foretold in both the law and the prophets, as does Honorius of Autun in the preceding century (*Gemma animae* Lib. III lxxiii, [*PL* 172, 662]). See also Bernoldus of Bregenz, *Micrologus*, from the end of the eleventh century (*PL* 151, 1015).
⁶ See Chapter 3, note 50.
⁷ See Chapter 3, note 56.
⁸ Schmidt, *HS*, p. 677. The change however, was not made in England, where the Sarum Missal still has John 12:1–36 as the Gospel for the Monday in Holy Week, the Gospel for the Saturday of the fifth week in Lent being John 6:54–72. (J. Wickham Legg, op. cit., pp. 92 and 99).
⁹ This was a prayer similar to and immediately following the Postcommunion. Once a feature of all Masses of the Roman rite, it died out in the early part of the Middle Ages except on the weekdays of Lent, where it survived until the 1970 reform, when it was finally abolished altogether.
¹⁰ Pontifical of Durandus, Lib. III, xxvii. 4 (Andrieu, PRM Vol. III, p. 658), OR xiv. 52 (*PL* 78, 1155).
¹¹ See Chapter 7.
¹² As found for example in the *Missale Lateranense* (Schmidt, *HS*, p. 674).
¹³ The first example is in a ninth century evangeliary from Salzburg, where John 13:1–32 has been amended in a later hand to the Passion according to St Mark (Schmidt, *HS*, p. 467).
¹⁴ OR xi. 38 (*PL* 78, 1040), Durandus, *Rationale* Lib. VI. lxxviii, 5 (Dura, p. 506). Durandus gives a wealth of allegorical explanations for the absence of lights, incense, blessing of the reader, *Dominus vobiscum* and *Gloria tibi Domine*, as well as for the various tones in which the Passion was sung. The whole passage is a classic of allegorizing (see Appendix to this chapter).
¹⁵ *Didache* 8. The date of this document is much disputed, but it appears to belong to either the first or the second century.
¹⁶ J. A. Jungmann, MRR Vol. I, p. 58. The name *deprecatio Gelasii* comes from Alcuin (*PL* 101, 560).
¹⁷ OR XXIV. 1–3, XXVII. 14–15, XXVIII. 4, XXIX. 3–4, XXXI. 4–5 (Andrieu, ORM Vol. 5, pp. 291–2, 351, 392, 437–8, 491–2). See also Canon 43 of the Council of Rispach-Freising-Salzburg (c.800), 'Ut si vobis videtur usum Romanum habere velle, fer. IV ante cenam Domini orationes quae scriptae sunt ad fer. VI parasceve ab episcopis vel presbyteris, hora tertia diei supradictae fer. IV,

dicantur in ecclesia cum genuflexione, nisi tantum pro Iudaeis' (quoted in Schmidt, *HS*, p. 707 n.2.)

18 Andrieu, ORM Vol. 5, pp. 183–4.

19 Schmidt, *HS*, p. 438.

20 Schmidt, *HS*, p. 707.

21 *OR* xii. 21 (*PL* 78, 1072).

22 At the time of St Hilarius I (461–468), according to Schmidt, *HS*, p. 707.

23 Both read in fourth-century Jerusalem on Good Friday. See Chapter 2, note 42.

24 Schmidt, *HS*, pp. 458–60.

25 St Leo, *Sermo* LIV c.5, 'in quartam feriam, qua lectio Dominicae Passionis iterabitur' (*PL* 54, 322). For the interpretation that the Passion according to St Matthew was read again on Wednesday, see Schmidt, *HS*, p. 673.

26 *PL* 54, 317.

27 *OR* XXIV 5, XXVII 18 and XXVIII 4, all from the eighth century, repeated in PRG XXIV 5 (Andrieu, *ORM* Vol. 5, p. 184), from the tenth. The first mention of the *Kyrie* is in *OR* XXIX 6 and *OR* XXXI 8, from the second half of the ninth century, where it has clearly been inserted into the text copied from earlier ordines.

28 Schmidt, *HS*, p. 708. See Chapter 4, note 74, for the Tracts of the First Sunday in Lent and Palm Sunday. In a typical medieval allegorical explanation, Honorius of Autun attributed the five verses of the Wednesday Tract to the five wounds of Christ (*Gemma animae* Lib. III, lxxiv).

29 For the text see Schmidt, *HS*, p. 393.

30 *OR* xiv 82 (*PL* 78, 1204); *OR* xv 62 (*PL* 78, 1305).

CHAPTER 6

TENEBRAE

The Office of Matins and Lauds

For Sundays and feast days, prior to the twentieth-century reform of the breviary, the Rule of St Benedict provided, after the silent recitation of the *Pater*, *Ave* and *Credo*, an opening versicle (*Domine, labia mea aperies, et os meum annuntiabit laudem tuam*) followed by two introductory psalms (3 and 94), a hymn, and then three nocturns. The first nocturn consisted of six psalms, each with an antiphon, then a versicle, the *Pater Noster* recited silently, a blessing of the lector and an Old Testament reading in four parts, each part followed by a responsory. The second nocturn was similar but the reading, also in four parts, comprised a patristic commentary or a hagiographical text. In the third nocturn, in place of the six psalms there were three Old Testament canticles, with a single antiphon at the beginning and end, followed by a versicle and blessing of the lector and a four-part reading from the New Testament. Each reading was succeeded by a responsory; the twelfth and final responsory was followed by the *Te Deum*, a Gospel reading, the hymn *Te decet laus*, and a final blessing.

Lauds began with a versicle (*Deus in adiutorium meum intende, Domine ad adjuvandum me festina*) and continued with psalms 66 and 50 (the *Miserere*), followed by two further psalms and an Old Testament canticle, variable according to the day. Then psalms 148, 149 and 150, from the *Laudate* series, were sung as a single psalm, followed by a short reading (known as a *capitulum*) with responsory, a hymn, versicle, and the *Benedictus*. The office concluded with the *Kyrie* and *Pater Noster*.

This monastic office for Sundays and feast days was adapted at an early date for urban liturgical practice. The basic structure of the office remained the same; the principal differences were that at Matins a single introductory psalm was sung, with three psalms and a three-part reading at each nocturn in place of six and four respectively. The office ended with the *Te Deum*.

The order of Matins and Lauds for the last three days of Holy Week (known collectively since at least the early twelfth century as Tenebrae) closely followed this pattern, with certain parts of the normal offices omitted. The office of Matins began, as usual, with the silent recitation of *Pater, Ave* and *Credo*. But the antiphon at the first psalm was then intoned immediately, omitting both the opening versicle and the invitatory psalm. The *Gloria Patri* normally sung at the end of each psalm was also omitted. No blessing was requested or given before the readings, and *Tu autem Domine miserere nobis* was not said after them. The readings for the first nocturn on each day were taken from the Lamentations of Jeremiah, those of the second nocturn from the treatise of St Augustine on the psalms, and those of the third nocturn from the letters of St Paul. The responsories following each reading consisted in free versions of texts taken from the psalms, the Old Testament prophets or the Gospels, appropriate to the season.[1] There was naturally no concluding *Te Deum*, which would have been wholly inappropriate during Holy Week.

Omitting the opening versicle, the antiphon at the first psalm of Lauds was intoned immediately following the responsory to the last reading of Matins. The office consisted of three psalms (of which the *Miserere*, Psalm 50, was always the first), followed by an Old Testament canticle and one further psalm taken from the *Laudate* series (psalms 145 to 150), and then the *Benedictus*. As at Matins, the *Gloria Patri* at the end of the psalms or canticles was omitted throughout. The *capitulum* with its responsory, hymn and versicle were all omitted. After the *Benedictus* Lauds concluded with the antiphon *Christus factus est*, the *Pater Noster* recited silently, the *Miserere* again, this time recited in a low voice, and the prayer *Respice, quaesumus, Domine*.

The omissions are ancient, being mentioned in several of the *Ordines Romani*, composed in the Frankish Kingdom mainly in the second half of the eighth century and reflecting both Roman and Gallican practice.[2] Similar omissions are found in the Office of the Dead. They appear to be a classic instance of Baumstark's Law ('Primitive conditions are maintained with greater tenacity in the more sacred seasons of the Liturgical Year.'), since those parts of the office which are omitted are in the main those which were added later.[3]

Lighting at Tenebrae

During Tenebrae the church was lit only by six large altar candles and a further fifteen arranged on a triangular 'hearse' situated before the Epistle (right) side of the altar. All these candles were of unbleached wax except for that at the apex of the hearse. At the conclusion of each of the psalms (nine at Matins and five at Lauds) one of the candles on the hearse was extinguished, on alternate sides, until at the end of the last psalm only the top candle was left alight. The six altar candles were likewise extinguished during alternate verses of the *Benedictus*. Finally, at the end of the *Benedictus* the single remaining candle was removed from the top of the hearse and hidden behind the altar, leaving the church in total darkness. After the prayer *Respice, quaesumus, Domine* the signal that the office had ended was given by the knocking of a book on the choir stalls (known as the *strepitus*), and the hidden candle was brought back and replaced on the top of the hearse.

Musical Settings at Tenebrae

The psalms, antiphons and readings were sung in the usual plainsong tones, the *Benedictus* each day being always in the first tone. However the Lamentations which comprised the readings at the first nocturn of Matins had their own individual melody, related to the sixth psalm tone, and one of the most strikingly beautiful in the whole plainsong repertoire. According to tradition this melody went back to the synagogue chant of apostolic times, but there is no evidence for this, and it is probably Gallican in origin. In the original Hebrew the first verse in the Lamentations began with the first letter of the alphabet (*Aleph*), the second verse with the second such letter (*Beth*), and so on, and this format was preserved in the Latin text by singing the appropriate letter of the Hebrew alphabet before each verse.[4] There are also many polyphonic settings, notably by Lassus, Victoria, Palestrina and Allegri, and by the English composers Thomas Tallis, William Byrd and Robert White and by the Portuguese de

Brito. These were seldom heard in practice, since, apart from the fact that only a shortened version and not the full text was normally set to music, Tenebrae lasted between one and a half to two hours, and to sing one of the polyphonic rather than the plainsong setting of the Lamentations would add some twenty minutes or more to this. The responsories also could be sung either in plainsong or in one or other of the polyphonic settings written for them by composers of the Renaissance period. The best known is that of Victoria, but there are also settings by Gesualdo, Croce, Palestrina and Charpentier. These were quite commonly heard in church, especially that of Victoria. The psalms and canticles were sung antiphonally, either between two choirs or between choir and congregation.[5]

The Timing and Texts of the Office

Matins was originally said during the night, beginning at midnight. St Benedict changed this to the eighth hour (approximately 2 a.m.) to enable his monks to get more sleep, and this timing was adopted in monasteries and in churches which followed the monastic practice. But about the beginning of the thirteenth century the Benedictines started to revert to the earlier time.[6] Eventually the timing of Tenebrae was advanced to the evening of the previous day, probably to allow the participation of the secular clergy and laity, a process which began in the thirteenth to fourteenth centuries. According to the *Caeremoniale Episcoporum* of 1600, Tenebrae should begin at 'the twenty-first hour or thereabouts', by which it means at around 4–5 p.m. in our time.[7] Lauds was originally a separate office sung at dawn, but by the second half of the eighth century it was already being sung immediately after the end of Matins.[8]

The *Liber Responsalis Compendiensis*, from the end of the ninth century, gives a full list of the psalms at Matins with their antiphons, from which it is clear that there were no changes in either until the abolition of Tenebrae in 1970.[9] The psalms for the Good Friday and Holy Saturday office were selected to reflect the feast, whereas those for Maundy Thursday are those which normally fall on a Thursday as part of a continuous reading (there is a gap of three psalms between the last psalm on Wednesday and the first on Thursday, which reflects the fact that there were originally twelve psalms, reduced to nine by omitting the last three). It seems likely therefore that the office of Tenebrae was originally celebrated only on the Friday and Saturday, and extended later to the Thursday in Holy Week, at some time before the closing years of the ninth century. This accords with the evidence that Maundy Thursday was the last day to which the ceremony of extinguishing the lights in the course of the office was extended (see below).

Evidence for the readings at Tenebrae in the eighth century comes from the *Ordines Romani*. At the first nocturn of Matins the whole of the Lamentations of Jeremiah were read over the three days, from 1:1 to 2:7 on Maundy Thursday, from 2:8 to 3:21 on Good Friday, and from 3:22 to the end on Holy Saturday. The readings at the second nocturn on Maundy Thursday and Good Friday consisted in extracts from St Augustine's *Treatise on the Psalms* (Psalm 54 on Maundy Thursday and Psalm 63 on Good Friday); on Holy Saturday they were taken from the homilies of the Fathers as appropriate to the day.[10] At the third nocturn on Maundy Thursday, the readings were from St Paul's First Letter to the Corinthians, starting at 11:23, on Good Friday from the Letter to the Hebrews starting at 4:11, and on Holy Saturday from the homilies of the Fathers as appropriate to the day. By the middle of the tenth century the three-part reading at the second nocturn on Holy Saturday was taken from the Letter to the Hebrews, commencing at 9:11.[11]

In monasteries during the Middle Ages the Lamentations seem to have been frequently recited rather than sung; there are provisions to this effect for example in the rules of the monastery of Farfa and in those of Cluny and in the Decrees of Lanfranc, all belonging to the eleventh century; the latter two also specify that the Hebrew letters should *not* be sung, an indication that the custom of doing so was normal.[12]

The responsories after the readings at Matins, described by Thurston as 'the very soul of the Tenebrae services',[13] appear to have been derived from Eastern liturgical poetry. The most ancient seem to be those from the Gospel of St Matthew. They may have been imported into the office during the seventh century when a succession of Eastern popes held the chair of St Peter.[14] The texts, however, are those of the old Latin Gospels rather than that of the Vulgate.[15] Amalarius of Metz in the mid-ninth century mentions them with admiration, and rightly calls them masterpieces, which dwell upon the guilt of Christ's betrayal and move the hearts of the faithful by the sorrow of his Crucifixion.[16]

From the above evidence it seems clear that although the readings, particularly those in the second and third nocturns, have varied to a certain extent over time, in other respects both the texts of the office and its structure remained essentially the same from the eighth century, at the very latest, until 1970.

The Gradual Extinction of Lights

The earliest evidence concerning the provision of light during the singing of the office comes from the *Ordines Romani*. It is difficult to interpret, because although it is possible to establish a relative dating for certain parts of the series, absolute dating is generally not possible, and it is also impossible to determine where each of the ordines was written except within very wide limits. Notwithstanding that their declared aim was the substitution of the Roman rite for the multiplicity of local rites, they appear to contain, to a varying degree, an admixture of Gallican and Roman practice.[17] The variety of ritual observances found in them is partly due to the varying dates of the ordines and partly to their different provenances.

According to *Ordo* XVI, which was composed in eastern France shortly before 787, 'on that night [Good Friday to Holy Saturday] no light is lit in the church until Saturday' and *Ordo* XVII, from between 790 and 800, expands upon this: 'on that night the light in the church is not lit but it is hidden so that it is invisible to everyone until Saturday'.[18] It would seem therefore that Matins and Lauds of Holy Saturday were sung entirely in the dark. Neither ordo contains any reference to the two preceding nights and it may therefore be inferred that the usual practice (whatever that may have been) was followed on those nights in the monastic communities where these ordines were in force. According to the approximately contemporary *Ordo* XXXB, however, one lamp or candle was permitted to assist the readers on Holy Saturday, and during the singing of Lauds at the Good Friday office on the previous night, six of the customary seven sanctuary lamps were extinguished one by one, the seventh being concealed and

reserved for Holy Saturday, presumably for the assistance of the
reader at the night office of that day, though this is not specifically
stated.[19] Both *Ordo* XXIII and *Ordo* XXXA (which also belong to
the eighth century but cannot be more closely dated) mention the
light concealed at the Good Friday office but in these cases it was
brought out only at the Easter Vigil, though in the case of the
former it was used to light the two large candles which formed
part of the papal rite, and in that of the latter to light the Paschal
candle, which at that time did not feature in the papal rite.[20] The
latter ordo also mentions the extinction of lights during Lauds on
both Good Friday and Holy Saturday, though without giving any
details.[21]

The practice of extinguishing lights during Matins as well, on
both Good Friday and Holy Saturday, is prescribed in *Ordo*
XXVIII, of about 800. One third of the church lights (we are not
told how many there are) is extinguished in the course of each
nocturn; during Lauds, the seven sanctuary lamps, as in *Ordines*
XXXA and XXXB, are also put out one by one as the psalms are
sung, beginning with the outside lamp on the right hand side,
then the corresponding lamp on the left hand side, and so on
working inwards and ending with the middle lamp.[22] *Ordines*
XXVI, XXVII, XXIX (all from the second half of the eighth century)
and XXXI (from the ninth) extend this practice to the office of
Holy Thursday.[23] *Ordo* XXIX not only prescribes that one third of
the church lights are to be extinguished during each nocturn of
Matins, but goes further and details the precise point at which
each of them is to be put out, beginning at the first antiphon of the
first psalm.[24] In none of these ordines is any reservation of the last
light mentioned.

According to the Pontifical of Poitiers, of around 900, on Good
Friday the church lights (whether candles or oil lamps is not clear)
were arranged in three rows with ten lights in each row. The
sacristan, standing near the door at the west end of the building,
gave the signal for the start of Matins by extinguishing a candle
which he held in his hand. As Matins progressed he gradually put
out the thirty church lights, one by one, working from west to
east. Although the pontifical does not say so (probably because
the author thought it too obvious to need mentioning) it is
virtually certain that ten lights would have been extinguished
during each nocturn. One light was extinguished at each of the

three antiphons to the psalms, one at the versicle between the last psalm and the first lesson, one at the beginning of each lesson and one at the beginning of each responsory. Each light was put out at the first or second syllable of the respective antiphon, lesson or responsory. There is no reference to any extinction of lights during Lauds.[25]

From the foregoing evidence it is possible to discern, if somewhat dimly, a development in the rite. It would seem that originally normal lighting was employed for Matins and Lauds of Holy Thursday and Good Friday, with the Holy Saturday office sung either entirely in the dark, or with a single light to assist in the reading of the lessons (the singing of the psalms in darkness would not have been a problem for a monastic community, whose members would have known them by heart). The custom then began of extinguishing the seven sanctuary lamps one by one during Lauds on Good Friday. This was extended to include the church lights during Matins, at first probably on Good Friday only, then on Holy Saturday and eventually on Maundy Thursday as well. In the absence of more precise evidence concerning the date and provenance of the various ordines it is not possible to be more specific than this. The process would in any case have taken place at different times in different places.[26] The desirability of liturgical unity was a concept which, notwithstanding the strong encouragement given by the imperial government, made headway only slowly and hesitantly, especially in a society where liturgical books were rare and expensive items.

The night office of the Triduum in eighth-century Rome does not seem to have been attended by the gradual extinction of lights. *Ordo* XXIII, which contains a description of the Holy Week ceremonies at the Lateran during that century, mentions the omissions at Lauds but has nothing to say on the subject of extinguishing lights at the night office. Neither does *Ordo* XXIV, which certainly reflects Roman practice and may represent an adaptation of the papal rite for use in the other city churches.[27] And Amalarius of Metz, in whose church the custom of extinguishing the lights on all three nights was already established, tells us that in the course of a visit to Rome during the year 832 he asked the Archdeacon, Theodore, what the contemporary practice was at the Lateran. According to Amalarius, Theodore replied that on the night of Maundy Thursday to Good Friday there was no formal ceremony of extinguishing the lights; all existing lights and fires were extinguished around noon on Good Friday, but new fire was kindled later in the day and this new fire was reserved for use at the night office of Holy Saturday (though it is not clear from his reply how many lights were actually in use at the time during this office).[28] However, as we shall see, on the evidence of *Ordo* L (which forms part of the Romano-German Pontifical) the custom of extinguishing the lights gradually on all three nights must have been adopted at Rome before the date of composition of this ordo, i.e before the middle of the tenth century.[29]

The purpose of the gradual extinction of lights appears to have been symbolic from the beginning. It has been suggested that it originally had a practical function, to save candles as the natural light grew stronger. This cannot however be the correct explanation since the total time required for the singing of Tenebrae is no more than two hours or so, and an office commencing at midnight or even 2 a.m. must have ended in the dark as it had begun.[30]

The form of the rite itself did not become standardized until the later Middle Ages.[31] Previously both the number of the candles and the manner of their extinguishing varied greatly between different churches and in different periods.[32] According to the Romano-German Pontifical, dating from about 950, the practice in certain places (*in quibusdam locis*) was to start with twenty-four lights on each night. It goes on to say that in the Roman Rite (*apud Romanos*) one third of the lights are put out at each of the three nocturns of Matins, leaving only the seven sanctuary lamps which were extinguished during Lauds (the same procedure in fact as in *Ordines* XXVI, XXVII and XXIX).[33] The phraseology suggests that the number of lights and the practice regarding their lighting and extinction was still not standardized throughout the Empire at the date of composition of this ordo.

The Hearse

The change from the practice of extinguishing the church lights during Matins and the sanctuary lights during Lauds to one of putting out candles on a wooden stand, or hearse, is not well documented. In the middle of the tenth century, when the

Romano-German Pontifical was composed, the former practice evidently still prevailed. However, in the Customary of Farfa and St Paul's Monastery in Rome, from the beginning of the eleventh century, we read

> On Holy Thursday, before the night office, thirty candles, the same number as there are psalms, should be lit on a wooden frame in front of the high altar. Fifteen psalms out of the total of thirty should be recited in silence before the start of the office after the three prayers. The sacristan should give the signals, as usual. When all have been said, accompanied by audible signals, the presiding priest should begin the antiphon *Zelus domus tuae*. And immediately a candle should be put out on one side, then another on the other side, and so on at the beginning of each psalm.[34]

What this appears to mean is that fifteen psalms (the so-called gradual psalms) were recited silently before the start of Matins proper, the sacristan giving a signal at the end of each one and, presumably, putting out one candle at the same time (it is not clear from the text how the sacristan knew when everyone was ready to go on to the next psalm). The remaining candles were put out, one by one, at the start of each of the fifteen psalms sung during Matins. The expression used for the hearse is *instrumentum lignorum*, which suggests a single apparatus formed from several pieces of wood, on which all thirty candles were mounted.[35] There is no mention of the sanctuary lights, which probably remained unlit for the whole of the office. The *Consuetudines* of Cluny, of about 1060, also refers to fifteen candles which are put out one by one at the beginning of each psalm, though they do not mention any hearse.[36] Neither do the contemporary *Decreta* of Lanfranc, which provide that before the start of the office as many candles should be lit as there are antiphons and reponsories to be sung, one to be extinguished at each antiphon and responsory.[37] From this time onwards we hear no more about any extinction of the ordinary church lights.

The Number of Lights at Tenebrae

In the later Middle Ages the number of lights used at Tenebrae (apart from the altar candles) varied considerably from place to place. The most common number seems to have been twenty-four, which are put out at the end of each psalm and each reading or responsory. The earliest authority for this number is Amalarius of Metz (c.830) and there are many other instances of this number up to the Council of Trent. As we have seen, it is found in the Romano-German Pontifical of the tenth century. It also occurs in the treatise *De Divinis Officiis* ascribed to Alcuin but actually an anonymous work of the tenth to eleventh century, an Ordinary of Canons Regular at Rouen (c.1050), John of Avranches (c.1065), Honorius of Autun (c.1150), John Beleth (c.1186), Sicardus of Cremona (c.1210), Durandus (c.1290), and in the Sarum Breviary of the thirteenth century.[38] This number survived at Rouen and Orléans into the eighteenth century and among the Premonstratensians into the twentieth.[39] In some places, particularly in England, the number was twenty-five.[40] These numbers are found in both the cathedral and monastic tradition.

Various allegorical interpretations were attached to the numbers, in particular the twelve prophets and twelve apostles (plus Christ in the case of twenty-five lights). Amalarius also identifies the twenty-four lights with the twenty-four hours of the day and the seventy-two lights lit over the whole Triduum with the three days spent by Christ in the tomb. The same explanation is given in Pseudo-Alcuin.[41] Other numbers are found less commonly. Where they occur they are, as one would expect, often divisible by three, corresponding to the three nocturns. In this category seventy-two, thirty-nine, thirty, twenty-seven, fifteen, twelve, and nine are mentioned in various sources, but forty-four, thirty-four, twenty-six, twenty-three, fourteen, thirteen, eleven, seven and five (the last in the Carmelite rite) are also found.[42] John Beleth in the twelfth century says that in some places there were seventy-two lights, in others twenty-four, fifteen, twelve, nine or seven.[43] Durandus mentions the same numbers as Beleth and goes on to say that in some places there was in fact no fixed number.[44] The first mention of fifteen lights, which seems to have been particularly associated with religious houses, is at Farfa at the beginning of the eleventh century, and other monasteries followed suit.[45] It is not clear when this number was adopted at Rome (there were twelve in use at St John Lateran in the twelfth century), the first documentary evidence of this number being the definitive Breviary of 1568, though it was probably well established there by then.[46]

Tempting as it may be to link the practice of putting out the six altar candles during the *Benedictus* with the custom of extinguishing the seven sanctuary lamps during Lauds in the early Middle Ages, particularly since the method of extinguishing them is reminiscent of that prescribed in *Ordines* XXXA and XXXB for the sanctuary lamps, there is in fact no evidence of any association between them. Its origin is obscure (it is difficult to find any record of it in any of the later medieval documents) and it seems to be relatively recent.[47] The first of the six candles, the outside one on the Gospel side, was put out at the end of the second verse of the *Benedictus*, the second, the corresponding one on the Epistle side, at the end of the fourth, and so on, at the end of each alternate verse, working inwards. A less common practice was to extinguish one candle at the end of each of the last six verses, in the same order.

Before the 1955 reform it was customary not to extinguish the fifteenth candle but to remove it from the hearse and hide it temporarily behind the altar, from where it was recovered at the end of the office and replaced on the top of the hearse.[48] In the beginning it seems that either the church was simply left in darkness after the extinction of the last candle, or another light was provided so that the community or congregation could find their way out of the church.[49] John Beleth says 'However, one [candle], located in the centre, is not put out, but is removed and hidden, and afterwards brought out again into the open, and from its flame all the church lights are relit'.[50] The purpose therefore seems to have been to provide a light, but inevitably it attracted symbolic interpretations, especially the obvious one of the burial and Resurrection of Christ.

The *strepitus*, which was usually made by knocking a book against a bench, probably originated simply in a signal that the office was over and that all present might leave.[51] In the later Middle Ages it naturally acquired symbolic interpretations. Durandus for example likens it to the ranting of Judas and to the noise made by the cohort which went out with swords and clubs to arrest Jesus in the Garden of Gethsemane. To this Sicardus adds the clamour of the crowd who mockingly adored him and the lamenting of the holy women.[52]

Origin of the Name

The first recorded mention of the name 'Tenebrae' is by Peter Abelard in the early twelfth century. He observes that 'these three days are spent in mourning, as though for the funeral of the Lord, hence the night office of these days is commonly called Tenebrae, since our grief is expressed by the putting out of the lights'.[53] The name was clearly well established by his time, and it is probably much older. Its origin is not recorded. However, since the word 'tenebrae' is used in both a literal and a metaphorical sense, and the themes of light giving way to darkness and darkness giving way to light are commonplaces of the Holy Week liturgy (the darkness over the whole earth at the Crucifixion mentioned in the Synoptic Gospels, reflected in the second responsory at the second nocturn of the Good Friday office, the ceremonies of the New Fire and the Paschal Candle, the *Exsultet*, the first Old Testament reading at the Paschal Vigil, etc.), the reasons for it are not hard to understand. Durandus, writing about the year 1290, says that the office of Tenebrae signifies not so much the physical darkness which covered the face of the earth while the Sun of Justice hung upon the Cross, as the spiritual darkness which during those three days possessed the hearts of the faithful.[54]

Appendix 1

Scriptural Sources for the Tenebrae Responsories

Maundy Thursday

First	Matt. 26:39, 41
Second	Matt. 26:38, Mark 14:41
Third	Is. 53:2, 5, 4
Fourth	Matt. 26:48, 27:6, 5, 26:24
Fifth	Matt. 26:15, 24
Sixth	Mark 14:18, Matt. 26:24, 23
Seventh	Jer. 11:19, 18:18
Eighth	Matt. 26:40, Luke 22:46
Ninth	Matt. 26:3–4, 55, John 11:47

Good Friday

First	Job 19:14, 30:13, 19:19, 16:10, Ps. 68:22, Job 16:14

Second	Matt. 27:51, Luke 23:42, Matt. 27:51–52
Third	Jer. 2:21, Matt. 27:26, Is. 5:2
Fourth	Mark 14:48–49, Matt. 27:26
Fifth	Matt. 27:45–46, John 19:30, Luke 23:46
Sixth	Jer. 12:7–11, Ps. 26:12
Seventh	Ps. 53:5
Eighth	Matt. 26:14–15, 58, 57
Ninth	Jer. Lam. 1:16, 12

Holy Saturday

First	Is. 53:7, 12
Second	Bar. 5:5, 4:36, Jer. Lam. 2:10, 18
Third	Joel 1:8, 13, Jer. 25:34, Joel 2:11, Soph. 1:14
Fourth	Rev. 7:17, Jer. 17:13, Luke 23:45
Fifth	Jer. Lam. 1:12
Sixth	Is. 57:1, 53:7–8
Seventh	Ps. 2:2, 1
Eighth	Ps. 87:5–6, 7
Ninth	Mark 14:46, Matt. 27:66, 62

Appendix 2

The Extinction of Lights in *Ordo Romanus* XXIX

In Section 12 (according to Andrieu's subdivision) of this ordo, which represents an adaptation of *Ordo* XXVII for use in a monastic community, we read that one third (*tertia pars*) of the church lights are extinguished during each nocturn of Matins. It goes on to say that thirteen lights are put out during each of the first two nocturns of Matins and six during the third, a total of thirty-two. It also specifies in great detail the exact point during each nocturn when each light is to be extinguished. However, Section 11 of the same ordo states that the church lights total twenty-eight. There are evidently two problems of interpretation here. First, there is a discrepancy between the twenty-eight lights mentioned in Section 11 and the thirty-two in Section 12. Secondly, the statement that one third of the lights are put out during each of the three nocturns does not tally with the further information that thirteen lights are extinguished during each of the first two nocturns and only six during the third.

The solution to this enigma proposed by MacGregor is that the number of lights originally mentioned in Section 11 was in fact thirty-nine. A copyist has assumed, wrongly, that this includes the seven sanctuary lamps, and in order to make the figures agree has reduced the number of lights extinguished during the third nocturn of Matins by seven, from thirteen to six, amending the points at which each light is put out to make his revised figure fit. The figure of twenty-eight in Section 11 is simply a scribal error for thirty-nine (i.e. XXVIII for XXXVIIII).

I can well believe that a careless or tired scribe could have copied XXXVIIII as XXVIII. It is much more difficult however to accept that a scribe who believed that the figure in Section 11 was meant to include the seven sanctuary lamps should go to all the trouble of altering not only the number of lights extinguished during the third nocturn but also the detailed arrangements for their extinction (especially since he then ended up with a figure which no longer represented one third of the church lights), when all he had to do in order to reconcile the numbers was to change the figure in Section 11 from thirty-nine to forty-six. I am inclined to believe therefore that the received text of Section 12, which is found in both of the surviving manuscripts of this ordo (*Vat Palat.* 417 and Petroburg. Q.V.II, n.5), is original and that the asymmetrical procedure recorded therein represents the genuine practice, idiosyncratic no doubt, in the monastic community for which the ordo was composed.

This would not however solve the problem of the discrepancy in the numbers between Sections 11 and 12, nor the fact that it is specifically stated that one third of the lights are put out at each nocturn. It is easier to suppose that XXVIII has been substituted by mistake for XXXVIIII than for XXXII. It may be however that the original author of the ordo did in fact intend to include the seven sanctuary lamps in his total, and that he simply copied the figure of one-third thoughtlessly from *Ordo* XXVII, his principal source, much of the text of which is reproduced word for word in *Ordo* XXIX.

Notes:

[1]   See appendix at the end of the chapter for the scriptural sources for each responsory.
[2]   References to the omissions are found in *ORs* XXIII. 1; XXVI. 11–12; XXVII.

3–4 (all Roman); XXVIII. 7–8 and 10 (Gallican); XXIX. 9–10; XXXA. 3–4; XXXB. 1–2, 4 and 26–7; and XXXI. 11–12 and 15. See *OHS*, p. 125 for the various dates at which the formulae omitted in Tenebrae were introduced into the office, and Righetti, op. cit., Vol. II. 95, pp. 154–5.

³ For Baumstark's Law, see Chapter 4, note 83.
⁴ The singing of the Hebrew letters of the alphabet before each Lamentation is mentioned in *OR* L. xxv. 3, xxvi. 1 and xxviii. 2, composed around the middle of the tenth century.
⁵ Music for Lamentations and responsories: see *The New Grove Dictionary of Music and Musicians*, ed. S. Sadie (Macmillan, 1980), Vol. X 410–412, XV 765.
⁶ A. J. MacGregor, *Fire and Light in the Western Triduum*, Alcuin Club Collection no. 71 (Collegeville, Minnesota, 1992), p. 31.
⁷ 'Hora vigesima prima vel circa', quoted in Righetti, op. cit., Vol. II. 95, p. 154. According to the old Italian system of counting the hours, the twenty-first hour was 4 p.m. in March and 5 p.m. in April; cf. MacGregor, op. cit., p. 32.
⁸ *OR* XXVI. 13, from the third quarter of the eighth century at the latest.
⁹ Paris BN lat. 17436: see Schmidt, *HS*, pp. 616–26.
¹⁰ Cf. *OR* XXVIII. 49 and *OR* XXXI. 53: 'omeliae sanctorum patrum ad ipsum diem pertinentes' (Andrieu, ORM Vol. 3, pp. 401 and 499).
¹¹ Evidence for the readings at Tenebrae: *OR* XXVIII. 9, 29 and 49 (ibid., pp. 393, 397 and 401); *OR* XXXA. 1 and 5 (ibid., pp. 455–6); *OR* XXXB. 3 and 26 (ibid., pp. 468 and 470); *OR* XXXI. 14, 34 and 53, (ibid., pp. 492, 496 and 499); *OR* L. xxv 3, xxvi 1 and xxviii 2 (ibid., Vol. 5, pp. 187, 244 and 260–1).
¹² *Disciplina Farfensis et Monasterii S. Pauli Romae* cap. ii (*PL* 150, 1197); Cluny, *Consuetudines* cap. xii (*PL* 149, 657); Lanfranc, *Decreta* cap. I, iv (*PL* 150, 458).
¹³ Thurston, op. cit., p. 255.
¹⁴ For the origin of the responsories see Baumstark, op., cit., Ch. VI, pp. 101–2; for eastern popes cf. *Liber Pontificalis*, 74–75, 84–90.
¹⁵ Thurston, op. cit., p. 257, Note 1.
¹⁶ Amalarius, *De ordine antiphonarum*, XLIII: 'Compositi sunt a magistris sanctae Romanae ecclesiae, in quibus compunctio traditionis eius frequentatur, et dolor crucifixionis eius stimulat corda fidelium' (*PL* 105, 1292).
¹⁷ For the intention to promote adoption of the Roman rite in the interests of liturgical unity, see the comments of Andrieu regarding *OR*s XV-XVI and XVIII-XIX: 'Conçus dans un esprit de propagande, ils sont destinés à promouvoir l'unité liturgique en faisant triompher la pratique romaine en des régions où s'opposaient des traditions rivales' (*ORM* Vol. 3, p. 4).
¹⁸ *OR* XVI. 36, 'Et ipsa nocte in ecclesia lumen non accenditur usque in sabato' (Andrieu, *ORM* Vol. 3, p. 152); *OR* XVII. 98, 'Et in ipsa nocte lumen in ecclesia non accenditur, sed absconditur, ut non ab omnibus videatur usque in sabbatum' (ibid., p. 189).
¹⁹ *OR* XXXB. 28, 'in primo psalmo tuta lampada de parte dextra, in secundo psalmo de parte sinistra, similiter per omnes psalmos usque vi aut vii, aut in finem evangelii reservetur absconsa usque in sabbato sancto' (Good Friday); id. 36, 'tantum una lampada accendatur propter legendum' (Holy Saturday) (Andrieu, *ORM* Vol. 3, pp. 470–1). For the origin of the seven sanctuary lamps see MacGregor, op. cit., pp. 48–51. There is undoubtedly a connection with Apocalypse 4:5 ('in front of the throne there were seven flaming lamps

burning, the seven spirits of God'), though the seven lamps mentioned therein may reflect existing liturgical practice, rather than the reverse.

20 OR XXIII. 24, 'accendent duo regionarii per unumquemque faculas de ipso lumine quod de VI feria absonditum est' (Andrieu, *ORM* Vol. 3, p. 272); *OR* XXXA. 15, 'accipiens de lumine quod VI feria absconsum fuit', (ibid., p. 457).

21 OR XXXA. 5, 'Deinde sequitur matutinum. Lucerne extinguntur' (Good Friday); id. 12, 'in lucernis accendendis vel extinguendis sicut superius diximus ita fiat' (Holy Saturday) (Andrieu, *ORM* Vol. 3, p. 456).

22 OR XXVIII. 30 and 49 (Andrieu, *ORM* Vol. 3, pp. 398 and 401).

23 OR XXVI. 13 (ibid., p. 328); *OR* XXVII. 5 (ibid., p. 348); *OR* XXIX. 11–12 (ibid., pp. 438–9); *OR* XXXI. 13 (ibid., p. 493).

24 OR XXIX. 11–12 (ibid., pp. 438–9). For the problems surrounding the interpretation of this passage see MacGregor, op. cit., pp. 96–101, and Appendix 2 to this chapter.

25 Pontifical of Poitiers: Martene *DAER* IV. cap. xxii I-II; MacGregor, op. cit., pp. 91–6.

26 For a detailed review of the evidence, see MacGregor, op. cit., Chapter 2.

27 OR XXIII. 1 (Andrieu, *ORM* Vol. 3, p. 269). For the Roman character of *OR* XXIV see ibid., pp. 280–2. *OR* XXVI, which does prescribe the practice of extinguishing lights at Tenebrae, is also Roman, but relates only to churches outside Rome, not those of the city itself.

28 Amalarius, *De ordine antiphonarum* XLIV, 2 (*PL* 105, 1292); id. *De ecclesiasticis officiis* Lib. IV, cap. xxi (*PL* 105, 1202).

29 OR L. xxv. 5 (Andrieu, *ORM* Vol. 5, pp. 187–8).

30 For the idea that the gradual extinction of lights was related to the increase of natural light in the church see A. Fortescue, *Holy Week* (London: Burns, Oates and Washbourne Ltd., 1951), Introduction, p. xvii.

31 For a detailed review of the evidence see MacGregor, op. cit., pp. 90–115.

32 Martene, *DAER* IV cap. XXII. For the number of lights see MacGregor, op. cit., pp. 52–66.

33 PRG cap. xxv 4–6, 'Lumen autem ecclesiae apud Romanos ab initio cantus nocturni inchoatur extingui, hoc tamen ordine ut ab introitu ipsius ecclesiae incipiat paulatim tutari, ut, verbi gratia, peracto primo nocturno, videatur eorum pars tertia esse extincta; medio nocturno, iterum tertia; tertio vero expleto, exceptis septem lampadibus, nihil luminis relinquantur' (Andrieu, *ORM* Vol. 5, pp. 187–8).

34 'Cena Domini quinta feria, ante nocturnos quindecim in instrumento lignorum ante maius altare totidem sint accensae candelae quot psalmi sunt imponendi. Et remanentibus triginta psalmis, ante nocturnas dicant quindecim sub silentio post ternas orationes factas. Signa sonet secretarius sicut solitus est. Quibus dictis sonantibus signis, priusquam dimissa fuerint hebdomadarius incipiat antiphonam, *Zelus domus tuae*. Et statim exstinguatur una candela hinc, alia inde, sicque fiat omnibus psalmis incipientibus.' (*PL* 150, 1197).

35 MacGregor (op. cit., pp. 79–80) suggests that the expression may be interpreted as meaning two stands, each carrying fifteen candles. If this were the case one would have expected 'instrumenta' rather than 'instrumentum'. However, as he points out, the text contains a number of grammatical and

orthographic errors, so we cannot be entirely certain about how many stands were involved.

36 Cluny, *Consuetudines* cap. xii (*PL* 149, 657).

37 'Per singulas antiphonas et singula responsoria exstinguantur singulae candelae' (*PL* 150, 458).

38 Twenty-four lights at Tenebrae: Amalarius, *Liber Officialis* IV, xxii (*PL* 105, 1202); Pseudo-Alcuin, *De divinis officiis* xvi (*PL* 101, 1203); Ordinary of the Canons Regular at Rouen (*PL* 147, 168); John of Avranches, *De officiis ecclesiasticis* (*PL* 147, 48); Honorius of Autun, *Gemmae animae* Lib. III lxxxvii (*PL* 172, 665–6); John Beleth, *Rationale divinorum officiorum* (*PL* 202, 105); Sicardus of Cremona, *Mitrale* Lib. VI, cap. xi (*PL* 213, 297). Sarum Breviary, F. Proctor and C. Wordsworth, (CUP, 1882).

39 Twenty-four lights still in use in Rouen and Orléans and among the Premonstratensians: MacGregor, op. cit., pp. 63–4.

40 The list of places where twenty-five lights were in use, in MacGregor's Table 2 (op. cit., p. 60), includes York, Norwich, Hereford and Lincoln, in addition to the *Decreta* of Lanfranc.

41 Pseudo-Alcuin, *De divinis officiis* xvi (*PL* 101, 1203).

42 Variation in the number of lights in later Middle Ages: MacGregor, op. cit., pp. 54–66.

43 Beleth, *Rationale* ci (*PL* 202, 105).

44 'secundum quosdam non est numerus certus' (*Rationale* Lib.VI, lxxii 15 [Dura, p. 514]).

45 *Disciplina Farfensis et Monasterii S.Pauli Romae* cap. ii (*PL* 150, 1197); cf. Cluny, *Consuetudines* cap. xii (*PL* 149, 657).

46 Fischer, *OEL*, p. 45, for twelfth century Rome; MacGregor, op. cit., pp. 62–3.

47 Righetti, op. cit., Vol. II. 96, p. 157.

48 The first mention of such a custom regarding the last light is in *Ordo XXXB*. 28, though in that instance the hidden light was not reproduced at the end of the office but reserved until Holy Saturday, apparently for use by the reader at the night office of that day. (id. 36). The same practice is prescribed in Pseudo-Alcuin, *De divinis officiis* xvi (*PL* 101, 1203).

49 Church left in darkness: Amalarius, *Liber officialis* IV, ii (*PL* 105, 1202); *Disciplina Farfensis* ii (*PL* 150, 1198); John of Avranches, *De officiis ecclesiasticis* (*PL* 147, 49). A separate light provided: Cluny, *Consuetudines* cap. xii (*PL* 149, 657); Lanfranc, *Decreta* cap. I, iv (*PL* 150, 458); Ordinary of the Canons Regular at Rouen (*PL* 147, 169).

50 'Una tamen quae in earum medio est collocata, non exstinguitur, sed absconditur et occultatur, posteaque in apertum profertur, ac eius luce omnia ecclesiae lumina rursus accenduntur' (Beleth, *Rationale* cl (*PL* 202, 106)).

51 Righetti, op. cit., Vol. II. 96, p. 158.

52 Durandus, *Rationale* Lib.VI, lxxii 27 (Dura, p. 516); Sicardus, *Mitrale* Lib.VI, cap. xi (*PL* 213, 299).

53 Ep. X to Bernard of Clairvaux (*PL* 178, 340).

54 Durandus, *Rationale* Lib.VI, lxxii 2 (Dura, pp. 511–12).

CHAPTER 7

MAUNDY THURSDAY

In the Roman Rite, the history of Holy Thursday (or Maundy Thursday as it is more commonly known in English-speaking countries) is characterized by three aspects: first, it was the day on which those who had been required to do public penance during Lent were reconciled and readmitted to the company of the faithful, in order to enable them to take a full part in the Easter ceremonies; secondly, it was the day on which Christ's institution of the Holy Eucharist in the course of the Last Supper was commemorated; and thirdly, it was the day on which the holy oils to be used in the baptism and confirmation of the catechumens during the Easter Vigil were blessed. This tripartite aspect of the day was established at an early date. Pope Silvester (314–355) is recorded as having said, in a letter to the Greek Church, 'On this day the sacrifice of the sacred Body and Blood of the Lord was initiated as a celebration by the Lord himself. On this day the holy chrism is consecrated throughout the world; on this day too pardon is granted to penitents, those at enmity are reconciled, those who are aggrieved are pacified.'[1] The letter may be apocryphal, but it undoubtedly reflects the practice in Rome at the time the *Vita Sylvestri* was composed, the second half of the fifth century.

In Pope Sylvester's letter the day is called simply *quinta feria*, and this is also the name under which it appears in a letter of the priest Uranus written in 431, in which he refers to the celebration of the Lord's Supper on this day.[2] About seventy years later St Avitus of Vienne calls it the 'Birthday of the Chalice' (*Natalis calicis*).[3] Around 620 St Isidore of Seville calls it the 'Lord's Supper' (*Coena Domini*), and some thirty years later St Eligius of Noyon tells us that it was known as both *Natalis calicis* and *Coena*

Domini.[4] The former name is also found in Ireland; an embolism in the Canon of the Stowe Missal of around 800 for this day reads *et diem sacratissimam celebrantes natalis calicis domini nostri Iesu Christi*.[5] In the Old Gelasian Sacramentary it is entitled *Quinta feria*, and in the eighth century Gelasians it is *Feria V coenae Domini*.[6] The contemporary Sacramentary of Prague calls it *Feria V in cena Domini*, as does the early ninth-century Gradual of Monza.[7] This became its official and virtually universal name.

The *Reconciliatio Pœnitentis*

The reconciliation of penitents in Rome on this day is documented from at least the fourth century by a passage in a letter of St Jerome to Oceanus, written around the year 399, in which he refers to the reconciliation of a certain Fabiola as having taken place before the day of the Pasch in the Lateran Basilica, in the presence of the whole population of Rome.[8] Jerome describes her as standing in the ranks of the penitents, while the bishop, priests and all the people shed tears with them.[9] Only slightly later than Jerome's letter is one from Pope Innocent I to Bishop Decentius of Gubbio, written in the year 416, in which he specifically mentions the reconciliation of penitents on this day as being a custom of the Roman Church.[10]

Unfortunately neither Jerome nor Innocent supplies any details of the accompanying ceremony, in particular whether or not it included a celebration of the Eucharist. Jerome indeed talks about the reception by Fabiola of communion in the presence of everyone,[11] but it is uncertain whether by 'communion' he means her readmission into the company of the faithful or specifically her reception of the Holy Eucharist. Innocent gives permission for the reconciliation of a penitent who is in danger of death to be brought forward in time 'lest he should depart from this world without communion',[12] but there is the same ambiguity in the use of the word 'communion'. Though it seems highly probable that the dying penitent would have received Holy Communion, this would most likely have been by way of Viaticum from the reserved Sacrament, rather than in the course of a celebration of the Eucharist.

The practice of reconciling penitents on Maundy Thursday is mentioned by St Eligius of Noyon around the middle of the seventh century,[13] but the first detailed account of the ceremony accompanying the reconciliation of a penitent at Rome is contained in the Old Gelasian Sacramentary, the prototype of which, as we have seen, was a Roman presbyteral sacramentary of the sixth to seventh century.[14] It takes place in the course of a morning Mass prescribed for this day, between the synaxis and the Eucharist proper,[15] and appears to have constituted an addition to the original sacramentary from which the Gelasian ultimately derives. The rite itself seems to have been borrowed from the papal liturgy, as evidenced by the use of the words *venerabilis pontifex* and *apostolice pontifex* in the opening prayer, although its complete absence from the Gregorian Sacramentary indicates that it had already become obsolete in the papal liturgy before the early part of the seventh century, when the Gregorian as we know it was composed.[16] The penitent presents himself 'in the bosom of the church' (*in gremio ecclesiae*), prostrate on the ground. The deacon addresses a lengthy petition to the bishop, beginning:

> The appropriate time has come, O venerable pontiff, the day of divine propitiation and human salvation, when death was destroyed and eternal life began, when in the vineyard of the Lord of Hosts such a planting of new shoots is to be made as will purify the corruption of the old. For although there is no time during which the riches of God's goodness and faithfulness are lacking, there is however at this time, thanks to His mercy, a wider forgiveness of sin and, thanks to His grace, a fuller reconciliation of the reborn.[17]

The prayer goes on to request that the sinner be reconciled, since he has 'eaten the bread of sorrow, watered his couch with tears, afflicted his heart with grief [and] his body with fasting'[18]. The bishop, or another priest, after admonishing the penitent not to repeat the sins for which he has been doing penance, says over him a number of prayers (the sacramentary gives seven in all), begging God to show mercy and forgive him.[19] There is no direct formula of absolution. The reconciliation ends with a final prayer, said either at this point or following the reception of communion by the penitent, asking God that, having obtained the forgiveness of all his sins, he might persevere in the sacramental life from that time on, and suffer nothing that would do harm to his eternal redemption (*ut percepta remissione omnium peccatorum in sacramentis tuis sincera deinceps devotione permaneat, et nullum redemptionis aeternae sustineat detrimentum*). Mass then continues with the Offertory.

The eighth-century Pontifical of Egbert of York[20] also contains a reconciliation rite for Maundy Thursday, though there is no hint of a reconciliation Mass as such. It begins with three of the prayers found in the Gelasian.[21] After a further prayer over the penitent, the bishop raises him from his position on the ground, and after the singing of the *Miserere* (Psalm 50) pronounces a formula of absolution, *Absolvimus vos vice beati Petri apostolorum principis*, which is clearly taken from the papal liturgy. The rite ends with a prayer begging God to 'forgive all crimes and universal sins' and grant to the penitent himself 'pardon in place of punishment, joy in place of grief, life in place of death'.[22]

In the eighth-century Gelasian sacramentaries the morning Mass of the day onto which the rite for the reconciliation of a penitent had been grafted has become a specific Mass for the Reconciliation of Penitents.[23] The tenth-century Sacramentary of Fulda not only includes the reconciliation Mass and rite according to the Gelasian tradition but also, uniquely, records the readings at the Mass: Romans 8:26–7 and John 8:1–26, as well as the Introit, taken from Psalm 24 (vv. 17 and 1), the Gradual, from Psalm 24 (vv. 17, 1 and 3), the Offertory verse, from Psalm 50 (vv. 3, 5 and 6) and the Communion verse, from Psalm 30 (v. 17).[24]

By the time of the Romano-German Pontifical, the rite itself had been greatly elaborated. There is no mention of any separate reconciliation Mass; at the third hour (approximately nine o'clock) the faithful gather at the church where the blessing of the oils is to take place, and the reconciliation is performed before the start of the morning Mass. The bishop sits in front of the church door where the penitents are gathered in the atrium. The archdeacon addresses him with the petition *Adest o venerabilis pontifex*, after which the bishop says to the penitents *Venite*. A deacon standing with the penitents replies with *Flectamus genua* and all kneel, rising again at the command *Levate* of a second deacon standing next to the bishop. The bishop says *Venite, venite*, the procedure is repeated and the penitents advance to the centre of the atrium. The bishop says *Venite, venite, venite* and the deacon once again commands them *Flectamus genua*, after which they advance (on their knees, presumably) to the feet of the bishop. There they remain prostrate until at a nod from the bishop the deacon orders them a third time *Levate*. The ministers then sing the antiphon *Venite, filii, audite me; timorem domini docebo vos* and Psalm 33 (*Benedicam domino*), repeating the antiphon at the end. During the singing the penitents are presented one by one first to the archdeacon and then by him to the bishop, who formally receives each penitent (lying prostrate on the ground) into the bosom of the Church. After this the bishop intones the antiphon *Cor mundum crea in me, Deus*, followed by the *Miserere*. Then the bishop and all the penitents prostrate themselves in prayer while the ministers sing a litany. When it is finished the bishop says the *Pater noster* and, after a series of nine versicles and responsories, he pronounces a number of prayers for reconciliation. No less than sixteen of these are provided, including most of those given in the Gelasian sacramentaries. Some of them are very long and it is difficult to believe that it was ever intended that all of them should be used in the same ceremony. In contrast to the Gelasian rite, the bishop then formally absolves the penitents, sprinkles them with holy water and incenses them, and, after reciting the brief prayer *Exsurge qui dormis, exsurge a mortuis et illuminabit te Christus*, admonishes them to amend their lives. For the absolution two formulae for several penitents are provided, and three for a single penitent, which are surely intended as alternatives.[25]

The rite contained in the Roman Pontifical of the Twelfth Century, which as we have seen in Chapter 3 was derivative on the Romano-German Pontifical, is almost identical to that found in the latter.[26] In the Pontifical of Durandus, however, the rite has reached still further heights of elaboration. In some churches, Durandus tells us, the penitents assemble in the morning outside the church to hear a Mass celebrated by a priest at an altar close by the church doors.[27] Priests then hear the individual confessions of the penitents, after which, in conjunction with the bishop, they decide which of the penitents have, by their diligent exercise of the penance imposed on them, deserved to be reconciled (the majority, one hopes) and which have not. The bishop, attended by an archdeacon, a deacon and four subdeacons, prostrates himself on a faldstool before the altar and, together with the attendant clergy, recites the seven penitential psalms and the litany of the saints, while the penitents wait outside, prostrate on the earth, barefooted and holding unlighted candles. At two specific points during the litany two of the subdeacons, with lighted candles, go to the doors and sing an antiphon,[28] then extinguish their candles and return to their places. Finally the bishop sends the deacon to the door with a large lighted candle; on his arrival he sings a third antiphon[29] and the penitents' candles are lit, after which he returns to the bishop and the litany ends with the *Agnus Dei*. The bishop, accompanied by the clergy, then proceeds to the middle of the church and takes his seat on another faldstool which has been made ready for him there, facing the door of the church; only then does the archdeacon, after calling for silence, address him with *Adest, o venerabilis pontifex*. When this is finished the bishop goes to the door of the church and admonishes the penitents. He then sings the antiphon *Venite, venite, venite, filii audite me, timorem domini docebo vos*, followed by the deacon with *Flectamus genua* and *Levate*. All this is repeated three times, after which the bishop takes up a position just inside the church and, while the antiphon *Accedite ad eum et illuminamini, et facies vestrae non confundentur* and Psalm 33 (*Benedicam domino*) are sung, the penitents enter and throw themselves at his feet, weeping. An archpriest formally requests him to reconcile them, confirming at his request that they are worthy of reconciliation. The penitents are commanded to rise; the bishop takes one of them by the hand, and the latter takes the hand of another penitent, and so on until all the penitents have joined hands. After a series of versicles and responsories and the antiphon *Dico vobis, gaudium est angelis Dei super uno peccatore paenitentiam agente*, he leads them to the faldstool in the centre of the church, where, after yet another antiphon, from the parable of the Prodigal Son,[30] he pronounces a formal absolution, followed by a prayer for God's mercy in the form of a Preface. The absolution notwithstanding, the ceremony is not yet over. Both clergy and penitents once again fall to the ground, the choir sings the antiphon *Cor mundum crea in me, Deus, et spiritum rectum innova in visceribus meis*, and after three more psalms, beginning with the *Miserere* (Psalm 50), the *Kyrie eleison, Pater noster* and another series of versicles and responsories, there follow seven prayers. After sprinkling the penitents with holy water and incensing them, he pronounces an indulgence, and the ceremony ends with a final short blessing.[31]

In addition to the detailed descriptions of the rite in the

pontificals, there are also references to it in many of the medieval commentators, such as Amalarius of Metz,[32] Pseudo-Alcuin,[33] Rupert of Deutz,[34] Honorius of Autun,[35] John Beleth[36] and Durandus of Mende,[37] but they add little to our knowledge, though Durandus mentions that following their reconciliation the penitents cut their hair and shave their beards, which they have allowed to grow long, and exchange their penitential garb for decent clothing.

In the later Middle Ages the custom of performing public penance during Lent seems to have gone into decline, coincidental with the growth in private confession (which the Lateran Council in 1215 made compulsory for all the faithful at least once a year) and in the practice of granting widespread indulgences. The rite according to the Pontifical of Durandus was reproduced exactly, however, in the post-Tridentine Roman Pontificals of 1570 and 1595 (together with the rite of formally ejecting the penitents from the church on Ash Wednesday) and thereafter it remained in every subsequent edition of the pontifical until the twentieth century, notwithstanding that it had by then fallen into complete desuetude.

The Morning and Evening Masses

One of the most striking features of the Holy Thursday liturgy is the celebration of a double Eucharist. The first reference to this is in the travel journal of Egeria, who tells us that at Jerusalem in the second half of the fourth century the Eucharist was first celebrated in the Martyrion at around two o'clock in the afternoon, lasting about two hours, and then again around seven o'clock in the evening 'behind the Cross'.[38] The people received Holy Communion at the second of these Masses. Egeria does not tell us the purpose of this dual celebration, nor whether the Mass liturgy was the same on both occasions. The Armenian Lectionary, which dates from only slightly later than Egeria's visit, gives us the readings at the first of these Masses, which was celebrated in the church itself, at around one o'clock (the seventh hour); the second Mass, which was celebrated 'before the holy cross', appears to have followed immediately upon the conclusion of the first, and, since no readings are given for it, seems to have consisted only in the Eucharist proper, without any preliminary synaxis.[39]

A double Eucharist is also found in North Africa at the time of St Augustine. There, the first Mass was celebrated in the morning, and the second in the evening. The reason for this custom is described in some detail by Augustine in a letter to Januarius.[40] The latter had asked whether it was appropriate on Maundy Thursday to dispense with the normal rules and take food before rather than after hearing Mass; it had come to his notice that this was done in some places, though it was not the practice in his own area.[41] In his reply, Augustine adopts a neutral position; some people argue that it makes for a more significant commemoration of the day if a meal is taken before Mass, but in his view nobody should be either compelled to eat before Mass or forbidden from eating. It is important that those who wish to attend Mass before breaking their fast should be able to do so. There is a widespread practice of taking a bath (evidently in preparation for Easter) on this day. Since it is difficult to bathe while fasting, those who bathe in the morning break their fast early, and a morning Mass is celebrated to accommodate them.[42] Others however prefer to follow the normal custom and maintain their fast (and presumably therefore also postpone their bath) until the ninth hour, and for these an evening Mass is provided (*ad vesperam vero propter ieiunantes*). St Augustine does not tell us whether the evening Mass was simply a repetition of the morning one, or had its own set of prayers and readings, or indeed provide any other information about them.

Evidence for the celebration of the Eucharist in both the morning and the evening of this day comes from southern Italy in the shape of a mid-sixth-century Capuan lectionary which contains two sets of readings, one *in cena domini mane* and the other *in cena domini ad sero*.[43] The reading for the morning Mass is 1 Corinthians 5:6–6:11 and for the evening 1 Corinthians 11:20–32. The former is about the need for penance as preparation for Easter, the latter is, not surprisingly, St Paul's account of the institution of the Eucharist. Although we do not know what the Gospels for the two Masses were, their different themes are clear from these Epistle readings. Gospels for both Masses are however prescribed in the Evangeliary of St Cuthbert which, notwithstanding its name, originated likewise in the Naples area some hundred years after the Capuan lectionary.[44] They were, for the morning Mass (*mane in coena domini ad missa*), the Passion according to St Luke and, for the evening Mass (*ieiunium de cena domini*), St John's account of the washing of the disciples' feet.

It was the custom in Rome for the priests of the various *tituli*, or parishes, to celebrate both a morning and an evening Mass, and sometimes, it would seem, a third Mass at which the oil of the sick and the oil of the catechumens for use in the parish were blessed.[45] The Old Gelasian Sacramentary contains three Masses for the day: a morning Mass (to which has been added the reconciliation of the penitents), a Chrism Mass, during which the holy oils are blessed, and an evening Mass. The opening Collect of the morning Mass looks forward to the coming of Easter,[46] and the subsequent celebrant's prayers of this Mass refer to the redemptive sacrifice of Christ.

As a rather curiously worded rubric in the Old Gelasian indicates, there was no psalmody and no greeting in this morning Mass.[47] The Mass must therefore have begun immediately with the Collects. There is no evidence as to whether or not there were any readings. It is possible, therefore, that the rite for the reconciliation replaced the readings (if there were any) when it was incorporated into the Mass. No Preface for this Mass is given in the sacramentary, but the Canon contains three embolisms:

> *Communicantes et diem sacratissimum celebrantes quo traditus est Dominus noster Iesus Christus, sed et memoriam venerantes ... ; Hanc igitur oblationem, Domine, cunctae familiae tuae, quam tibi offerunt ob diem ieiunii Coenae Dominicae, in qua Dominus noster Iesus Christus tradidit discipulis suis corporis et sanguinis sui mysteria celebranda, quaesumus, Domine, placatus intende, ut per multa curricula annorum salva et incolumis munera sua tibi domine mereatur offerre, diesque nostros in tua pace disponas ... ; [and in place of Qui pridie quam pateretur] Qui hac die antequam traderetur, accepit panem in suis sanctis manibus, elevatis oculis ...* [48]

The evening Mass in the Roman *tituli* seems originally to have contained no synaxis, but to have started immediately with the Offertory. This is indicated by the *Missa ad vesperum* in the Old Gelasian, which begins with the Secret prayer and the Preface.[49] Later a synaxis was added, the Introit being borrowed from Tuesday's Mass, the Collect from Good Friday and the Gradual from Lauds, the readings (the institution of the Eucharist and the washing of the disciples' feet) being those prescribed for the evening Mass in the Capuan lectionary and the Evangeliary of St Cuthbert.[50] This change seems to have occurred during the eighth century. It can be documented in the pages of the so-called 'eighth century' Gelasian sacramentaries, in which the Good Friday Collect (*Deus a quo et Iudas*) has been added to the celebrant's prayers prescribed for the evening Mass.[51] The Preface in the Old Gelasian is lengthy and rhetorical in form, in the Gallican manner, and must represent an addition to the original Roman sacramentary after it had crossed the Alps. It concentrates exclusively on the treachery of Judas, omitting all reference to the most important aspect of the celebration, the institution of the Eucharist. The embolisms of the morning Mass are however repeated verbatim in the Canon.[52]

The liturgical policies of Pepin and Charlemagne in the Frankish Empire eventually led, as explained in Chapter 3, to the emergence in their dominions of a Romano-Gallican liturgy based on the Gregorian sacramentary as expanded by the supplement of Alcuin. From the beginning of the ninth century the Gelasian tradition in Gaul gradually died out. The Romano-Gallican liturgy, as exemplified in the Romano-German Pontifical, was finally adopted in Rome itself, towards the end of the tenth century. It is therefore the papal and not the presbyteral liturgy which is at the root of subsequent development, and it is the papal Mass to which we must now turn.

The Papal Mass

Only one Mass was celebrated at the Lateran on this day, which was attended by the priests from the *tituli*. The Gregorian sacramentary thus contains only one Mass for the day, at which the pope blessed the oils.[53] This Mass, too, like the evening Mass in the *tituli*, originally appears to have had no synaxis, as the absence of the latter from the eighth century Pontifical of Egbert, which describes the papal rite in some detail, indicates.[54] At the sixth hour, around noon, the pope begins the Mass with the word *Oremus*, after which the offerings are placed on the altar. Then the pope intones *Sursum corda*, and the usual dialogue, Preface, Sanctus and Canon follow. At the appropriate point in the Canon, immediately before the prayer *Per quem haec omnia*, a cardinal deacon collects the oil of the sick from the people and brings it to the pope who blesses it with the prayer *Emitte Domine spiritum.* This was the point at which, in the early days of the Church, it had been customary to bless the people's offerings, and where in some places it seems the practice of blessing grapes still continued.[55]

Just before the Communion the pope goes to his seat, whereupon the archdeacon approaches with the chrism in a gold flask covered by a white cloth the end of which is draped over his right shoulder. The bishops, priests and deacons present stand round in a circle. The pope breathes three times on the flask of oil, touching it with his hand, and intones *Sursum corda,* the people replying with *Habemus ad dominum.* He continues with *Gratias agamus Domino Deo nostro,* and the people reply *Vere dignum et iustum est.* He then consecrates the chrism with the prayer *Qui in principio.* At the end he makes the sign of the cross with his thumb three times over the flask and again breathes three times on it, also in the form of a cross. A subdeacon then takes the flask from the archdeacon and conveys it to all the persons in the sanctuary, each of whom kisses it. When this is finished, another cardinal deacon brings forward the flask containing the oil of the catechumens, covered with a cloth the end of which is draped over his left shoulder, and the pope blesses it with the prayer *Deus qui virtute,* after which it is carried around by acolytes for veneration by the assembled clergy. The Mass then concludes with the communion of clergy and people. The titular priests return to their own churches to celebrate their own Mass there.

Writing in the middle of the ninth century, Amalarius of Metz records the concelebration of the Maundy Thursday Mass by the pope and the priests of his diocese. He says that it is the custom of the Roman Church for the priests to be present at the consecration and to co-consecrate the bread and wine with the pope, as well as joining him in blessing the holy oils.[56]

No proper Preface for this day seems to have been provided in the papal Mass; at least none of the sacramentaries in the Gregorian tradition contains any. The Canon of the Mass included three embolisms. The first differed only slightly in wording from that in the Old Gelasian Sacramentary,[57] but the second and third are quite different:

> *Hanc igitur oblationem servitutis nostrae sed et cunctae familiae tuae, quam offerimus ob diem in qua dominus noster Iesus Christus tradidit*

*discipulis suis corporis et sanguinis sui mysteria celebranda, quaesumus
domine ut placatus accipias, diesque nostros in tua pace disponas* ... and
*qui pridie quam pro nostra omniumque salute pateretur, hoc est hodie,
accepit panem in sanctas ac venerabiles manus suas.*[58]

This papal Mass also acquired a synaxis during the course of
the eighth century. The first recension of the Roman Evangeliary,
from around 645, gives no Gospel for this day,[59] but both the mid-
eighth century recensions prescribe St John's account of the
washing of the disciples' feet.[60] The earliest lectionaries all give St
Paul's account of the institution of the Eucharist as the Epistle
reading.[61] As in the Gelasian tradition, the Collect, *Deus a quo et
Iudas*, was borrowed from that for Good Friday. The eighth
century antiphonals are also in agreement on the other scriptural
texts of the Mass, texts which survived unchanged until the 1970
reform.[62]

Ordines Romani XVI and XVII, which date from the late eighth
century and were written for a monastic community, still
prescribe a Mass without any synaxis for Maundy Thursday,
which suggests that the monastic rite retained the older form after
it had gone out of use elsewhere. Neither is there any *pax* during
the Mass.[63] But the description of the rite in Ordo XXIII, which
represents an unofficial account by a liturgically-minded Frankish
monk of the papal ceremonies of the Triduum which he had
witnessed in the course of a visit to Rome at some time during the
eighth century, includes the *Kyrie eleison, Gloria in excelsis Deo*,
'and everything as on other feastdays, except for the Alleluia and
the chrism which is blessed on this day'. The Body of the Lord is
divided into two parts, one of which is reserved for the following
day, a proceeding in which all the priests present take part. The
pope communicates on his own, and after doing so he blesses the
chrism, which is distributed to the various city churches. Finally
the assisting priests make their own communion and depart for
their own churches.[64]

The Blessing of the Oils

According to the rite of baptism contained in the *Apostolic
Tradition* of Hippolytus, the holy oils were blessed immediately
before baptism took place. A simple prayer of thanksgiving was

said over what he calls the 'oil of thanksgiving' (the chrism) and an exorcism over the 'oil of exorcism' (the oil of catechumens). At an early date however we find them being blessed, in anticipation of the Paschal Vigil, on the Thursday of Holy Week.[65] In the course of the Middle Ages various explanations were given for assigning the blessing to this day. In the early seventh century for example St Isidore tells us that it is because it was on this day that Mary of Magdalen anointed the head and feet of the Lord with oil.[66] The true reason is undoubtedly that given by Rupert of Deutz, namely that this is the last opportunity for doing so before the Easter Vigil, when they are to be used in the baptisms which take place on that night.[67] The blessing of the oil of the sick at the same time was no doubt done as a simple matter of convenience.

The *Ordines Romani* supply some details of the eighth-century Roman rite which are missing from the rather terse account of the blessing of the oils in the Pontifical of Egbert. The chrism and the balsam are mixed by the pope before the Mass begins.[68] He faces east while blessing the chrism.[69] The flasks containing the oil of the sick are left by the people on the floor outside the sanctuary; some are collected by deacons and handed to the pope for blessing, the remainder are placed to right and left on the balustrade which surrounds the sanctuary and blessed collectively by the other bishops and senior priests present.[70]

This rite corresponds closely to that described in the ninth century by Amalarius, though he mentions an exorcism of the oils as well as a blessing.[71] No such exorcism is found in any of the earliest Roman books, except for the Gregorian Sacramentary itself.[72] Amalarius quotes the rubric from the Gregorian Sacramentary for the blessing of the oil of the sick[73] and mentions as a specifically Roman practice the joint consecration of the chrism by the pope and all the priests present.

The Romano-German Pontifical, composed in the Abbey of St Alban at Mainz around the middle of the tenth century, reflects a hybridization of Roman and Gallican customs. In the Roman rite, the oil which is to become the chrism and the oil of the catechumens are simply handed to the pope by the archdeacon for blessing without undue solemnity, but in the Romano-Gallican rite they are brought from the sacristy in a solemn procession. After the bishop has communicated he goes to his seat with the deacons. Twelve priests and other clergy, as many as are required to bring the two oils to the church with all decorum, go to the sacristy. Two acolytes pick up the two ampullae, holding them in their left hands, with the silk covers draped first over their left and then their right shoulders, so as to hang down in front, and a procession is formed, first two acolytes with lighted candles, then the chrism between two crosses, then the oil of the catechumens between two thurifers, then the Gospel book; behind them come the twelve priests, two by two, and the choir singing the hymn *Audi iudex mortuorum* with the refrain *O redemptor sume carmen temet concinentium.* During the hymn the readers, doorkeepers, acolytes and subdeacons take up their places in order of rank on the altar steps, with a subdeacon and the archdeacon at the highest point. One ampulla is passed up the row to the archdeacon. The vessel with balsam is handed by a subdeacon to a deacon who hands it to the bishop. The deacons stand behind the bishop, the priests to right and left, and between them the crosses, candles, thuribles and Gospel book around the bishop. The latter, or someone deputed by him, then preaches a sermon about the blessing of the chrism, before the blessing itself takes place. Other differences from the papal rite include an exorcism of each of the oils before their blessing, the co-consecration of the oil of the sick with the bishop by all the priests present, and the mixture of the balsam with the chrism accompanied by the prayers *Oremus dominum nostrum omnipotentem* and *Haec commixtio liquorum* immediately prior to its blessing, rather than before the beginning of the Mass. [74]

This rite entered the Roman rite proper at the end of the tenth century, when the Romano-German Pontifical was introduced to Rome. The Roman Pontifical of the Twelfth Century has survived in three separate ordines which differ in detail. *Ordo* XXXA reproduces the rite of the Romano-German Pontifical almost exactly.[75] *Ordo* XXXB, however, omits the procession with the oils altogether, and prescribes the mixture of the balsam with the chrism before the beginning of Mass, as was traditional at Rome,[76] while *Ordo* XXXC states that in some churches it is the custom to sing *O Redemptor sume carmen* during the procession, but that in the Roman church silence is preserved at this point.[77] This silence is confirmed by all the other Roman documents, none of which mentions any hymn or chant during the procession.

The rite contained in the late-thirteenth-century Pontifical of Durandus is a combination of Gallican exuberance and the medieval love of the dramatic. Since, with some minor variations, it found its way into the post-Tridentine Roman Pontificals, and became standard throughout the west for the next 400 years, it is worth describing in some detail. Three flasks containing the three oils are prepared before the beginning of the Mass. That containing the oil which is to become the chrism must be larger than the other two, and covered with a cloth of white silk; the others are covered in silk of a different colour. When the bishop reaches the appropriate point in the Canon he goes to a seat in the sanctuary in front of a table, with the sacred ministers standing on either side, seven priests, seven deacons and seven subdeacons.[78] An archdeacon announces three times in a loud voice, *Oleum infirmorum*. The oil is brought from the sanctuary by a subdeacon accompanied by two acolytes, handed to the archdeacon and placed by him on the table, where it is exorcized and blessed by the bishop, the other priests joining in the exorcism and blessing. Mass then proceeds. After the bishop has made his communion, he is joined by five more priests, to make twelve in all. As many of the ministers as necessary go to the sacristy to fetch the chrism and the oil of the catechumens. The archdeacon again announces three times *Oleum ad sanctum chrisma* and *Oleum catechumenorum*. The flasks containing these oils are then brought from the sacristy in solemn procession. It is headed by two acolytes with lighted candles; then come a subdeacon with the cross and an acolyte with thurible and incense, followed by two archdeacons carrying the flasks of oil under a canopy borne aloft by four priests, then two more candle bearers, and another subdeacon with a cross and a thurifer with thurible and incense, and a deacon with the Gospel book. Then come two cantors singing the first four verses of *Audi iudex mortuorum,* to which the whole choir responds with the refrain *O Redemptor sume carmen* (the remaining four verses are sung after the blessing of the chrism). Finally come the rest of the subdeacons, two by two, and the twelve priests. The archdeacons hold the flasks of oil in their left arms, wrapped in their coverings which are draped first over their left and then over their right shoulders, with the ends again wrapped around the flasks.

The ritual accompanying the blessing itself, a further elaboration of the rite of the Romano-German Pontifical, is minutely specified. The archdeacons and some of the deacons and subdeacons take up their position on either side of the bishop. The priests form a semicircle, in front of the bishop and to both sides of him. Other deacons position themselves behind the bishop, and the subdeacons on the altar steps. Those carrying the crosses, candles, thuribles and Gospel book stand between the priests and subdeacons. The flask with the chrism and the vessel containing the balsam are placed on the table in front of the bishop, who blesses the balsam with the prayer *Deus mysteriorum,* mixes some of it with a portion of the chrism with the prayer *Oremus Deum nostrum omnipotentem, qui incomprehensibilem,* and then adds the mixture to the rest of the oil with the prayer *Haec commixtio liquorum.* Followed by each of the priests present, he breathes three times on the mixture, and then exorcizes and blesses it with the usual prayers. Bishop and priests salute the chrism individually with the words *Ave sanctum chrisma,* repeated three times, followed by a kiss, a feature also found in *Ordo* XXXC of the Roman Pontifical of the Twelfth Century. The blessing of the oil of the catechumens follows immediately; after the bishop and each of the priests has breathed upon it three times it is exorcized and blessed with the usual prayers and saluted in the same way as the chrism with the words *Ave sanctum oleum.*[79]

Interestingly, no matter how complex the accompanying ritual became in the later Middle Ages, the blessings themselves were never multiplied, as they were for example in the case of the ashes on Ash Wednesday and palms on Palm Sunday. One exorcism and one blessing for each oil, plus two prayers said over the mixing of the chrism and the balsam, remained the norm.

The 1586 Roman Pontifical repeats the Pontifical of Durandus with a few variations. The announcement of each oil by the archdeacon is made once, not three times. The exorcism and blessing of the oil of the sick is carried out by the bishop alone. The blessing of the chrism takes place after the communion of all the clergy, not just the bishop. The order of the procession is somewhat different, and there is no canopy held over the oils. The position of the various grades of clergy during the blessing itself is also slightly different. There are two prayers said over the balsam, *Deus mysteriorum* and *Creaturam omnium,*[80] and the mixture of balsam with some of the oil is added to the rest of the chrism after the exorcism and blessing, not before. The final four verses of *Audi iudex mortuorum* are sung after the blessing of the oil of the catechumens. With these variations Durandus' rite remained the norm throughout the Roman Church from 1586 until the reform of 1970.

The papal rite of the later Middle Ages is recorded in the Ordinary of the Papal Chaplains, the Missal of the Thirteenth Century,[81] and the various ordines compiled by the masters of the ceremonies at the Lateran between the twelfth and fourteenth centuries.[82] By contrast with the elaborate rite of the Pontifical of Durandus, it retained much of its primitive simplicity. After reciting the office of None with his cardinals and the curial clergy in the chapel of St Thomas, located in the atrium of the Lateran basilica (or in the chapel of St Gregory, when the ceremony is performed at St Peter's) the pope vests and then mixes the oil which is to become the chrism with the balsam. The three flasks containing the oils remain in the chapel, while the Pope and all the clergy enter the basilica in procession and begin the Mass. At the beginning of the Canon[83] the junior cardinal deacon and several of the subdeacons return, preceded by a cross bearer and an acolyte with incense, to the chapel. There the cardinal deacon takes the flask of the chrism and two subdeacons those containing the other two oils, and all return to the main altar. Before the *Per quem haec omnia* the subdeacon holding the oil of the sick hands it to the pope who, together with all the bishops and cardinal priests present, pronounces the exorcism and the blessing. After making his communion he goes to his seat where he is approached by two acolytes, carrying the chrism and the oil of the catechumens, covered in cloth of white silk, in their left hands. The acolyte holding the chrism hands it to the assistant deacon who passes it on to the pope, who breathes on it three times, followed by all the bishops and cardinal priests present, after which all together pronounce the exorcism and blessing of the oil. The oil of the catechumens is exorcized and blessed in exactly the same way. After the blessing all present salute the oils in turn, with the words *Ave sanctum crisma* and *Ave sanctum oleum* respectively, repeated three times, bowing their heads and kissing the flasks containing them. The oils are then taken to the place where they are to be kept.

The Chrism Mass

It seems to have been customary at Rome for the oils of the sick and of the catechumens to have been blessed in at least some of the Roman *tituli* by the titular priests as well as by the pope at the Lateran. For the Mass at which these blessings took place a separate Mass formula, in addition to those of the morning and evening Masses, was provided. This is first recorded in the Old Gelasian Sacramentary, where it appears in second place, between the morning Mass, at which the penitents were reconciled, and the evening Mass of the Lord's Supper, and then in the Gelasian sacramentaries of the eighth century, which are derivative upon it. The original Roman Mass contained no blessing for the chrism, being a presbyteral and not a papal Mass, so a blessing was added locally, for use by the bishops of the Frankish kingdom.[84] The celebrant's prayers provided are general in tone; only the preface of the Mass refers to the oils:

It is right and fitting, proper and salutary, to beseech Thee that in Thy clemency Thou wouldst transform this created thing, chrism, into a sacrament of perfect salvation and life for those who are to be renewed in the spiritual washing of baptism, so that when, through the sanctification of their anointing, the corruption of their first birth is wiped clean, the holy temple of each one may be filled with the innocent odour of an acceptable life and, imbued with the dignity of kings, priests and prophets through the sacrament of Thine institution, they may be clothed in the robes of incorruptibility.

This Preface seems to have been of Gallican origin and probably originated as a blessing of the chrism rather than as a Preface for the Mass.[85] The Canon contains the same three embolisms as the morning Mass.[86] The oils are blessed in the same place and with the same prayers as in the papal rite, though the balsam and chrism are mixed immediately before the blessing, rather than before the start of the Mass.

Features Peculiar to the Mass of Maundy Thursday

The angelic hymn *Gloria in excelsis Deo* did not originally form part of the liturgy of the Roman Mass; it appears to have been introduced by Pope Symmachus (498–514) on Sundays and the feasts of martyrs, but only at Masses where the celebrant was a bishop. A priest was allowed to say it only at the Mass of Easter Day.[87] The first reference to its use on Maundy Thursday is in the eighth-century *Ordo Romanus* XXIII, in the context of the papal Mass.[88] It is absent from the interrelated *Ordines* XXIV, XXVI, XXVII, XXIX or XXXI, though the compiler of *Ordo* XXVIII, which represents a Gallicanized version of *Ordo* XXVII, has added it on his own initiative.[89] Most of the later liturgical books however, such as the tenth century Gregorian of St Eligius, its contemporary Romano-German Pontifical and the successive Roman Pontificals, as well as the later medieval series of *Ordines Romani*, indicate that it should be said (though *Ordo* XXXC of the Pontifical of the Twelfth Century adds cautiously that it is not the practice to do so in some churches, except at a Mass where the chrism is blessed).[90] John of Avranches, Archbishop of Rouen in the mid-eleventh century, tells us that the *Gloria* was sung only when the celebrant was a bishop, as does his English contem-porary Lanfranc, and Bernold of Bregenz that it was said only *ubi chrisma consecratur*. A century later Honorius of Autun says that the *Gloria* is sung *ad chrisma*, implying the same limitation.[91] In the Pontifical of Durandus of the late thirteenth century the *Gloria*, the Creed and the *Ite Missa est* are all omitted except at the Mass where the chrism is blessed.[92] The 1474 Missal and that of Pius V prescribe both the *Gloria* and the Creed at all Masses, regardless of the status of the celebrant.[93]

The ringing of the bells at the beginning of or during the *Gloria* does not appear to be an ancient practice. Originally, following the conclusion of the *reconciliatio poenitentis*, the bells were rung for the start of the Maundy Thursday Mass, after which they remained silent for the rest of the triduum. This for example is the rubric in the Romano-German Pontifical, the *Disciplina* of Farfa and St Paul's at Rome, the Roman Pontifical of the Twelfth Century, the Pontifical of the Roman Curia, in *Ordo Romanus* x and in the Pontifical of Durandus.[94] In some places, according to Durandus, the silence of the bells was observed from the end of Vespers or Compline, or even from the end of Prime, after which they were replaced for the rest of the triduum with a clapper.[95] The use of the latter as a signal appears to be monastic in origin; it is found at Monte Cassino in the sixth century, and in the context of the Maundy Thursday Mass it is prescribed in the *Consuetudines* of Cluny, the *Disciplina* of Farfa and St Paul's, and in the *Decreta* of Lanfranc.[96] From the monastic milieu it was adopted in the late Middle Ages in the cathedral and parish liturgy as a replacement for the bells during the Triduum. The practice of ringing the bells solemnly for the last time at the *Gloria* of the Maundy Thursday Mass belongs to the end of the medieval period, and is probably due to a desire for symmetry with their reappearance at the *Gloria* of the Easter Vigil Mass.[97]

The Creed was not incorporated into the Mass of the Roman rite until 1014, though it appeared very much earlier in the Gallican Mass. In the context of the Maundy Thursday Mass it first appears at Rome in the *Ordo Ecclesiae Lateranensis* of about 1120 and in the Pontifical of the Roman Curia. Thereafter it figures regularly in this Mass. Durandus however says that it should be left out if there is no blessing of the oils at the Mass in question.[98]

The omission of the kiss of peace is prescribed in almost all the documents.[99] The reason seems to be symbolic: on this day it called to mind the kiss whereby Judas betrayed his master.[100] Sometimes the Agnus Dei was also left out, or alternatively if it were said the second repeat would, in view of the omission of the *Pax*, conclude with *miserere nobis* instead of *dona nobis pacem*, the ending which had replaced *miserere nobis* on other days in the year during the tenth-eleventh century, though this practice was alien to Rome, which retained the ending *dona nobis pacem* until the 1955 reform.[101]

The practice of communion by the faithful at every celebration of the Eucharist declined at a very early date; the Synod of Agde in 506 was compelled to enjoin the receipt of communion at Easter, Pentecost and Christmas as an absolute minimum.[102] If we may trust the evidence of the *Ordines Romani*, in eighth-century Rome and Gaul the communion of the people on this day was still commonplace.[103] Thereafter it appears to have declined. But in monastic communities it seems to have remained the practice for many centuries more for all their members to receive communion on Maundy Thursday.[104] The *Ordo Ecclesiae Lateranensis* of about 1120 is particularly eloquent on the importance of all the brethren, both monks and lay brothers without exception, communicating on this day, quoting from a letter which it attributes to Pope Soter,

> On the day of the Lord's Supper the reception of the Eucharist is neglected by some. But the custom of the Church demonstrates that on this day it should be received by all the faithful, excepting only those to whom, because of serious crimes, it is forbidden, since even the penitents are reconciled on this same day to the reception of the Body of the Lord.

It is extremely unlikely that this represents an excerpt from a genuine letter of Soter, who occupied the Apostolic See in the third quarter of the second century, but it does illustrate the importance attached in the twelfth century by the community of canons attached to the Lateran Basilica to the receiving of communion on this day by all its members.[105] But for the papal Mass at the same basilica the contemporary *Ordo Romanus* x merely says, 'The Pope from his seat gives communion to those who wish it', implying that the numbers who did so wish would be few.[106] Only after the reforms of St Pius X did it become commonplace once again for the faithful attending the Maundy Thursday Mass to receive communion.

A few documents prescribe the omission of the *Ite missa est*, a dismissal being considered inappropriate when Vespers were to follow immediately upon the conclusion of the Mass.[107] Normally, however, it seems to have been said as usual. The Roman Pontifical of the Twelfth Century prescribes the *Ite missa est* when the *Gloria* has been said and the *Benedicamus domino* when it has not, a practice which became universal in the Roman rite at every Mass.[108]

The Procession

The reserved Sacrament was originally removed from the altar without ceremony. Not until John of Avranches in the eleventh century do we find any mention of a procession, with lights and incense, to a side altar where the Body of the Lord was kept, with clean altar cloths and a light burning before it until the extinction of lights at Matins of the following day.[109] His contemporary Lanfranc, like John a native of Normandy, stipulates that the place of reservation should be 'most appropriately prepared'. He does not attach any particular ceremony to the process of transfer, except that the place itself should be incensed both before and after it takes place, and that thereafter a light should be kept burning before the Blessed Sacrament.[110] However the *Consuetudines* of Cluny from the same period speak of the Lord's Body being conveyed to a place behind the altar with candles and incense, and placed on a golden paten placed between golden salvers, themselves within silver tablets, fashioned in the form of the Gospel text.[111] The Roman Pontifical of the Twelfth Century still says merely that an unbroken portion of the Lord's Body is reserved for communion on the following day, with no reference to any procession, but in the long recension of the Pontifical of the Roman Curia we read that after the communion the junior cardinal-deacon takes the Body of the Lord in a pyx under a canopy to a prepared place, preceded by cross and candles.[112] This is identical to the rite contained in *Ordo Romanus* x, except that there the junior cardinal-priest is specified; the procession similarly takes place immediately after the Communion.[113] This was still its position at the time of *Ordo* xv, approximately two centuries later, though the Sacrament is now conveyed in a great golden chalice instead of in a pyx, and the use of a chalice subsequently became the rule.[114] The change in the timing of the procession until after the end of Mass is attributable to Sixtus IV, in the late fifteenth century. At first this seems to have obtained only when the pope himself was present, but from the middle of the sixteenth century it became universal.[115]

The singing during the procession of the *Pange lingua gloriosi corporis mysterium*, composed by St Thomas Aquinas as the hymn for Vespers for the feast of Corpus Christi, is first prescribed in the *Caeremoniale Episcoporum* of 1516, though the custom of doing so is doubtless older. It was sung either in the original plainsong version or, later, in a polyphonic setting such as that by Palestrina, sometimes in both plainsong and polyphony in alternate verses. The 1516 edition of the *Caeremoniale* lays down very elaborate instructions for the procession, including the precise order of all the various ranks of both clergy and laity. The later edition of 1600 specifies that the last two verses of the *Pange lingua*, beginning *Tantum ergo sacramentum*, should not be sung until the procession reaches the place of reservation, and this practice became standard until the reform of 1970.[116]

With the growth in the popularity of Eucharistic worship it became customary for the faithful to visit their parish church during the afternoon and evening of Maundy Thursday for private prayer at the so-called Altar of Repose, and even, for those living in towns and cities, to make a round of all the churches within reasonable distance of their homes, visiting as many as they could within the time at their disposal, for the same purpose. It also became customary to decorate the altar itself with banks of candles and large numbers of flowers. The *Caeremoniale Episcoporum* of 1600 indeed prescribes that 'a sanctuary inside the church should be prepared and decorated as beautifully and magnificently as possible, adorned with many lights'.[117]

It was probably inevitable that the transfer of the Blessed Sacrament from the tabernacle on the principal altar to that in a subsidiary chapel should have become associated during the Middle Ages in the minds of the faithful, by anticipation as it were, with the burial of Christ in the tomb. Various attempts were made, not always successful, to correct this misconception, and to suppress some of the customs to which it had given rise in certain places, such as draping the altar with black hangings, or exhibiting representations of the crucifixion or burial of Our Lord.[118] The prohibition of these practices was repeated in connection with the 1955 reform.[119]

Vespers

These were normally sung either immediately after the end of the Mass of the Lord's Supper, or within the Mass itself after the Communion and before the Postcommunion prayer, and in either case before the *mandatum* in most monastic establishments and those churches where the *mandatum* was performed.[120] At the Lateran, however, they were normally sung by cantors during the *mandatum* while the pope washed the feet of twelve subdeacons.[121] Like Tenebrae, they were of archaic form. They began with the antiphon to the first psalm *Calicem salutaris accipiam et nomen Domini invocabo*, omitting the opening versicle and response and the *Gloria Patri*. The psalms were 115, 119, 139, 140 and 141, sung without the *Gloria Patri*. There was no *capitulum*, hymn or versicle. After the *Magnificat* the office ended simply, as at Lauds, with the *Christus factus est*, the silent recitation of the *Pater Noster* and the prayer *Respice quaesumus Domine*.[122] The stripping of the altars followed at once.

The Stripping of the Altars

The stripping of the altars, now associated with the final phase of the Maundy Thursday liturgy, probably reflects what was originally the normal practice after any liturgical celebration.[123] H. A. P. Schmidt comments, 'The reason why the altars remain bare from after the Mass of Holy Thursday until Saturday is clear, because the Eucharist is not celebrated'.[124] The stripping on this particular day is first recorded in *Ordo Romanus* XXIV from the eighth century, and thereafter it recurs regularly in the *Ordines Romani* and other liturgical books, as well as in the medieval commentators.[125] The first reference to the recital of Psalm 21 *Deus Deus meus respice in me* with the antiphon *Diviserunt sibi vestimenta mea* seems to be in the Lateran Missal of around 1230.[126] By this time the procedure, which was carried out after the conclusion of Vespers, had long since acquired a symbolic significance.[127]

The colour of white seems to have been associated with the day from an early date, even before the system of liturgical colours was formalized by Innocent III around the beginning of the thirteenth century.[128] *Ordo Romanus* XXIII, from the first half of the eighth century, says *subdiaconi cum albis vestibus procedunt et diaconi cum dalmaticis*.[129] Durandus says that white is used on this day 'on account of the production of the chrism, which is consecrated for the cleansing of souls, for the Gospel reading also on that feast especially commends purity'.[130]

As we have seen, the papal Mass, from which the Mass of the Lord's Supper in the Tridentine Missal of Pius V was ultimately derived, originally took place at the sixth hour, around noon. This time was chosen to enable those titular priests who attended the Mass and concelebrated it with the pope, to return to their churches in time to celebrate their own evening Mass. With the adoption in Rome at the end of the ninth century of the Romano-German Pontifical, these separate Masses (in so far as they had continued to be said at all during the period of anarchy) were replaced by a single Mass, which began with the reconciliation of penitents at either the third or sixth hour. Durandus, at the end of the thirteenth century, also gives the sixth hour as the correct time for the beginning of the Mass, following both the *mandatum* and the reconciliation of penitents.[131] In the course of the Middle Ages the starting time for Mass was advanced to the third hour, around nine o'clock in the morning, where it remained until the 1955 reform transferred it to the evening.[132]

The *Mandatum*

A washing of the feet seems to have been practised at this time in the fourth century, since St Augustine mentions it, though there appears to have been some diversity of opinion in his day as to whether it should be carried out during Holy Week or Easter Week.[133] St Eligius, Bishop of Noyon from 640–659, refers to a 'fraternal washing of feet' on Holy Thursday, but supplies no further details.[134] From Canon III of the seventeenth Council of Toledo, held in 694, however, we learn that in Spain, at least, the rite had been performed long enough for it to have fallen into some decay; after complaining about its neglect the Council goes on to quote from St Cyprian as to the particular necessity for it to be carried out on the day when Christ had instituted it, and ends by declaring 'This holy synod decrees and ordains that from this time forth in all the churches of Spain and Gaul the feast should not be observed without each bishop and priest taking care to wash the feet of those subject to him according to this holy example'.[135] No details of the rite (if indeed a formal rite existed at this time) are given. However the decree illustrates the character of the *mandatum*; it was, and remains, like the action of Christ in washing the feet of his disciples, an act of humility. As a rubric in the Gilbertine Ordinal puts it, 'He [the prior] performs in this office the role of Him who although he was the Master and Lord of all made Himself the servant of all'.[136]

According to a later addition in the Pontifical of St Egbert, the pope was accustomed on Maundy Thursday to wash the feet of the members of his personal household, and each ecclesiastic to do likewise in his own home. This notice was probably inserted in the Pontifical around the middle of the eighth century. It would appear, therefore, that there was no formal ceremony at Rome at that time, merely a private rite conducted in the pope's own apartments, and in those of the senior ecclesiastics.[137]

The first detailed account of the *mandatum* rite that we have comes from the Romano-German Pontifical of about 950, though there are references to it in the *De ecclesiasticis officiis* of Amalarius from the ninth century and in the Pontifical of Poitiers of about 900. Its appearance in the pontificals indicates that its observance had by this date spread from the monasteries to at least some of the cathedrals of the Frankish kingdom.[138] That of Poitiers gives few details, but the Romano-German Pontifical tells us that after the conclusion of Vespers the bishop goes in procession with his ministers to the location where the *mandatum* is to take place. There the Gospel from John 13:1–15 is read, and the bishop says a prayer:

O God, whose most holy supper we celebrate, make us worthy of it we pray by cleansing us from the filth of sin, Thou who, in order to instil in us an example of humility, didst condescend on this day to wash the feet of Thy disciples.

He then lays aside his vestments and girds himself with a towel. Beginning with the bishop, those present wash one another's feet and dry them, while they sing antiphons and psalms 118 (*Beati immaculati in via*), 47 (*Magnus Dominus*), 66 (*Deus misereatur nostri*), 83 (*Quam dilecta*), 50 (*Miserere mei Deus*), 132 (*Ecce quam bonum*) and 150 (*Laudate Dominum in sanctis eius*). When the washing is finished, a deacon or lector continues the reading from the Gospel according to John, from 13:16 to the end of chapter 17. The ceremony concludes with a series of responsories and prayers.[139] As we shall see, the rite is parallel to that observed in the monastic environment, and is clearly derived therefrom.

Evidence from monastic sources includes the *Disciplina* of the Abbey of Farfa, the Decrees of Lanfranc and the *Consuetudines* of Cluny. At Cluny, the feet of the monks are washed by the *hebdomadarii*, who leave them wet, then again by the abbot, who dries them. If there are too many monks for the abbot to attend to, one or more of the brethren are deputed to assist him. The *mandatum* takes place in the chapter house, but the feet of the abbot and his assistants, if any, are first washed outside by monks nominated to do so. Apart from those antiphons appropriate to the *mandatum* (we are not told what they were), it was customary to sing the hymn *Tellus et aethera iubilent in magni coena Principis*, composed by Bishop Flavius of Chalon-sur-Saône (also mentioned in the Pontifical of Poitiers).[140] At the end a signal is given and a deacon wearing alb and stole and carrying a Gospel book enters in procession with lights and incense. The community rises and the deacon reads chapters 13 and 14 of St John's Gospel. After the first verse has been read, all sit down. At the end of the reading another sign is given, and the brethren, preceded by the deacon, go in procession to the refectory.[141]

At both Farfa and Cluny there was a separate ceremony in which the feet of poor men were washed by the brethren in the cloister; in addition to having his feet washed, each received a sum of money.[142] In those houses which followed the *Decreta* of Lanfranc the monks also washed the feet of poor men in the cloister, each monk washing the feet of one man, except for the abbot, who washed those of two, before having their own feet washed. Each poor man received a drink, a blessing and the sum of two denarii, or whatever other sum the abbot decided was appropriate.[143] In the twelfth-century *Ordo Ecclesiae Lateranensis* there are also two separate ceremonies. While the monks are singing Prime in the chapter house everything is made ready in the cloister by the lay brothers, who then bring in one hundred poor men. When the office is over the monks take up a position in the porch before the chapter house, facing one another as if they were in choir. Each of the lay brothers washes the feet of two or three poor men while a cantor sings the antiphon *Mandatum novum do vobis*. When they have finished, two of the monks lay aside their hoods and, after girding themselves with a towel, 'humbly and devoutly' wash the feet of three or four of the poor men, drying them and then kissing them. Two more monks then take their place and do the same, and so on throughout the community, ending with the prior, who must wash the feet of any poor men who may remain. Each man receives a gift of one denarius. The ceremony ends with a prayer said by the prior and a *Pater noster*.

The feet of the monks and lay brethren are washed in the chapter house by the prior, in a separate ceremony, but thereafter until the Octave of Pentecost only the feet of the poor are washed (a procedure which, we are told, also takes place on every Saturday of the year). If for any good reason this washing of the feet of the poor has to be omitted on any particular occasion, they must still be given the alms which they are accustomed to receive during the ceremony. As in other houses, the rite concludes with the reading by a deacon of chapters 13 and 14 of St John's Gospel. The community stands until they hear the words 'when He had sat down once more' (13:12). At the words 'Come now, let us go', they proceed to the refectory, the deacon continuing the reading from the start of chapter 15. When they reach the refectory there is a pause in the reading for wine to be blessed by the prior and served. While it is being drunk 'with sobriety' the Gospel reading continues until the end of chapter 17 is reached, whereupon the community proceed to the church to sing Compline.[144] The custom of blessing and drinking a cup of wine while the interrupted Gospel reading is continued was known as the 'Caritas' and appears to be first documented at St Benedict's own abbey of Monte Cassino.[145]

According to the Pontifical of the Twelfth Century and the Pontifical of the Roman Curia the pope washes the feet of twelve subdeacons after the end of Mass, while his chaplains sing Vespers. In the former case the ceremony takes place in his private chapel, and in the latter in the basilica of St Laurence, or in the chapel of St Martin if he happens to be at St Peter's.[146] *Ordo Romanus* xi, also from the twelfth century, mentions St Laurence as the location for the papal rite. After washing the feet of the twelve subdeacons the pope gives each one five solidi. At the end of Vespers he also gives each bishop present four solidi, each cardinal three solidi and each cantor two solidi.[147] This sounds more like a development of the practice recorded in the addition to the Pontifical of St Egbert than an adoption of the Frankish rite found in the Romano-German Pontifical.[148] The first mention that we have of the pope washing the feet of poor men as well as those of the twelve subdeacons comes from *Ordo Romanus* xii from the end of the twelfth century. In an entirely separate ceremony, which takes place after supper, he washes the feet of thirteen poor men, drying and kissing them. Each man then receives a drink and alms.[149]

In the Pontifical of Durandus from the end of the thirteenth century, we find a double ceremony, as in the *Ordo Ecclesiae Lateranensis*. In the morning the bishop presides in the chapter house where thirteen poor men have their feet washed and receive alms, while the schola sings antiphons and psalms, including Psalm 118 and all the penitential psalms. The evening ceremony is confined entirely to the clergy who have their feet washed while the schola sings appropriate antiphons including *Mandatum novum do vobis*. At the end the archdeacon reads chapters 13 and 14 of St John's Gospel, after which the clergy go to the refectory where they receive the 'Caritas' while the archdeacon completes the Gospel reading up to the end of chapter 16. Both the morning and the evening ceremony end with the recitation by the bishop of the prayer *Adesto quaesumus Domine officio servitutis nostrae.*[150]

At Rome, the second ceremony in which the pope washed the feet of thirteen poor men seems to have gone out of use quite soon after its first mention in *Ordo Romanus* xii. *The Caeremoniale*

Episcoporum of 1600 however says that in some places it is the custom to wash the feet of thirteen poor men and give them food, drink and alms, and in others for the bishop to wash the feet of thirteen of his canons; the decision as to which practice to follow is left to local custom, or the decision of the bishop, though the former displays the greater humility and charity.[151] Outside Rome the Franciscan Missal of 1243 seems to have been influential in formalizing as well as disseminating the rite, and it is here that we find a specific mention of the hymn *Ubi caritas et amor* in connection with the *mandatum* itself; of Benedictine origin, it seems previously to have been associated with the drinking of the 'Caritas' in the refectory, on Maundy Thursday as well as on other days.[152]

The rubric in the 1474 Missal presents the *mandatum* as an exclusively clerical affair:

> After the stripping of the altars at the proper hour a sign is given with a clapper and the brethren assemble to perform the mandatum; those of higher rank wash the feet and kiss them, and meanwhile the following [chants] are sung, either wholly or in part as the cantor decides.[153]

A large number of antiphons based on the Gospel text, beginning with *Mandatum novum do vobis*, are provided, each followed by verses from psalms and ending with *Ubi caritas et amor*. A shortened version of this rite, with the addition of *Adesto quaesumus Domine officio servitutis nostrae* as a concluding prayer, remained the standard rite of the *mandatum* until 1970, performed in monasteries and cathedrals but rather seldom at parish church level.

The Washing of the Altars

St Isidore of Seville, writing around the year 620, tells us that it was the custom on Holy Thursday to wash the walls and pavements of the church, and to purify the sacred vessels, because it was on this day that Christ had washed the feet of his apostles.[154] Some two hundred years later Rabanus Maurus repeats Isidore word for word, except that he adds 'the altars of the church' as well as the walls and pavements.[155] The custom is also mentioned in Pseudo-Alcuin of the tenth to eleventh century.[156] John of Avranches (c.1060–1070) is the first to mention that the altars are washed in both water and wine (but the walls and pavements in water only).[157] John Beleth also records the use of both water and wine to wash the altars, adding that they are brushed with hard branches (*asperis ramis*), particularly of yew or box.[158]

Descriptions of the accompanying rite (if any) are rare. But one such is found in a Sarum Missal of about 1300. Water is first blessed, then two priests with deacon and subdeacon and candle bearers wash all the altars with wine and water, starting with the principal altar. During the washing of each altar the schola sings various chants, beginning with the responsory *In monte Oliveti* and verse *Verumtamen*.[159] Another responsory and verse are sung while the washing takes place, and when it is completed, the priest recites the Collect of the saint to whom the particular altar is dedicated, after which the responsory *Circumdederunt me* and versicle *Quoniam tribulatio* are sung.[160] This rite is repeated at each altar in the church.[161]

In the Gilbertine Ordinal, also from England, of the first half of the fifteenth century, the prior, vested in surplice and stole and barefooted, is directed to wash both the altars and the crucifixes on them with boughs of hyssop or yew, as a symbol of the flagellation of Christ, first pouring wine over each of the five crosses inscribed on the altar and each of the wounds in the figure on the crucifix, and then scattering water over and around the altars and the crucifixes, representing the blood of redemption and the water of regeneration which flowed from the side of Christ.[162]

According to Durandus' Rationale of about 1290, the custom of washing the altars was widespread but not universal. Where it obtains, the altars are washed with water and wine and rubbed with boughs, especially boughs of yew, while one of the penitential psalms, or another chant appropriate to the Passion, is sung. In some places the pavement of the church is washed as well.[163] But in his pontifical he states bluntly that the altars are not to be washed, to which one manuscript adds 'except where it has been customary to do so', which looks like an addition by a scribe anxious not to interfere with established custom.[164]

It seems therefore that the tradition was already beginning to die out in the time of Durandus. There is no trace of it in any of the late medieval series of Roman ordines, so it was evidently not observed at the Lateran Basilica at this time. Neither is it found in the first printed missal of 1474. Eventually it went out of use everywhere except at St Peter's in Rome, where it continued until the mid-twentieth century. After Tenebrae the clergy of the basilica went in procession to the Altar of the Confession, on which had been placed seven ampullae of white wine mixed with water. The officiating canon and six others ascended the steps of the altar, to the antiphon *Diviserunt sibi* and Psalm 21, and poured the contents of the ampullae over the altar. The cardinal arch-priest then sprinkled water around with a sprinkler made of yew branches, in which he was followed by each of the other canons. They then returned to the altar and dried it with sponges and towels. Finally, all kneeled and the officiating canon said the antiphon *Christus factus est*. The *Pater noster* was recited silently and the rite ended with the prayer *Respice*.[165]

Appendix

The Blessing of the Oils in the Gelasian Tradition

In the Gregorian tradition, as exemplified for instance in the Roman Pontifical of the Twelfth Century (*Ordo* XXXB and XXXC), the oil of the sick is exorcized and blessed, with the prayers *Exorcizo te, immundissime spiritus* and *Emitte, domine, spiritum tuum para-clytum* respectively, during the Canon of the Mass, between the *Nobis quoque peccatoribus* and *Per quem haec omnia, domine, semper bona creas*. The chrism is likewise exorcized and blessed with the prayers *Exorcizo te, creatura olei, per Deum patrem omnipotentem* and *Qui in principio, inter caetera* after the celebrant's communion, and this is immediately followed by the exorcism and blessing of the oil of catechumens, with the prayers *Exorcizo te, creatura olei, in nomine Dei patris omnipotentis* and *Deus incrementorum*. The rite in the Romano-German Pontifical and the Roman Pontifical of the Twelfth Century (*Ordo* XXXA) is the same except that the balsam is mixed with the chrism before the start of Mass instead of just before the latter is exorcized and blessed.

There appear however to be significant differences in the rite enshrined in the Old Gelasian Sacramentary. The oil of the sick is blessed at the same point in the Canon, with the prayer *Emitte, domine, spiritum tuum paraclytum*, though no exorcism is given. After the fraction, but before the commixture, the deacon offers 'the other oil' to the celebrant for blessing, and the latter blesses it with the prayer *Deus incrementorum* followed by *Qui in principio, inter caetera*. The latter appears to be intended as a blessing of the chrism; not only is this the function which it invariably performs in the Gregorian tradition, but it also includes the words *Christi tui, a cuius sancto nomine chrisma nomen accepit*. There follow the heading *Item olei exorcizati confectio* and a rubric prescribing the admixture of the balsam, and then the exorcism *Exorcizo te, creatura olei, in nomine Dei patris omnipotentis* and a blessing *Omnipotens aeterne Deus, qui mysteriorum tuorum*. This also appears to relate to the chrism, in view of the heading and rubric and because the blessing contains the words *et olivae chrisma mundo liberationis gloriam reversuram*. The celebrant is then instructed to return to the altar and proceed with the Mass.

Schmidt concludes that in the Gelasian tradition the Roman formula for the blessing of the chrism has been adopted as the blessing of the oil of the catechumens, with the prayers *Exorcizo te, creatura olei, in nomine Dei patris omnipotentis* and *Omnipotens aeterne Deus, qui mysteriorum tuorum* representing that of the chrism. At first sight this seems to be the most natural interpretation. However, not only is this in conflict with all our other sources (including the account of Amalarius), but if it were really the case one would have expected the reference to the chrism in the prayer *Qui in principio, inter caetera* to have been omitted or at least suitably amended.

A more convincing explanation for the confusion has been proposed by Chavasse. The Gelasian tradition originally contained no blessing of the chrism, which at Rome was carried out only in the course of the papal mass. The 'other oil' was the oil of the catechumens which was blessed with the prayer *Deus incrementorum*, as in the Gregorian tradition.[166] The lost archetype from which the Old Gelasian was derived was however amended twice, in order to supply a blessing for the chrism. The first interpolator inserted, immediately after the blessing of the oil of the catechumens, the heading *Item olei exorcizati confectio* and the rubric prescribing the admixture of the balsam, followed by the prayers *Exorcizo te, creatura olei, in nomine Dei patris omnipotentis* and *Omnipotens aeterne Deus, qui mysteriorum tuorum*. A second interpolator, wishing to include the Gregorian prayer for the blessing of the chrism, and reposition this blessing before that of the oil of the catechumens, as at Rome, clumsily inserted *Qui in principio, inter caetera* after *Deus incrementorum,* treating *Exorcizo te, creatura olei, in nomine Dei patris omnipotentis* and *Omnipotens aeterne Deus, qui mysteriorum tuorum* as the exorcism and blessing of the oil of the catechumens instead of that of the chrism. However, he failed to move the heading and the rubric or to amend the reference to chrism in the prayer *Omnipotens aeterne Deus, qui mysteriorum tuorum.* We are therefore left apparently with two blessings of the chrism, with the rubric and exorcism falling in between the two.

The author of the Sacramentary of Angoulême has noticed that something has gone wrong in the sequence of blessings and has attempted to correct it, in a somewhat maladroit manner, by moving the rubric for the admixture of the balsam (though not the heading) to before *Qui in principio, inter caetera,* and adding to it a note that the latter is the blessing of the chrism (*Post hoc misces balsamum cum alio oleo et benedices chrisma in his verbis*). Otherwise he has simply followed the Old Gelasian, thus treating *Deus incrementorum,* the blessing for the oil of the catechumens in the Roman rite, as a sort of preliminary blessing of the chrism before the admixture of balsam.

The author of the Sacramentary of Gellone has fallen into even deeper confusion. He too has moved the rubric, correctly, to before *Qui in principio, inter caetera,* but then resumes the Mass with the *Pater noster* and the embolism, which thus appear twice, both before and after the blessing of the chrism. He then proceeds with the rest of the Mass to its conclusion. Evidently realizing at the end that he has omitted the blessing of the oil of the catechumens, he attempts to insert it at this point, but with the heading and rubric (again) for the blessing of the chrism, which he has blindly copied from his source, concluding with *Exorcizo te, creatura olei, in nomine Dei patris omnipotentis* and *Omnipotens aeterne Deus, qui mysteriorum tuorum,* as in the Old Gelasian.

In conclusion, therefore, it seems that the apparent differences between the Gregorian and Gelasian traditions are largely due to copyists' blunders and inept attempts to correct them. The principal remaining differences are: first, that in the Gregorian tradition the balsam is mixed with the chrism before the Mass begins instead of immediately before the chrism is blessed, and, secondly, that the blessings of the chrism and the oil of catechumens occur after the communion of the celebrant, whereas in the Gelasian tradition they take place after the *fractio.*

Notes

1 'In hac etiam die sacrificium sacri corporis et domini sanguinis ab ipso domino celebrationis sumpsit initium. Hac die in toto orbe sanctum chrisma conficitur, hac etiam die pœnitentibus per indulgentiam subvenitur, discordes ad concordiam redeunt, pacificantur irati' (*Vita Silvestri*, quoted in Schmidt, *HS*, p. 7 14).

2 'eodem die, id est quinta feria, ... sanus dominicam coenam celebravit' (John, Bishop of Naples) (*PL* 53, 865).

3 *Sententiae* VII (*PL* 59, 302, 308).

4 Isidore, *Etymologiarum* Lib.VI, cap. xviii (*PL* 82, 251); Eligius, *De ecclesiasticis officiis* Lib. I, cap. xxix (*PL* 87, 628).

5 The Stowe Missal is the oldest known Mass book of the Irish Church. It survives in a manuscript (D.II.3) kept in the library of the Royal Irish Academy in Dublin. Modern edition, HBS, Vols XXXI-XXXII, ed. G. F. Warner, 1906–1915.

6 Old Gelasian, Mohlberg, 349, 375, 391; Sacramentary of Angoulême, CC CLIX, Vol. C 598; Sacramentary of Autun, id. CLIX, Vol. B 465; Sacramenary of Gellone, id. CLIX, Vol. A 588.

7 Sacramentary of Prague: Schmidt, *HS*, p. 414; Gradual of Monza: ibid., p. 486.

8 'tota urbe spectante Romana, ante diem Paschae in basilica quondam Laterani' (Ep. lxxvii, *Ad Oceanum de morte Fabiolae* [*PL* 22, 692]). By the 'diem Paschae' Jerome almost certainly meant the Triduum, beginning on Good Friday. (See Chapter 1, notes 50 and 51.)

9 'staret in ordine pœnitentium, episcopo, presbyteris, et omni populo collacrymantibus' (ibid.).

10 'De pœnitentibus autem ... si nulla interveniat aegritudo, quinta feria ante pascha eis remittendum, Romanae Ecclesiae consuetudo demonstrat' (*PL* 20, 559).

11 'Recepta sub oculis omnium communione' (*PL* 22, 694).

12 'si quis in aegritudinem incurrerit, atque usque ad desperationem devenerit, ei est ante tempus Paschae relaxandum, ne de saeculo absque communione discedat' (*PL* 20, 559).

13 Eligius, Homilia X, 'Hac etiam die ... penitentibus per indulgentiam subvenitur, discordes ad concordiam hodie redeunt' (*PL* 87, 629).

14 See Chapter 3, pp. 49–51, Schmidt (*HS*, pp. 723–6), consistently with his view that the Gelasian tradition originated in Gaul and not in Rome, argues that the rite found in the Old Gelasian Sacramentary is a fusion of a Roman reconciliation rite with a Gallican reconciliation Mass which could be celebrated on other days besides Maundy Thursday. Righetti believed that the reconciliation rite began as an aliturgical synaxis which was developed into a Mass in Gaul after the middle of the sixth century, the reconciliation rite taking the place of the synaxis of the Mass (op. cit., Vol. II, p. 153). Chavasse has, I

believe, shown conclusively that the entire rite including the Mass is of Roman origin (op. cit., pp. 149–53).

[15] As indicated by the rubric which follows the conclusion of the rite: 'Post haec offert plebs et conficiuntur sacramenta' (Mohlberg, 368).

[16] Chavasse, op. cit., p. 149. The eighth-century Pontifical of Egbert of York has a reconciliation rite, though no Mass (Schmidt, *HS*, pp. 554–5). Its solitary appearance in the *Ordines Romani* is in *Ordo* XXXI. 20, where it takes place after the Gospel during the ordinary Mass at which the oils are blessed (Andrieu, *ORM* Vol. 2, p. 494).

[17] 'Adest, o venerabilis pontifex, tempus acceptum, dies propitiationis divinae et salutis humanae, qua mors interitum et vita accepit aeterna principium, quando in vinea Domini Sabaoth sic novorum plantatio facienda est ut purgetur execratio vetustatis. Quamvis enim a divitiis bonitatis et pietatis Dei nihil temporis vacet, nunc tamen et largior est per indulgentiam remissio peccatorum et copiosior per gratiam assumptio renascentium' (Mohlberg, 353). I have assumed that the manuscript reading 'et curatio' is a copyist's error for 'execratio', the reading found in the Romano-German Pontifical.

[18] 'manducavit panem doloris, lacrimis stratum rigavit, cor suum luctu, corpus afflixit ieiuniis' (ibid.).

[19] For the misplacing here of formulae designed for the reconciliation of a penitent on his deathbed, see Chavasse, op. cit., pp. 151–3. However, the words 'in sacramentis tuis sincera deinceps devotione permaneat' in the final prayer (Mohlberg, 368) appear to me to rule out his contention that this prayer can relate to a reconciliation *ad mortem*. Chavasse also believes that the first three of the seven prayers (Mohlberg, 356–8) actually belong to a rite of admission to penitence rather than to one of reconciliation, notwithstanding that the rubric specifically directs them to be said immediately after the admonishment to the sinner not to return to his old ways.

[20] See Chapter 4, note 25.

[21] Mohlberg, 356, 357 and 358.

[22] Full text in Schmidt, *HS*, pp. 554–5.

[23] The Mass formula in the Sacramentary of Angoulême is headed, 'Missa ad reconciliandum penitentem' (CC CLIX, Vol. C 607), and that in the Sacramentary of Autun, 'Missa ad reconciliandum' (CC CLIX, Vol. B 473). (The scribe of the Sacramentary of Gellone has altered the rubric from 'egreditur poenitens' to 'egrediuntur poenitentes' but has characteristically overlooked amending the singulars 'gessit' and 'presentatur' to the plurals 'gessunt' and 'presentantur' [CC CLIX, Vol. A 588]).

[24] Schmidt, *HS*, pp. 423–4. The slightly later Pseudo-Alcuin gives the same Gradual, Gospel and Communion verse, but a different Introit, Epistle and Offertory verse (*PL* 101, 1204).

[25] PRG cap. xxv 24–59 (Andrieu, *ORM* Vol. 5, pp. 192–207).

[26] Andrieu, PRM Vol. I, pp. 215–19. The number of prayers for reconciliation has been reduced from sixteen to eleven. Otherwise there are only very minor differences.

[27] The Mass is a hybrid one, with texts culled from a number of different feast days. See Andrieu, PRM Vol. III, p. 559.

[28] 'Vivo ego, dicit dominus, nolo mortem peccatoris, sed ut magis convertatur

et vivat' and 'Dicit dominus: penitentiam agite, appropinquabit enim regnum celorum'.

29 'Levate capita vestra, quia appropinquabit redemptio vestra'.

30 'Oportet te, fili, gaudere quia frater tuus mortuus fuerat et revixit; perierat et inventus est' (Luke 15:32).

31 Andrieu, PRM Vol. III, pp. 559–69.

32 Amalarius, De ecclesiasticis officiis Lib. I, cap. xii (PL 105,1011).

33 Pseudo-Alcuin, De divinis officiis xvi (PL 101, 1204).

34 Rupert, De divinis officiis V, xv (PL 170, 139).

35 Honorius, Gemma animae Lib. III lxxv (PL 172, 662).

36 Beleth, Rationale xcv (PL 202, 95).

37 Durandus, Rationale Lib. VI, lxxiii, 7 (Dura, pp. 518–19).

38 See Chapter 2, p. 35.

39 Conybeare, op. cit., 76.

40 Augustine, Ep. liv, 7(9) (PL 33, 204).

41 It was permitted, though not enjoined, for Africa in the twenty-ninth canon of the third council of Carthage, held in the year 397, and for Gaul in the Council of Macon, held in 585.

42 It is not altogether clear why it should be difficult to bathe and fast at the same time. However, very few people would have had a private bathroom at home, and their opportunities for bathing would therefore have been restricted by the opening hours of the public baths. By St Augustine's time there would also have been separate hours for men and women.

43 Schmidt, HS, p. 471.

44 Ibid. The evangeliary is so called because both the surviving manuscripts in which it is preserved, which date from around 700, appear to have been written in Lindisfarne.

45 Chavasse, op. cit., p. 128. The consecration of the chrism was the exclusive prerogative of the bishop, who in the case of Rome was, of course, the pope. Numerous attempts were however made by priests to encroach on this prerogative of the bishop, condemned in the strongest terms in the second and third Councils of Carthage, the first Council of Toledo and the Council of Worms (Martène, DAER IV, cap. XXII, cols. 243–4).

46 'Omnipotens sempiterne Deus, da, quaesumus, universis famulis tuis plenius atque perfectius omnia festi paschalis introire mysteria ...' (Mohlberg, 349). The sacramentary provides two collects (id. 349 and 350) and an oratio super sindonem (id. 351) for the Mass, which indicates that it belongs to the oldest liturgical stratum in the book (cf. Chavasse, op. cit., pp. 131–2). All three are also found in the Bobbio Missal, the third under its Gallican name of Post nomina (Lowe, op. cit., nn. 136–198).

47 'Eodem die non psallitur, nec salutat, id est non dicit Dominus vobiscum' (Mohlberg, 349).

48 Mohlberg, 370–372. Chavasse points out that the phrase 'accepit panem in suis sanctis manibus' is a reflection of the oldest known text of the Roman Canon, that found in St Ambrose's De Sacramentis ('in sanctis manibus suis accepit panem'), and thus an indication of the antiquity of this Mass (Chavasse, op. cit., p. 132).

49 Mohlberg, 391–392.

[50] The Gospel therefore duplicated that read on the Tuesday of Holy Week, until the Passion according to St Mark was substituted for the latter around the year 900.

[51] CC CLIX Vol. A 633, id. Vol. B 642, id. Vol. C 495 (Sacramentaries of Gellone, Angoulême and Autun), Schmidt, *HS*, pp. 391 and 408 (Sacramentaries of Reichenau and St Gall). The Gellone scribe has, characteristically, mislabelled this Collect as 'secreta'.

[52] Mohlberg, 392.

[53] The rubric in the Gregorian sacramentary is 'In ipso die conficitur chrisma in ultimo ad missam antequam dicatur *per quem haec omnia domine semper bona creas*, levantur de ampullis quas offerunt populi, et benedicit tam domnus papa quam omnes presbiteri' (Wilson, op. cit., p. 49). It is followed by the prayer for the blessing of the oil of the sick. As it stands the rubric is misleading; it was in fact only the oil of the sick that was presented by the people. A further rubric, 'Incipit benedictio chrismatis principalis' then precedes the prayer for the blessing of the chrism, followed in turn by 'Exorcismus olei' and the prayer for the blessing of the oil of catechumens.

[54] See Schmidt, *HS*, pp. 552–4.

[55] 'In eo loco ubi solemus uvas benedicere, ibi consecratur oleum pro infirmo' (Amalarius, *De ecclesiasticis officiis* Lib.I cap. xii [PL 105, 1013]). Repeated almost verbatim by Rupert of Deutz, *De divinis officiis* Lib.V, xv (*PL* 170, 141) and in a Pontifical of Rouen (*PL* 78, 328). A relic of the practice remains to this day in the wording of the Roman Canon, 'It is through Him that Thou dost create, sanctify, give life to, bless and provide all these good things (*haec omnia*) for us'.

[56] 'Mos est Romanae Ecclesiae ut in confectione immolationis Christi adsint presbyteri, et simul cum pontifice verbis et manis conficiant, at quia in ipsa periocha concluditur consecratio olei huius, oportet ut simili modo sicut et caetera, cum pontifice presbyteri oleum conficiant ' (Amalarius, *De ecclesiasticis officiis* Lib.I cap. xii (*PL* 105, 1016)). Repeated virtually word for word in the approximately contemporary Pontifical of Rouen (*PL* 78, 329). Cf. Jungmann, *MRR* Vol. I, p. 198 n.14.

[57] 'quo dominus noster Iesus Christus pro nobis est traditus' instead of 'quo traditus est dominus noster Iesus Christus'.

[58] Wilson, HBS, Vol. XLIV, pp. 48–9. The Cambrai manuscript reading 'pro nostra omnium salute' must be an error for 'pro nostra omniumque salute'. This embolism (without *hoc est hodie*) was probably originally used on every day of the year, only later being restricted to Maundy Thursday (Schmidt, *HS*, p. 754).

[59] Schmidt, *HS*, p. 458.

[60] Schmidt, *HS*, pp. 459–60.

[61] Lectionary of Würzburg (Schmidt, *HS*, p. 458), Lectionary of Corbie (ibid., p. 462), Lectionary of Alcuin (ibid., p. 463), *Comes* of Murbach (ibid., p. 464), *Comes* Theotinchi (ibid., p. 465).

[62] Antiphonals of Mont Blandin (Schmidt, *HS*, pp. 482) and Rheinau (ibid., p. 484), Gradual of Monza (ibid., p. 486).

[63] *OR* XVI. 31, *OR* XVII. 92 (Andrieu, *ORM* Vol. 2, pp. 151 and 188).

[64] *OR* XXIII. 4–8 (ibid., p. 269).

[65] L. Deiss, *Early Sources of the Liturgy* (London: Chapman, 1967), pp. 57–8. Schmidt believed that at Rome in the time of Hippolytus Maundy Thursday as well as Good Friday were aliturgical days, and that the blessing of the oils was transferred from the Easter Vigil during the fifth century (Schmidt, *HS*, p. 661).

[66] Isidore, *De ecclesiasticis officiis*, Lib. I cap. xxix.2 (*PL* 83, 764). Repeated by Rabanus Maurus, *De clericorum institutione* Lib. II, cap. xxvi (*PL* 107, 547).

[67] Rupert, *De divinis officiis* Lib. V, xvii (*PL* 170, 141). A wealth of allegorical explanations for the various aspects of the ceremony is given by the medieval commentators. For example, the two lights, two crosses and two thuribles which accompany the procession refer to the Law and the Prophets, the two cantors to the Old and New Law, the acolyte with the candle to the angel in the column of fire. The flasks when they are presented for blessing are half covered and half bare because Christ lay hid for a while before his Passion, but they are wholly bare after the blessing because Christ on the Cross was exposed for all to see. There is a great deal more in the same vein (cf. John of Beleth, *Rationale divinorum officiorum*, xcv [*PL* 202, 306–307]).

[68] *OR* XXIV. 8, *OR* XXVII. 22, *OR* XXVIII. 12 (Andrieu, *ORM* Vol. 2, pp. 289, 352 and 394).

[69] *OR* XXIV. 17, *OR* XXVII. 30, *OR* XXVIII. 20 (ibid., pp. 291, 354 and 396).

[70] *OR* XXXB. 11 (ibid., p. 468).

[71] Amalarius, *De ecclesiasticis officiis* Lib. I, xii (*PL* 105, 1013–1016).

[72] Wilson, op. cit., p. 50. There are two exorcisms in the surviving manuscript of the Old Gelasian, but both of them are additions to the original text (see appendix to this chapter). There is no exorcism mentioned in the Pontifical of Egbert or in any of the *Ordines Romani*.

[73] See note 46 above for the text of this rubric. It is also reproduced in Pseudo-Alcuin xvii (*PL* 101, 1206).

[74] PRG cap. xxv. 70–97 (Andrieu, *ORM* Vol. 5, pp. 212–25).

[75] *Ordo* XXXA. 36–59 (Andrieu, PRM Vol. I, pp. 220–6).

[76] *Ordo* XXXB. 1–9 (ibid., p. 227). The Pontifical of the Roman Curia follows *Ordo* XXXB on both these points (XLII, 10–27 [ibid., Vol. II, pp. 458–63]).

[77] *Ordo* XXXC, 7–17 (ibid., Vol. I, pp. 230–2).

[78] The number of each grade of ministers probably derives ultimately from the seven *regionarii* who had the charge of the seven districts into which the City of Rome was divided for administrative purposes.

[79] Andrieu, PRM Vol. III, pp. 571–9.

[80] Durandus says that this prayer is added in some churches (Andrieu, PRM Vol. III, p. 577).

[81] Andrieu, PRM Vol. II, Appendix ii, pp. 543–50.

[82] *OR* x, 2–11 (*PL* 78, 1010–1013), *Ordo Ecclesiae Lateranensis* (Fischer, *OEL*, pp. 50–2), *OR* xii, XI.24 (*PL* 78, 1073–1074), *OR* xv, LXV (*PL* 78, 1307–1310).

[83] This appears to be the meaning of the words 'postquam dominus papa intrat ad sacrificandum'. Other ordines specify during the Preface (*OR* xii), after the Sanctus (*Ordo Ecclesiae Lateranensis*), and either after the elevation or after the Sanctus (*OR* xv).

⁸⁴ See appendix to this chapter.

⁸⁵ Schmidt, *HS*, p. 727.

⁸⁶ Some of these sacramentaries omit the third embolism, and some delete the words *ieiunii Coenae Dominicae* in the second.

⁸⁷ Jungmann, *MRR* Vol. I, pp. 356–7.

⁸⁸ 'Et post *Kyrie eleison* domnus apostolicus dicit *Gloria in excelsis Deo*' (Andrieu, *ORM* Vol. 2, p. 269).

⁸⁹ Ibid., p. 394. *OR*s XXIX and XXXI prescribe the omission of the *Kyrie eleison* also (ibid., pp. 440 and 493–4).

⁹⁰ Sacramentary of St Eligius 51 (Schmidt, *HS*, p. 439); PRG cap. xxv. 62 (Andrieu, *ORM* Vol. 5, p. 208); Roman Pontifical of the Twelfth Century XXXA. 28 and XXXC. 5 (Andrieu, *PRM* Vol. I, pp. 219 and 230); Pontifical of the Roman Curia XLII. 9 (ibid., Vol. II, p. 458); Pontifical of Durandus Lib. III, ii. 51 (ibid., Vol III, p. 570). The *Gloria* was not however said at Cluny (*PL* 149, 658–659).

⁹¹ John of Avranches, *Lib. de officiis ecclesiasticis* (*PL* 147, 49–50); Lanfranc, *Decreta* cap. I iv (*PL* 150, 459–460); Bernoldus, *Micrologus* cap. lii, 28 (*PL* 151, 1015–1016); Honorius, *Gemma animae* Lib. III, lxxxv (*PL* 172, 665).

⁹² Lib. III, ii. 51 (Andrieu, *PRM* Vol. III, p. 570).

⁹³ *Missale Romanum* 1474, HBS, Vol. XVII (1899), p. 156.

⁹⁴ PRG cap. xxv. 100 (Andrieu, *ORM* Vol. 5, p. 207); *Disciplina Farfensis* (*PL* 150, 1198–1199); Pontifical of the Twelfth Century XXXC. 3–4 (Andrieu, *PRM* Vol. I, p. 229); Pontifical of the Roman Curia XLII. 3 (ibid., Vol. II, p. 455); Pontifical of Durandus Lib.III, ii. 47 (ibid., Vol. III, p. 570); *OR* x (*PL* 78, 1009).

⁹⁵ *Rationale*, Lib.VI, lxxii, 3–4 (Dura, p. 512).

⁹⁶ Monte Cassino, *De coenobiorum institutis* Lib. III, cap. xi, xii (*PL* 49, 114–115, 164–165) (cf. Righetti, op. cit., Vol. II.97, p. 159); *Disciplina Farfensis* cap. iii (*PL* 150, 1199); Cluny, *Consuetudines* cap. xii (*PL* 149, 658–9); Lanfranc, *Decreta* cap. I, iv (*PL* 150, 459–460).

⁹⁷ Thurston, op. cit., pp. 279–80; *OHS*, p. 130.

⁹⁸ Fischer, *OEL*, p. 50; Pontifical of Roman Curia XLII. 9 (Andrieu, *PRM* Vol. II, p. 458); Pontifical of Durandus Lib. III, ii. 51 (ibid., Vol. III, p. 570).

⁹⁹ For example Old Gelasian Sacramentary (Mohlberg, 390); *OR* XVI. 31 (Andrieu, *ORM* Vol. 2, p. 151); *OR* XVII. 91 (ibid., p. 188); *OR* XXIX. 23 (ibid., p. 441); *OR* XXXI. 18 (ibid., p. 493); PRG cap. xxv. 100 (ibid., Vol. 5, p. 225); John of Avranches, *Lib. de officiis ecclesiasticis* (*PL* 147, 49–50); Roman Pontifical of the Twelfth Century XXXC. 10 (Andrieu, *PRM* Vol. I, p. 231); Pontifical of Durandus Lib. III. ii. 90 (ibid., Vol. III, p. 580); 1474 Missal (HBS, Vol. XVII, p. 158).

¹⁰⁰ Righetti, op. cit., Vol. II.98, p. 160. Of the omission, John of Avranches says, 'pax non accipiatur; quod enim de sexta feria servetur, falso enim pacis osculo traditur' (*Lib. de officiis ecclesiasticis* [*PL* 147, 49–50]).

¹⁰¹ Jungmann, *MRR* Vol II, pp. 338–9. The omission of the *Agnus Dei* entirely is found for example in John of Avranches, (ibid.) and in *OR* XXIX. 23 (Andrieu, *ORM* Vol. 2, p. 441).

¹⁰² Canon xviii (*PL* 84, 266). Cf. Jungmann, *MRR* Vol. II, pp. 361–2.

¹⁰³ *OR* XXIV. 21 (Andrieu, *ORM* Vol. 2, p. 291); *OR* XXVII. 34 (ibid., p. 354); *OR*

XXVIII. 24 (ibid., p. 396); *OR* XXIX. 25 (ibid., p. 441); *OR* XXXB. 24 (ibid., p. 470); *OR* XXXI. 28 (ibid., p. 495).

[104] Cf. for example the *Regularis Concordia* of St Dunstan, 'communicatio praebetur tam fratribus quam cunctis fidelibus' (*PL* 137, 491), the *Disciplina Farfensis et Monasterii S. Pauli Romae* 'communionemque cuncti debent etiam infantes accipere' (*PL* 150, 1199), the *Consuetudines* of Cluny, 'omnesque communicant' (*PL* 149, 659), the *Decreta* of Lanfranc, 'nullus a communione se subtrahat, nisi subtrahendi rationabilis causa existat' (*PL* 150, 459–460), and the *Missale de Lesnes* (around 1200), 'Omnes enim sacerdotes quam alii canonici ad sacram communionem accedunt' (HBS, Vol. XCV, 1962, ed. Dom Philip Jebb, p. 42).

[105] 'In cena domini a quibusdam perceptio eucharistiae negligitur. Quae quoniam in eadem die ab omnibus fidelibus exceptis his, quibus pro gravibus criminibus inhibitum est, percipienda sit, ecclesiasticus usus demonstrat, cum etiam penitentes eadem die ad percipienda corporis et sanguinis domini sacramenta reconcilientur' (Fischer, *OEL* pp. 47–8).

[106] 'Pontifex vere in sede sua communicat illos qui communicare volunt' (*PL* 78, 1013).

[107] *OR* XXXA. 4 (Andrieu, *ORM* Vol. 2, p. 455); Pontifical of Durandus Lib. III. ii. 94 (at a Mass where the chrism has not been blessed), (id. PRM Vol. III, p. 580).

[108] Roman Pontifical of the Twelfth Century XXXC. 19 (Andrieu, PRM Vol. I, p. 233).

[109] John of Avranches, *Lib. de officiis ecclesiasticis* (*PL* 147, 50).

[110] Lanfranc, *Decreta* cap. I, iv (*PL* 150, 460).

[111] 'reconditur Dominicum corpus a sacerdote retro altare. Ponitur in patena aurea, et patena inter scutellas aureas, et adhuc scutellae inter tabulas argenteas, quae facta sunt ad textum evangelii' (Cluny, *Consuetudines*, cap. xii [*PL* 149, 659]).

[112] Pontifical of the Twelfth Century XXXA. 60 (Andrieu, PRM Vol. I, p. 226); Pontifical of the Roman Curia XLII. 29 (ibid., Vol. II, p. 463).

[113] *OR* x. 12 (*PL* 78, 1013).

[114] *OR* xv. LXVI (*PL* 78, 1309–1310).

[115] W. Lockton, *The Treatment of the Remains of the Eucharist after Holy Communion* (CUP, 1920), pp. 89–90.

[116] Ibid.

[117] 'Praeparandum igitur ornandumque erit aliquod sacellum intra ecclesiam, quo pulchrius magnificentiusque poterit, multis luminibus ornatum'. Quoted in Righetti, op. cit., Vol. II.102, p. 166.

[118] Examples in J. Monti, *The Week of Salvation* (Huntington, Indiana, 1993), p. 131.

[119] 'externa signa cuiusdam *sepulcri* penitus prohibentur ... Iuxta novas dispositiones huiusmodi repraesentationes funereae nequeunt amplius tolerari' (*OHS*, p. 142).

[120] After Mass: PRG cap. xxv. 105 (Andrieu, *ORM* Vol. 5, pp. 226–7); Pseudo-Alcuin xvii (*PL* 101, 1206); Cluny, *Consuetudines* cap. xii (*PL* 149, 659); Lanfranc, *Decreta* cap. I, iv (*PL* 150, 460). Before the Postcommunion: Roman

Pontifical of the Twelfth Century XXXA. 61 (Andrieu, PRM Vol. I, p. 226); Pontifical of the Roman Curia XLII. 32 (ibid., Vol. II, p. 464); Durandus, *Rationale* Lib. VI, lxxv. 13 (Dura, p. 528). The Roman Pontifical of the Twelfth Century (*Ordo* XXXC. 19) says that Vespers are sung 'in omnibus aliis ecclesiis, praeter in ecclesia romana' before the Postcommunion, but from the following paragraph it appears that by 'ecclesia romana' it means not the Roman rite generally but only as celebrated by the pope in person. (Andrieu, PRM Vol. I, p. 233).

121   Roman Pontifical of the Twelfth Century XXXC. 20 (Andrieu, PRM Vol. I, p. 233); Pontifical of the Roman Curia XLII. 32 (ibid., Vol. II, p. 464); *OR* x. 12 (*PL* 78, 1013); *OR* xi. 41 (ibid., 1041); *OR* xii. XI 26 (ibid., 1074); *OR* xiv. LXXXIV (ibid., 1207).

122   The silent recitation of a *Pater* and *Ave* before the start of the office, and of the *Miserere* before the final prayer, seem to have been additions to the primitive office (*OHS*, p. 125). They were removed in the 1955 reform.

123   Righetti, op. cit., Vol. II.103, p. 168.

124   Schmidt, *HS*, p. 777.

125   Amalarius, *De ecclesiasticis officiis*, Lib. I xii (*PL* 105, 1012); John of Avranches, *Liber de officiis ecclesiasticis* (*PL* 147, 150); Durandus, *Rationale* Lib. VI, lxxvi (Dura, p. 529). John of Avranches says that it takes place after dinner, Durandus after Vespers.

126   Schmidt, *HS*, p. 777.

127   For example, in the ninth century Amalarius tells us that the bare altars represented the flight of the apostles (*De ecclesiasticis officiis* Lib. I, xii [*PL* 105, 1023]).

128   Innocent III, *De sacro altaris mysterio*, Lib. II, cap. xv (*PL* 217, 799–802).

129   *OR* XXIII. 3 (Andrieu, *ORM* Vol 2, p. 269).

130   *Rationale*, Lib. III, xviii 1, 'Albis indumentis utendum est ... in coena Domini, propter confectionem chrismatis, quod ad mundationem animae consecratur; nam et evangelica lectio munditiam principaliter in illa solemnitate commendat' (Dura, pp. 129–30).

131   Roman Pontifical of the Twelfth Century XXXC. 3 (Andrieu, PRM Vol. I, p. 229); Pontifical of Durandus Lib. III ii. 47 (ibid., Vol. III, p. 570).

132   *OR* xv of about 1390 gives the starting time as the third hour (*PL* 78, 1307).

133   Ep. 55.18.33 (*PL* 33, 220).

134   Eligius of Noyon, *Homilia* viii (*PL* 87, 623).

135   'Proinde haec sancta synoda decernit et instituit ut deinceps non aliter per totius Hispaniae et Galliae ecclesias eadem solemnitas celebretur nisi pedes unusquisque pontificum seu sacerdotum secundum hoc sacrosanctum exemplum suorum lavare studeat subditorum' (*PL* 84, 557).

136   *Ordinale Gilbertinum*, De mandato conventus, 'Gerit enim in hoc officio figuram eius qui cum esset Magister et dominus omnium factus est omnium servus' (HBS, Vol. LIX, p. 35). The ordinal dates from the first half of the fifteenth century.

137   Schmidt, *HS*, pp. 554, 744, 766 & 884–5. The addition occurs in a single manuscript of the Pontifical, now lost, from the monastery of St Remigius in Reims, where Schmidt suggests the insertion actually took place.

138   Amalarius, *De ecclesiasticis officiis*, Lib. I cap. xii (*PL* 105, 1011); Pontifical of

Poitiers: Martène, *DAER* IV, cap. XXII, col. 286.
[139] PRG xxv. 111–136 (Andrieu, *ORM* Vol. 5, pp. 228–32).
[140] Martène, *DAER* IV, cap. XXII, col. 286.
[141] Cluny, *Consuetudines* cap. xii (*PL* 149, 659–660).
[142] *Disciplina Farfensis* cap. ii (*PL* 150, 1199–1200).
[143] Lanfranc, *Decreta* cap. I, iv (*PL* 150, 460–461).
[144] Fischer, *OEL* pp. 46–7 and 53–4.
[145] Schmidt, *HS*, pp. 768–9.
[146] Pontifical of the Twelfth Century XXXC. 20 (Andrieu, PRM Vol. I, p. 233); Pontifical of the Roman Curia XLII. 31–32 (ibid., Vol. II, pp. 463–4).
[147] *OR* xi. 41 (*PL* 78, 1041).
[148] Schmidt's comment, 'Hic ordo magis aulicus quam liturgicus dicendus est' is apposite (*HS* p. 771).
[149] *OR* xii. XI, 27 (*PL* 78, 1075).
[150] Pontifical of Durandus Lib. III, ii. 2–6, 98–101 (Andrieu, PRM Vol. III, pp. 558–9, 581–2).
[151] Schmidt, *HS*, p. 775.
[152] Ibid., pp. 651–3 and 775. The language of verses 1 and 8 of the hymn is clearly related to that of Rules 4 and 72 of St Benedict. For the full text of the hymn see Schmidt, *HS*, pp. 652–3.
[153] *Missale Romanum* 1474, 'Post nudationem altarium hora competenti facto signo cum tabula conveniunt fratres ad faciendum mandatum; maiores abluunt pedes et osculantur et interim hec subscripta cantantur vel omnia vel in parte pro dispositione cantoris' (HBS, Vol. XVII, p. 158).
[154] Isidore, *De ecclesiasticis officiis* Lib. I cap. xxix. 2 (*PL* 83, 764).
[155] Rabanus, *De clericorum institutione* Lib. II cap. xxxvi (*PL* 107, 547).
[156] Pseudo-Alcuin, *De divinis officiis* xvii (*PL* 101, 1204).
[157] John of Avranches, *Lib. de officiis ecclesiasticis* (*PL* 147, 50).
[158] Beleth, *Rationale* ciii (*PL* 202, 108).
[159] R. In monte Oliveti oravi ad patrem, 'Pater, si fieri potest, transeat a me calix iste; spiritus quidem promptus est, caro autem infirma. Fiat voluntas tua'. V. 'Verumtamen non sicut ego volo sed sicut tu vis' (Matt. 26:39, 42)
[160] R. Circumdederunt me vituli multi, tauri pingues obsederunt me. V. Quoniam tribulatio proxima est, quoniam non est qui adiuvet (Ps. 21, vv.12–13).
[161] J. Wickham Legg, op. cit., pp. 106–7.
[162] *Ordinale Gilbertinum*, de lavacione altarium (HBS, Vol. LIX, p. 35).
[163] Durandus, *Rationale*, Lib. VI, lxxvi.5, 7, 'In plerisque locis lavantur altaria vino et aqua et ramis fricantur, praesertim cum ramis de savina' (Dura, pp. 529–30).
[164] Pontifical of Durandus, Lib. III, ii. 97, 'Post haec altaria denudentur, non tamen laventur <nisi lavari fuerit consuetum>" (Andrieu, PRM Vol. III, p. 581).
[165] Righetti, op. cit., Vol. II.103, p. 168.
[166] In the oldest Gregorian tradition the words 'incrementorum et profectuum spiritalium munerator' are omitted, the prayer beginning simply 'Deus qui virtute sancti spiritus tui …'

CHAPTER 8

GOOD FRIDAY

The Synaxis

As we have seen in Chapter 1, there were originally only two
weekday services held in Rome during Lent, the synaxes on
Wednesdays and Fridays. The Friday of Holy Week was not celebrated, as it came to be later, as a separate commemoration of the
Crucifixion, separate that is from the commemoration of the
mysteries of our redemption which took place at the Easter Vigil.
This is clearly seen from the two non-Gospel readings prescribed
for the Friday synaxis. The earliest surviving record of these
comes from the Lectionary of Würzburg,[1] dating from the early
eighth century, though they almost certainly go back much earlier
than this.[2] The readings are from Hosea: 6:1–6 and Exodus
12:1–11.[3] Neither relates to the Crucifixion; both were chosen for
their Paschal connotations. The passage from Hosea contains the
words 'after a day or two he will bring us back to life, on the third
day he will raise us and we shall live in his presence', understood
as a prophecy of the Resurrection, and that from Exodus is the
familiar one concerning the first Passover. Isaiah 53:1–12,
regarded from the earliest times as a prophecy of the Crucifixion,
was read not on Friday but at the Wednesday synaxis two days
earlier. The Gospel reading in all the earliest evangeliaries is the
Passion according to St John, the culmination of the readings from
St John's Gospel which characterize the second half of Lent in the
Roman rite. The Passion according to St Matthew was read on the
previous Sunday and that according to St Luke on Wednesday. Of
these three Passion readings it was that of the Sunday which was
regarded, in Rome at least, as the most important.

The form of the synaxis in the Roman *tituli* is preserved in the

Old Gelasian Sacramentary, and in the Gelasians of the eighth century which derive from it.[4] It begins at the ninth hour, the time in the afternoon at which Christ died. A cross is placed upon the altar. The priest and other ministers enter without ceremony, in silence. Then after asking the people to pray for him the priest says *Oremus* and the deacon bids the people *Flectamus genua*, and, after a short pause, *Levate*. The priest then says the first Collect *Deus a quo et Iudas reatus sui poenam*. The first lesson is read, followed by a responsory. The process is then repeated, the second Collect being *Deus qui peccati veteris haereditatem mortem*. After the second responsory the Passion is read, and the *Orationes Sollemnes* follow immediately.

The responsories after each reading are given in the eighth-ninth century antiphonaries.[5] That following the first reading was taken from Habacuc 3:1–3, *Domine audivi et timui*, evidently on account of the words 'In the midst of two creatures Thou shalt be revealed',[6] understood as a prophecy of Christ between the two thieves. The responsory following the second reading consisted of verses 2–10 and 14 of Psalm 139, *Eripe me, Domine, ab homine malo*.

Over the course of time it became customary to celebrate the Eucharist after the Lenten Wednesday and Friday synaxes, and this was extended first to Monday, then to Tuesday and Saturday, and finally to Thursday, so that by the middle of the eighth century Mass was celebrated on every weekday of Lent, with the exception of Good Friday and Holy Saturday. The reason why there was no Mass on either of these two days is given in the letter of Pope Innocent I to Bishop Decentius of Gubbio, written in 416,

> It is certain that the apostles spent these two days in grief and hid themselves from fear of the Jews. It is equally clear that they fasted on the two aforementioned days, so that the tradition of the Church holds that there can be absolutely no celebration of the sacraments on those days.[7]

At a later date the medieval commentators added various allegorical explanations. John Beleth for example in the twelfth century gives us four reasons: first, because, since Christ is the true sacrifice, offered on this day, the type must give way to the reality; secondly, because it was on this day that the Church's Bridegroom was taken away and descended into the lower regions; thirdly, that because the veil of the temple was rent in two and the horns of the altar thrown down, there is no place to offer the sacrifice of the Lord's Body; and fourthly, because Moses says in the Book of Exodus, 'Another will fight for you, and you will be silent', the other referred to being Christ.[8]

On this day the pope presided at a synaxis held at the stational church, Santa Croce in Gerusalemme (also known as the Basilica Sessoriana). According to *Ordo Romanus* XXIII he left the Lateran Palace at about the eighth hour and entered the Basilica of St John, together with the other ministers, all in their bare feet. Here two candles were lit from reserved fire, and these were carried before him as all went in procession to Santa Croce, singing Psalm 118 *Beati immaculati in via*, the archdeacon holding the pope's left hand. The pope himself carried a thurible with incense in his right hand, and behind him walked a deacon carrying the relic of the True Cross in a jewelled reliquary. On arrival at Santa Croce the reliquary was placed on the altar and the pope opened it. He then prostrated himself before the altar in silent prayer. This preliminary silent prostration appears to have been a feature of the ancient Roman synaxis, before the introduction of the Introit some time before the beginning of the sixth century.[9] After this he rose and kissed the relic, followed by all the clergy and people present. Meanwhile, as soon as the pope had kissed the relic, a subdeacon ascended the ambo and read the first lesson, followed by a cantor who intoned the first responsory from the same place, a procedure then repeated for the second reading and responsory. After this a deacon, barefoot and flanked by two subdeacons, read the Passion according to St John.[10]

By the time of the Roman Pontifical of the Twelfth Century, however, the ceremony begins at the sixth hour, and the pope is followed in procession not by a deacon carrying a relic of the True Cross but by the junior of the cardinal priests bearing a receptacle with hosts consecrated at the Mass of the previous day. The procession is still made barefoot. The Veneration of the Cross takes place after the synaxis has concluded with the *Orationes Sollemnes*.[11] This is followed by all the later series of *Ordines Romani*, though they differ as to what takes place before the beginning of the procession from the Lateran.[12]

A curious feature of the papal synaxis seems to have been that it originally contained no Collects. None is given in the Gregorian Sacramentary and there is no mention of any in the eighth-century *Ordines Romani* XVI, XVII, XXIII, and XXIV. The author of *Ordo* XXVII however has added, immediately before the second reading, the words *Et dicit pontifex*: *Oremus. Diaconus Flectamus genua. Levate. Et dat orationem Deus a quo et Iudas*, to the text which he has taken from earlier ordines. It would appear therefore that this was an innovation in the papal liturgy at the time that *Ordo* XXVII was composed, in the second half of the eighth century.[13] The innovation was followed in all the liturgical books of the Gregorian tradition.

The Gelasian tradition of two Collects persisted in some places; for example the *Disciplina Farfensis et Monasterii Sancti Pauli Romae* of around 1000 prescribes the same two Collects as in the Old Gelasian Sacramentary, and they seem to have survived at Benevento until the tenth century.[14] In England, Lanfranc's *Decreta* for Canterbury of about 1070 also prescribe two Collects, though it seems that only one was in use at Sarum and York.[15] With the replacement of the Gelasian by the papal Gregorian tradition, the single Collect form eventually became standardized in the Roman rite, and persisted until 1955, in which year the Gelasian practice of two Collects was restored, though, curiously, in the reverse order.[16]

The first responsory in the papal rite was the same as that in the presbyteral, but the second appears to have consisted originally in Psalm 90 *Qui habitat in adiutorio Altissimi*, or at least part thereof. This is prescribed in *Ordo* XXIII and *Ordo* XXXB.[17] *Ordo* XXIV however gives either this or *Eripe me, Domine ab homine malo* as alternatives.[18] The manuscripts of *Ordines* XXVII and XXVIII are divided between *Qui habitat* and *Eripe me*.[19] The somewhat later *Ordines* XXXI and XXXIII have only *Eripe me*, and this became the norm, though the Romano-German Pontifical of the tenth century gives both alternatives, describing *Eripe me* incorrectly as 'a very recently composed tract' (*tractum nuperrime compilatum*).[20]

The lessons were read without introduction[21] and the Gospel narrative commenced with the simple announcement by the deacon *Passio domini nostri Iesu Christi secundum Iohannem*, without any of the usual preliminaries.[22] In contrast to Palm Sunday, this seems to have been the practice on Good Friday from the very beginning. The custom of having the narrative read or sung by three deacons, which began during the tenth century, was not adopted in Rome itself until the end of the Middle Ages.

In the Pontifical of the Roman Curia, the Pontifical of Durandus and the later series of *Ordines Romani*, as well as in the first printed missal of 1474, it is specified that the pulpit from which the gospel is read must be bare.[23]

At the end of the Gospel two deacons snatched away (*in modum furantis*) the cloth which had been placed on the altar (left bare after the evening Mass of Holy Thursday) at the start of the synaxis.[24] This covering and uncovering of the altar at the beginning and end of the Good Friday synaxis in all probability had originally no symbolism attached to it but was simply a repetition of the practice at every synaxis which at a later date acquired an allegorical significance appropriate to Good Friday.[25] The uncovering of the altar was sometimes carried out, for obvious symbolic reasons, at the words *Partiti sunt vestimenta mea sibi*, the point in the Gospel where the division of Christ's garments between the soldiers is related.[26] This was later dramatized still further in some churches: two cloths were placed on the altar at the start of the Gospel, and each of the deacons pulled off one of them, as if tearing Christ's garments apart.[27] The Gallican custom of interrupting the narrative at the words *tradidit spiritum* for a few minutes' silent meditation is not found in Rome until the fourteenth century, at first on Good Friday and slightly later on Palm Sunday also.[28]

In the Ordinary of the Papal Chaplains, from the first quarter of the thirteenth century, there is a pause in the recitation immediately before the words *Post hoc autem rogavit Pilatum Joseph ab Arimathea* while the pope puts incense into a thurible; this is then carried to the Gospel book together with two lighted candles, which are held by acolytes until the end of the reading. Afterwards the book is taken to the pope who kisses it.[29] From this source the practice was incorporated into the long recension of the Pontifical of the Roman Curia, dating to the late thirteenth century, and the papal rite of the later Middle Ages.[30] But it remained confined to the papal rite; the Pontifical of Durandus does not have it, and the rubric in the Missal of 1474 merely prescribes that from this point on the remainder of the Passion should be sung in the normal gospel tone.[31] In the Missal of Pius V the *Munda cor meum* is also said at this point, and this remained the custom until the 1955 reform. Sometimes in the later Middle Ages a sermon followed the Passion.

The time at which the papal synaxis commenced appears to have varied over the years. The eighth century *Ordines Romani* XXIV, XXVII, & XXVIII all agree on the third hour, around nine o'clock in the morning.[32] According to the first of these, the pope is accompanied by all the clergy of both the city and the suburban churches, who celebrate a second synaxis in their own churches in the evening (which could mean any time after about three o'clock). This evening synaxis is also mentioned in *Ordines* XXVII and XXVIII. It seems therefore that the start of the papal synaxis may have been advanced from the eighth to the third hour in order to enable the priests of the *tituli* to take part in it and then return to celebrate it again in their own churches. According to *Ordo* XXXB, however, the papal synaxis begins at the fifth hour and the synaxes in the *tituli* at the ninth.[33] The fifth hour is also the time specified in the Romano-German Pontifical, which mentions too the second synaxis in the individual churches.[34] The Roman Pontifical of the Twelfth Century, the Pontifical of the Roman Curia and the Pontifical of Durandus all agree in specifying the sixth hour (around midday) as the correct starting time for the Good Friday liturgy, and there is no mention in any of them of any later synaxis. The sixth hour is also given as the starting time in the first printed missal of 1474.[35] Later it became the usual practice to celebrate the liturgy in the morning.

The liturgical colour associated with the Good Friday rite seems to have been black from the beginning. Black was the normal colour in use from Septuagesima until Holy Saturday.[36] Durandus, however, tells us that it was permissible to use violet instead of black and this was in fact the custom of the Roman Church, except on Holy Thursday and Good Friday, when white and black were used respectively.[37] It seems therefore that black was not specifically adopted as a colour of mourning, as one might have supposed, but was simply the original penitential Lenten colour which was retained on this day after the substitution of violet on the other days of Lent. In this respect it paralleled the prostration before the altar in silent prayer, which was originally not an expression of grief but the normal practice at the beginning of every synaxis, retained on Good Friday alone because this was the only day of the year when the ancient synaxis survived in its pure form.[38] Black remained the proper colour for the day until the 1970 reform, when red was substituted for it.[39]

The *Orationes Sollemnes*

Originally every synaxis concluded with a series of prayers, known as the *orationes sollemnes* or, more generally, as the prayer of the faithful, after the homily.[40] This seems to have been the norm throughout the Christian world. St Augustine, for example, tells us that they were in use throughout the Church.[41] St Prosper of Aquitaine, in a treatise written around the middle of the fifth century, says that with the universal concurrence of both clergy and laity there is no part of the world in which prayers of this kind are not offered by Christian people.[42]

As time went by, however, it became more and more frequent to celebrate the Eucharist after the synaxis on days other than Sundays and feast days. This resulted in a certain amount of duplication between the prayer of the faithful and the intercessions contained within the Canon. Moreover, Pope Gelasius (492–496) inserted into the fore-mass after the Introit a litany, the so-called *deprecatio Gelasii*, whose petitions were very similar to those of the prayer of the faithful. As a consequence the latter went out of use completely except on the few remaining days when there was no celebration of the Eucharist following the synaxis. Although by the time of Gregory the Great the *deprecatio Gelasii* had been reduced on non-festal days to only the concluding *Kyrie eleison*, the prayer of the faithful was not restored, and it survived only on Wednesday and Friday of Holy Week.[43]

Before the 1970 reform there were nine petitions in all, for the Church, for the pope (sometimes substituted by or combined with the local bishop), for the clergy and people, for the emperor (or emperors), for the catechumens, for those in affliction or danger, for heretics and schismatics, for the Jews and for pagans. Each petition included a bidding prayer, a pause for silent prayer, and a Collect. The earliest text of the prayers that has come down to us is contained in the so-called *Missale Gallicanum Vetus*, a Gallican sacramentary of the eighth century, and in the Old Gelasian and Gregorian sacramentaries.[44] Where the texts of the latter two differ from each other the *Gallicanum Vetus* sometimes agrees with one and sometimes with the other. This indicates that it is not derived from either the Gelasian or Gregorian but from an earlier Roman version of the prayers which reached the Frankish kingdom before either of these.

Although the sacramentaries are themselves later compilations, the text itself can be dated on internal evidence to the fourth or early fifth century. The words *subiciens ei* [i.e. to the Church] *principatus et potestates* in Prayer I, and in particular *pro christianissimo imperatore* in the original Prayer IV, cannot be earlier than Constantine, the first Christian emperor. Some texts of the latter prayer have the plural *pro christianissimis imperatoribus*, which suggests the joint reign of either Gratian and Theodosius (379–395) or Arcadius and Honorius (395–408).[45] It is not clear which of these two versions, the singular or the plural, is the earlier. However, the references in Prayer III to 'confessors' (which signifies those who are suffering for the faith) immediately after the clerical orders and in Prayer VI (for those in affliction and danger) to the opening of prisons and the breaking of chains are redolent of the age of persecution, which points to an earlier rather than a later origin for these prayers.

The format of the prayers was certainly known in the time of St Augustine, who, in the course of a letter to Vitalis of Carthage (who had denied their efficacy) refers to the priest bidding the people to pray for the faithful, catechumens, heretics and unbelievers, in terms which reflect the language of our prayers.[46] The text that has come down to us was certainly in existence well before the middle of the fifth century. Some time between 435 and 442 St Prosper of Aquitaine supplied an appendix to a letter of Pope Celestine I to the bishops of Gaul. In it he gives an account of the prayers then in general use which have clear linguistic similarities, in both the bidding prayers and the Collects, to the Good Friday prayers reproduced in the eighth century sacramentaries. Prosper also describes these prayers, with similar linguistic echoes, in his treatise *De vocatione gentium*, written a few years later.[47] The style of the prayers suggests that the bidding prayers and the Collects are by different hands. The latter contain many examples of the so-called *cursus*, the rythmical prose which was a feature of Roman composition between the fourth and the seventh centuries, but this is almost entirely absent from the bidding prayers.[48]

In the suburban areas of Rome the priests of the *tituli* substituted the name of their own bishop for that of the pope in Prayer II.[49] Outside Rome, the prayers underwent some modification to adapt them to local requirements. In particular, the local bishop as well as the pope was mentioned in Prayer II. The original text of the bidding prayer, still found in the *Gallicanum Vetus*, has simply *Oremus et pro beatissimo papa nostro*, as does the Gregorian; in this context the word *papa* seems to retain its original meaning of the local bishop (who in the city of Rome was of course the pope). But in the Old Gelasian we find *Oremus pro beatissimo papa nostro et pro antistite nostro*, which the sacramentaries of Angoulême and Gellone, as if to put the meaning beyond all doubt, expand to *Oremus et pro famulo dei papa nostro sedis apostolicae et pro antistite nostro*.[50]

Prayer IV also was adapted in Gaul to include the Frankish king or kings as an alternative to the Roman emperor. So the *Gallicanum Vetus* has *Oremus et pro christianissimis regibus* in the bidding prayer instead of *Oremus et pro christianissimis imperatoribus*, although the relevant passage in the Collect still reads *respice propitius ad Romanum benignus imperium*. The Old Gelasian and the Sacramentary of Angoulême have *Oremus et pro christianissimo imperatore vel rege nostro* and *respice propitius ad Romanum sive Francorum benignus imperium* in the bidding and the Collect respectively.[51] By contrast, *Ordo Romanus* XXIV prescribes a separate prayer for the king of the Franks in addition to that for the Roman emperor, and the Sacramentary of Gellone contains a text for this prayer.[52]

There was no change in the text of the prayers until 1955. Even that for the Roman emperor continued to be said; first the rulers of the Holy Roman Empire and then the Habsburgs, who claimed to be their successors, interpreted it as referring to themselves. It ceased to be said only after the banishment of the last emperor of Austria in 1918, and was replaced in the 1955 reform by a prayer for the rulers of states in general.

Almost all the sources indicate that the genuflection at the prayer for the Jews is to be omitted.[53] The only exception is the Old Gelasian.[54] The Gelasian sacramentaries of the eighth century, however, which derive ultimately from it, prescribe the omission of the genuflection at this point. This may be due to an increase in anti-Judaism in the period after the compilation of the Old Gelasian; however, anti-Judaism within the Christian Church began at a very much earlier period and there is no evidence of any particular increase at the time of which we are speaking. Bearing in mind that the Old Gelasian survives in a single manuscript, the apparent exception may therefore be due to no more than scribal oversight. According to the *Ordo Ecclesiae Lateranensis* of about 1120 and *Ordo Romanus* xii of around 1190, the genuflection is omitted because the Jews bent their knees in mockery of Christ during the crucifixion, and because of our horror at this crime.[55] There is no reason to doubt that this is the true reason for the practice, which was retained in the 1955 reform, along with the words *perfidis* and *perfidiam* in the text of the prayer, notwithstanding efforts to have them removed.[56]

The rubrics in the Old Gelasian and its eighth century successors prescribe that the prayers be said standing, but between the bidding prayer and the collect the deacon, with the words *Flectamus genua . . . Levate*, commands the people to kneel, evidently for a brief private prayer, and then rise again. According to *Ordo Romanus* XXIV, which dates from the second half of the eighth century, however, the pope (or other celebrant) introduces the prayers with the single word *Oremus*, and the deacon immediately commands the people to kneel with *Flectamus genua* and rise with *Levate*. The bidding prayer and Collect follow, both seemingly said standing. The prayer for the pope himself is omitted when he is present. *Ordo Romanus* XXVII says the same but adds that there is a long pause after *Flectamus genua* during which he, and presumably also the people, pray silently. The Romano-German Pontifical repeats this rubric exactly, but the pause for silent prayer takes place only at the commencement of the series, not before each prayer. The bidding prayers are recited standing, but the Collects (other than that for the Jews) are said kneeling, except for the endings *Per dominum nostrum . . .*[57] In the thirteenth-century Pontifical of Durandus the preliminary silent prayer, said kneeling, has disappeared and the deacon simply recites *Flectamus genua, Levate* between each bidding prayer and its Collect, both of which are said standing.[58] Similarly the 1474 and subsequent missals merely prescribe the recitation of *Oremus. Flectamus genua. Levate* before each Collect (apart of course from that for the Jews).[59] This fairly meaningless genuflection continued until the 1955 reform, when, in an attempt to revive the pause for silent prayer, the rubric requires a brief interval for such prayer between *Flectamus genua* and *Levate*. In the 1970 reform however it was done away with altogether, and the Collect now follows upon the bidding prayer with no interval between them.

The *Adoratio Crucis*

The ancient Roman synaxis ended on Good Friday, as it did on all Wednesdays and Fridays, with a sermon and the *orationes sollemnes*. Apart from the choice of readings, there was nothing to distinguish it from the synaxes held on other ferias. It was several hundred years before the fourth-century Jerusalem custom of venerating a relic of the True Cross on Good Friday, so graphically described by Egeria, was adopted at Rome.[60] The custom had however long been known in the West. In a letter sent by St Paulinus of Nola in 402/3 to his friend Sulpicius Severus, enclosing a sliver of the True Cross to be enshrined in the complex of churches which the latter was building at Primuliacum, near Toulouse, he refers to

> the basilica built upon the site of the Passion, which, glowing with gilded coffering and rich in golden altars, preserves in an inner sanctuary the Cross which the bishop of that city every year, when the Pasch of the Lord is celebrated, displays to the people for their veneration, after first venerating it himself.[61]

We do not know exactly when this custom was adopted in Rome. However, from 687 to 715, and again from 731 to 752, the See of Peter was occupied continuously by popes of Greek or Syrian origin, and it seems likely to have been one of these who introduced the rite to the Roman Church.

Our first description of it is contained in *Ordo Romanus XXIII*, composed in the eighth century, possibly before 750. This ordo represents an account by a Frankish monk of the papal ceremonies of the Triduum which he had personally witnessed in the course of a visit to Rome. As described above, the pope and his attendants walked in the morning in procession from the Lateran to the Basilica of Santa Croce, the pope carrying a thurible with incense in his right hand, and behind him a deacon carrying the relic of the True Cross in a jewelled reliquary. This is the only occasion in the liturgy of the Roman Church when the pope followed the eastern practice of carrying a thurible in person. The relic itself may well have been the one which, housed in a cruciform golden reliquary adorned with jewels, was, according to a curious story in the *Liber Pontificalis*, originally donated by Pope Symmachus (498–514) to the Basilica of St Peter, then mislaid and miraculously rediscovered by Pope Sergius (687–701), one of the series of popes of eastern origin.[62]

The veneration of the relic takes place immediately after arrival at Santa Croce. The rite is very simple. The reliquary is placed on the altar and the pope opens it. After prostrating himself before the altar in silent prayer, he rises and kisses the relic. He is followed, in order, by all the other bishops, priests, deacons and subdeacons present. It is then placed on a small folding stand[63] for veneration by the men present in the congregation, and afterwards taken outside the sanctuary for veneration by the women. Meanwhile, the scriptural readings of the synaxis are taking place.[64]

There are some clear similarities between this rite and that of Jerusalem. There too the veneration begins before the synaxis; the relic is placed on a table and venerated by everyone individually, with a kiss. At Jerusalem, however, the veneration ends before the synaxis begins; at Rome they appear to take place concurrently.[65] But this must have proved distracting to the participants, because very soon the two were separated. According to *Ordo Romanus* XXIV, from the second half of the eighth century, the veneration takes place in the evening. A cross is prepared a little way in front of the altar, supported on each side by an acolyte, with a prie-dieu in front of it. The cross is kissed first by the pope and then by the clergy, bishops, priests and deacons, in order of rank, and finally by the people.[66] In the city and suburban churches, according to the Gelasian Sacramentary, the veneration takes place at the same time of day and in a similar manner. Immediately after the completion of the evening synaxis the deacons fetch the reserved sacramental elements and place them upon the altar, after which the priest venerates the cross with a kiss, and immediately says the *Pater Noster* and the embolism. Then everyone else present venerates the cross and makes his own communion.[67] This rite soon spread outside Rome; it is for example faithfully reproduced in the Gelasian sacramentals of the eighth century from Gaul. Few churches would have possessed a relic of the True Cross, so in the majority an ordinary cross was venerated instead for, as Amalarius says, 'Although every church cannot have one [a relic of the True Cross], the power of the Holy Cross is nevertheless not lacking in those crosses which are made in the likeness of the Lord's Cross.'[68]

There is no mention either in *Ordo* XXIII or in any of the Gelasian books of any prayers or chants during the veneration. In *Ordo* XXIV however we are told that during the veneration by the priest and people the antiphon *Ecce lignum crucis* and Psalm 118 (*Beati immaculati in via*) are sung. The Pontifical of Archbishop Egbert of York, which dates from between 732 and 766, has a set of one long prayer and five short ones to be recited during the ceremony; the long prayer reads

> O Lord Jesus Christ, most glorious creator of the world, Who, whilst equal in the splendour of glory to the Father and the Holy Spirit, didst condescend to take on the purest flesh, and didst allow Thy most glorious and holy hands to be pierced on the gibbet of the Cross, in order that Thou mightest tear down the gates of the underworld and free the human race from death, have mercy on me, weighed down as I am by the shame of my sin and sullied with the stain of my misdeeds; do not abandon me, most glorious Lord, but deign to pardon that evil which I have done, hear me, prostrate in adoration of Thy life-giving Cross, so that I may be worthy to take part with a clean heart in these sacred rites.[69]

Presumably this longer prayer was said by the priest alone; one or more of the shorter ones may have been said by the people also as they took part in the ceremony.

By the time of the ninth-century *Ordo* XXXI the original simple rite has been embellished and elaborated. It takes place in the morning now, following the synaxis. After the conclusion of the *orationes sollemnes*, two priests go to the sacristy and return with the Body of the Lord and a cup of unconsecrated wine which they put upon the altar, on which has already been placed a covered reliquary containing the relic of the True Cross. The pope venerates the relic and then says the *Pater Noster* and the embolism, after which he makes the commixture of the Body of the Lord with the wine and receives his own communion. Then a covered cross is positioned behind the altar, supported on each side by an acolyte. Two cantors bow before it and begin the *Trisagion* (Thrice-Holy) with the Greek *Hagios ho Theos* to which the choir responds with the Latin *Sanctus Deus*. Meanwhile the cross is carried to a point closer to the altar and the procedure is repeated. Finally, the cross is carried to the altar itself, and it is repeated once more. The cross is then uncovered by the pope who begins in a high voice the chant *Ecce lignum crucis*. The clergy take up the chant, *in quo salus mundi pependit. Venite adoremus*, upon which the people genuflect. The two cantors carry the cross to a convenient place where it can be venerated by the clergy and the people; during the veneration Psalm 118 is sung.[70] With some modifications and rearrangements, described below, this is the rite which endured for a thousand years until the 1970 reform.

The use of a covered cross which is unveiled in the course of the ceremony is first found in *Ordo Romanus* XXXI and in the roughly contemporary Pontifical of Poitiers.[71] It is in all likelihood connected with a change from the use of a plain cross to one bearing a figure of Christ crucified. In any event the latter is certainly in use by the eleventh century since in Lanfranc's *Decreta* of about 1070 it is prescribed that each person venerating the cross should kiss the feet of the image.[72]

In the tenth-century Roman-German Pontifical from Mainz the ceremony still takes place in the evening, as it does in the earlier *Ordines Romani* XXIV to XXIX. There are other differences with *Ordo* XXXI, mainly in the direction of further elaboration, evidently added to the rite in the Gallican milieu. The cross is not covered and remains in the same place, in front of the altar, throughout the ceremony, as in the earlier Roman rite, and it is supported on either side by two acolytes. So far the rubric is taken verbatim from *Ordo* XXIV. Some manuscripts of the pontifical however prescribe three genuflections for each person venerating the cross, and each genuflection is accompanied by a lengthy prayer which, if actually recited individually by each person making the genuflections, must have stretched the whole procedure out to an interminable length. During the veneration the *Trisagion* is sung, in Greek and Latin, alternately with the *Improperia* (Reproaches), the antiphon *Ecce lignum crucis* with Psalm 118 (*Beati immaculati in via*), the antiphon *Crucem tuam adoramus* with Psalm 66 (*Deus misereatur*), the antiphon *Dum fabricator mundi* with verse *O admirabile pretium*, and the hymn *Pange lingua gloriosi lauream certaminis*, with its responsories *Crux fidelis* and *Dulce lignum*, which in the rite according to *Ordo* XXXI is sung during the general communion.[73]

The rite described in the Ordinary of the Papal Chaplains, the Roman Missal of the Thirteenth Century and (with very minor variations) in the Pontifical of Durandus is something of a hybrid between the earlier Roman rite of *Ordo* XXXI and that of the Romano-German Pontifical.[74] The idea of beginning with a covered cross which is then unveiled comes from *Ordo* XXXI, that of a triple obeisance from the Romano-German Pontifical. The pope (or other celebrant) takes off his chasuble and goes to the right hand (Epistle) side of the altar, where he receives from his ministers a covered cross. He unveils the top of the cross, raises it slightly and begins the antiphon *Ecce lignum crucis*. The ministers join in and, at the words *Venite adoremus*, all present fall to their knees and bow deeply. The antiphon is repeated by cantors. The pope then proceeds a little further and unveils a further portion of the cross, as far as the middle, raising it again slightly and beginning the *Ecce lignum crucis* in a higher key. Once again the latter is taken up by the ministers and repeated by the cantors, and all genuflect and bow at the words *Venite adoremus*. He goes to the centre of the altar and uncovers the remainder of the cross, holding it higher again and beginning the antiphon for a third time in a still higher key, which the ministers and cantors take up once more, and all genuflect and bow as before. The pope then carries the cross to a prepared place in front of the altar where he venerates it first himself, taking off his shoes and prostrating himself three times. He is followed by the clergy in order of rank. Meanwhile two separate groups of cantors sing the *Trisagion* and the *Improperia*, as well as the antiphons *Adoramus te Christe, Crucem tuam adoramus* and *Salva nos Christe salvator*, with Psalms 66 and 118 and the hymn *Pange lingua*. The chants are continued until all present have venerated the cross.[75] At the end of the ceremony the cross is placed upon the altar.

Except for the repetition of the *Ecce lignum crucis* by the cantors, the rubric in the 1474 Missal is the same. In the 1955 reform the triple genuflection ('creeping to the cross' as it was known in medieval England)[76] was abolished, except for the clergy and ministers, and it was provided that prior to its unveiling the cross should be brought to the altar in procession accompanied by two acolytes with lighted candles, who accompany it throughout the ceremony; otherwise the rite remained unaltered until 1970.

The *Trisagion* as an accompaniment to the Veneration of the Cross appears in *Ordo Romanus* XXXI, probably composed in northern France during the second half of the ninth century, in which it constitutes an addition to the material taken from earlier ordines, and in the Antiphonal of Corbie of about 900.[77] The singing of the *Improperia* alternately with it is first found in the Antiphonal of Senlis of around 880 and in the Pontifical of Poitiers, which is also ninth century in date.[78] The *Trisagion*, sung in both Greek and Latin, formed part of the opening ceremony of the Gallican Mass rite.[79] It is unquestionably of Eastern origin, and the *Improperia*, though in their present form they appear to be of Western composition, probably also originated in the liturgical poetry of the East.[80] The evidence suggests that they entered the Roman liturgy via Gaul, through the medium of the Romano-German Pontifical, towards the end of the tenth century. The preservation of the Greek text of the *Trisagion* in the liturgy, alongside a Latin translation in the West, may be due to the legend that it is the song of the angels in heaven, miraculously revealed in a vision in fifth-century Constantinople.[81] The first instance of the use of a double choir for the *Improperia* and *Trisagion* seems to be in the thirteenth-century Pontifical of Durandus, where the *Improperia* are sung alternately by two cantors from each choir, the whole ensemble joining in with *Parasti crucem Salvatori tuo*, and the *Trisagion* is sung in Greek by all four cantors and repeated in Latin by the entire ensemble. As with so much else in the Pontifical of Durandus, the use of a double choir for these chants became standard practice until the reforms of the mid-twentieth century.

The *Improperia* originally contained only three verses, *Quia eduxi te de terra Ægypti*, *Quia eduxi te per desertum* and *Quid ultra debui facere*. The remaining nine verses (all beginning *Ego*) were composed later. They are not found earlier than the eleventh century. Their text shows similarities in both theme and language with an antiphon in a Beneventan antiphonal of the same century, described as an *antiphona graeca*, which is a Latin version of a seventh-century Canon of the Jerusalem church, and it seems likely therefore that the inspiration for them was derived from the East via southern Italy.[82] Outside Rome it took time for them to be adopted; for example the Irish Rosslyn Missal of about 1400 still has only the first three verses.[83] The hymn *Pange lingua*, first found in *Ordo Romanus* XXXI as an accompaniment to the communion of the minor clergy and the people and in the Romano-German Pontifical and later documents as an accompaniment to the Veneration of the Cross, is attributed to

Venantius Fortunatus, Bishop of Poitiers in the fifth century, who composed it on the occasion of the gift of a relic of the True Cross.[84]

The antiphon *Ecce lignum crucis* makes its first appearance in *Ordo* XXIV as an accompaniment, with Psalm 118, to the veneration by priest and people.[85] In *Ordo* XXXI it is intoned, after the singing of the *Trisagion*, by the pope as he uncovers the cross, and is then taken up by the clergy who sing it, followed by Psalm 118, during the veneration.[86] In the Romano-German Pontifical (where, as in *Ordo* XXIV, the cross is uncovered from the start) it is also sung between the *Trisagion* and Psalm 118 during the veneration.[87] In the Roman Pontifical of the Twelfth Century however it is sung three times during the triple unveiling of the cross, before the *Improperia* and *Trisagion*, and this is the position it occupies in the liturgy from that time onwards.[88]

The Communion

The ancient non-eucharistic synaxes seem to have normally concluded with the receipt of Holy Communion from the reserved Sacrament. This was the practice in the Eastern rites on every weekday of Lent in ancient times, and it still obtains on the Wednesdays and Fridays of that season in those rites. The rite celebrated on Good Friday in the Roman *tituli* likewise concluded with the distribution of Holy Communion, although in the papal rite there was no communion before the eighth-ninth century.[89]

In our earliest source, the Old Gelasian Sacramentary, the communion rite is extremely simple. At the end of the afternoon synaxis, immediately following the *orationes sollemnes*, the deacons go to the sacristy and fetch the Body and Blood of the Lord, consecrated the previous day, which they place upon the altar. After making his own veneration of the cross, the priest says the *Pater Noster* and the embolism. Then everyone venerates the cross and communicates.[90] This rubric is repeated word for word in the Gelasian sacramentaries of the eighth century.[91] It is noteworthy that, in contrast to subsequent practice, the Sacrament is reserved under both kinds, and presumably communion was made under both kinds also.

According to *Ordo Romanus* XXIII (first half of the eighth century), after the conclusion of the morning synaxis the pope and his deacons simply returned to the Lateran, without communicating. Anyone else however who wished to communicate might do so from the reserved Sacrament, or alternatively communicate at one of the titular churches. It is not clear whether the Sacrament was reserved under one or both kinds.[92] In any event, reservation under both kinds did not survive very much longer. By the time of *Ordo* XXIV (second half of eighth century) reservation was restricted to the Body of Christ alone. John Beleth (c.1186) and Sicardus of Cremona (c.1210) give us three reasons why the Precious Blood was not reserved in their day: first, the danger of spillage; secondly, because the bread and wine respectively signify the New and Old Testaments, and the sacrifices of the latter have now been superseded by that of the former; and thirdly, because of Christ's comment that he would not drink of the fruit of the vine again until he drank it new with his disciples in the kingdom of his Father. The first of these reasons is without any doubt the true reason why the practice was discontinued.[93]

In *Ordo Romanus* XXIV communion takes place in the evening, after the Veneration of the Cross. Two senior priests, immediately after venerating the cross, go to the sacristy and bring back the Body of the Lord consecrated the previous day. They return with two subdeacons, one carrying the Body of the Lord on a paten and the other a chalice of unconsecrated wine, which are placed on the bare altar. At the end of the Veneration of the Cross the bishop says the *Pater Noster* and its embolism and then places a portion of the consecrated host in the chalice. This is done in silence, in other words without the usual prayer recited during the intinction, which, since it refers to the Body and Blood of Christ, would have been inappropriate given that, up to that point at least, the wine was unconsecrated.[94] All then make their communion, in silence.[95] The reason why a portion of the host is placed in the chalice is made explicit in the Romano-German Pontifical – the purpose is to consecrate the wine.[96] This seems to have been regarded as the only acceptable method of consecrating it on Good Friday, since otherwise the rule against celebrating the Eucharist on this day would be breached.[97] The rite contained in this pontifical is the same as that in *Ordo* XXIV, though it is provided that the celebrant may say a silent prayer during the intinction.

The first hint of an elaboration of the rite comes, perhaps

surprisingly, from monastic sources of the eleventh century. According to the Disciplina of Farfa and the Monastery of St Paul at Rome (c.1000) two priests and a deacon go to the designated altar of reservation with candles and incense, and there they make ready the Body of the Lord and prepare a chalice with wine and water. They return to the main altar, on which an altar cloth and corporal have been placed, and all present prostrate themselves. The priest incenses the chalice and says the *Pater Noster* followed by the embolism, which he says silently, except for the ending *Per omnia saecula saeculorum*.[98] Then he places a portion of the Body of the Lord in the wine. All then make their communion. The rubric in the *Consuetudines* of Cluny (c.1060) is similar, except that it adds that if after the general communion any part of the Body of the Lord is left over it must be reverently consumed by the two priests involved in the procession. In the *Decreta* of Lanfranc (c.1070) the celebrant, having resumed his chasuble and stole after the conclusion of the Veneration of the Cross, goes with a deacon to the place of reservation and there incenses the Body of the Lord, which the deacon then takes back to the main altar, while the community all genuflect. Water and wine are mixed in a chalice. The celebrant and deacon recite the Confession, the former says a prayer and incenses the Body of Christ (again, evidently) together with the chalice, and says the *Pater Noster* and embolism. He then places a particle of the host in the chalice and communicates, followed by the rest of the community.[99]

The course of the twelfth century saw major changes to the rite, especially in the form of greater elaboration of the procession and the expansion of the rite with additional prayers. In the *Ordo Ecclesiae Lateranensis* of Prior Bernard (c.1120–1140) the Body of Christ and a chalice of wine are carried by a deacon in procession from the place of reservation, accompanied by a thurifer and two candle bearers and a subdeacon with a flask of water. During the procession the deacon recites quietly *Hoc corpus quod pro vobis tradetur. Hic calix novi testamenti est in meo sanguine dicit Dominus. Hoc facite, quotiescumque sumitis in meam commemorationem.*[100] Before reciting the *Pater Noster* the celebrant mixes water and wine in the chalice, saying the prayer *In spiritu humilitatis*, which made its appearance in the Offertory section of the Mass at around this time.[101] It is somewhat inappropriate in the context of

Good Friday in view of the words *sic fiat sacrificium nostrum ut a te suscipiatur hodie* on a day when no sacrifice actually takes place. The instruction to say it is repeated in the Roman Pontifical of the Twelfth Century, though it is absent from the short recension of the Pontifical of the Roman Curia and is specifically prohibited in that of Durandus.[102] Nevertheless it recurs in *Ordo Romanus* xiv of about 1350 and in the first printed missal of 1474 and that of Pius V, remaining part of the rite until the 1955 reform.

It was not long before the rite was further expanded. The early thirteenth-century Ordinary of the Papal Chaplains prescribes an incensation of the elements upon the altar, accompanied by the prayers *Incensum istud a te benedictum* and *Dirigatur Domine* respectively, and followed by the *Orate fratres* (though without the response *Suscipiat Dominus sacrificium de manibus tuis*), which like *In spiritu humilitatis* contains an inappropriate mention of sacrifice. The long recension of the Pontifical of the Roman Curia, compiled later in the same century, also prescribes the incensation of the elements, accompanied by the same prayers and succeeded by *In spiritu humilitatis* and *Orate fratres* (also without the usual response).[103] There is however no blessing of the incense, as there is at this point in the ordinary liturgy of the Mass. In both documents the pope alone communicates, reciting the usual prayers which accompany communion, except *Domine Jesu Christe, fili Dei vivi*, since it contains the words *hoc sacrosanctum corpus et sanguinem tuum*, and the prayer which accompanies the communion from the chalice. Afterwards he washes his hands or fingers and says the prayer *Quod ore sumpsimus*, but not *Corpus tuum Domine quod sumpsi* or *Placeat tibi sancta Trinitas* since the former refers to the Blood of Christ and the second to sacrifice. With some modifications (the incorporation of a washing of hands by the celebrant before the incensation[104] and an elevation of the Host after the embolism), this is the rite which was followed in the Missal of Pius V and remained in force until the 1955 reform.

The reason why references to the Blood of Christ in the Good Friday communion rite were deemed inappropriate is that towards the end of the twelfth century doubts were beginning to be expressed about the validity of consecration by intinction. The practice of breaking off a portion of the Body of the Lord and placing it in the cup of unconsecrated wine continued, however, being now regarded as a means of hallowing the wine rather than of consecrating it. Writing about 1186 John Beleth attempts to explain it thus:

> If anyone should ask how the wine which is consumed during communion can be consecrated by contact with the Body of the Lord ... we, following rather the truth and that which has been handed down from the holy Fathers, say that the wine is certainly not consecrated by the contact in question, but sanctified ... quite apart from the fact that if the wine were to be consecrated by contact with the Body of the Lord, it would go against the decree which prohibits any consecration on this day.[105]

The theological shift is documented in the texts of the Ordinary of the Papal Chaplains and the Pontifical of the Roman Curia, from the early and late thirteenth century respectively. The former states, in words echoing the Romano-German Pontifical, 'He breaks the host in the normal way, placing a portion of it in the chalice, in silence. The unconsecrated wine is sanctified by the commixture of the Body of the Lord'; the latter repeats the first sentence almost word for word but omits the second entirely.[106]

It was during the same twelfth century that the custom began of elevating the Host for adoration by the people during Mass after the priest had pronounced the words of consecration.[107] Eventually the custom was extended to Good Friday also. The first mention of this appears to be in *Ordo Romanus* xv, composed about 1392.[108] Since there was no consecration on that day *Ordo* xv prescribes that it should be done during the *Pater Noster*, at the words *sicut in caelo et in terra*, the idea presumably being that the elevated Host forms a link between earth and heaven. In the Missal of Pius V and subsequently the elevation takes place after the embolism.

The practice of elevating the Host seems to have been seen as a substitute for the general communion of the people, the decline in which had begun as early as the sixth century and continued during the early Middle Ages, to the point where the Lateran Council of 1215 had to insist on the reception of communion by the laity at least once a year, at Easter.[109] In the eleventh century communion on Good Friday however seems to have been still widespread; John of Avranches, Archbishop of Rouen c.1060–1070, tells us that on this day everyone communicates 'a maiore ad minorem'.[110] The Roman Pontifical of the Twelfth Century says simply that all who wish to do so should communicate in silence, the implication being that some still do.[111] But *Ordo Romanus* x, also from the twelfth century, says that the pope alone communicates, and this becomes the norm from then onwards.[112] However, communion by the laity on Good Friday survived in some places, particularly in France, Germany and Spain, and was not formally proscribed until as late as 1622, and even this proscription was not wholly effective.[113]

It seems to have been around the start of the eleventh century that the practice began on other days of reciting the embolism in a low voice or silently.[114] Apart however from some monastic contexts this practice was never followed on Good Friday, so from this time onwards we find specific directives in the liturgical books to say it out loud.[115]

The *Vexilla Regis*, composed like the *Pange Lingua* by Venantius Fortunatus, began as, and remains, the hymn for Vespers of Palm Sunday. The practice of singing it during the procession from the place of reservation to the high altar is not found before the very end of the Middle Ages. There is no mention of it in the first printed missal of 1474, where the procession still takes place in silence.[116] The practice was suppressed in the 1955 reform, which restored the silent procession.

Vespers

Vespers were normally sung or recited immediately after the conclusion of the liturgy of the day. Apart from the Magnificat antiphon, they were until the 1970 reform exactly the same as those of Maundy Thursday. At various times and in various places they were either said privately and in silence, or, when said in choir, recited and not sung.[117] The latter seems to have been the practice at St John Lateran during most of the later Middle Ages.[118]

The Origin of 'The Mass of the Presanctified'

The practice of distributing Holy Communion from the reserved Sacrament following the conclusion of a non-Eucharistic synaxis seems, from the minimal evidence available, to have begun in the

East at an unknown date, though not later than the seventh century. The first certain recorded mention of it is in Canon 52 of the Quinisext Synod (also known as the Council *in Trullo*) of 692, which prescribes that it should be celebrated in place of the ordinary Eucharist on every day of Lent except Saturdays, Sundays and the Feast of the Annunciation, but it probably began much earlier than this.[119] The cessation of the ancient practice of each member of the congregation taking a portion of the Sacrament home with him after the Sunday Eucharist for self-communication during the week provides a likely context. St Theodore Studites has left us a detailed description of the rite as celebrated in eighth-century Constantinople.[120] The reason why the Eucharist itself was not celebrated on the ordinary weekdays of Lent seems to have been a feeling that to do so would represent a breach of the Lenten fast.[121]

The name given in the East to the celebration of a *synaxis didactica* followed by a general communion was 'η θεια λειτουργια των προηγιασμενων, of which the Latin name *Missa Praesanctificatorum* is a direct translation. The evidence for the rite in the West is even more meagre than it is for the East. In Africa it is attested as early as the time of Tertullian.[122] However, the earliest mention that we have of it at Rome is in the Old Gelasian Sacramentary, seventh century and Gallican in its present form, but reflecting the rite contained in an older Roman presbyteral sacramentary of the sixth century, now sadly lost. But at Rome, as in the East, it is probably much older. It is unclear whether it was ever celebrated at Rome on any other day than Good Friday, though it was certainly confined to the latter by the time of the Old Gelasian. As mentioned above, the communion rite was not added to the papal Good Friday synaxis until two or three hundred years later.

There is a curious dearth of evidence concerning the use of the name *Missa Praesanctificatorum* in the Latin West; it is not used in any of the liturgical books, and its first appearance in print seems to be as late as 1648.[123]

The Easter Sepulchre

In many parts of Europe an aliturgical ceremony took place immediately after the conclusion of Vespers on Good Friday,

involving the symbolic burial of a crucifix, sometimes accompanied by a consecrated host, in a special place in the chancel of the
church, known as the Easter Sepulchre.[124]

The first surviving record of this custom, which evidently arose
as a result of the medieval passion for the dramatic, comes from
Anglo-Saxon England, in the *Regularis Concordia* of about 973,
though it appears to have originated on the continent at a rather
earlier date. It prescribes a triple ceremony: after the Veneration of
the Cross on Good Friday a cross is buried (*depositio*), on Easter
Sunday morning it is raised (*elevatio*) and later on the same day
there is a dramatic representation of the visit of the women to the
tomb.[125]

In the later Sarum Rite, the *depositio* took place with considerable
solemnity. On Holy Thursday three hosts were consecrated at the
evening Mass, two of which were reserved for the following day,
one for consumption by the priest during the Good Friday liturgy
and the other for the Easter Sepulchre.[126] A pyx enclosing the
consecrated host is placed on the altar during the adoration of the
cross. After Vespers the priest lays aside his chasuble and his shoes
and assumes a surplice. Carrying the pyx and the cross, wrapped in
linen cloths, he proceeds barefoot, together with another priest if
one is present, to the sepulchre, in which he solemnly lays the pyx
and the cross, and then kneels while the choir sing the antiphon 'I
am numbered among those who go down to the Pit, a man bereft of
strength, a man alone, down among the dead' (Ps. 87:5–6).[127] Then,
rising, he intones the responsory which follows the ninth reading
at Matins of Holy Saturday, 'When the Lord was buried, they
sealed the sepulchre, rolling a stone before the mouth of the sepulchre, and placed soldiers to guard Him. The chief priests went to
Pilate, and having asked him, placed soldiers to guard Him', to
which is added 'For fear His disciples come and steal Him away
and tell the people "He has risen from the dead"' (Matt. 27:64).[128]
The sepulchre is then incensed and the door to it closed, after which
the same antiphon is sung again. The priest and choir then sing, in
the form of a dialogue, *In pace: in idipsum. In pace factus est: locus eius.
Caro mea: requiescet in spe.* All then retire.[129]

Instead of a pyx it was the custom in some places (Durham,
Lincoln and Wells for instance), to use a specially made receptacle
fashioned in the image of Christ, with the Host visible through a
pane of rock crystal in his breast.[130]

After the *depositio* it was customary to leave at least one light burning before the sepulchre, and to keep a watch, not so much it appears for the purpose of private prayer as to guard against the possibility of the pyx being stolen, since there are numerous instances in medieval churchwardens' accounts of money being paid to the watchers, as well as for bread, ale and fire to keep them fed and warmed. Wills also often contain bequests both for maintaining the light and for payments to the watchers. The maintenance of the light and of the watchers was sometimes undertaken by a guild.[131]

The *elevatio* in the Sarum Rite took place early on Easter Sunday morning, before Matins. The priest and any other clergy present go in procession to the sepulchre, from which, after incensing it, they remove the pyx to the altar. They then remove the cross also and carry it round the church while the choir sings

> Christ, rising again from the dead, now dies no more. Death shall have no more dominion over him, for in that he lives, he lives unto God. Alleluia, Alleluia. Now let the Jews tell how the soldiers who were guarding the sepulchre came to lose the king at the placing of the stone, since they did not preserve the rock of justice. Let them either produce Him buried, or adore Him rising, saying with us, Alleluia, Alleluia.[132]

The third element in the ceremony, the dramatization later on Easter Sunday of the visit of the women to the tomb, seems to have been rare in England, and does not figure at all in the Sarum Rite, but it was very common on the continent, more common in fact than the *depositio* and *elevatio*. It took the form of a dialogue between the women and the angel, sometimes with the addition of Peter and John, or of Peter and John with the risen Christ.[133]

The Easter sepulchre was always situated on the north side of the chancel, at least in England. It usually took the form of a timber structure, handsomely adorned with hangings depicting scenes from the Passion and Resurrection. During the rest of the year it would be stored, and brought out only at Holy Week and Easter. Not a few churches however, both in England and on the continent, had permanent stone sepulchres, in the form of a richly carved niche set into the wall north of the high altar; there are good surviving examples at Heckington and Gosberton in Lincolnshire, Hawton in Nottinghamshire, Sparsholt in Berkshire,

Holcombe Burnell in Devon, Patrington in Yorkshire, Westhampnett in Sussex and Otford in Kent, amongst others.[134] Even before the Reformation, it was quite common for structures such as these, designed as Easter sepulchres, to double up as tombs for local gentry.

In England the rite did not survive the Reformation. It was not affected by Thomas Cromwell's injunctions of 1538, which suppressed all the lights in the church bar three, the one on the rood-loft, the one before the Sacrament of the altar and the one before the Easter Sepulchre, which were allowed to remain 'for the adorning of the church and divine service'.[135] But it was abolished completely in 1549, with the imposition of the new Prayer Book, after having been suppressed by Cranmer in the Archdiocese of Canterbury on his own initiative in the preceding year. In some places however it seems to have continued for a while, contrary to the law.[136] Although it was restored by Mary, it was abolished again, this time for good, by Elizabeth in 1559.[137]

Appendix

Texts of antiphons sung during the *Adoratio Crucis*.

Ecce lignum crucis in quo salus mundi pependit. Venite adoremus.

Behold the wood of the cross, on which hung the saviour of the world. Come let us adore.

1. Populе meus, quid feci tibi, aut in quo contristavi te, responde mihi. Quia eduxi te de terra Ægypti, parasti Crucem Salvatori tuo (Mich. 6:3–4).
2. Quia eduxi te per desertum quadraginta annis, et manna cibavi te, et introduxi te in terram satis bonam, parasti Crucem Salvatori tuo (Deut. 8:2–3, 7).
3. Quid ultra debui facere tibi et non feci? Ego quidem plantavi te meam vineam speciosissimam, et tu facta es mihi nimis amara; aceto namque sitim meam potasti et lancea perforasti latus Salvatori tuo (Is. 5:4; Jer. 2:21; Ps. 68:22).

Agios ho Theos. Sanctus Deus.
Agios Ischyros. Sanctus Fortis.
Agios Athanatos, eleison imas. Sanctus immortalis, miserere nobis.

1. My people, what have I done to you, or how have I offended you, tell me. Because I led you out of the land of Egypt, you have prepared a Cross for your Saviour.
2. Because I led you through the desert for forty years, and fed you with manna, and brought you into a prosperous land, you have prepared a Cross for your Saviour.
3. What more should I have done for you which I have not done? It was I who planted you, my most beautiful vine, and you have become most bitter to me, for you have given me vinegar for my thirst and have pierced the side of your Saviour with a spear.

Holy God (*in Greek and Latin*)
Holy strong one (*ditto*)
Holy immortal one, have mercy upon us (*ditto*)

Adoramus te Christe et benedicimus tibi, quia per Crucem tuam redemisti mundum.

We adore you, Christ, and we bless you, because through your Cross you have redeemed the world.

Crucem tuam adoramus, domine, et sanctam resurrectionem tuam laudamus et glorificamus. Ecce enim propter Crucem venit gaudium in universo mundo.

We adore your Cross, O Lord, and we praise and glorify your holy Resurrection. For indeed it was through your Cross that joy came into the whole world.

Salva nos, Christe Salvator, per virtutem Crucis; qui salvasti Petrum in mari, miserere nobis.

Save us, Christ our Saviour, through the power of the Cross; you who saved Peter in the sea, have mercy on us.

Dum fabricator mundi mortis supplicia pateretur in cruce, clamans voce magna tradidit spiritum, et ecce velum templi divisum est, monumenta aperta sunt, terraemotus enim factus est magnus, quia mortem filii Dei clamabat mundus se sustinere non posse. Aperto ergo lancea militis latere crucifixi domini, exivit sanguis et aqua in redemptionem salutis nostrae.

V. O admirabile pretium cuius pondere captivitas redempta est mundi, tartarea confracta sunt claustra inferni, aperta est nobis ianua regni.

While the creator of the world suffered the torments of death on the cross, crying out with a loud voice he gave up his spirit; and behold the veil of the temple was torn in two, the graves of the dead were opened, and a great earthquake occurred. For the world was proclaiming that it could not endure the death of the Son of God. When the side of the crucified Lord was opened by a soldier's lance there came forth blood and water, for our redemption and salvation.

V. O wonderful price whose value redeemed the captivity of the world, shattered the hellish gates of the underworld, and opened the doors of the kingdom to us.

Super omnia ligna cedrorum tu sola excelsior in qua vita mundi pependit, in qua Christus triumphavit et mors mortem superavit in aeternum.

Above all the trees of the cedar wood you alone raise your head higher than the rest, you on which the Life of the World hung, on which Christ triumphed, he whose death overcame death for ever.

Notes

[1] Schmidt, *HS*, p. 458.

[2] See note 6 below. Dom Gregory Dix believed that they were originally read at the Roman Easter Vigil and transferred to Good Friday when the Roman church began to observe that day as a commemoration of the Passion separate from that of the Resurrection, some time after the papacy of St Leo. (G. Dix, *The Shape of the Liturgy*, London: A. & C. Black, 1986, p. 440). There is however no evidence for this hypothesis, and the reasons given in support of it by the same author in *The Mass of the Presanctified* (London: Church Literature Association, 1933) are highly speculative.

[3] The reading from Philippians 2:5–11 prescribed in the *Lectionum Capitulare et Notae Capuenses* of about 545 is not found in any other source and is probably simply a local variation.

[4] Old Gelasian, Mohlberg, 395–418; Sacramentary of Gellone, CC CLIX Vol. A, 642–666; Sacramentary of Autun, id. CLIX Vol. B, 500–518; Sacramentary of Angoulême, id. CLIX Vol. C, 648–678.

[5] Schmidt, *HS*, p. 482 (Mont Blandin), 487 (Monza), 489–490 (Senlis), 494 (Compiègne), 498 (Corbie).

6   The text, 'In medio duorum animalium innotesceris' comes from the Old
    Latin version; the Vulgate of St Jerome has a quite different reading: 'In
    medio annorum notum facies'. No doubt this is at least part of the reason
    why the Old Latin text was retained for this responsory when the Vulgate
    was substituted for the remaining scriptural texts in the Good Friday liturgy.
    The obvious alternative, to replace it with a different responsory, was
    evidently regarded as unacceptable. This suggests that the reading of this
    text from Habacuc was already ancient. In any event, it must have formed
    part of the liturgy from the fourth century at the latest.

7   'Nam utique constat apostolos biduo isto et in maerore fuisse et propter
    metum Iudaeorum se occuluisse. Quod utique non dubium est, in tantum
    eos ieiunasse biduo memorato, ut traditio ecclesiae habeat isto biduo sacra-
    menta penitus non celebrari' (*PL* 20, 559). Innocent's words are echoed by
    Rabanus Maurus writing in the year 819: 'In hac die sacramenta penitus non
    celebrantur; sed Eucharistiam in coena Domini consecratam, peracto officio
    lectionum et orationum et sanctae crucis salutatione, resumunt, quia, ut
    Innocentius papa testis est, ex eo quod apostoli et amatores Christi eo biduo
    quo crucifixus et sepultus salvator est, in moerore constituti, ab omni cibo
    abstinuerunt se, hinc traditio Ecclesiae habet biduo memorato sacramenta
    non celebrari' (*De clericorum institutione*, Lib. II cap. xxxvii [*PL* 107, 349]). See
    also Pseudo-Alcuin, xviii (*PL* 101, 1208).

8   'Corpus Christi non conficitur hoc die quatuor de causis: prima est quia
    Christus hoc die pro nobis re vera immolatus est et, veritate veniente, debet
    cessare figura, ac ei dare locum; secunda, quod istiusmodi die reipsa
    Ecclesiae Sponsus sublatus sit, descendit enim ad inferos; tertia est quoniam
    tum temporis velum templi disruptum est, et cornua altaris sunt transversa,
    ita ut nobis non esset ubi corpus Christi conficeretur; quarta, quia Moyses
    dixit in Exodo: *Alius pugnabit pro vobis, et vos tacebitis (Exod. xiv)*; alius, id est
    Christus ...' (Beleth, *Rationale* xcvii [*PL* 202, 99]).

9   Righetti, op. cit., Vol. II.106, p. 172. The attribution of the Introit to Pope
    Celestine I (422–432) in the *Liber Pontificalis* may be historically unreliable,
    but it was evidently added to the Mass long enough before the composition
    of the latter (around the middle of the sixth century) for its origin to have
    been forgotten.

10 *OR* XXIII. 9–19 (Andrieu, *ORM* Vol. 3, pp. 270–1).

11 Roman Pontifical of the Twelfth Century XXXI. 1–9 (Andrieu, PRM Vol. I,
    pp. 234–6).

12 According to the twelfth century *OR* x, beginning at the sixth hour (around
    midday) the seven penitential psalms are recited in the Lateran Basilica
    before the procession to Sta. Croce in Gerusalemme begins (*PL* 78, 1013). On
    the other hand *OR* xii, of about 1192, has the pope and his chaplains
    gathering at dawn to recite the entire psalmody, then going to the Basilica of
    St Laurence at the sixth hour with all the cardinals to venerate the heads of
    SS. Peter and Paul, and only then returning to the Lateran Basilica to begin
    the procession (*PL* 78, 1075). *OR* xiv of about 1350 is similar to *OR* x except
    that instead of the seven penitential psalms the pope and ministers recite the
    office of Sext, and the pope bestows an indulgence on the people from his

window, once in the morning and again in the evening (*PL* 78, 1214). This practice also features in *OR* xv of about 1392, which also has the pope and his chaplains reciting the entire psalmody in the morning (*PL* 78, 1315). It seems that the preliminaries varied considerably from one papacy to another.

13   *OR* XXVII. 37 (Andrieu, *ORM* Vol. 3, p. 355).

14   *Disciplina Farfensis* cap. iii (*PL* 150, 1201). Survival at Benevento; Righetti, op. cit., Vol. II.106, pp. 172–3.

15   Lanfranc, *Decreta* cap. I, iv (*PL* 150, 464); J. Wickham Legg, op. cit., p. 109; Tyrer, op. cit., p. 121.

16   This arrangement is found in the Pontifical of Durandus Lib. III, iii. 4–8 (Andrieu, PRM Vol. III, pp. 582–3), and prior to this only in one manuscript (Paris BN Lat. 14088) of *OR* XXXII (Andrieu, *ORM* Vol. 3, p. 519). This manuscript however displays other differences in the rite which are peculiar to it. The other surviving manuscript of this ordo (Cambridge, CCC Cod. lat. 192) faithfully follows the Gelasian order of the Collects.

17   *OR* XXIII. 18 (Andrieu, *ORM* Vol 3. p. 271); *OR* XXXB. 31 (ibid., p. 471).

18   *OR* XXIV. 24 (ibid., p. 292).

19   *OR* XXVII. 37 (ibid., p. 355); *OR* XXVIII. 33 (ibid., p. 399).

20   *OR* XXXI. 38 (ibid., p. 496); *OR* XXXIII. 4 (ibid., p. 531). PRG cap. xxvii 10 (ibid., Vol. 5, p. 247).

21   The first reference to this reading 'sine titulo' on Good Friday seems to be in the Roman Pontifical of the Twelfth Century XXXI. 2 & 4 (Andrieu, PRM Vol. I, pp. 234–5), but it is undoubtedly of ancient origin. It is attested for the Easter Vigil readings in the eighth century *Ordines Romani* (see Chapter 9 note 118 for the references). The practice of prefacing the reading with a title and ending with *Deo gratias* is a later development (cf. Jungmann, *MRR* Vol. I, p. 420). The rubric is repeated in the Pontifical of the Roman Curia XXIII. 8 & 10 (ibid., Vol. II, p. 466), the Pontifical of Durandus Lib. III, iii. 5 & 8 (ibid., Vol. III, p. 583), *OR* x. 14 (*PL* 78, 1013–1014), *OR* xii. 13 (*PL* 78, 1075–1076), *OR* xiv. 93 (*PL* 78, 1214–1217), *OR* xv. 75 (*PL* 78, 1315–1317) and the Missal of 1474 (HBS, Vol. XVII, p. 162). The ancient practice survived until the 1970 reform.

22   *OR* XXVIII. 34 (Andrieu, *ORM* Vol. 3, p. 399); *OR* XXIX. 32 (ibid., p. 442); *OR* XXXI. 39 (ibid., p. 497); *OR* XXXIII. 4 (ibid., p. 531); PRG cap. xxvii. 6 & 11 (ibid., Vol. 5, pp. 247–8); *Ordo Ecclesiae Lateranensis* (Fischer, *OEL*, p. 55); *OR* x. 14 (*PL* 78, 1013–1014); *OR* xii. 13 (*PL* 78, 1075–1076); Roman Pontifical of the Twelfth Century XXXI. 5 (Andrieu, PRM Vol. I, p. 235); Pontifical of the Roman Curia XLIII. 11 (id. Vol. II, p. 466); Pontifical of Durandus Lib. III, iii. 11 (id. Vol. III, p. 583); *OR* xiv. 93 (*PL* 78, 1214–1217); *OR* xv. 75 (*PL* 78, 1315–1317). The practice is also mentioned in several of the medieval commentators, who naturally attach all sorts of allegorical meanings to it.

23   Pontifical of the Roman Curia XLIII. 11 (Andrieu, PRM Vol. II, p. 466); Pontifical of Durandus Lib. III, iii. 11 (ibid., Vol. III, p. 583); *OR* x. 14 (*PL* 78, 1013–1014); *OR* xii. 13 (*PL* 78, 1075–1076); *OR* xiv. 93 (*PL* 78, 1214–1217); *OR* xv. 75 (*PL* 78, 1315–1317); *Missale Romanum* 1474 (HBS, Vol XVII, p. 163).

24   *OR* XXIV. 39 (Andrieu, *ORM* Vol. 3, p. 356); *OR* XXVIII. 35 (ibid., p. 399); PRG cap. xxvii. 12 (ibid., Vol. 5, p. 248).

25 Jungmann, *Public Worship*, p. 195.

26 Pontifical of Poitiers of the ninth century (Martène, *DAER* IV, cap. XXIII, col. 375); *OR* XXXI. 40 (Andrieu, *ORM* Vol. 3, p. 497); Roman Pontifical of the Twelfth Century XXXI. 5 (Andrieu, PRM Vol. I, p. 234). There is no mention of the custom however in the Pontifical of the Roman Curia, or in any of the later series of *Ordines Romani*.

27 *OR* XXXI. 40 (Andrieu, *ORM* Vol. 3, p. 497); PRG cap. xxvii. 12 (Andrieu, *ORM* Vol. 5, p. 248); Pontifical of Durandus Lib. III. iii. 12 (id. Vol. III, p. 583), Sarum Missal (J. Wickham Legg, op. cit., p. 110 n. 1–1). In the PRG it is described as an alternative to the more usual practice, and in the Pontifical of Durandus it is said to obtain only in some churches.

28 *OR* xiv 93 (*PL* 78, 1215) for Good Friday; *OR* xv. 60 & 75 (*PL* 78, 1303–1304, 1315–1317) for both days.

29 Ordinary of the Papal Chaplains, II.12 (Andrieu, PRM Vol. II, Appendix ii, p. 558).

30 Pontifical of the Roman Curia XLIII. 12 (ibid., pp. 466–7); *OR* xii. 13 (*PL* 78, 1075–1076); *OR* xiv. 93 (*PL* 78, 1214–1217); *OR* xv. 75 (*PL* 78, 1315–1317).

31 Pontifical of Durandus Lib. III, iii. 11 (Andrieu, PRM Vol. III, p. 583); *Missale Romanum* 1474 (HBS, Vol. XVII, p. 167).

32 *OR* XXIV. 22 (Andrieu, *ORM* Vol. 3, p. 291); *OR* XXVII. 35 (ibid., p. 355); *OR* XXVIII. 31 (ibid., p. 398).

33 *OR* XXXB. 29 and 34 (ibid., pp. 470–1).

34 PRG cap. xxvii. 2 and 34 (ibid., Vol. 5, pp. 245 and 252).

35 *Missale Romanum* 1474 (HBS, Vol. XVII, p. 161).

36 'Nigris autem indumentis utendum est ... a Septuagesima usque ad Sabbatum Paschae' (Innocent III, *De sacro altaris mysterio* Lib. II cap. xv (*PL* 217, 802). The systematization of the liturgical colours is normally ascribed to Innocent III. However, there is an earlier instance of the use of black for Lent (except for the final two weeks) in twelfth-century Jerusalem (J. W. Legg, 'An Early Sequence of Liturgical Colours, hitherto but little known, apparently following the Use of the Crusaders' Patriarchal Church in Jerusalem in the 12th Century', in *Essays Liturgical and Historical* [SPCK, 1917]).

37 Durandus, *Rationale* Lib. III, xviii 6 & 9 (Dura, p. 131); Pontifical of Durandus Lib. III, xxvii. 3–4 (Andrieu, PRM Vol III, p. 658).

38 Righetti, op. cit., Vol. II.106, p. 172.

39 Red seems however to have been the colour in use in medieval England. It is prescribed in the Sarum Missal of 1526 (F. E. Warren, *The Sarum Missal in English* [London, 1911], p. 251).

40 For the history of these prayers see Jungmann, *MRR* Vol. I, pp. 480–90.

41 Sermo XLIX, 8 (*PL* 38, 324).

42 Prosper of Aquitaine, *De vocatione gentium*, Lib. I cap. xii, 'Quam legem supplicationis ita omnium sacerdotium et omnium fidelium devotio concorditer tenet, ut nulla pars mundi sit in qua huiusmodi orationes non celebrentur a populis christianis' (*PL* 51, 664–665). He makes a similar comment in his appendix to the letter of Pope Celestine to the bishops of Gaul, 'Ab apostolicis tradita in toto mundo atque in omni ecclesia catholica uniformiter celebrantur' (G. G. Willis, 'The Solemn Prayers of Good Friday',

in *Essays in Early Roman Liturgy*, Alcuin Club Collections No. XLVI, SPCK, 1964, pp. 39–41).

43 For the *deprecatio Gelasii* see Jungmann, *MRR* Vol. I, pp. 336–9. For the history of the Wednesday *orationes sollemnes* and their eventual disappearance on this day see Chapter 5.

44 *Missale Gallicanum Vetus*: PL 72, 358–360 (cf. Willis, op. cit., pp. 14–17); Old Gelasian: Mohlberg, 400–417; Gregorian: Wilson, HBS, Vol. XLIV, pp. 51–3. The *Missale Gallicanum Vetus* and another Gallican sacramentary, the *Missale Gothicum*, also have a series of similar prayers to be said at the Easter Vigil, following the blessing of the Paschal Candle (*Missale Gallicanum Vetus*, PL 72, 365–367; Missale Gothicum, ed. Bannister, HBS, Vol. LII (1917), p. 69).

45 Sacramentaries of Gellone, CC CLIX Vol. A 652, p. 88; St Gall and Prague, Schmidt, *HS*, p. 789. In the *Missale Gallicanum Vetus*, the word 'regibus' is substituted for 'imperatoribus'.

46 'Et quando audis sacerdotem Dei ad altare exhortantem populum Dei orare pro incredulis, ut eos Deus convertat ad fidem, et pro catechumenis, ut eos desiderium regenerationis inspiret, et pro fidelibus, ut in eo quod esse coeperunt, eius munere perseverent'; 'Numquid et orare prohibebis Ecclesiam pro infidelibus, ut sint fideles, pro iis qui nolunt credere, ut velint credere, pro iis qui ab eius lege doctrinaque dissentiunt, ut legi eius doctrinaeque consentiant' (Ep. 217 [*PL* 33, 978, 988]).

47 Willis, op. cit., pp. 39–41.

48 Willis, op. cit., pp. 45–6. For the cursus see also Jungmann, *MRR* Vol. I, pp. 376–8.

49 *OR* XXIV. 28 (Andrieu, *ORM* Vol. 3, p. 293). Repeated word for word in the tenth century Sacramentary of St Eligius (Schmidt, *HS*, p. 441).

50 In the Collect, the Gellone scribe has, with his characteristic carelessness, failed to change the singular 'electum nobis antistitem' to the plural 'electos nobis antistites', so that although the bidding prayer calls for prayer for both the pope and the local bishop, in the Collect only one of them is actually prayed for. Evidently the manuscript from which the scribe was copying contained the older text found in the Gregorian and the *Gallicanum Vetus*.

51 Willis, op. cit., p. 15.

52 OR XXIV. 3 (Andrieu, *ORM* Vol. 3, p. 288); Sacramentary of Gellone, CC CLIX Vol. A, 654–655, pp. 88–9.

53 For example, *OR*s XXIV. 2; XXVII, 15; XXVIII., 35; XXIX. 4; XXXI. 41 (Andrieu, *ORM* Vol. 3, pp. 288, 351, 399, 438, 497); PRG cap. xxvii. 14 (ibid., Vol. 5, p. 249); Pontifical of Poitiers (Martène, *DAER* IV, cap. XXIII col. 375); Amalarius, *De ecclesiasticis officiis* Lib. I, xiii (*PL* 105, 1027); Lanfranc, *Decreta* cap. I, iv (*PL* 150, 464); Beleth, *Rationale* xcviii (*PL* 78, 102).

54 Mohlberg, 414–415.

55 *Ordo Ecclesiae Lateranensis*, Fischer, *OEL* p. 55; *OR* xii. XIII (*PL* 78, 1075–1076). The same reason is also given in the Roman Pontifical of the Twelfth Century, XXXI. 6 (Andrieu, PRM Vol. I, p. 235).

56 Schmidt, *HS*, p. 790. They were unofficially dropped during the papacy of John XXIII, and disappeared entirely when the prayer for the Jews was completely rewritten in the 1970 reform.

57   *OR XXIV.* 2 & 26; *OR XXVII.* 39; *OR XXIX.* 33 (Andrieu, *ORM* Vol. 3, pp. 288, 293, 356, 442); PRG cap. xxvii. 13–32 (ibid., Vol 5, pp. 248–52).

58   Pontifical of Durandus, Lib. III, iii. 13 (Andrieu, PRM Vol. III, p. 583–4).

59   *Missale Romanum* 1474, (HBS, Vol XVII, pp. 167–70).

60   *PE* 36. 1–3.

61   Ep. 31 ad Severum: 'condita in passionis loco basilica, quae auratis corusca laquearibus, et aureis dives altaribus, arcano positum sacrario crucem servat: quam episcopus urbis eius quotannis cum Pascha Domini agitur, adorandum populo princeps ipse venerantium promit' (*PL* 61, 329).

62   At the time the *Liber Pontificalis* was compiled this relic was venerated in the Lateran Basilica on the feast of the Exaltation of the Holy Cross. Another such relic was donated by Pope Hilarus (461–468) to the oratory of the Holy Cross which he had constructed in the Lateran baptistery. Cf. *The Book of Pontiffs*, transl. R. Davis, Liverpool University Press, 1989, pp. 39, 45 & 85. See also Righetti, op. cit., Vol. II.107, pp. 176–7).

63   Assuming this to be the meaning of the obscure phrase 'super arcellam ad rugas'.

64   *OR XXIII.* 9–22 (Andrieu, *ORM* Vol. 3, pp. 270–2).

65   At Jerusalem in the early fifth century however, as at Rome later, there may have been some overlap between the *adoratio crucis* and the synaxis; the Armenian Lectionary says, confusingly, 'At dawn on the Friday the holy wood of the cross is set before holy Golgotha, and the congregation adore until the ninth hour. The adoration is completed, and at the sixth hour they assemble in holy Golgotha, and repeat eight psalms and five gospel lections' (Conybeare, op. cit., 86a).

66   *OR XXIV.* 29–35 (Andrieu, *ORM* Vol. 3, pp. 293–4).

67   Mohlberg, 418.

68   Amalarius, *De ecclesiasticis officiis* Lib. I cap. xiv: 'Quamvis omnis ecclesia eam non possit habere, tamen non deest eis virtus sanctae crucis in eis crucibus quae ad similitudinem Dominicae crucis factae sunt' (*PL* 105, 1029).

69   *Pontificale Egberti* 7.1: 'Domine Iesu Christe, gloriosissime conditor mundi, qui cum splendore gloriae aequalis Patri Sanctoque Spiritu carnem immaculatam assumere dignatus es, et gloriosissimas tuas sanctas palmas crucis patibulo permisisti configi, ut claustra dissipares inferni et humanum genus liberares a morte: miserere mihi misero oppressum facinore ac nequitiarum labe sordidatum, non me digneris derelinquere, gloriosissime domine, sed dignare mihi indulgere quod malum egi, exaudi me prostratum ad adorandum vivificam crucem tuam, ut in his sacris sollemniis tibi merear assistere mundus. Qui vivis etc.' (Schmidt, *HS*, p. 556).

70   *OR XXXI.* 42–49 (Andrieu, *ORM* Vol. 3, pp. 497–8).

71   *OR XXXI.* 46 (Andrieu, *ORM* Vol. 3, p. 498); Pontifical of Poitiers (Martène, *DAER* IV, cap. XXIII, cols. 375–376.

72   Lanfranc, *Decreta* cap. I, iv (*PL* 150, 464–466).

73   PRG cap. xxvii. 34–49 (Andrieu, *ORM* Vol. 5, pp. 252–9).

74   The rite found in the Roman Pontifical of the Twelfth Century is similar, except that the pope removes his shoes and venerates the covered cross with a triple prostration before unveiling it (Andrieu, PRM Vol. II, p. 236).

75 Ordinary of the Papal Chaplains and Roman Missal of the Thirteenth Century, II.14 (Andrieu, PRM Vol. II, Appendix ii, pp. 559–60); Pontifical of Durandus Lib. III, iii. 14–21 (ibid., Vol. III, pp. 584–5).

76 Cf. Thurston, op. cit., p. 359. This 'creeping to the cross' was particularly detested by the Protestant reformers, and was effectively abolished in England, along with the other Holy Week ceremonies, in 1548 (E. Duffy, *The Stripping of the Altars*, Yale UP, 1992, p. 457).

77 OR XXXI. 46 (Andrieu, *ORM* Vol. 3, p. 498); Antiphonal of Corbie: Schmidt, *HS*, p. 498.

78 Schmidt, *HS* p. 490; Martène, *DAER* IV, cap. XXIII, cols. 375–376.

79 Dix, op. cit., pp. 465–7; Jungmann, *MRR* Vol. I, p. 47.

80 Schmidt, *HS*, pp. 794–5. See also Baumstark, op. cit., pp. 101–2. The name is taken from Ps. 68:21 'Improperium exspectavit cor meum et miseriam, et sustinui qui simul contristaretur et non fuit, et qui consolaretur et non inveni'.

81 Dix, op. cit., p. 451.

82 Schmidt, *HS*, p. 795. The Beneventan antiphon reads in part, 'Pro columna ignis, in cruce me configitis. Pro nube, sepulcrum mihi foditis. Pro manna, fel me potatis. Propter aquas, acetum mihi in poculo porrigitis'. Compare *Improperia* 7, 8 and 9.

83 The Rosslyn Missal, ed. H. J. Lawlor, HBS, Vol. XV (London, 1898), p. 32.

84 Schmidt, *HS*, pp. 793–4; Righetti, op. cit., Vol. II.107, pp. 177–8.

85 OR XXIV. 35 (Andrieu, *ORM* Vol. 3, p. 294).

86 OR XXXI. 47 (ibid., p. 498).

87 PRG cap. xxvii. 39 (ibid., Vol. 5, p. 252).

88 Roman Pontifical of the Twelfth Century XXXI. 8 (Andrieu, PRM Vol. I, p. 236).

89 Righetti, op. cit., Vol. II.108, pp. 178–9. Cf. also Amalarius of Metz, 'De qua observatione interrogavi Romanum archdiaconum, et ille respondit; In ea statione ubi apostolicus salutat crucem, nemo ibi communicat' (*De ecclesiasticis officiis* Lib. I. cap. xv [PL 105, 1032]). It seems likely that in the beginning there was no distribution of communion anywhere on Good Friday, and that the papal liturgy preserved this more ancient practice. Cf. Righetti, ibid., and Schmidt, *HS*, p. 797.

90 Mohlberg, 418.

91 Sacramentary of Gellone, CC CLIX Vol. A 666; Angoulême, CC CLIX Vol. C 679–681; Prague, Schmidt, *HS*, p. 415. In the Sacramentary of Angoulême, uniquely, the rite concludes with a Postcommunion prayer (*Refecti vitalibus alimentis*), borrowed from Maundy Thursday, and a prayer over the people (*Adesto domine propitius plebi tuae*), borrowed from the Friday of the second week in Lent. The Sacramentary of Prague also has the Postcommunion and prayer over the people, but apparently misplaced by the scribe from Maundy Thursday.

92 OR XXIII. 21–22 (Andrieu, *ORM* Vol. 3, p. 272). The papal Gregorian Sacramentary, in contrast to the presbyteral Gelasian, contains no communion rite.

93 Beleth, *Rationale* xcix (PL 202, 103–104); Sicardus, *Mitrale* Lib. VI, cap. xiii (PL 213, 319–320).

94   The original text of this prayer was 'Fiat commixtio et consecratio corporis et sanguinis Domini nostri Iesu Christi accipientibus nobis in vitam aeternam.' The Council of Trent changed it to its present form to meet the objections of reformers who claimed that it implied that receipt under both kinds was necessary to salvation. Cf. Jungmann, *MRR* Vol. II, pp. 315–16.

95   *OR* XXIV. 32–38 (Andrieu, *ORM* Vol. 3, p. 294). Repeated word for word in *ORs* XXVII, XXVIII and XXIX.

96   'Sanctificat autem vinum non consecratum per sanctificatum panem.' (PRG cap. xxvii. 53 [Andrieu, *ORM* Vol. 5, p. 260]). 'Sanctificatum' in this context evidently means 'consecrated' since it is used also of the bread.

97   The Roman archdeacon mentioned by Amalarius evidently disapproved since he told Amalarius that 'qui iuxta ordinem libelli *per commistionem panis et vini consecrat vinum* non observat traditionem Ecclesiae, de qua dicit Innocentius isto biduo sacramenta penitus non celebrari' (*De ecclesiasticis officiis* Lib. I. cap. xv [PL 105, 1032]).

98   The silent recitation of the embolism began around the year 1000. It continued however to be said aloud on Good Friday (Jungmann, *MRR* Vol. II, pp. 289–90). The practice at Farfa and Cluny of saying it silently on Good Friday as well appears to be purely monastic. It occurs also in the monastic *Ordo Ecclesiae Lateranensis* (Fischer, *OEL*, p. 58).

99   *Disciplina Farfensis* cap. iii (*PL* 150, 1202); Cluny, *Consuetudines* cap. xiii (*PL* 149, 662); Lanfranc, *Decreta* cap. I, iv (*PL* 150, 466).

100 Fischer, *OEL*, p. 58. This processional rite is also found in the thirteenth century Codex of Fonte Avellana (*PL* 155, 882).

101 F. M. Quoëx, 'Historical and Doctrinal Notes on the Offertory of the Roman Rite', in the Proceedings of the Fifth International Colloquium of CIEL, p. 62; Jungmann, *MRR* Vol. II, pp. 51–2. The text of this prayer is taken from the prayer of Azarias in the Book of Daniel (Dan. 3:39–40).

102 Roman Pontifical of the Twelfth Century, XXXI. 11 (Andrieu, PRM Vol. I, p. 237); Pontifical of Durandus Lib. III, iii. 24 (ibid., Vol. III, p. 586). According to Bugnini and Braga this prayer, and the incensation of the offerings, were removed by Innocent III, which would explain their absence from the short recension of the later Pontifical of the Roman Curia, though they reappear in the long recension (*OHS*, p. 168).

103 Pontifical of the Roman Curia XLIII, 17 (Andrieu, PRM Vol II, p. 468); Ordinary of the Papal Chaplains, II.17 (ibid., Appendix ii, p. 562). The rubrics make it clear that both the Body of Christ and the chalice of unconsecrated wine are incensed together.

104 First mentioned in the Pontifical of Durandus Lib. III, iii. 24 (Andrieu, PRM Vol. III, p. 586).

105 'Si quis autem roget num istud vinum quod in communione sumitur ex Dominici corporis contactu consacretur … nos tamen, veritatem magis sequentes et ea quae sancti Patres tradiderunt, dicimus vinum illud omnino non esse consecratum ex illo contactu, sed sanctificatum … Iam etiam praetereo, si Dominici corporis tactu vinum consecraretur, contra decretum fieri quod prohibet, ne hoc die consecratio fiat' (Beleth, *Rationale* xcix [PL 202, 104]).

[106] 'Frangit hostiam secundum consuetudinem ponens de ea in calice nihil dicens. Sanctificatur enim vinum non consecratum per corpus domini inmistum' (Ordinary of the Papal Chaplains, II.18 [Andrieu, PRM Vol. II, Appendix ii, p. 562]); 'Frangat hostiam more solito et ponat particulam in calice nihil dicens' (Pontifical of the Roman Curia, XLIII. 18 [ibid., Vol. II, p. 468]).

[107] Jungmann, *MRR* Vol. II, pp. 206–8.

[108] *OR* xv, LXXVIII (*PL* 78, 1320).

[109] Cf. Jungmann, *MRR* Vol. II, pp. 359–67.

[110] John of Avranches, *Lib. de officiis ecclesiasticis* (*PL* 147, 52).

[111] 'Et omnes qui volunt communicent cum silentio' (Roman Pontifical of the Twelfth Century XXXI. 11 (Andrieu, PRM Vol. II, p. 237).

[112] *OR* x. 15 (*PL* 78 1014). For the thirteenth century see the Pontifical of Durandus Lib. III, iii 26–28 (Andrieu, PRM Vol. III, pp. 586–7), and for the fourteenth *OR* xiv. XCIII (*PL* 78, 1217).

[113] *OHS*, p. 167.

[114] Jungmann, *MRR* Vol. II, p. 289.

[115] The Roman Pontifical of the Twelfth Century XXXI. 11 for instance prescribes that the embolism should be said 'non sub silentio sed media voce' (Andrieu, PRM Vol I, p. 237).

[116] *Missale Romanum* 1474 (HBS, Vol. XVII, p. 173).

[117] Said privately, *OR* XXI. 51, XXXII. 15 (Andrieu, *ORM* Vol. 3, p. 498 & 520); *Disciplina Farfensis* (*PL* 150, 1202); John of Avranches, *Lib. de officiis ecclesiasticis* (*PL* 147, 152); PRG cap. xxvii. 54 (Andrieu, *ORM* Vol. 5, p. 260); Pontifical of the Twelfth Century XXXI. 12 (Andrieu, PRM Vol. I, p. 237).

[118] 'Non cantando sed recitando', *OR* x. 15 (*PL* 78, 1014); *OR* xiv XCIII (*PL* 78, 1217); *OR* xv. LXXVIII (*PL* 78, 1320). Of the later series of *Ordines Romani* only *OR* xii. XIII prescribes that they should be sung (*PL* 78, 1076).

[119] I. Ziadé in *Dictionnaire de Théologie Catholique* (Paris, 1936) Vol. xiii Part I, pp. 82–4.

[120] *Explicatio Divinae Liturgiae Praesanctificatorum* (*PG* 99, 1687–1688).

[121] L. Allatius, *De Missa Presanctificatorum*, in his *De ecclesiae occidentalis et orientalis perpetua consensione* (Cologne, 1648), pp. 1543–7.

[122] 'Similiter de stationum diebus non putant plerique sacrificiorum orationibus interveniendum, quod statio solvenda sit accepto corpore Domini' (Tertullian, *de Orat.* 19); Righetti, op. cit., Vol. II.108, p. 178.

[123] In Allatius; see note 121 above.

[124] For a detailed account of the custom in this country see P. Shenigorn, *The Easter Sepulchre in England* (Medieval Institute Publications, 1987). Cf. also E. Duffy, *The Stripping of the Altars* (Yale University Press, 1992), pp. 29–37.

[125] Shenigorn, op. cit., pp. 18–23.

[126] 'Ponantur a subdiacono tres hostiae ad consecrandum, quarum duae reserventur in crastinum, una ad percipiendum a sacerdoto, reliqua ut ponatur cum cruce in sepulchro' (quoted in A. Heales, 'Easter Sepulchres: their Object, Nature and History', in *Archaeologia* XLI, 1869, p. 5).

[127] 'Aestimatus sum cum descendentibus in lacum, factus sum sicut homo sine adiutorio, inter mortuos liber'.

[128] 'Sepulto domino, signatum est monumentum, volventes lapidem ad ostium monumenti, ponentes milites qui custodirent illum. Accedentes principes sacerdotum ad Pilatum, petierunt illum, ponentes milites qui custodirent illum. Ne forte venirent discipuli eius et furentur eum, et dicant plebi surrexit a mortuis'.

[129] Heales, op. cit., p. 5.

[130] Ibid., pp. 7–8.

[131] Examples in Heales, op. cit., pp. 9–15.

[132] 'Christus resurgens ex mortuis iam non moritur, mors illi ultra non dominabitur; quod enim vivit, vivit Deo. Alleluia, Alleluia. Dicant nunc Iudaei quomodo milites custodientes sepulcrum perdiderunt regem ad lapidis positionem, quare non servabant petram iustitiae. Aut sepultum reddant aut resurgentem adorent nobiscum, dicentes Alleluia, Alleluia'. Heales, op. cit., pp. 5–6; Shenigorn, op. cit., pp. 28–30.

[133] Shenigorn, op. cit., pp. 31–2.

[134] Heales, op. cit., pp. 26–9, 36–7; Duffy, op. cit., Plates 7–10.

[135] Duffy, op. cit., p. 407.

[136] D. MacCulloch, *Thomas Cranmer* (Yale University Press, 1996), pp. 384, 410; Duffy, op. cit., pp. 457–65; Heales, op. cit., pp. 42–3.

[137] Duffy, op. cit., pp. 543–8, 566; Heales, op. cit., pp. 44–5.

CHAPTER 9

THE EASTER VIGIL

The New Fire

As we saw in Chapter 2, in fourth-century Jerusalem there took place every evening a ritual, known as the Lucernare, which involved a solemn lighting by the bishop of the lamps in the Anastasis from the flame kept burning permanently in the shrine enclosing the Tomb of Christ, accompanied by the singing of antiphons, psalms and prayers. This rite appears to have been derived from earlier synagogue practice.[1] From Palestine it spread to the West, in a simpler form and somewhat modified inasmuch as it became the function of a deacon rather than the local bishop, and entailed the production of new fire rather than the use of fire from a reserved supply. This was the source of the rite with which the Paschal Vigil now begins. Originally performed at dusk on every evening of the year, it now takes place only once a year.[2] In an age when the only source of light was fire, and the onset of darkness was feared for the latent terrors it was believed to conceal, the symbolism that came to surround the kindling in total darkness of the new fire, from which first the Paschal Candle and then the church lights were lit, followed by the previously extinguished domestic fires, would have been far more potent than we can easily imagine in an era when darkness is no longer feared and light and heat can be supplied at the flick of a switch.

In the course of a letter to St Boniface,[3] Pope Zacharias (741–752) relates that the light for the blessing of the font at the Vigil in the basilica of St John Lateran was reserved at the Maundy Thursday Mass by collecting the oil from all the lamps in the building, at the time of the consecration (or at the blessing of the chrism),[4] into three large lamps which were kept in a remote part of the church and carefully tended until required on the evening of Holy Saturday. He attributes considerable antiquity to the practice, saying that it goes back to the holy Fathers of old. Since all the other lamps were by implication put out, and remained so for the rest of the Triduum, the fire from these three large lamps must also have been used (though Zacharias does not say so) for other liturgical purposes during the intervening period, in particular for lighting the candles borne before the pope in the procession to the basilica of Santa Croce on Good Friday morning.[5] There is no indication that the fire was blessed either when it was reserved or when it was produced for use at the Vigil.[6] Nor can we be sure what the contemporary practice was in the other basilicas and churches of the city, though it may well have been the same.

Some eighty years later, in 832 to be precise, Amalarius of Metz visited Rome. In the course of his visit he questioned Archdeacon Theodore about the extinction of lights during the Triduum at St John Lateran. In Amalarius' own region it was the custom for the church lights to be extinguished in the evening of each of the three days. Theodore replied that at Rome there was no ceremonial extinction of lights on Maundy Thursday, but all fires, including domestic fires, were put out on Good Friday, for symbolic reasons, at about the sixth hour. The afternoon liturgy on Good Friday was conducted without lights of any kind, either of lamps or of candles. At the ninth hour new fire was kindled, from which the domestic fires were relit, and some of this fire was reserved until required for Matins and Lauds of Holy Saturday.[7] In the evening of the latter day one candle was lit from the reserved fire (symbolising, Amalarius says, the pillar of fire which went before the Israelites during the crossing of the Red Sea); it was then blessed and the second candle lit from it. The lamps in the basilica remained extinguished until the end of the litanies, when they and the candles of the neophytes were lit.[8]

At first sight it would appear that the custom described by Theodore had replaced that followed in the time of Pope Zacharias. However, the matter is not quite so simple as that. Theodore does not say that the lights at St John Lateran were not put out on Maundy Thursday, only that there was no ritual extinction of these lights (*nihil autem ibi in eadem nocte observatur de extinctione luminum*), which leaves it open as to whether they were left burning or simply put out without ceremony. It is possible, therefore, that the custom at the Lateran of reserving fire in the three large lamps, kept continuously burning, still continued, and that it was this fire which was used to light the church lamps and the candles of the neophytes, although Zacharias himself mentions its use only in connection with the blessing of the font. However, if Amalarius is being precise when he says that all fire (*totus ignis*) was extinguished at noon on Good Friday, then the previous practice must have been superseded by his time. In any event the notion of having two separate sources of supply, one for the Holy Saturday night office and another for the Vigil, in the same basilica, seems an unnecessary duplication, out of character with the traditional simplicity and economy of the Roman rite.

A rubric in the Old Gelasian, which in its present form is a Gallican document of the early eighth century, but which is based on an earlier Roman presbyteral sacramentary, appears to reflect a custom similar to that described by Amalarius, since the archdeacon is instructed to take fire 'from the light which was hidden away on Good Friday' for the lighting of the Paschal Candle at the start of the Vigil.[9] The rite found in the relevant *Ordines Romani* varies, according to their date and provenance. The oldest, *Ordo* XXIII, though composed in Gaul in the first half of the eighth century, is an eye-witness account of the papal Holy Week ceremonies as carried out at the Lateran. Light for the Vigil is obtained from fire reserved on Good Friday.[10] *Ordines* XXXA and XXXB, from the end of the eighth century, also prescribe the use of fire reserved on Good Friday; the latter adds that the reservation takes place at the end of Lauds.[11] The text in *Ordo* XXXA is identical to the rubric in the Old Gelasian, and is evidently copied from it. But according to another group of Romano-Gallican ordines, XXVI, XXVII, XXVIII, XXIX and XXXI, which vary in date from the second half of the eighth century to the second half of the ninth, fire is reserved on Maundy Thursday, not existing fire this time, but fire newly kindled from flint, and kept in a single lamp until required to light the Paschal Candle at the start of the Vigil. In three of these five ordines (XXVI, XXVII and XXIX) new fire is kindled on Good Friday and Holy Saturday as well.[12] *Ordo* XXVI (the source from which the other two ordines were derived) reflects Roman practice, not however that of any of the city churches but of those in the surrounding countryside.[13] The purpose of rekindling fire on each of the three days is evidently to supply light for the liturgy of the day following the extinction of all lights during the night office (Tenebrae), the flame reserved on Maundy Thursday apparently being strictly restricted to lighting the Paschal Candle. On each day the new fire is kindled in a place outside the church; a candle is lit from it and borne in procession through the church to the sanctuary where it is used to light first the seven sanctuary lamps and then the lights in the rest of the church for the celebration of the liturgy, after which they remain alight until the start of the night office.

This kindling of new fire on each of the three days of the Triduum appears to have been widespread outside Rome. For example it is mentioned by John of Avranches, Archbishop of Rouen in the eleventh century: 'On these three days new fire is kindled in the church from a stone, and from there it is taken to other habitations'.[14] And in the following century Rupert of Deutz (near Cologne) says that

> on these three days we have recourse to a stone; either by striking a stone, we extract the fire which lies hidden in its innermost veins, or by offering the transparent stone of a crystal to the sun in a clear sky, we convert the ray passing through the little circle of the crystal into the nourishment hidden within in a manner wonderful to behold.[15]

In England there is evidence of the practice in the thirteenth century from Canterbury, Norwich, Worcester and Evesham, and in the fourteenth from York.[16] The first English reference to the practice however appears to be in the *Decreta* of Lanfranc, Norman Archbishop of Canterbury in the eleventh century, who may well have introduced it from Rouen. The new fire was used on each day to relight all the other monastery fires which had been previously put out.[17]

The first reference to any blessing of the new fire appears to be in the Homily on Pastoral Care of Pope Leo IV (847–855): 'On Holy Saturday let the old fire be put out and let new fire be blessed and divided among the people, together with water'.[18] In the rite found in the Pontifical of Poitiers, from the end of the ninth century, a candle is first lit at the west end of the church from the new fire reserved on Good Friday, and then blessed by a deacon. A second candle, mounted on a reed, is lit from this and then carried in procession and used to light the Paschal Candle prior to the blessing of the latter.[19] The use of two candles is no doubt precautionary, in case one of them should blow out.[20]

In the Romano-German Pontifical, from the following century, the rite is an elaboration of that contained in the second group of *Ordines Romani* mentioned above. New fire is kindled on Maundy Thursday, in a place outside the church, at the ninth hour when the days are long and at the fifth when they are short; this fire is blessed, three prayers of blessing (probably intended as alternatives) being provided, *Deus qui per filium tuum angularem scilicet lapidem; Domine Deus pater omnipotens, lumen indeficiens, conditor omnium luminum* and *Domine sancte, pater omnipotens, aeterne Deus, benedicentibus nobis hunc ignem, in nomine tuo.* The blessing is followed by another prayer, *Veniat, quaesumus, omnipotens Deus super hoc incensum*, which originated as the final part of the blessing of the Paschal Candle in the Old Gelasian Sacramentary, but is now detached therefrom and recited as a separate prayer after the lighting of a candle from the new fire. As in the ordines, this candle is borne in procession into the church, where it is used to light the seven altar lamps in preparation for the evening Mass. Meanwhile some of the new fire is reserved in a single lamp until the Vigil on Holy Saturday.

New fire is also kindled on Good Friday and Holy Saturday for use at the liturgy of the day, as prescribed in the ordines from which this rite derives. At the start of the Easter Vigil a candle is also lit from the fire reserved on Maundy Thursday and then blessed (again) with the prayer *Deus mundi conditor*, from the Gelasian tradition, or *Domine sancte, pater omnipotens, aeterne Deus, in nomine tuo*, while the schola sings the seven penitential psalms. As in the Pontifical of Poitiers, a second candle, mounted on a reed, is then lit from the first and carried in procession to light the Paschal Candle.[21] In the monastic context, the kindling and blessing of new fire on each of the three days is also prescribed in the *Disciplina* of Farfa and the Monastery of St Paul and in the *Consuetudines* of Cluny, both from the eleventh century.[22]

A large number of prayers of blessing for the new fire have survived (even discounting those which are more or less minor variations). A recurrent theme in many of these prayers is the appearance of God to Moses in the form of a burning bush and the pillar of fire that went before the Israelites during the crossing of the Red Sea. The second prayer from the Romano-German Pontifical, *Domine Deus pater omnipotens, lumen indeficiens*, has linguistic similarities with a prayer for the blessing of the lamp in the Mozarabic rite, and both may well be derived from the Jerusalem prayer at the Lucernare.[23] As time went by the practice became established in many places of employing two, three or even four of these prayers, originally simply alternatives, at the same ceremony.[24]

It was the practice in some places, the Romano-German Pontifical tells us, to sing Prudentius' hymn *Inventor rutili dux boni luminis* (originally composed for the Lucernare) during the procession. Most of the churches for which there is evidence for this practice are in England or Germany. It is prescribed for example in the *Decreta* of Lanfranc,[25] the Magdalen College Pontifical of the twelfth century,[26] the Sarum Missal of the thirteenth[27] and the Westminster Missal of the fourteenth century,[28] as well as in the Gilbertine Ordinal of the fifteenth.[29] It is never found in Rome, nor indeed anywhere in southern Europe with the solitary exception of Aquileia.

The method employed to kindle the new fire was normally that of striking metal against stone, but in some places it was produced by concentrating the sun's rays with a lens of glass or crystal.[30] Pope Zacharias in his letter to Boniface, who had evidently asked him whether a lens was used in Rome, states that no such practice was known there.[31] In those places where a lens was the principal means used for kindling the fire, the alternative method of flint and metal was usually permitted, a reasonable enough provision given that even in southern Europe a sunny day cannot always be relied upon. Rupert of Deutz, in the extract quoted above, refers to the use of either a flint or a lens, calling them both a 'lapis' (stone).[32] In Rome itself during the later Middle Ages either a flint or a lens could be used.[33]

With the arrival of the Romano-German Pontifical in Rome towards the end of the tenth century, its rite was incorporated into the liturgy of the Roman Vigil, with the change that the ceremony of blessing the fire was transferred from Maundy Thursday to the start of the Easter Vigil itself. The custom of kindling new fire on Maundy Thursday and Good Friday was eventually abandoned. It was still practised at Rouen in the eleventh century, as John of

Avranches attests,[34] but in the Roman Pontifical of the Twelfth Century the rubric for the Easter Vigil merely says that the new fire should be lit 'if it has not been kindled on Maundy Thursday, as is the custom in some churches'.[35] In subsequent pontificals and the later series of *Ordines Romani* however there is no reference at all to the kindling of new fire on any other day than Holy Saturday, though there is some variation in the timing; in the Roman Pontifical of the Twelfth Century, it takes place at the fifth or sixth hour, though the fire is not blessed until the start of the Easter Vigil, whereas in that of Durandus the kindling is effected between the offices of Sext and None. More usually, as for example in the Pontifical of the Roman Curia, both kindling and blessing immediately precede the blessing of the Paschal Candle at the start of the Vigil. The new fire is lit outside the church or, in the case of the papal rite, in the atrium of the Lateran Basilica or the papal chapel.[36]

In the Roman Pontifical of the Twelfth Century the same three prayers as in the Romano-German Pontifical are used for the blessing, but the rite has been transferred from Maundy Thursday to Holy Saturday, and all three prayers are said. The fourth prayer, *Veniat, quaesumus, omnipotens Deus super hoc incensum*, has been transmuted into a blessing of the grains of incense which are to be infixed in the Paschal Candle as well as of the fire, the word 'incensum' having undergone a shift in meaning from 'fire' to 'incense'. The Pontifical of the Roman Curia reproduces this rite and adds a sprinkling of the fire with holy water and an incensation, a practice which seems to have originated in northern Europe.[37] This became the final form of the Roman rite which, via the Pontifical of Durandus, entered the first printed missal of 1474 and the Missal of Pius V, and survived until the reform of 1955.

Origins of the Paschal Candle

There is little doubt that the ceremonies surrounding the lighting and blessing of the Paschal Candle, as well as those pertaining to the production of new fire at the Easter Vigil, represent an elaboration of the evening rite of Lucernare which was celebrated, on a daily or weekly basis, throughout the Christian world during the early centuries. However, the evidence as to when and where the Lucernare was transmuted into a ceremony of solemnly blessing and lighting a single large candle, specifically associated with the Easter Vigil, is somewhat meagre. The first mention of it is in a letter sent to St Jerome in 384 by the deacon Praesidius, asking him to compose a 'praise of the candle' (*laus cerei*) which he could use in conjunction with the blessing of the candle in his church at Placentia (Piacenza). His letter has not survived but Jerome's reply has. He refuses the request, and treats Praesidius to a lengthy denunciation of the use of candles, as distinct from oil lamps, in liturgical celebrations on the grounds that it is quite unscriptural, objecting also to the high-flown language found in the sort of composition which Praesidius is asking for, with its praise of bees who procreate without sex and its Virgilian imagery of these creatures as soldiers advancing in column under the leadership of their king, most inappropriate, in Jerome's opinion, to the office of a deacon, to the sacraments of the Church, and to the solemnity of the Easter observance.[38] From this we can infer that the custom of blessing the Paschal Candle at the Vigil and of singing a hymn in its praise was already well established, at least in Praesidius' part of Italy, by the late fourth century, and that there was no fixed format, but each deacon was at liberty to compose his own hymn, or, as in the case of the unlucky Praesidius, ask someone else to do so for him. It also appears from the same source that an encomium of bees regularly figured in such hymns, a feature which is also found consistently in later *laudes cerei*, including the original text of the one in use today, the *Exsultet*.

St Augustine clearly had no such reservations as his older contemporary since he tells us that he actually composed such a hymn as Jerome refused. This statement seems to be the source of the later notion that Augustine was the author of the *Exsultet*, which is surprising since he not only says that his composition was in verse but also quotes three lines from it.[39] We cannot be certain however that the blessing of a Paschal Candle formed part of the Easter Vigil in North Africa in Augustine's time since he may have composed his hymn at the request of and for use in some other church. In any case it seems to have been known at Rome by the time of Pope Zosimus (417–418), who is recorded in the *Liber Pontificalis* as having given permission for the blessing of the candle to be performed *per parrocias*, which probably means in the seven suburbicarian dioceses outside the city, since we know from *Ordo Romanus* XXVI that even in the eighth century, when this ordo was composed, no such ceremony took place in the city itself.[40] This ruling of Zosimus seems to have become widely known outside Italy, since, according to the ninth-century writers Rabanus Maurus and Amalarius, it was responsible for the introduction of the rite into their local churches. However, apart from the evidence that it was already taking place in northern Italy before the time of Zosimus, this kind of Roman control over the liturgies of Fulda and Metz is an anachronism for the early fifth century.[41]

There is further evidence for the existence of the ceremony from Pavia, whose bishop, Ennodius, composed two lengthy prose *laudes cerei* soon after the start of the sixth century. They deal with the creation of the world and of man, his fall and redemption, and the offering of light to God, and contain an encomium of the bees and their supposed chastity in the manner which Jerome found so repugnant.[42] From the archdiocese of Milan at around the same time we have the Ambrosian version of the *Exsultet*. And there is further evidence for the custom, this time from Ravenna towards the end of the sixth century, in the shape of a letter from St Gregory to Marinianus, bishop of that city, in which he advises him to avoid lengthy ceremonies, such as the blessing of the candle, if he is unwell.[43]

It is noteworthy that up to this point in time most of the evidence we have comes from northern Italy. But from about 590 we have a poem in praise of the Paschal Candle by the Gallican Drepanius Florus, and by 633 at the latest the custom had become widespread in Spain, since the Fourth Council of Toledo, held in that year, extended it to those churches where it was not already being observed, particularly those of Galicia. In fact we have the text of a Mozarabic blessing from the same century, in rhyming verse, whose themes are the joy of the approaching baptisms, the equality of all men in the sight of God, who is praised as the creator of light itself and implored to grant his blessing to the candle, an encomium of the bees and a final prayer for salvation.[44] By the eighth century the rite was well established in Gaul, since it features in the *Missale Gothicum*, the *Missale Gallicanum Vetus* and in the Bobbio Missal. The first named, dating from between 690 and 715, gives us the oldest known text of the Romano-Gallican *Exsultet*, which it attributes to Augustine.[45] None of these books contains any rubric, but in the Gelasian sacramentaries we read:

> Firstly in the middle of the eighth hour of the day they go to the church, enter the sacristy and put on their vestments in the customary manner. Then the clergy begin a litany and the priest proceeds from the sacristy with the sacred ministers. They come to the altar and stand there with bowed head until the *Agnus Dei*. Then the priest, rising from prayer, goes behind the altar and takes his seat. Then the archdeacon, coming before the altar, takes a light from the fire concealed on Good Friday, makes a cross over the candle, lights and blesses it.

There follows a long prayer of blessing, commencing *Deus mundi conditor auctor luminis*, the themes of which are broadly similar to those of the *laudes cerei* of Ennodius (including an encomium of the bees); the eighth-century Gelasians (though not the Old Gelasian) follow this with the *Exsultet*.[46]

Evidence for the rite also comes from Ireland in the form of a hymn included in an antiphonary from the monastery at Bangor, County Down, compiled between 680 and 691. This remarkable composition comprises nine four-line stanzas in a highly idiosyncratic Latin. It refers *inter alia* to the crossing of the Red Sea, comparing the candle to the column that went before the Israelites on that occasion, and continues

> Hoarding the hidden breath of the divine honeycomb, and cleansing the innermost cells of our hearts, Thou hast filled them with Thy word, as a swarm of new-born bees, chosen by the breath of the spirit, leaving its burden behind, seeks heaven on tranquil wings.[47]

The antiphonary also contains a prose prayer for the blessing of the candle; its theme is the column of fire which defended the chosen people from Pharaoh and his army.

But the *laus cerei* which eventually supplanted all others, and survives to this day as the only blessing of the Paschal Candle in use in the Roman rite, is the *Exsultet*. This is known in three forms, the Ambrosian, the Beneventan and the Romano-Gallican. The first part, the Prologue, followed by the Eucharistic Dialogue, is the same in all three; the second, the Preface, being specific to each of these rites. The style of the text, containing many examples of the *cursus*, suggests a composition date between the fourth and seventh centuries, and it probably belongs earlier rather than later in this period. According to Honorius of Autun and Durandus it was composed by St Ambrose, a belief shared in modern times by Dom Bernard Capelle; other scholars however attribute it rather to an unknown author influenced by the work of St Ambrose.[48]

The Prologue begins with three strophes, in a type of free verse or rhythmic prose. The first strophe invokes the heavenly powers, the second the earth, and the third the Church, calling on each in turn to rejoice in the Resurrection of the Eternal King. It then concludes with an exhortation to the people to pray for him, the deacon, so that he might 'worthily accomplish the praise of this candle'.

After the Eucharistic Dialogue, the Ambrosian *Exsultet* continues with praise of the Lamb of God, the column of fire that led God's people through the waves which drowned their persecutors, and the Bread of Heaven prefigured by the manna which fed the people of Israel in the desert. The old has passed away, and all is made new, 'It befits us therefore, on this night when the Resurrection of our Lord and Saviour draws near, to offer up this waxen richness, radiant in its appearance, sweet in its odour and brilliant in its light'.[49] It ends with a prayer that the faithful 'may greet the day of the Lord's Resurrection sanctified by the prayers or merits of Thy high priest and bishop Ambrose, and with the help of Christ in all things'.[50]

The Beneventan *Exsultet* (also known as the Old Italian or the *Exsultet* of Bari) has verbal parallels with the first of Ennodius' two *laudes cerei*, and like the Ambrosian may have been composed in northern Italy.[51] After the Eucharistic Dialogue and the usual introductory words of the Preface, it proceeds:

> Who hast condescended to preserve us until this night, the mother not of darkness but of light, in which the resurrection of the dead into the eternal day has begun, inasmuch as, unloosing His bonds and crushing below His heel the sting of death, He Who was down amongst the dead has risen from the dead.[52]

After a lengthy eulogy of the bees, it continues with praise of the candle itself and ends with a prayer for the pope, the bishop, the clergy, the emperor and all the people. During the eleventh century this Beneventan *Exsultet* was largely supplanted by the

Romano-Gallican *Exsultet*, though it seems to have survived for a while as an alternative to the latter, since it last appears in two missals from Salerno of the fifteenth century.[53]

It was the custom in southern Italy for the *Exsultet* (at first the Beneventan version, later the Romano-Gallican one) to be sung by the deacon from an ambo, round the base of which the congregation gathered. The deacon chanted the text from a long roll, which was illuminated with illustrations based on paschal themes such as the sin of Adam, the Crossing of the Red Sea, the Crucifixion, the Harrowing of Hell and (naturally) the Resurrection, as well as Christ in Glory, the Madonna and Child, Mother Church and others relevant to the text, including charming beekeeping scenes. The illuminations are, in relation to the text, upside down and on the right instead of the left hand side. The reason for this was that as the singing of the *Exsultet* progressed, the scroll would, as it was unrolled, gradually descend among the congregation, who would be able to examine the scenes portrayed the right way up from their standpoint. Twenty-seven such rolls, in whole or in part, survive, ranging from the tenth to the fourteenth century.[54]

The text of the Romano-Gallican *Exsultet*, the one in use in the Roman rite today, has undergone some changes in the course of time. The reference to the 'fortunate sin of Adam' gave rise to theological objections, and is omitted in some sources.[55] Likewise the lengthy eulogy of the bees which appears in the earliest sources is increasingly excluded and eventually disappears altogether in the later Middle Ages, probably under the influence of the thirteenth-century Franciscan Missal, which included the reference to the sin of Adam but omitted the praise of the bees.[56] Only a brief reference to the bees as the producers of wax for the candle remained until 1970, when it was finally excised. The conclusion of the hymn was sometimes modified to include prayers for other individuals beside the pope and the local bishop; the Westminster Missal of 1362–1386 for example mentions the king, the queen, their children, their firstborn son and the abbot of Westminster.[57]

The Paschal Candle in Rome and Gaul

The first mention that we have of the Roman rite comes in *Ordo Romanus* XI, dating from the seventh century, or possibly even the second half of the sixth. There is no Paschal Candle as we know it. Instead, two candles, each the size of a man, are, following the reading of the lessons, carried in procession to the font by two ministers, called *notarii* in the ordo.[58] Later ordines add further details. In the monastic *Ordo* XVI the Vigil commences with a blessing of candles by a deacon, though it seems likely that this is a general blessing of candles rather than of these two specific ones.[59] In *Ordo* XXIII (where the bearers are called *regionarii*) the two large candles are lit from the fire reserved on Good Friday, a practice which as we have seen is prescribed in the Old Gelasian Sacramentary and noted by Amalarius during his visit to Rome.[60] In *Ordines* XXIV and XXVII the two *notarii* take up a position to the left and right respectively of the altar, until the lessons have been read, at which point, still carrying their candles, they precede the procession to the font.[61] *Ordo* XXXB calls the candle bearers subdeacons (which the *notarii* may well have been) and says that they stand behind the altar until the end of the readings.[62] Apart from the single uncertain reference in *Ordo* XVI, there is no reference to any blessing of the candles in any of these documents, or in the Gregorian Sacramentary, nor are they ever referred to as Paschal Candles.

The remaining ordines reflect the rite obtaining either in the suburban area outside the city of Rome or in the particular Gallican milieu in which the ordo in question was written. *Ordines* XXV and XXVI are concerned with the practice in the suburban churches; according to the former the Paschal Candle is blessed by a deacon, who sings the *Exsultet* over it, while the latter tells us that it is lit from fire reserved on Maundy Thursday.[63] In the Gallican *Ordo* XXVIII however the candle is lit in the sacristy and then carried in silent procession into the church, placed in a candle holder in front of the altar, and then blessed by a deacon, after he has asked one of the ministers present to pray for him.[64] In *Ordo* XXXI we find a hybrid rite: the candle is lit in the sacristy from newly kindled fire, carried silently into the church, placed in a candle holder before the altar and blessed by the archdeacon, after asking those present to pray for him, with the *Exsultet*. But as soon as this is finished, two *notarii* light two man-sized candles from the Paschal Candle and then take up position on either side of the altar, while all the church lights are lit with fire from these two candles, which they hold while the lessons are read, after the conclusion of which they precede the procession to the font.[65] A similar hybrid rite is also found in the Pontifical of Poitiers, though it appears to be employed only when a bishop presides over the ceremony.[66]

The Paschal Candle in the Later Middle Ages

It is an elaborated version of this hybrid rite which we find in the Romano-German Pontifical of the tenth century. The priests and ministers enter the sacristy at the seventh hour and robe themselves in their most solemn vestments – the deacons in dalmatics, the subdeacons in albs of linen or silk. They all proceed, in order of rank, from the sacristy to a place outside the basilica, where a candle is lit from the new fire blessed and reserved on Maundy Thursday, and the priest, making the sign of the cross over the candle, blesses it in a low voice, but one which can be heard by the bystanders, beginning *Dominus vobiscum. Et cum spiritu tuo*, while the schola sings the seven penitential psalms. The prayer of blessing is *Deus mundi conditor*, as in the Gelasian tradition (an alternative prayer, *Domine sancte, pater omnipotens, aeterne Deus, in nomine tuo*, is also provided). Then a candle placed on a reed is lit from the first candle, and the clergy and people enter the church in silence. The seven lamps before the altar are lit from the second candle, and the Paschal Candle itself is placed in a candelabrum before the altar in the centre of the church, both clergy and people gathering around. The archdeacon makes a cross upon it, lights it from the new fire and bowing humbly asks one of the priests or ministers who are standing reverently around to pray for him. He then rises and blesses the Paschal Candle, first reading the introductory prayer *Exsultet iam angelica turba*. Raising his voice, he sings first the Eucharistic Dialogue, and then, in the tone of the canon, *Vere quia dignum et iustum est invisibilem Deum omnipotentem patrem filiumque eius*, etc. After the blessing of the candle, two other candles the size of a man in two candelabra are lit from it and the fires in every house (which have been previously extinguished) are relighted from the new fire. But this rite does not take place, the Pontifical tells us, within the city of Rome; there the two *notarii* merely take the candles lit from the new fire and hold them, one at the right hand corner of the altar and the other at the left, until the blessing of the font.[67] This hybrid rite, featuring both an individual Paschal Candle and two great candles which are lit from it, also appears in the *Regularis Concordia* of St Dunstan and at the monasteries of Farfa and St Paul at Rome.[68]

The rubric for the blessing of the candle in the Gelasian Sacramentary includes, as we have seen, an instruction to make the sign of the cross over it. However, by the time of the Romano-German Pontifical the words *super cereum* have become *in cereo*, i.e. a cross is to be made upon the candle itself. This was probably done by incision, though the rubric does not make this clear. In the Sacramentary of Ratoldus (or Corbie) of about 980 we read that the cross in question is to be made with incense, and that the year of the Lord, together with the Greek letters A and Ω, should also be inscribed on the candle.[69] The tracing of the cross with five grains of incense, which are embedded by the deacon at the words *Suscipe sancte pater incensi huius sacrificium vespertinum* into holes previously inscribed on the candle, seems to have been first recorded at Cluny around the year 1060.[70] Rupert of Deutz, writing about fifty years later, also says that the grains of incense are inserted into a small cross cut into the candle, though he does not specify at what point in the rite this takes place.[71] The association of the five grains with the five wounds of Christ is first mentioned by Durandus towards the end of the thirteenth century, though the analogy is an obvious one and must have been made earlier, possibly even from the beginning.[72] At Rome the first mention of the five grains of incense is in the Pontifical of the Twelfth Century, where they are blessed with the prayer *Veniat quaesumus* immediately after the blessing of the new fire in the atrium of the Lateran basilica. Since they are embedded in the candle during the singing of the *Exsultet* at the words *Suscipe sancte pater incensi huius sacrificium* they must presumably have been carried in the procession from the atrium to the altar.[73] This is the rite which, with the addition in the 1570 Missal of a sprinkling and incensation of the five grains, endured until the reform of 1955.[74]

The practice of inscribing the year at least seems to be much older than its first appearances in the tenth-century Pontifical of Poitiers and Sacramentary of Ratoldus might lead us to suppose.[75] In the year 701 a group of monks from the monastery at Jarrow who happened to be visiting the basilica of St Mary Major in Rome on Christmas Day of that year noticed candles carrying the inscription 'From the Passion of Our Lord Jesus Christ there are 668 years'.[76] Although we are not told which candles in particular bore this inscription, they would have to have been larger than the ordinary candles in use at the basilica to accommodate such an inscription, and it is tempting to believe, especially in view of the reference to the Passion rather than the Incarnation, that they were in fact the two large candles blessed and carried at the previous Easter Vigil at St Mary Major, as well as at other churches within the city of Rome. If so, it would have been natural for the custom to have spread to the single large candle which featured in the extra-urban rite, and from there to other dioceses within and eventually outside Italy.[77] The first certain indications however of the inscription of the year of Our Lord on the Paschal Candle are those in the Pontifical of Poitiers and the Sacramentary of Ratoldus. Slightly later the *Disciplina* of the Monastery of Farfa and St Paul at Rome of around 1000 prescribes that both the year of Our Lord and the epact should be inscribed on the candle.[78] Rupert of Deutz mentions the year of Our Lord but not the epact.[79] In the city of Rome itself however there is no mention of any custom of inscribing the year of Our Lord on the candle.[80]

The Paschal Candle was usually lit from a smaller candle which had itself been lit from the new fire and borne in procession from the church door to the place, normally the sanctuary, where the Paschal Candle had been set up, as we have seen in the Pontifical of Poitiers and in the Romano-German Pontifical. The device used to hold the smaller candle during the procession seems originally to have been a reed (*arundo* or *canna*), referred to in both of these documents; at Poitiers the candle was moulded into the shape of a serpent.[81] The transport of new fire by means of a reed is also mentioned in several of the earlier *Ordines Romani*.[82] Later, other instruments were used in different places: a pole or rod, sometimes carved in the shape of a serpent, or, particularly in Normandy and England, a spear.[83]

The use of multiple candles to transmit the new fire probably originated in the necessity of providing a fall-back in the case of a single candle being inadvertently extinguished; thus the English order of Gilbertines used five candles and the *Ordo Ecclesiae Lateranensis* mentions several, though without specifying any particular number, which the compiler tells us are provided in case the wind should blow one or more out.[84] But the device which came to be most commonly used and eventually was to supplant all others in the Roman rite was the triple candle, the so-called *trikirion*, first mentioned in the Roman Pontifical of the Twelfth Century, but occurring several centuries earlier in Eastern liturgies, from which it probably reached Rome via southern Italy.[85] From there it spread throughout Europe.[86] It consisted of three small candles the stocks of which were softened and wound around one another. The ready interpretation of the trikirion as a symbol of the Blessed Trinity was probably the factor that earned it such widespread acceptance. Originally all three candles seem to have been lit simultaneously, but as the practical purpose of the triple candle was forgotten in favour of its symbolism, the practice (first recorded in the Missal of 1571) began of lighting one candle at each of the three stations made in the course of the procession, the first at the church door, the second in the centre of the church and the third on arrival at the front of the altar.

None of the early Gregorian sacramentaries contain any reference to the Paschal Candle. The rite was eventually incorporated into the liturgy of the city of Rome itself around the end of the tenth century, under the influence of the Romano-German Pontifical. The ceremony as we find it carried out in the Lateran according to the Roman Pontifical of the Twelfth Century is similar to that of the former but there are a few important differences. Instead of a single candle lit from a supply of fire reserved on Maundy Thursday, a triple candle is lit from the new fire kindled outside the church, and this is then placed on a reed and carried by the junior cardinal deacon in procession into the building and up the aisle to the ambo. Three pauses are made, at the door of the church, between the door and the ambo, and at the foot of the ambo itself, at each of which the deacon sings *Lumen Christi* in a slightly higher voice each time, to which the schola and the subdeacons accompanying him reply with *Deo gratias*.[87] The deacon then ascends the ambo where he lights the Paschal Candle, incenses the book, and begins the *Exsultet*. When he comes to the words *Suscipe sancte pater incensi huius sacrificium vespertinum* he attaches firmly to the candle five grains of incense in the shape of a cross, and when he reaches the verse *Qui licet sit divisus in partes mutuati luminis detrimenta non novit*, the seven sanctuary lamps and the two candles in two candelabra are lit from it.

Meanwhile the pontiff goes in procession to the altar with all his clergy. After the blessing of the candle, the domestic fires, which have been extinguished, are lit from the new fire. The compiler of the pontifical adds that this is the rite performed in the Roman church, but elsewhere there is an alternative rite, which he wrongly ascribes to Zosimus, in which the Paschal Candle is placed in a candelabrum before the altar and the clergy and people gather nearby. The deacon makes a cross on the candle with a stylus, together with A and Ω and the year from the Incarnation of the Lord. He bows humbly to the priest who gives him a blessing and then, rising and turning to the choir, sings three times in an ascending tone *Lumen Christi*. The rest follows as in Rome.[88]

The source of the triple cry of *Lumen Christi* with the response *Deo gratias* is unclear. It may have originated in the custom found in the eighth century in some Benedictine houses at the evening meal, when a light was required, for the brother who brought in the light to announce *Lumen Christi*, to which the assembled community replied *Deo Gratias*.[89] The triple cry is first recorded in a liturgical context around the year 1000 in the liturgy of Benevento, though it did not take place during the procession but only after the deacon had arrived at the ambo and lit the Paschal Candle. The first instance of its use during the procession is from Vallombrosa about the year 1040, approximately a hundred years before its first appearance in Rome.[90]

In all essentials the rite of the Pontifical of the Twelfth Century is the one which eventually, via the 1474 Missal, was incorporated into the Tridentine Missal of Pius V and remained in use until 1955.[91] The only changes were that before beginning the *Exsultet* the deacon asked for a blessing from the celebrant, which the latter bestowed in the words used at the Gospel on other days (substituting *praeconium paschale* for *evangelium*), and the candle was not lit from the *trikirion* until the words *Qui licet sit divisus in partes*, the church lights being then lit at the words *O vere beata nox*. A genuflection at each *Lumen Christi* was also added in the fourteenth century.[92] The custom of lighting two other large candles, a relic of the ancient Roman rite which preceded the adoption in the city of the Paschal Candle, was discontinued.[93]

In the course of time it became customary in many places outside Rome, including some religious communities, to add all sorts of additional information as well as the current year to the inscription on the candle. There is evidence from Poitiers in the ninth century that the year of the indiction (fifteen-year cycle) was included, and from the eleventh century it became customary to add the epact (age of the moon on 1st January).[94] Once the practice had begun there was no restraining it, and in many places a paper, known as the *charta*, was attached to the candle or its holder, containing a wealth of information concerning, *inter alia*, the (supposed) age of the universe, the solar and lunar cycles, the golden number, the liturgical calendar, the number of years from the Nativity and the Assumption of the Blessed Virgin, the names of the current pope, bishop, and ruler with their respective regnal years, the dates of important historical events, etc. The practice was especially popular in France, where exceptionally long *chartae* were in vogue (that of Rouen in 1678 contained no less than forty-eight dates, beginning with the 5,678th year from the creation of the world and ending with the 35th year of the reign of Louis XIV), and where in some places they survived into recent times.[95] But it was never adopted at Rome.

The Liturgical Colours

Durandus in his *Rationale divinorum officiorum*, written around 1290 says,

> White vestments should be used ... on Holy Saturday, at the Mass ... And it should be understood that for the whole of the rites which take place on Holy Saturday before the Mass, violet should be used, with a single exception; the deacon who blesses the candle and the assistant subdeacon should wear a white dalmatic and tunicle respectively, because this blessing, like the Mass, appertains to the Resurrection. But once the blessing of the candle is finished, the deacon removes his dalmatic and puts on a violet planeta, which he wears until the beginning of the Mass. The subdeacon however does not change his vestments.[96]

The same rubric, in virtually identical words, is contained in *Ordo Romanus* xiv, of about 1350.[97] With the exception of the provisions regarding the subdeacon the same rule has endured to this day. The ministers' violet vestments are changed for white ones in the sacristy during the singing of the second part of the litany (from *Peccatores, Te rogamus audi nos*).[98]

The Readings

The system of scriptural readings during the foremass, or Mass of the Catechumens, during the early Christian centuries followed that of the Jewish Synagogue, in which there were two readings, the first from the Law and the second from the Prophets, and a homily after either the first or second reading, with psalms and prayers in between.[99] The first Christians added a third reading, from one of the four Gospels, and frequently replaced either the reading from the Law or that from the Prophets, or both, with readings from the other books of the New Testament. These readings were followed by a psalm and prayer. This primitive pattern of reading, psalmody and prayer could still be discerned in the Masses for the Ember Saturdays in the Roman Missal in use down to 1970. The pattern persisted in the Roman rite during the first few centuries, but eventually the three readings were reduced on most days to two, including of course the Gospel. According to the *Liber Pontificalis* this reduction had already taken place before the time of Pope Celestine (422–432). Although this may be no more than guesswork on the part of the compiler, we can at least be sure that the change had taken place long enough before the relevant section of this work was compiled, around 540, for the date when it had actually occurred to have been forgotten.[100]

The primitive number of readings remained, however, on certain days, the Ember Wednesdays, the Wednesdays of the fourth week in Lent and of Holy Week, and on Good Friday, until the reform of 1970. On a few other days, by contrast, it was the practice to have more than two readings before the Gospel. For the Ember Saturdays the heading to the list of readings in the seventh-century *Comes* of Würzburg is 'Sabb. in XII lect.', which suggests an original number of twelve, though in the extant copy of this lectionary only six are given. For the Vigils of Easter and Pentecost the number varied according to the Gregorian, early Gelasian and later Gelasian traditions between five and thirteen. The readings for these vigils were chosen as prophetic of the institution of the New Covenant and of the Eucharist, of Resurrection and of the Baptism into new life which the neophytes were about to receive.

We have almost no information before the beginning of the fifth century as to the choice of readings at the Easter Vigil. The solitary exception is from the beginning of the sermon of Melito of

Sardis, probably belonging to the second half of the second century, 'The scripture from the Hebrew Exodus has been read, and the words of the mystery have been plainly stated, how the sheep is sacrificed, how the people is saved, and how Pharaoh is scourged through the mystery'.[101] The reference is plainly to the passage concerning the institution of the Passover in Exodus 12:1–11. The first complete selection of readings that has survived is the Jerusalem series contained in the Armenian Lectionary of the early fifth century. This contains twelve Old Testament readings, the first being the account of the creation of the world in Genesis 1:1–3:24 and the last the story of the three young men in the fiery furnace from Daniel 3:1–90. The first three and the fifth readings are taken from the Pentateuch and are in scriptural order, which means that, except for the insertion of Jonah 1:1–4:11 in the fourth place, they may well be part of the primitive series of the Jerusalem church. The remaining seven are not in scriptural order and have evidently undergone some rearrangement. The choice of Daniel 3 as the last reading is probably due to the desire to round off the whole series with the canticle *Benedictus es, Domine patrum nostrorum*. The readings were preceded by Psalm 117, with the antiphon 'This is the day which the Lord has made, let us exult and rejoice in it', and between each reading there was a psalm and a prayer, said kneeling.[102]

Between the Armenian Lectionary of Jerusalem and the earliest Roman documents there is a gap of some two hundred years which, in the present state of knowledge, it is impossible to fill. In seventh-century Rome it appears that the system of readings at the Paschal Vigil differed as between the papal and the presbyteral rites. The evidence of the Gregorian Sacramentary indicates that the former had four readings, from Genesis 1–2 (the creation of the world), Exodus 14 (the crossing of the Red Sea), Isaiah 4 (the judgement and restoration of Sion) and Isaiah 54–55 (God's covenant with his people). Exodus 14 and Isaiah 4 are followed by the canticles *Cantemus Domino* and *Vinea facta est* respectively. There is no introductory prayer. The first two readings correspond with two of those in the Jerusalem series, and all are followed by a Collect, as at Jerusalem. The first line of each reading is given in the sacramentary, and in two of the earliest manuscripts the text is taken not from the Vulgate of St Jerome but from the Old Latin translation which preceded it.[103]

By contrast to the Gregorian, the Old Gelasian Sacramentary has an introductory prayer and ten readings, including the four found in the Gregorian. Since there are no headings, as in the latter, it is not possible to tell whether the text of the readings was from the Old Latin or the Vulgate. The canticles which follow the readings from Exodus 14 and Isaiah 4 in the Gregorian are also found in the Old Gelasian.[104] So are the Collects, but the second is attached to a reading from Ezekiel 37 and there are significant differences in the wording of both.[105] The Frankish Gelasians of the eighth century have all the readings of the Old Gelasian plus a further two of their own, making a system of twelve Old Testament readings altogether. The number of Collects is made up to twelve by borrowing the two from the Gregorian not already employed in the Old Gelasian. The Old Gelasian had six readings in common with the Jerusalem series, including those four which it shares with the Gregorian, and the Frankish Gelasians had seven. In both series the final reading was the account of the preservation of the young men in the fiery furnace from Daniel 3.[106]

Antoine Chavasse has produced an ingenious explanation to account for the difference in the number of readings between the Gregorian and Gelasian traditions at Rome. He believed that the reduction in the pre-Gospel Mass readings from two to one took place at different times in different Roman churches. All churches however had six readings (excluding the Gospel) on Holy Saturday, with the result that in some churches there would have been four extra readings (as in the papal liturgy) and in others five. In addition some churches were bilingual; each reading, including those of the Mass, were read in both Greek and Latin, a practice which originated in the period of Byzantine influence at Rome between 550 and 750. This meant that the churches where there were five extra readings and one customary pre-Gospel reading, would have had ten extra and two customary readings, if we count the same reading in both Greek and Latin as being equivalent to two readings. The monolingual churches made up the total number by adding further readings in Latin, to take the place of those which in the bilingual churches were read in Greek. The Roman prototype of the Old Gelasian Sacramentary would have represented the combination of five extra readings and one customary reading, in a church that was monolingual. However there was no bilingualism in Gaul, and when the Gallican liturgy was Romanized it was not realized that the Roman system represented a codification of different local customs, with the result that it was misinterpreted as requiring twelve readings. In addition the customary pre-Gospel reading was erroneously omitted from the total, as a result of the gap in the liturgy created by the Blessing of the Font. The extra readings were accordingly fixed at twelve, with two further readings added to make up the number, together with two Collects taken from the Gregorian.

In support of his theory Chavasse invoked the evidence of the Roman lectionary known as the *Comes* of Würzburg relating to the system or readings on the Saturdays of the four Ember weeks. As noted above, they are headed 'Sabb. in XII lect.', though only six readings follow. Chavasse concluded from this that they were read in both Greek and Latin. On two of the days in question, there are four Old Testament and two New Testament readings, and on the remaining two there are five Old Testament and one New Testament readings. In the later Lectionary of Alcuin however there are five Old Testament readings and one New Testament reading on all four days. Chavasse argued that this reflected a gradual change from two customary readings plus four extra readings to one customary reading plus five extra ones. He also pointed to a comment by Amalarius of Metz that 'six readings were read in Greek and Latin by the Romans of old ... They are referred to as twelve readings because there are twelve lectors'. Finally he argued that by a careful analysis of the texts of the ten Collects in the Old Gelasian it was possible to show which were the original ones and which were additional, and that the latter were edited versions of texts found elsewhere in the Roman sacramentaries.[107]

Ingenious as this hypothesis is, it involves some serious difficulties. There appears to be no sound evidence for bilingualism outside the Easter Vigil and one or two other important feasts,[108] and then mainly in the papal liturgy (there is no mention of it, for example, in *Ordo Romanus* XXIV, which seems to be an adaptation of the papal liturgy for use by a bishop). Amalarius' statement that the Romans of old had a bilingual system of readings is pure speculation on his part, on a par in fact with his statement that Zosimus was the originator of the blessing of the Paschal Candle.[109]

But the main argument against Chavasse's hypothesis is the timing. There is no doubt that the bilingual readings belong to the period of Byzantine influence at Rome, between 550 and 750, but the question is at what precise point within that period were they introduced? It is true that Byzantine influence in the field of art began to be felt in Rome from about the middle of the sixth century, after the reconquest of most of Italy for the empire, but this alone would not have supplied a good reason for introducing readings in a language understood by very few Romans. The Roman liturgy did not go in for pointless liturgical innovations. The change must have taken place at a time when there was a significant number of people in the congregation who had no Latin, or at least not enough to be able to understand readings in that language. This can only have been after the iconoclastic emperor Leo II banned the use of images in 730 and instigated a fierce persecution of their supporters, an action that led to a large influx of Greek-speaking refugees to Rome. The pontificate of either Gregory III (731–741) or Zacharias (741–752), both popes of eastern origin, is the likely context for the introduction of the practice to Rome. But by this date the Old Gelasian system of readings was already well established.

Schmidt believed that the pre-Gregorian Paschal Vigil had six Old Testament readings, from Genesis 1, Genesis 22, Exodus 14, Deuteronomy 31, Isaiah 4 and Isaiah 54–5, to which a seventh, from Baruch 3, was later added (he believed by St Gregory himself). The readings were in scriptural order and the third, fourth and fifth were each followed by a canticle. This scheme of seven readings was then divided between the Paschal and the Pentecost Vigils (the latter being a later imitation of the former) though, in order to supply each vigil with four readings and two canticles Isaiah 4 was duplicated. This division produced the scheme of readings for the Easter and Pentecost Vigils which endured in the Roman Missal until the twentieth century.

In support of his theory Schmidt argued that the themes of the readings from Deuteronomy 31, Isaiah 4 and Baruch 3, all relate to Baptism and are appropriate at least as much to Easter as they are to Pentecost, and that the reading from Genesis 22 (the sacrifice of Abraham) is entirely appropriate to Easter but has little relevance to Pentecost. However, in some of the early liturgical books there is evidence of a desire to retain all three canticles at the Easter

Vigil: the author of the Romano-German Pontifical for instance adopts the papal system of four Old Testament readings for the Vigil but in order to retain all the canticles bizarrely attaches *Attende caelum*, the canticle of Moses from the end of Deuteronomy 31, to the end of the reading from Isaiah 54 (he also, equally bizarrely, attaches the canticle *Cantemus Domino* from the end of Exodus 14 to the end of the reading from Genesis 22 at Pentecost, thus providing, in his own curious way, for all three canticles at each of the vigils).[110]

Elsewhere the purpose was achieved, more logically, by reading Deuteronomy 31 with its canticle at Easter, either in substitution for or as well as Isaiah 54–5. In constructing his hypothesis Schmidt ignores the evidence from the Old Gelasian, since he believed that this sacramentary originated in Gaul and is therefore not relevant to his reconstruction of the Roman system. He also accepts readily that his reconstruction is highly speculative.[111]

If we look at the evidence from other Western rites, we find that the Mozarabic *Liber Comicus* and the Gallican Lectionary of Luxeuil, both of the seventh century, have a system of twelve readings, as at fifth-century Jerusalem.[112] Six of the Mozarabic readings are identical to those of Jerusalem. Unfortunately, owing to a gap in the manuscript of the Lectionary of Luxeuil, the first two readings have been lost, but the concordance of other lectionaries and the fact that the readings from the Pentateuch appear to be in scriptural order makes it almost certain that the first reading was the creation of the world from Genesis 1. If so, then Jerusalem, Spain and Gaul all have a twelve-reading system with six readings common to all three. Moreover the first, and more significantly the last, of these common readings are the same in all three cases. Genesis 1 is perhaps a natural choice for the first reading, but Daniel 3 is not so for the last. The Old Gelasian has only ten readings, but again six of these are identical to those in the other three systems and the first and last readings are the same. The Frankish Gelasians and the contemporary *Comes* of Murbach and *Comes* Theotinchi have a twelve-reading system, adding to the ten from the Old Gelasian Jonah 1–3 from the Gallican and Deuteronomy 31 from the Gregorian tradition, and preserving Daniel 3 in the final place.[113] The interdependence of all these systems, as against the four-reading Gregorian tradition, seems inescapable.

Our most detailed source for the rite surrounding the reading of the prophecies, as they came to be known later, in eighth-century Rome is the Appendix to *Ordo Romanus* XXVIII, which dates from shortly before the end of that century. The pope, preceded by the two great candles, goes up to the altar and prays silently. Then he takes his seat, and a subdeacon goes up into the ambo and begins the first reading, from Genesis 1, in Greek; he is followed by another subdeacon, who reads it in Latin. The pontiff rises and says *Oremus*, and the deacon follows him with *Flectamus genua* and *Levate*. The pope then recites the Collect. The same procedure is followed for each of the four readings, including the canticles after Exodus 14 and Isaiah 4. The final reading is that from Deuteronomy 31.[114]

When the Roman liturgy was reformed, around the year 1000, under the influence of the Romano-German Pontifical, it was, perhaps surprisingly, not the Gregorian system of four Old Testament readings which was adopted but the Frankish Gelasian system of twelve such readings.[115] This became the standard for almost a thousand years, until the 1955 reform during the pontificate of Pius XII restored the Gregorian four-reading system.

Once established, the tradition in the Roman liturgy of repeating the readings in Greek persisted for a long time. The Roman Pontifical of the Twelfth Century still indicates that at Rome there are twenty-four readings, twelve in each language, as does *Ordo Romanus* xi of the same century.[116] But the approximately contemporary *Ordo* x specifies that they are to be read in both languages only if the pope so wishes, as do the thirteenth-century Pontifical of the Roman Curia, the Ordinary of the Papal Chaplains and the Roman Missal of the same century. So too does *Ordo Romanus* xiv of about 1350.[117] But there is no mention of bilingualism in *Ordo* xv of around 1392, or in any subsequent documents. It seems therefore that it became increasingly rare in the later Middle Ages and died out altogether in the second half of the fourteenth century.

Until 1970 the readings were always proclaimed without any title at the beginning. The authorities are unanimous on this point.[118] According to Sicardus and Durandus this was done either because Christ our head has not yet been restored to us, or because those who are to be baptized are still in ignorance of the scriptures. Honorius on the other hand says that it is because the neophytes have not yet received the sign of the Kingdom of God on their foreheads, The true reason of course is simply that it reflects the ancient practice, preserved at the Easter Vigil by the operation of Baumstark's Law.[119]

Outside Rome, the number of readings at the Vigil was subject to some variation. The Pontifical of Poitiers of about 900 prescribes the regular four readings for those who follow the Gregorian system and twelve for those who follow the Gelasian. Some other churches, however, in France had five or six.[120] Outside Rome, Sicardus tells us that in some churches there were as many as twenty-four (i.e. those where a bilingual system obtained), in others only six. Durandus says that there were four in some churches, and six, twelve or fourteen in others.[121] In the tenth-eleventh centuries Pseudo-Alcuin, Farfa and Cluny all still followed the Gregorian system of four readings, and four is also the number found in the Sarum Rite in England, as in the Gregorian system but substituting Deuteronomy 31, with its canticle, for Isaiah 54–5.[122]

The Litanies

The most ancient known practice, found in the Old Gelasian Sacramentary and in the Frankish Gelasians of the eighth century, as well as in the Romano-German Pontifical, was for the reading of the lessons to conclude with the Tract *Sicut cervus* (Psalm 41:2–4) and the prayer *Omnipotens sempiterne Deus, respice propitius ad devotionem populi renascentis*. During the procession to the baptistery which followed a litany was sung. After the blessing of the font another litany was sung during the return procession.[123] But according to some of the later Roman medieval documents, the procession to the baptistery takes place immediately after the conclusion of the readings. *Sicut cervus* is sung by the schola, which heads the procession; they are followed by the subdeacons singing or reciting a litany (presumably in a low tone) and finally by the pope and the cardinal deacons. The prayer *Omnipotens sempiterne Deus, respice propitius* is said on arrival at the baptistery.[124]

The Roman rite in the first printed Missal of 1474 and the 1570 Missal of Pius V was similar to that in the later Roman medieval documents. After the end of the readings *Sicut cervus* was sung during the procession to the baptistery and the prayer *Omnipotens sempiterne Deus respice propitius* was recited on arrival at the entrance. The litany was not begun until after the procession had returned to the altar.[125]

As a form of prayer the litany appears to have been of eastern origin. It seems to have been incorporated into the Roman Mass by Pope Gelasius I (492–496), who inserted a litany consisting of eighteen petitions, to which the people responded with *Kyrie eleison,* after the Introit. Somewhat later this litany seems to have been restricted to feast days only, and subsequently it went out of use altogether, surviving in the ordinary Mass liturgy only in the recitation of the vestigial *Kyrie* at this point.[126] But, thanks to the operation of Baumstark's Law, the litany survived as part of the Easter Vigil liturgy, as well as on certain other days in the year, such as the feast of St Mark (25 April), the Rogation Days and at ordinations to the priesthood.

In the rite according to the Old Gelasian Sacramentary a litany is sung at the very beginning of the Vigil: 'The clergy begin a litany, and the priest proceeds from the sacristy with the sacred ministers. When they reach the altar they stand there with bowed head until they say *Agnus Dei, qui tollis peccata mundi, miserere'*.[127] After the conclusion of the readings, a litany accompanies the procession to the font: 'Then they proceed, with a litany, to the font for the baptisms'.[128] When the baptisms are over 'the priest returns with all the ministers to the sacristy, and after a short while they begin a third liturgy'.[129] In the eighth century Frankish Sacramentary of Angoulême these rubrics are repeated virtually word for word, except that two separate litanies are mentioned after the baptisms.[130] Both these sacramentaries contain a rubric to the effect that the number of the litanies should conform to that of the Blessed Trinity, which seems to mean that they should be threefold, i.e that each invocation should be repeated three times.[131]

Neither the Old Gelasian nor the Frankish Gelasians supply any text for the litanies, with the exception of the Sacramentary of Autun, in which, after a threefold *Christe audi nos* and *Sancta Maria ora pro nobis* there are sixty-two invocations of archangels, angels, apostles, evangelists, martyrs and confessors, followed by eleven female saints. The litany continues with nine petitions, with the response *parce nobis Domine, libera nos Domine* or *te rogamus audi nos*, and concludes with *Agnus Dei qui tollis peccata mundi miserere nobis*, a threefold *Christe audi nos* and the *Kyrie eleison*.[132] The litany in the ninth century Pontifical of Poitiers contains invocations of fifty-two saints, of whom around twenty appear to be local, and fourteen petitions, including to 'preserve the Frankish army' and to 'grant them life, health and victory'.[133] The litanies sung in other places are likely to have been substantially the same, with some variations naturally to take into account local saints. These sometimes extended to very large numbers; the litanies sung in the Frankish Empire during the reign of Louis the Pious, for example, contained no less than 532 saints.[134]

There is no reference in the Gregorian Sacramentary to any litanies, and for our knowledge of them in the papal liturgy of the Vigil we depend on the eighth century *Ordines Romani*, in particular *Ordo* XXIII and *Ordo* XXXB. There is no entrance litany and, since this is the papal liturgy, no blessing of the Paschal Candle. The two *regionarii* light their two great candles from the fire reserved from Good Friday and the readings begin at once. After they are finished the schola proceeds to the entrance portico of the Lateran baptistery where they sing a threefold litany. At the *Agnus Dei* the pope enters the baptistery with his deacons, the two large candles borne before him, and the blessing of the font and baptisms take place. After the baptisms a sevenfold litany is sung, followed, when the pope gives the signal, by a threefold litany while the sacred ministers are vesting for the Mass. At the *Agnus Dei* the pope and the deacons, preceded by the two great candles, emerge from the sacristy and stand before the altar with heads bowed until the litany ends with the *Kyrie eleison*, whereupon the Vigil Mass begins.[135]

In *Ordo* XXIV, which probably represents an adaptation of the papal ceremonies for use in other Roman churches or dioceses of central Italy, there is no entrance litany. Before the blessing of the font and the baptisms the schola, accompanied by the sub-choir-master carrying a gold vessel containing the chrism to be mixed with the baptismal water, sings a threefold liturgy. *Ordo* XXVII adds that they continue singing the *Agnus Dei* until the bishop nods to them to be silent. After the baptisms they sing a sevenfold, fivefold and threefold litany before the altar. When they reach the final *Agnus Dei* the choirmaster says *Accendite* and the church lights are immediately lit. The bishop comes from the sacristy, preceded by two candle bearers, and at the conclusion of the litany he intones the *Gloria* of the Mass.[136]

The rite in the Romano-German Pontifical is similar to that in *Ordo* XXIV, except that the litany sung at the font by the schola is a sevenfold one, and after it the clergy and people proceed from the church to the font, while a fivefold litany is sung. After the baptisms they begin a threefold litany and the bells are rung for the Mass. When they reach *Agnus Dei*, the choirmaster says in a loud voice *Accendite*, whereupon the candles held by the newly baptized are lit, and the whole church is illuminated. *Christe audi nos* and *Kyrie eleison* are repeated while the ministers proceed from the sacristy to begin the Mass. The celebrant is preceded all the time by two candle bearers.

The method of singing a multiple litany is described in detail in the *Ordo Ecclesiae Lateranensis*. During the readings the senior subdeacon with six other ministers goes to the font. He begins a sevenfold litany by singing *Christe audi nos* and this is repeated by each of the other six in turn. Each petition is sung in the same manner. When this sevenfold litany is finished two of the ministers depart and a fivefold litany is sung in the same way, after which two more ministers leave and the remaining three sing a threefold litany. These litanies can be extended or shortened as the occasion requires.[137] A different method is prescribed in the *Decreta* of Lanfranc: after the conclusion of the readings there is a threefold litany; two cantors intone *Kyrie eleison*, which is repeated first by those of the monks on the right hand side of the choir and then by those on the left, and so on throughout the litany.[138] In the Sarum Missal seven choristers sing a sevenfold litany of the saints; this is followed immediately by a fivefold litany of the saints sung by five deacons, while the procession goes to bless the font. During the return from the font three senior clerics sing a litany comprising ten petitions cast in a trochaic metre of eight feet, commencing *Rex sanctorum angelorum totum mundum adiuva*, which is repeated by the choir after each subsequent petition.[139]

In the Roman Pontifical of the Twelfth Century and in that of the Roman Curia seven subdeacons proceed to the font during the readings, and there sing a sevenfold, fivefold and threefold litany. According to the former, these litanies are omitted if there are no baptisms, a threefold litany being substituted instead, immediately after which the Mass begins.[140] In the Pontifical of Durandus, however, we find a variant practice. After the reading of the lessons comes the *Sicut cervus* and the prayer which follows it, in the accustomed way. Then two cantors begin the litany before the altar of Saint Privatus, patron of Mende (of which Durandus was bishop). When they reach *Sancte Private, ora pro nobis* they return to the sanctuary with cross, candles and thurible, and then continue the litany as far as *Propitius esto*, at which point they break it off while the font is blessed. Upon the return of the procession to the sanctuary they resume the litany at the point where they broke it off, and continue it to the end.[141]

In the first printed missal of 1474 there are no litanies before the blessing of the font, but following the return procession to the altar (or immediately after the readings if there is no blessing) two cantors in the centre of the choir begin a litany containing, in addition to invocations of the Trinity and the Blessed Virgin, twenty-two saints and twenty-four petitions. It is a double litany; each invocation or petition and the response is first sung by the cantors in the centre of the choir and then repeated in full by both sides of the choir simultaneously.[142] The litany continued in the sanctuary down to the *Kyrie* with which the Mass commenced. With only minor changes this passed into the Missal of Pius V and thus became the standard practice in the Roman rite down to 1955.

The Blessing of the Baptismal Waters

The blessing of the baptismal waters (or blessing of the font as it is usually, though not altogether correctly, known), and the baptisms which followed, originally took place not in the cathedral or church where the Vigil was being held but in an adjacent baptistery. With the extension of the baptismal rite from the Easter and Pentecost Vigils to other times of the year, and the growing preponderance of infant over adult baptisms which followed the spread of Christianity, the number of baptisms taking place at the Easter Vigil declined to the point where they ceased altogether, and the blessing of the water assumed the character of an annual general blessing of baptismal water rather than that of a specific blessing of the water to be used in baptisms which followed immediately.

As mentioned above, the rite begins with the singing of Psalm

41 (*Sicut cervus*) either in full or simply verses 2–4, followed by the prayer *Respice propitius*

> Almighty and Eternal God, look with loving kindness upon the devotion of those in process of rebirth who, like the deer, seek the fount of Thy waters, and grant in Thy mercy that their thirst for faith may through the mystery of baptism sanctify them in both soul and body.[143]

The blessing then follows by means of a lengthy prayer first recorded in the Old Gelasian Sacramentary. With only minor variations in wording it also appears in the Gregorian Sacramentary. It begins with a brief introductory prayer (*Omnipotens sempiterne Deus*), followed by the prayer of blessing proper, beginning *Deus qui invisibili potentia* and ending *qui venturus est iudicare vivos et mortuos et saecula per ignem*.

Originally this prayer of blessing was not cast in the form of a Preface. The Eucharistic Dialogue and *Vere dignum et iustum est* is not found in either the Old Gelasian or in the earliest *Ordines Romani*. It first appears in the so-called Sacramentary of Reichenau of about 800 from northern Switzerland and in *Ordo XXVIIIA* (which adds *Dominus vobiscum, Et cum spiritu tuo*), composed at Wissembourg in Alsace at around the same time.[144] It does not occur in the oldest surviving manuscript of the Gregorian Sacramentary, written in 811/812, nor in a somewhat later manuscript of 867–872, but it is found in a third such manuscript of the third quarter of the same century, all of them from Gaul.[145] It seems therefore to have been a Gallican innovation of the late eighth or early ninth century which was adopted over a period of time. Some manuscripts of the Romano-German Pontifical (mainly those of Group β) have it and some (those of Group α) do not.[146] From the former group it was copied into the Roman Pontifical of the Twelfth Century and its successors, remaining a feature of the Roman rite until 1970.[147]

Notwithstanding this remarkable consistency over a very long period of time, the prayer shows signs of amendment and editing prior to its first recorded appearance in the Old Gelasian.[148] The first section, down to *perfectae purgationis indulgentiam consequantur*, is addressed to God the Father, and takes the form of a petition for the sanctification of the water, quoting two paradigms from Genesis, namely the Spirit of God brooding over the waters and the story of the Flood. It may once have contained more, suppressed to avoid duplication when the next section of the prayer was added. Whether this is so or not, the language at this point clearly goes back to that of a fourth century blessing quoted by St Optatus and the blessing in the Leonine Sacramentary of the fifth to sixth century.[149] This first section concludes with an exorcism, the language of which suggests that it may be derived in part from a pre-Christian apotropaic formula, suitably adapted.[150]

The next section, beginning *Unde benedico te* and ending *in nomine Patris et Filii et Spiritus Sancti*, contains the blessing proper, first in the name of the Father, quoting five Old Testament paradigms, then in the name of the Son, mentioning five from the New Testament. This section began life as an exorcism (a role which it continued to play in the blessing of water outside the Easter and Pentecost Vigils); it was adapted for its present purpose by changing the word *exorcizo* to *benedico*. As is common in exorcisms, the subject of the exorcism, in this case the baptismal water, is addressed directly.

The third section is in effect an epiklesis; after a brief introductory prayer in a reading tone (*Haec nobis praecepta servantibus*), the celebrant prays in the preface tone that the power of the Holy Spirit may descend upon the font and make fruitful the entire substance of the water it contains 'so that every man entering upon this sacrament of regeneration may be born again in a true innocence and a new infancy'.

The only rubrics given in the Old Gelasian are for a gesture towards the water at the words *Unde benedico te, creatura aquae* and for a change of tone at *Haec nobis praecepta*. It seems likely however that the Paschal Candle was dipped into the water at the words *luminis admixtione*. This phrase was later changed to *numinis admixtione*, and the change probably came about as the result of a transfer in the point at which the candle was so dipped from here to the epiklesis. The Gregorian Sacramentary also reads *luminis admixtione*, adding a direction to breathe three times on the water at the words *Descendat in hanc plenitudinem fontis*.[151] In *Ordines* XXIII and XXXB the two large candles of the papal rite are dipped into the water at the latter point, though there is no mention of any breathing on the water; after the blessing the pope scatters the newly blessed water over the people.[152] According to *Ordines* XXIV, XXVII, XXVIII and XXXI the celebrant is to divide the water with his hand in the form of a cross three times at the words *qui hanc aquam, unde benedico te* and *benedico te per Iesum Christum* respectively.[153]

All the gestures found in the *Ordines Romani* are faithfully reproduced in all the manuscripts of the Romano-German Pontifical; those of Group β add that the water should also be divided into four parts at the words *et in quattuor fluminibus totam terram rigare praecepit,* and that the celebrant should breathe three times on the water at the words *Descendat in hanc plenitudinem fontis* in the form of the Greek letter ψ.[154] Since both *Ordines* XXVIIIA and XXXI also have this triple insufflation, but simply in the form of a cross,[155] it seems clear that the rubric in the Romano-German Pontifical is simply a misunderstanding of this prescription, though an attempt was later made to rationalize it as representing the initial letter of the word ψυχη.[156] The error was in any case perpetuated and remained a feature of the Roman rite until 1970.

In some places it seems that it was the custom for those awaiting baptism to dip their unlit candles in the font. According to Amalarius this was done at the words *Descendat in hanc plenitudinem fontis.*[157] The custom is also recorded in the Pontifical of Poitiers, but at the words *Qui hanc aquam regenerandis hominibus;* it adds that they are held in the water by an acolyte until the blessing of the font is finished.[158] There is no trace of the practice at Rome.

The text and rubrics of the blessing found in the manuscripts of Group β of the Romano-German Pontifical endured in the Roman rite for over a thousand years, until the reform of 1970. The only additions were a direction to the celebrant to touch the water with his hand at the words *Sit haec sancta,* a preliminary triple insufflation at the words *Tu has simplices aquas* (taken from the Pontifical of Durandus), a triple rather than a single dipping of the Paschal Candle at *Descendat in hanc plenitudinem fontis,* and a direction to scatter the water to the four points of the compass after its division at *Qui de te paradisi fonte manare fecit* (also from the Pontifical of Durandus).[159]

The admixture of chrism with the baptismal water after the conclusion of the blessing is first recorded in *Ordo Romanus* XI, from the end of the sixth or beginning of the seventh century. The rite is very simple, and appears to take place in silence:

When all this is finished, he pours chrism from a gold vessel upon the water in the fonts in the shape of a cross. And he mixes the said chrism and the water with his hand and sprinkles it over each font and the people present. All those who wish may take some of the blessed water in their own receptacles, before the children are baptised, for sprinkling in their house or vineyards or fields or orchards.[160]

St Leo too mentions, in a sermon preached around the year 850, the custom of allowing those present to take away some of the water in their own vessels after it has been blessed.[161]

This simple rite is repeated in similar terms in most of the later eighth- and ninth-century Romano-Gallican ordines, and in the Frankish Gelasian sacramentaries. It appears also in the Bobbio Missal, the *Missale Gothicum* and the *Missale Gallicanum Vetus*, all of Gallican provenance.[162] In *Ordo* XXXB the chrism is mixed with other holy oil (presumably that of the Catechumens).[163] The complete absence of the rite of admixture from the Roman sacramentaries and from *Ordo* XXIII, where the blessing of the water concludes with a simple sprinkling of the people, suggests that it is Gallican in origin, and did not reach Rome until the end of the tenth century, under the influence of the Romano-German Pontifical.[164] In the latter the rite is somewhat elaborated:

a subdeacon, taking the gold vessel from which the chrism is to be poured into the font, and pouring into it oil from both flagons, that is some of the holy oil and of the chrism, hands it to the deacon who passes it to the bishop. The latter pours the chrism from the gold vessel over the water in the form of a cross, saying in a low voice 'May this font be rendered holy and fruitful for those reborn from it into eternal life'. And with the gold vessel he mixes the chrism with the water and sprinkles it with his hand throughout the font, and over all the people standing around. Afterwards all who wish may receive the blessing from the same water, each one in his own container, before the baptism of the children, to sprinkle in their homes, their vineyards, their fields and their crops.[165]

The custom of sprinkling the blessed water over the people and allowing them to take some of it away is not found in the Pontifical of the Twelfth Century or in that of the Roman Curia, nor is it mentioned in any of the later medieval *Ordines Romani*. In the 1571 Missal of Pius V however the sprinkling takes place immediately after the blessing of the water and before the admixture of the holy oils. This remained its place until 1952, when it was transferred to form a conclusion to the new rite of the renewal of baptismal promises.

The ceremony of mixing the chrism with the water is, according to the Pontifical of Durandus, omitted in some churches when there are to be no baptisms.[166] The admixture is prescribed however without qualification in both the Pontifical of the Twelfth Century and in that of the Roman Curia, though in both of these it is followed by an order of baptism.[167] It became a standard feature of the Roman rite, even after the conferral of baptism at the Easter Vigil died out altogether, until the reform of 1970 abolished it altogether.

The Baptisms

It is impossible, within the scope of the present survey, to do justice to the development of the Roman baptismal rite itself over a period of two millennia.[168] All we can do is give a succinct account of the rite as it appears in its developed form in the Roman Pontifical of the Twelfth Century (the rite in the Pontifical of the Roman Curia is similar).

While the godparent holds the child, the minister asks *Quis vocaris?* and the godparent replies with the child's baptismal name. The minister, addressing the child by name, proceeds to question him: *N., credis in Deum patrem omnipotentem, creatorem coeli et terrae?, Credis et in Jesum Christum filium eius unicum dominum nostrum natum et passum?, Credis et in spiritum sanctum, sanctam catholicam ecclesiam, sanctorum communionem, remissionem peccatorum, carnis resurrectionem, vitam aeternam?* To each question the answer is *Credo.* He then ask *Vis baptizari?*, to which the answer is *Volo.* Then each one is baptized with a triple immersion, in the following manner: *Et ego baptizo te in nomine patris* (first immersion), *Et filii* (second immersion), *Et spiritus sancti* (third immersion), *ut habeas vitam aeternam. Amen.* At the Lateran, the pontiff baptizes one or two or three of the children, as he chooses, and the remainder are baptized by a priest or deacon.

After the baptism the godparent presents the child to the bishop or to a priest, who makes the sign of the cross in chrism with his right thumb on the child's forehead saying, *Pax tecum. Et cum spiritu tuo. Deus omnipotens, pater domini nostri Jesu Christi, qui te regeneravit ex aqua et spiritu sancto, quique dedit tibi remissionem omnium peccatorum, ipse te linit chrismate salutis in Christo Jesu domino nostro, in vitam aeternam.* Reply, *Amen.* After this he puts a white gown on the child saying, *Accipe vestem sanctam candidam et immaculatam, quam perferas ante tribunal domini nostri Jesu Christi, ut habeas vitam aeternam. Amen.* He then gives him a candle saying, *Accipe lampadem irreprehensibilem, custodi baptismum tuum, ut, cum dominus venerit ad nuptias, possis occurrere ei in aula coelesti. Amen.*

If the bishop is present, he confirms the candidates, by placing his hand on their heads one by one, and praying for the sevenfold grace of the Holy Spirit, saying,

> *Spiritus sanctus super vos descendat et virtus altissimi sine peccato vos custodiat. Amen. Dominus vobiscum.* Reply, *Et cum spiritu tuo. Omnipotens sempiterne Deus qui regenerare dignatus es hos famulos tuos et famulas ex aqua et spiritu sancto, quique dedisti eis remissionem omnium peccatorum, emitte in eos septiformem spiritum tuum, sanctum paraclitum de coelis.* Reply, *Amen. Spiritum sapientiae et intellectus.* Reply, *Amen. Spiritum consilii et fortitudinis.* Reply, *Amen. Spiritum scientiae et pietatis.* Reply *Amen. Adimple eos spiritu timoris tui et consigna eos signo crucis Christi in vitam propitiatus aeternam Per dominum nostrum ... in unitate spiritus sancti ...*

He then dips his finger in the chrism and, after asking each one his name, makes the sign of the cross on his forehead, saying *N. signo te signo crucis, confirmo te chrismate salutis, in nomine patris et filii et spiritus sancti. Amen. Pax tecum.* Reply, *Et cum spiritu tuo.* After all have been anointed he gives them a blessing, saying,

> *Ecce sic benedicetur omnis homo qui timet dominum. Benedicat vos dominus ex Sion, ut videatis bona Jerusalem omnibus diebus vitae vestrae. Gloria patri ... Pax vobis.* Reply, *Et cum spiritu tuo. Deus qui apostolis tuis sanctum dedisti spiritum et per eos eorumque successores ceteris fidelibus tradendum esse voluisti, respice propitius ad humilitatis nostrae famulatum et praesta ut horum corda, quorum frontes sacro chrismate delinivimus et signo crucis designavimus, idem spiritus sanctus adveniens templum gloriae suae dignanter inhabitando perficiat. Qui cum Deo patre et eodem spiritu sancto vivis et regnas Deus, per ...*

Finally he makes the sign of the cross over them saying *Benedicat vos pater et filius et spiritus sanctus. Amen.*[169]

The Mass

Mass did not always begin as soon as the baptisms were over. The rubric in the Old Gelasian instructs the celebrant and sacred ministers to return to the sacristy where they are to begin a third litany, re-entering the church to start the Mass only when the first stars appear in the sky.[170] Since by this time, in contrast to the ancient practice, the Vigil began at around half past two in the afternoon, the gap could have been quite a long one.[171] We are not told whether the congregation remained in church during the interval or went home for a rest. The Old Gelasian rubric is repeated word for word in the eighth-century Sacramentary of Gellone, which also prescribes the same starting time for the Vigil, and the same practice is found in *Ordo Romanus* XVII, written for a monastic community around 790–800.[172] In the latter case, since the Vigil begins in the afternoon at the ninth hour and there is no blessing of the font or baptisms, the interval must have been a long one. There is a similar provision in *Ordines Romani* XXXA, which is also monastic, and XXXII, which relates to the rite cele-brated in an ordinary church.[173] In the latter case the interval is filled either with the recitation of Vespers or the singing of three litanies, sevenfold, fivefold and threefold. According to the Romano-German Pontifical the monastic practice is to sing Vespers at this point, after which there is a *modicum intervallum* until the first star appears and Mass can begin, though in the cathedral rite Mass begins at once without any such interval.[174]

The Pontifical of Poitiers supplies a reason for deferring the beginning of Mass until the appearance of the stars, for which it claims apostolic authority; it is so that the people should not have to leave the church before midnight, since the Second Coming would occur on this night at this time.[175] Since apostolic authority for the practice is also invoked by St Jerome in the fourth century, it may be genuine, and is at least very early.[176] The Romano-German Pontifical also says that the people should not be dismissed before midnight, though without giving any reason for it, other than *canonum sanctiones*.[177] But in none of the eighth-century Gelasian sacramentaries besides that of Gellone, nor in the other *Ordines Romani*, is any such interval prescribed; in these Mass begins immediately after the baptisms are finished, as it does in the papal liturgy at the Lateran, where after the pope has confirmed the newly baptized and a second and third litany have been sung, he intones the *Gloria* of the Mass.[178]

In the Romano-Gallican *Ordo Romanus* XXIV, and those other ordines which are derivative upon it, when the *Agnus Dei* of the final litany is reached the choirmaster announces *Accendite* and the church lights are immediately lit for the start of Mass. A similar rubric occurs in the Pontifical of Poitiers, the Romano-German Pontifical and in the Pontifical of Durandus.[179]

The *Kyrie* which concludes the last repetition of the litanies also doubles as the opening *Kyrie* of the Mass. There is no Introit.[180] The *Kyrie* is followed by the *Gloria*, during which the bells are rung, for joy at the Resurrection of the Lord. The first mention we have of this custom appears to be in *Ordo Romanus* XXXI, from northern France in the second half of the ninth century.[181] Thereafter we find it in the *Regularis Concordia* from tenth century England, in the *Disciplina* of the Monastery of Farfa and St Paul's in Rome of around the year 1000, and in the *Consuetudines* of Cluny of about 1060. It is also mentioned by John of Avranches, the contemporary Archbishop of Rouen.[182] However, there is no reference to it either in the Romano-German Pontifical (where the bells are rung for the beginning of Mass) or in any of the Roman Pontificals prior to that of Durandus, towards the end of the thirteenth century. Thereafter it is prescribed for the first time in the papal liturgy in *Ordo Romanus* xv of about 1392.[183]

The *Gloria* itself originally belonged only to a Pontifical Mass; it was not sung at any Mass celebrated by an ordinary priest. The only exception to this was at the Easter Vigil Mass, when the presiding priests in the Roman *tituli* had the right to sing the *Gloria* and to sit in the episcopal chair.[184] This rule is confirmed by a rubric in the Gregorian Sacramentary, which reads, 'The *Gloria in excelsis Deo* is said on Sundays and feast days only, whenever the bishop is present, but it is never to be said by priests, except only at Easter'.[185] According to the same *Ordo* each of the titular priests then dispatched his mansionarius to the Lateran, whence he returned after the *fractio* with a portion of one of the hosts consecrated by the pope, which the celebrant then placed in his own chalice, a survival of the rite of the *fermentum* which was at one time a feature of the liturgy of the city every Sunday of the year.[186]

Prior to its modernization in the reforms of 1970 the Easter Vigil Mass presented a number of very ancient features. As well as the absence of any Introit, there was no Creed, no Offertory verse, no kiss of peace, no *Agnus Dei* and no Communion verse.[187] Incense was carried as normal at the Gospel but no lights. The medieval commentators supplied allegorical interpretations for these omissions; Durandus, for example, tells us that the absence of lights at the Gospel signifies that Christ has not yet risen but still lies in the tomb, and the omission of the Creed indicates the uncertainty of weak minds.[188] The real reason is once again the operation of Baumstark's Law. Almost all the features which were omitted in the Easter Vigil Mass had been adopted into the Roman Mass from outside sources in the period between the late fourth century and the twelfth century.[189] What survived in the Easter Vigil liturgy prior to 1970, therefore, represented, at least externally, the form of Mass as it was celebrated in Rome around the middle of the fourth century, modified only by a few later additions such as the prayers said silently by the celebrant at the Offertory and before his communion, and, until 1955, the Last Gospel.[190]

The Epistle for the Mass according to the earliest lectionaries is St Paul's letter to the Colossians 3:1–4.[191] The Gospel similarly is Matthew 28:1–7.[192] These remained the readings at the Easter Vigil Mass until the reform of 1970. Likewise the verse (Psalm 117:1) and tract (Psalm 116:1–2) sung between the Epistle and the Gospel is that found in the earliest antiphonaries.[193] The Old Gelasian Sacramentary gives two Collects and two Secret prayers; one of each of these (*Deus qui hanc sacratissimam noctem* and *Suscipe, quaesumus, Domini preces populi tui*) is also found in the earliest Gregorian sacramentaries.[194] Two alternative Postcommunion prayers are given in the Old Gelasian, and a single, different, one (*Spiritum nobis, Domine, tuae caritatis*) in the Gregorian.[195] Of these Gregorian prayers, which became standard in the Roman rite, only the Collect survived the 1970 reform.

The reading of the Epistle is immediately followed by the singing of *Alleluia*, for the first time since the eve of Septuagesima. The Roman Pontifical of the Twelfth Century prescribes that this should first be sung by the celebrant *nobiliter*, then repeated twice by the choir.[196] The Ordinary of the Papal Chaplains and the Roman Missal of the Thirteenth Century contain an elaborate rite; the primicerius says to the pope in a low voice 'I proclaim to you a new song, Alleluia', and kisses his foot, the pope then sings the

Alleluia, and the primicerius repeats the procedure twice. Each time the pope sings the Alleluia in a higher voice, joined at each repeat by his assistants. Finally the primicerius sings the Alleluia once again and begins the verse *Confitemini* which is taken up by the choir.[197] This practice however seems to have been confined to the papal chapel. Durandus in his pontifical simply says that the Alleluia should be sung by the bishop, followed by the choir, three times, each time in a higher key; after the verse *Confitemini* and before the Tract *Laudate Dominum* it is sung again by everyone present.[198] With the exception of the congregational repeat, this is the custom which finally became established and was perpetuated in the Missal of Pius V.

The Old Gelasian contains two Prefaces, presumably at the option of the celebrant. The second of the two (*Te quidem omni tempore sed in hac potissimum nocte gloriosius praedicare*) is abbreviated in the Gregorian Sacramentary by omitting the words *Propterea profusis paschalibus gaudiis totus in orbe terrarum mundus exultat*.[199] The Preface in the Sacramentary of Fulda, from the tenth century, which is also found in a number of Gregorian sacramentaries of the period, appears to be a blend of the two Old Gelasian prefaces, and that in the contemporary Sacramentary of St Eligius from the abbey of Corbie is a shortened version of the same Preface.[200] But it was the Preface from the Gregorian Sacramentary which prevailed and became via the Missal of Pius V the standard Preface for the Mass until the 1970 reform.

The Canon contains two embolisms: *Communicantes, et noctem sacratissimam celebrantes resurrectionis Domini nostri Jesu Christi secundum carnem, sed et memoriam venerantes . . .* and

> *Hanc igitur oblationem servitutis nostrae sed et cunctae familiae tuae, quam tibi offerimus pro his quoque quos regenerare dignatus es ex aqua et Spiritu sancto, tribuens eis remissionem omnium peccatorum, ut invenires eos in Christo Jesu Domino nostro, quaesumus, Domine, ut placatus accipias. Pro quibus maiestati tuae supplices fundimus preces, ut nomina eorum ascribi iubeas in libro viventium, diesque nostros . . .*[201]

Some of the Frankish Gelasian sacramentaries also have a blessing of the lamb after the *Nobis quoque peccatoribus*.[202] The Gregorian Sacramentary has the same two embolisms, but shortens the second by omitting the words between *ut invenires* and *nostro*, and between *Pro quibus* and *viventium*. Some of the Frankish

Gelasians, as well as all the subsequent Gregorian books, follow the Gregorian version, which became the standard one.[203]

The practice of singing an abbreviated form of the First Vespers of Easter Day after the distribution of Holy Communion is not primitive. It appears to have originated in Gaul towards the end of the ninth century. *Ordo Romanus* XXIX, composed about 870 probably at the abbey of Corbie, prescribes the singing of Vespers between the end of the baptisms and the beginning of Mass. In the approximately contemporary *Ordo* XXXI, also from north-eastern France, they are sung during the Communion.[204] In neither of these documents is the precise form of Vespers indicated, though in the former the *Magnificat* antiphon is given as *Vespere autem sabbati* and in the latter they are described as *vespertinalibus hymnis vel laudibus quae cum alleluia cantantur*, so in the latter case at least the First Vespers of Easter Day are clearly intended.[205] But in one of the two surviving manuscripts of *Ordo* XXXII, of around 900 from the same area, the abbreviated form of Vespers familiar from the pre-1955 rite, namely Psalm 116 with the antiphon *Alleluia* followed by the *Magnificat* with its antiphon, is sung after the distribution of communion, which takes place in silence. The Postcommunion prayer of the Mass doubles as the concluding prayer of Vespers.[206] In the Romano-German Pontifical we find exactly this form of Vespers, but sung during communion, as in *Ordo* XXXI. In the same document however it is stated that this is not the practice at Rome, where no Vespers are sung either before or after the Mass.[207]

The Timing of the Vigil

As mentioned above, it was already the practice at the time of the Old Gelasian Sacramentary (seventh to eighth century) for the Vigil to begin in the early afternoon. The tendency continually to advance the starting time is confirmed by our other documents. In *Ordo Romanus* XVI, from the eighth century, it is given as the ninth hour, or around three o'clock, and this is still the time mentioned in *Ordo* XXVIII, of about 800.[208] But in *Ordo* XXXB, around a century later, it has become the eighth hour, and in the Romano-German Pontifical of about 950 it is the seventh.[209] In the Pontifical of the Roman Curia the time has crept back to the sixth hour, and this is also the time in the Pontifical of Durandus (though in the latter the ceremony begins with Sext); the Pontifical of the Twelfth Century prescribes either the fifth or the sixth hour.[210] Assuming a period of around four to five hours for the Vigil and the Mass, beginning at the fifth hour would mean finishing in mid-afternoon. By the end of the Middle Ages it was customary to begin the Vigil early on Holy Saturday morning, with the consequent anomaly that the Resurrection of Our Lord was celebrated by way of anticipation even before the official end of Lent, at midday.

Appendix 1

Mozarabic Prayer for the Blessing of the Lamp

Exaudi nos, lumen indeficiens, Domine Deus noster, unici luminis lumen, fons luminis, lumen auctor luminum quae creasti et inluminasti, lumen angelorum tuorum, sedium, dominationum, principatuum, potestatum et omnium intelligibilium quae creasti, lumen sanctorum tuorum. Sint lucernae tuae animae nostrae, accedant ad te, inluminentur abs te, luceant veritate, ardeant caritate, luceant et non tenebrescant, ardeant et non cinerescant. Benedic hoc lumen, o lumen, quia et hoc quod portamus in manibus tu creasti, tu donasti. Per haec lumina quae accendimus de hoc loco expellimus noctem; sic et tu expelle tenebras de cordibus nostris. Simus domus tua lucens de te; sine defectu luceamus et te semper colamus, in te accendamur et non extinguamur.

Hear us, undying light, O Lord our God, light of the one light, the fount of light, light who is the source of the lights which you have created and made to shine, light of your angels, thrones, dominions, principalities, powers and all sentient beings whom you have created, light of your saints. May our minds be your lamps, may they draw close to you, may they be set alight by you, may they shine with truth, may they burn with love, may they glow and not be darkened, may they burn and not be consumed. Bless this light, O Light, because this too which we bear in our hands you have created, you have provided. By means of these lights which we are kindling, we drive the night out of this place; do you also in the same way drive the darkness out of our hearts. May we be your home, drawing its light from you, may we glow without ceasing and may we ever worship you; may we be illumined by you and never extinguished.

Note. This prayer from *CC* CLXI 499.

Appendix 2

Easter Vigil Readings

	I	II	III	IV	V	VI	VII	VIII	IX	X	XI
Genesis 1	1	1	1	1?	1	2	1	1	1	1	1
Genesis 2–3				2?	2						
Genesis 5–8			2	3	4	1	2	2	2		
Genesis 22	2		3	4	6	3	3	3	3		2
Genesis 27				5	8						
Exodus 12	3		8	6	9	4	9	9	9		
Exodus 14–15	5	2	4	7	5	5	4	4	4	2	3
Deuter. 31			9		7		11	11	11	4	
Joshua 3				10							
2 Kings 2	8										
2 Chron. 34–5					10						
Job 38	7										
Isaiah 1						6					
Isaiah 4		3	7	9			8	8	8	3	
Isaiah 54–5		4	5		3		5	5	5		4/5
Isaiah 60	6										
Jeremiah 31	9										
Baruch 3							6	6	6		6
Ezekiel 36											7
Ezekiel 37	11		6	8	11		7	7	7		
Daniel 3	12		10	12	12		12	12	12		
Josiah 1	10										
Jonah 1–4	4			11			10	10	10		

References

I.   Jerusalem: Armenian Lectionary: ms 121 (417–439 AD)
II.   Gregorian
III. Old Gelasian
IV.   Gallican: Lectionary of Luxeuil (end 7th C)
V.   Mozarabic: *Liber Comicus* (2nd half of 7th C)
VI.   Ambrosian: *Lectionum Capitulare Ambrosianum* (12th C)
VII. Romano-Gallican: *Comes* of Murbach (late 8th C) and of Theotinchi (c. 800).
VIII. Gelasians of the 8th Century
IX.   1474 Missal and Missal of Pius V (1571)
X.   Missal of Pius XII (1955)
XI.   Missal of Paul VI (1970)

Appendix 3

Preface from Sacramentary of Fulda

Vere dignum et iustum est, aequum et salutare, nos tibi semper et ubique gratias agere, Domine sancte, Pater omnipotens, aeterne Deus, te quidem omni tempore, sed in hac potissimum nocte gloriosius collaudare et praedicare, per Christum Dominum nostrum, qui inferorum claustra dirumpens, victoriae suae clara vexilla suscepit, et triumphato diabolo victor a mortuis resurrexit. O noctem, quae finem tenebris ponit, et aeternae lucis viam pandit. O noctem quae videre meruit et vinci diabolum et resurgere Christum. O noctem in qua tartara spoliantur, sancti ab inferis liberantur, caelestis patriae aditus aperitur; in qua in baptismate delictorum turba perimitur, filii lucis oriuntur. Quos, exemplo dominicae matris, sine corruptione sancta mater ecclesia concipit, sine dolore parit, et cum gaudio ad meliora provehit. Et ideo...

It is truly right and fitting, proper and salutary, that we should always and everywhere give you thanks, holy Lord, almighty Father, eternal God, and at all times, but most particularly on this night, praise you and extol you more gloriously, through Christ our Lord, who, breaking apart the bolts of the underworld, grasped the shining standards of his victory, and, triumphing over the devil, rose victorious from the dead. O night, which put an end to darkness, and opened up the way of eternal light! O night, which was worthy to see both the defeat of the devil and the resurrection of Christ! O night in which hell was harrowed, the saints set free from the underworld, and the way opened to our heavenly fatherland, in which through baptism a multitude of sins is wiped out, and the sons of light arise! Those whom Holy Mother Church, like the Lord's own mother, conceives without corruption, brings forth without pain, and raises with joy to better things. And therefore...

Appendix 4

The Pentecost Vigil

The Vigil commenced with the reading of six of the lessons from the Old Testament read at the Easter Vigil, in the ancient manner without introductory title or *Deo gratias* at the end. When the readings were sung by a cantor they were read simultaneously by the celebrant in a low voice at the Epistle side of the altar. The readings were Genesis 22:1–19, Exodus 14:24 – 15:3, Deuteronomy 31:22 – 32:4, Isaiah 4:1 – 5:2, Baruch 3:9–38 and Ezekiel 37:1 – 14. The texts of the canticles with which Readings II, III and IV concluded were in the Old Latin version, as at the Easter Vigil, and each reading ended with an appropriate Collect, though without the preceding *Flectamus genua, Levate*. After the conclusion of the readings the celebrant, who had hitherto worn a violet chasuble, put on a cope of the same colour, and accompanied by the other ministers went in procession to the font, while the antiphon *Sicut cervus* was sung. On arrival at the font the baptismal waters were blessed with the same prayer and the same ritual gestures as at the Easter Vigil. On returning to the altar the celebrant took off his cope and the ministers prostrated themselves before the altar while the litanies were sung, in the same manner as at Easter, each petition with its response being sung by the cantors and repeated in full by the choir or congregation. Actual baptisms at the Pentecost Vigil, which had in early times been normal, had long since ceased to be carried out, though the embolism in the Canon of the Mass, which implied that such baptisms had taken place, remained. After the conclusion of the litanies, the celebrant put on a red chasuble and the Mass of the Pentecost Vigil began with the singing by the choir of the *Kyrie eleison*, solemnly, after which the celebrant intoned the *Gloria*.

The Pentecost Vigil, which like its counterpart at Easter had come to be celebrated in the morning rather than the evening of the day before the feast, was abolished as part of the 1955 reform of the liturgy, but the Vigil Mass itself continued to be celebrated until the general abolition of vigils in 1970.

Notes

[1] Cf. Wilkinson, op. cit., pp. 66–70; MacGregor, op. cit., pp. 299–301; Baumstark, op. cit., pp. 133–5.
[2] Baumstark comments that it is one of the phenomena which were once universal and now survive only in great liturgical celebrations. He sees a trace of the originally utilitarian character of the rite in the words of the *Exsultet*, 'ut cereus iste ad noctis huius caliginem destruendam indeficiens perseveret' (op. cit., p. 135).
[3] PL 89, 951.

4   Depending on whether 'sacrum chrisma' or simply 'sacrum' is the correct reading in the text.

5   These candles were lit, according to OR XXIII. 10, which is approximately contemporary with Zacharias, with flame taken 'ex ungiario', which presumably refers to one of the three lamps mentioned by the Pope (Andrieu, *ORM* Vol. 3, p. 270; cf. ibid., pp. 318–19).

6   MacGregor (op. cit., p. 232) believes that the words 'per sacerdotem renovabitur' imply that the fire was blessed immediately before use at the Vigil. He may be right, though as he himself says 'renovabitur' seems an odd word to choose instead of 'benedicetur'. I am inclined to think that it merely means that the priest recovered the flame from the place where it had been hidden and restored it to the sight of the congregation. In either case, the language is somewhat odd.

7   'Mos ecclesiae nostrae obtinet per tres noctes, id est per feriam quintam, quae vocatur cena Domine, et per sextam, quae vocatur parasceve, et per septimam, quae vocatur sabbatum sanctum, ut extinguantur luminaria ecclesiae in nocte. De more sanctae matris nostrae Romanae ecclesiae interrogavi archidiaconum Theodorum memoratae ecclesiae, scilicet Romanae, qui respondit: *Solo esse cum apostolico in Lateranis quando officium celebratur de cena Domini. Nihil autem ibi in eadem nocte observatur de extinctione luminum. In feria sexta nullum lumen habetur lampadum sive cereorum in ecclesia in Jerusalem, quamdiu domnus apostolicus ibi orationes solemnes facit aut quamdiu crux salutatur, sed tamen in ipsa die novus ignis accenditur de quo reservatur usque nocturnale officium* ... Et, propter necessitatem communem, reaccenditur in sancta Romana ecclesia eodem die, ut ex illo cibi coquantur et reservetur ad usum noctis necessarium' (Amalarius, *De ordine antiphonarum* XLIV, 2 [*PL* 105, 1292–1293]). 'In Romana ecclesia extinguitur totus ignis in sexta feria et reaccenditur ... ignis iste qui nostris usibus procuratur potest extingui in sexta feria circa sextam horam diei et renovari circa nonam horam diei' (id. *De ecclesiasticis officiis* Lib. IV cap. xxii [*PL* 105, 1202]). The 'ecclesia in Jerusalem' is of course Santa Croce in Gerusalemme which was the station for the Good Friday liturgical action. The extinction of domestic fires is also mentioned in OR XXVIII. 63, where however they are relit on Holy Saturday with fire taken from the Paschal Candle (Andrieu, *ORM* Vol. 2, p. 404).

8   'reservetur ignis de sexta feria, ut illuminetur cereus qui ponitur in vice columnae ignis ad benedicendum, qui ab initio benedictionis illuminatus est, et cum benedictus est, ab eo illuminetur secundus cereus. Cetera luminaria extincta permaneant usque ad novissimam laetaniam quae pertinet ad officium missae de resurrectione Domini; tunc accendantur luminaria ecclesiae et neophytorum' (id. *De ordine antiphonarum* XLIV, 2 [*PL* 105, 1293]).

9   Mohlberg, 425. For the original text of this rubric see note 46 below.

10   OR XXIII. 24 (Andrieu, *ORM* Vol. 3, p. 2 72).

11   OR XXXA. 15 (ibid., p. 457); OR XXXB. 28 (ibid., p. 470).

12   Ibid., pp. 325–9 (*OR XXVI*); 348–51 (*OR XXVII*); 396–7 (*OR XXVIII*); 440–3 (*OR XXIX*); 495 (*OR XXXI*). The lighting of the Paschal Candle from new fire kindled and reserved on Maundy Thursday also features in Pseudo-Alcuin xvi (*PL* 101, 1205).

13 Cf. the distinction made between the 'forenses civitates' and the 'catholica ecclesia infra civitatem romanam' in section 6 (Andrieu, *ORM* Vol. 3, pp. 311–2).

14 John of Avranches, *Lib. de officiis ecclesiasticis*: 'In his tribus diebus novus ignis de petra excussus in ecclesia accenditur, et inde per ceteras domos' (*PL* 147, 49). For the extinction of fires during the Triduum cf. also Durandus, *Rationale* Lib.VI. lxxx (Dura, p. 543).

15 Rupert of Deutz, *De divinis officiis* Lib. V cap. xxviii: 'ad lapidem per eosdem tres dies confugimus, ut vel lapidem percutientes, ex abstrusis eius venis ignem occultum eliciamus, vel liquidum crystalli lapidem sereno coelo soli obicientes, radium eius traiectum per eiusdem crystalli orbiculum spectaculi miraculo in subiectam suscipiamus escam' (*PL* 170, 148–9).

16 For a full list of the sources see MacGregor, op. cit., p. 148, Tables 8a and 8b.

17 Lanfranc, *Decreta* cap. I, iv: 'ex hoc igne omnes foci in omnibus officinis prius exstincti iterum accendantur' (*PL* 150, 467).

18 'In sabbato Paschae, extincto veteri, novus ignis benedicatur et per populum dividatur, et aquae similiter' (*PL* 115, 681–682). The Pontifical of Egbert, from the eighth century, contains a blessing of fire, but this has no specific link with the Vigil (Schmidt, *HS*, p. 555).

19 Martène, *DAER* IV, cap. XXIV, col. 434.

20 In Lanfranc's *Decreta*, cap. I, iv it is specifically provided that a second candle should be lit inside a lantern as a precaution in case the first, which is carried in the procession, should blow out (*PL* 150, 466).

21 PRG cap. xxv 16–20, xxvii 2, xxix 11 (Andrieu, *ORM* Vol.5, pp. 191–2, 245, 264).

22 *Disciplina Farfensis* cap. iii (*PL* 150, 1198, 1201 and 1203); Cluny, *Consuetudines*, caps. xii and xiii (*PL* 149, 658 and 661). Curiously, there is no mention of any new fire on Holy Saturday in the latter, but its existence can be inferred from the description of the lighting of the Paschal Candle.

23 MacGregor op. cit., pp. 163–5. For the text of the Mozarabic prayer see Appendix 1 to this chapter.

24 Ibid., pp. 158–64, tables 15, 16, 17 and 18, containing a full list of all the known instances. For the texts of the various prayers cf. Appendix 4 to the same work.

25 Lanfranc, *Decreta* cap.I, iv (*PL* 150, 466). There is a comprehensive list of those places where the *Inventor rutili* was sung during the procession in MacGregor, op. cit., pp. 280–1.

26 Pontifical of Magdalen College (1151–1200), from southern England, possibly Canterbury (ed. H. A. Wilson, HBS, Vol. XXXIX [1910], p. 169).

27 J. Wickham Legg, op. cit., p. 117.

28 Westminster Missal (1362–1386), (ed. H. W. Legg, HBS, Vol. II [1891], col. 578).

29 *Ordinale Gilbertinum, de sabbato sancto pasche* (HBS, Vol. LIX [1921], p. 40).

30 For a comprehensive list of the relevant churches see MacGregor, op. cit., tables 36 and 37 on pp. 208–9 and 218.

31 'De crystallis autem, ut asseruisti, nullam habemus traditionem' (*PL* 89, 951).

32 In classical Latin poetry 'lapis' can have the meaning of 'gemstone' (e.g. Catullus, 69, 3; Horace, *Carmina* III, 24, 48).

33 Fischer, *OEL*, p. 60; Roman Pontifical of the Twelfth Century XXXII. 1 (Andrieu, PRM Vol. I, p. 238), Pontifical of the Roman Curia XLIV. 1 (ibid., Vol. II, p. 470), *OR* x. 16 (*PL* 78, 1014), *OR* xiv. XCIV (ibid., 1218), *OR* xv. LXXVI (ibid., 1321).

34 See note 14 above.

35 Roman Pontifical of the Twelfth Century XXXII. 1, 'novus ignis, si non fuerit excussus in caena domini, iuxta morem quarumdam ecclesiarum, excutiatur hoc die' (Andrieu, PRM Vol. I, p. 238).

36 Fischer, *OEL*, p. 60; Roman Pontifical of the Twelfth Century XXXII. 1 (Andrieu, PRM Vol. I, p. 238); Pontifical of the Roman Curia XLIV. 1 (ibid., Vol. II, p. 470; Pontifical of Durandus Lib. III, iv. 1 (ibid., Vol. III, p. 587); *OR* xii. 30 (*PL* 78, 1076); *OR* xv. LXXVII (*PL* 78, 1321). In *OR* xii, from about 1192, it takes place 'in atrio ante portas Lateranensis ecclesiae', in *OR* xv, from around two hundred years later, 'benedicitur in capella, praesente domino papa'.

37 Roman Pontifical of the Twelfth Century XXXIII. 2–5 (Andrieu, PRM Vol. I, p. 238); Pontifical of the Roman Curia XLIV. 2–6 (ibid., Vol. II, p. 470). The first mention of sprinkling the fire with holy water seems to be in Lanfranc's *Decreta* of about 1070 (*PL* 150, 466). The combination of both sprinkling and incensation is first found in the same century at the monastery of St Bénigne at Dijon (MacGregor op. cit., pp. 171–2).

38 Full text of Jerome's letter in *PL* 30, 182 and Schmidt, *HS*, pp. 629–33 The source of the Virgilian imagery is Book IV of the *Georgics*, in particular lines 56–7, 82–3 and 160–4. Compare for example line 86 of the original text of the *Exsultet* (ingentes animos angusto versat in pectore) with line 83 of *Georgics* IV (ingentis animo angusto in pectore versant), and lines 99–103 (aliae inaestimabili arte / cellulas tenaci glutino instruunt / aliae liquantia mella stipant / aliae vertunt flores in ceram / aliae ore natos fingunt)) with lines 160–4 (narcissi lacrimam et lentum de cortice gluten / prima favis ponunt fundamina, deinde tenacis / suspendunt ceras; aliae spem gentis adultos / educunt fetus; aliae purissima mella / stipant et liquido distendunt nectare cellas). The notion that bees reproduce without sexual intercourse is found in lines 198–201 of the same poem (ed. F. A. Hirtzel, OUP, 1955).

39 *De civitate Dei*, Lib. XV. cap. 22. (*PL* 41, 467). Augustine's canticle was, like Virgil's Georgics, in hexameters, which would no doubt have added further fuel to Jerome's indignation, had he ever got to hear of it. A note in the Pontifical of Poitiers preserved a legend that Augustine composed the *Exsultet* and that Jerome reprimanded him for his Virgilianisms and amended it to exclude them (Martène, *DAER* IV, cap. XXIV, col. 409).

40 *OR* XXVI. 6 (Andrieu, *ORM* Vol. 3, p. 326). MacGregor (op. cit., Appendix 14) believes that this permission related not to the suburbicarian dioceses but to the dioceses of central Italy outside the immediate vicinity of the city, or even to more distant regions converted to Christianity by Roman missionaries. But in the letter of Innocent I to Decentius of Gubbio, written in 416, the expression 'per parroccias' evidently refers to that part of the diocese of Rome outside the city itself (*PL* 56, 516–517; see Chavasse, *Le Sacramentaire Gélasien*, pp. 77–8). The biography of Zosimus is included in that part of the

Liber Pontificalis which was written around 540. The expression may have changed its meaning somewhat during the intervening years, but it is hard to believe that it could refer to anywhere a long way from Rome. For the eighth century the author of *OR* XXVI is quite specific; the consecration of the candle was carried out 'in forensibus civitatibus' but not 'infra civitatem romanam'.

41   Rabanus Maurus, *De clericorum institutione* Lib. II cap. xxviii, 'secundum institutionem Zosimi papae' (*PL* 107, 350); Amalarius, *De ecclesiasticis officiis* Lib. I cap. xviii, 'nobis quoque praeceptum est a papa Zosimo benedicere cereum ... quod a diacono benedicitur morem sequitur romanum' (*PL* 105, 1033–1034).

42   Full texts in CC CLXI 499 (*Corpus Praefationum*) nos. 1646 and 1637; also in Schmidt, *HS*, pp. 633–7 and *PL* 63, 258–262.

43   Ep. XI. 33, (*PL* 20, 1169).

44   Drepanius Florus, *De cereo paschali* (*PL* 61, 1087–1088); Fourth Council of Toledo, Canon IX (*PL* 84, 369); Mozarabic blessing of candle: Escorial, Codex del Camarin fo. 1–2, (CC CLXI 499 [Corpus Praefationum], no. 766bis).

45   *Missale Gothicum*: 'Benediccio cerae beati Augustini episcopi quam adhuc diaconus cum esset edidet et caecinit' (HBS, Vol. LII, p. 67, original spelling). This expression, or words to the same effect, is repeated in the *Missale Gallicanum Vetus*, (*PL* 72, 364–365), the Bobbio Missal (HBS, Vol. LVIII, pp. 69–70) and many later liturgical books.

46   'Primitus enim viii hora diei mediante procedunt ad ecclesiam et ingrediun-tur in sacrario et induunt se vestimentis sicut mos est. Et incipit clerus litania *(sic)* et procedit sacerdos de sacrario cum ordinibus sacris. Veniunt ante altare stantes inclinato capite usquedum dicent *Agnus Dei qui tollis peccata mundi miserere*. Deinde surgens sacerdos ab oratione vadit retro altare sedens in sede sua. Deinde veniens archidiaconus ante altare, accipiens de lumine quod vi feria absconsum fuit, faciens crucem super cereum et illuminans eum, et completur ab ipso benedictio cerei.' The Old Gelasian Sacramentary omits 'Deinde surgens sacerdos ab oratione vadit retro altare sedens in sede sua', but this is probably a scribal error arising from the repetition of 'Deinde' at the start of the next sentence (Old Gelasian, Mohlberg, 425–429; Sacramentary of Angoulême, CC CLIX Vol C 730–733; Sacramentary of Rheinau, Schmidt, *HS*, p. 391; Sacramentary of Gellone (omitting the first part of the rubric), CC CLIX Vol A 675–677; Sacramentary of Autun (reversing the order of the *Deus mundi conditor* and the *Exsultet*), CC CLIX Vol B 520–522).

47   'Secretis iam condis favi / divini mellis alitus / cordis repurgas intimas / verbo replisti cellolas. Examen ut foetus novi / ore praelectum spiritu / relectum caelum sarcinis / querat securis pinnulis'; translated reading 'secretos' for 'secretis', 'condens' for 'condis', 'repurgans' for 'repurgas', 'spiritus' for 'spiritu' and 'relictis' for 'relectum'. The composition is headed 'Ymnum quando caeria benedicitur' (Ambrosian Library of Milan, C.5 inf.; modern edition HBS, Vol. IV, ed. F. E. Warren, 1892).

48   Honorius, *Gemma animae* Lib. III, cii (*PL* 172, 668); Durandus, *Rationale* Lib. VI. lxxx (Dura, p. 543); B. Capelle, 'L'Exsultet Paschal, oeuvre de St

Ambrose', in *Studi e Testi* 121, Vatican City, 1946; B. Fischer, 'Ambrosius der Verfasser des österlichen Exsultet?', in Archiv für Liturgiewissenschaft 2, 1952; C. Mohrmann, 'Exsultent divina mysteria', in *Eph. Lit.* 66, 1952.

49 'Decet ergo in hoc Domini salvatoris nostri vespertinae resurrectionis adventu, ceream nos adolere pinguedinem, cui suppetit candor in specie, suavitas in odore, splendor in lumine'. Text in CC CLXI 499 (*Corpus Praefationum*) no. 1159 and Schmidt, *HS*, pp. 646–7. The earliest manuscript dates from the ninth century (Bergamo, Biblioteca di S. Alessandri in Colonna, 524).

50 'quae summi sacerdotis et antistitis tui Ambrosii oratione sanctificata vel meritis resurrectionis dominicae diem, Christo in omnibus prosperante, suscipiat'.

51 For a detailed account of the Beneventan *Exsultet* see T. F. Kelly, *The Exultet in South Italy* (OUP, 1996).

52 'Qui nos ad noctem istam, non tenebris sed luminis matrem, perducere dignatus est, in qua exorta est ab inferis in aeterna die resurrectio mortuorum. Solutis quippe nexibus et calcato mortis aculeo, resurrexit a mortuis qui fuit inter mortuos liber' (CC CLXI 499 [Corpus Praefationum], no. 1094bis). The last phrase is a reference to Psalm 87 v. 5, 'factus sum sicut homo sine adiutorio, inter mortuos liber', the eighth psalm at Matins of Good Friday.

53 Kelly, op. cit., pp. 59–69. It also appears slightly earlier in the Ragusa Missal of the thirteenth century. However, the chant melody given in these late medieval missals differs from those in the earlier ones. On the whole question of the *Exsultet* chants, cf. G. Benoit-Castelli, 'Le Praeconium Paschale', in *Eph. Lit.* 67, pp. 309–34.

54 There is a full list in Kelly, op. cit., Appendix I. Many of the illuminations are reproduced in G. Cavallo, *Rotoli Liturgici del Medioevo Meridionale* (Istituto Poligrafico e Zecca dello Stato, Rome, 1994).

55 It is omitted for instance in the Romano-German Pontifical and in the Sacramentary of Fulda, and it is strongly deprecated in the *Consuetudines* of Cluny (*PL* 149, 663).

56 Omitted first in the Romano-German Pontifical (c.950) and in the Sacramentary of Fulda (c.975). It appears in the Missal of Robert of Jumièges of c.1000, which is from England in spite of its name (ed. H.A. Wilson, HBS Vol. XI (1896), pp. 91–2) but is omitted from the Westminster Missal (c.1370) and the later Sarum missals. It does not appear in the first printed missal of 1474 or in any subsequent edition of the Roman Missal.

57 Westminster Missal, ed. H. W. Legg, HBS, Vol. II, col. 583. On the origin in twelfth-century Germany or north-eastern France of the present chant for the *Exsultet*, cf. Benoit-Castelli, op. cit., pp. 333–4.

58 *OR* XI. 89–90 (Andrieu, *ORM* Vol. 2, p. 444).

59 *OR* XVI. 40 (ibid., Vol. 3, p. 152).

60 *OR* XXIII. 24 (ibid., p. 272).

61 *OR* XXIV. 41 (ibid., p. 295); *OR* XXVII. 51 (ibid., p. 359).

62 *OR* XXXB. 38 (ibid., p. 471). The two great candles, as well as the Paschal Candle itself, figure in the rite described in the Pontifical of Poitiers of about

900, where they are held to symbolize the two angels seated in the empty tomb of Christ (Martène, *DAER* IV, cap. XXIV, col. 434).

63   *OR* XXV. 1–3 (Andrieu, *ORM* Vol. 3, p. 301); *OR* XXVI. 5 (ibid., p. 326).

64   *OR* XXVIII. 59–60 (ibid., p. 403).

65   *OR* XXXI. 63–67 (ibid., p. 500).

66   Martène, *DAER* IV, cap. XXIV, col. 434.

67   PRG cap. xxix, 11–31 (ibid., Vol. 5, pp. 264–73).

68   *Regularis Concordia*, (*PL* 137, 494); *Disciplina Farfensis* cap. iii (*PL* 150, 1203).

69   *PL* 78, 336. The inscription of a cross with A and Ω on the candle in the tenth century is also found in the Mozarabic Antiphonary of Leon. Cf. MacGregor, op. cit., pp. 366–8.

70   Cluny, *Consuetudines* cap. xiv, 'diaconus in eo foraminibus ante praecavatis crucem facit cum quinque granis incensi' (*PL* 149, 663).

71   Rupert of Deutz, *De divinis officiis* Lib. VI, xxxi (*PL* 170, 173).

72   *Rationale*, Lib. VI. lxxx (Dura, p. 543).

73   Roman Pontifical of the Twelfth Century XXXXII. 5–8 (Andrieu, *PRM* Vol. I, pp. 239–40). MacGregor (op. cit., p. 350) says that there was no procession according to this document, but in fact one is mentioned specifically in para. 7 ('processionaliter procedens cum schola cantorum et aliquibus subdiaconis').

74   MacGregor, op. cit., p. 350.

75   Pontifical of Poitiers, Martène, *DAER* IV, cap. XXIV col. 434; Sacramentary of Ratoldus, *PL* 78, 336. The former directs specifically that the deacon is to cut the year of Our Lord, together with the indiction (fifteen year cycle) into the candle with a stylus.

76   'A Passione Domini nostri Jesu Christi anni sunt DCLXVIII', Bede, *De temporum ratione*, cap. XLVII (*PL* 90, 495).

77   MacGregor, op. cit., pp. 368–70.

78   *Disciplina Farfensis* cap. iv (*PL* 150, 1203).

79   Rupert of Deutz, *De divinis officiis* Lib. VI. xxix (*PL* 170, 171).

80   The practice is mentioned in the Roman Pontifical of the Twelfth Century XXII. 10, but only as one observed outside Rome itself (Andrieu, *PRM* Vol. I, pp. 240–1).

81   Pontifical of Poitiers, 'ferente in arundine candelam instar colubri' (Martène, *DAER* IV, cap. XXIV col. 434); PRG cap. xxix. 16 (Andrieu, *ORM* Vol. 5, p. 267).

82   *OR* XXVI. 4, 9 (Andrieu, *ORM* Vol. 3, pp. 326–7); *OR* XXVII. 7 (ibid., p. 349); *OR* XXVIII. 26 (ibid., p. 397); *OR* XXIX. 15 (ibid., p. 440); *OR* XXXI. 30 (ibid., p. 495).

83   Cf. MacGregor, op. cit., tables 39, 40, 41 and 42 (pp. 254–62) for comprehensive lists of the places where there is evidence for the use of these instruments. Of the twenty instances of the use of a spear cited in table 41, fifteen are in England or Normandy.

84   *Ordinale Gilbertinum, de sabbato sancto pasche*: 'diacono cum hasta in qua figuntur quinque candele in ceree in summo' (HBS, Vol. LIX, p. 39); *Ordo Ecclesiae Lateranensis*: 'plures candelas in unum glomeratas, ne a vento leviter exstinguantur' (Fischer, *OEL*, p. 61).

[85] Pontifical of the Twelfth Century XXIII. 10 (Andrieu, PRM Vol. I, pp. 240–1); Baumstark, op. cit., pp. 147–8. It also makes an appearance in the Pontifical of Apamea, an early thirteenth century pontifical of the Roman rite from Syria (Martène, *DAER* IV, cap. XXIV, col. 433).

[86] MacGregor, op. cit., table 43 on p. 269.

[87] The threefold cry of 'Lumen Christi', 'Deo gratias' is also mentioned in the contemporary *Ordo Ecclesiae Lateranensis*. The rite as described therein closely follows that of the Roman Pontifical of the Twelfth Century except that the Paschal Candle is not lit until the words 'Quem in honorem Dei rutilans ignis accendit' (Fischer, *OEL* p. 61).

[88] Roman Pontifical of the Twelfth Century XXXI. 7–10 (Andrieu, PRM Vol. I, pp. 239–41).

[89] *OR* XIX. 22 (Andrieu, *ORM* Vol. 3, p. 212); cf. MacGregor, op. cit., p. 284.

[90] MacGregor, op. cit., pp. 281–7 and Table 46.

[91] *Missale Romanum* 1474, HBS, Vol. XVII, p. 175.

[92] *OR* xv. LXXVII (*PL* 78, 1321–1322).

[93] The two man-sized candles of the ancient Roman rite had become by the end of the twelfth century simply 'duobus parvis aliis cereis' (Beleth, *Rationale* cvi (*PL* 202, 110)). Thereafter they disappear entirely. There is no trace of them in the detailed description of the rite in *OR* xiv of about 1350 (*PL* 78, 1218–1219), or subsequently.

[94] Martène, *DAER* IV, cap. XXIV, col. 434.

[95] Martène, *DAER* IV, cap. XXIV, cols. 410–11. For a detailed account of the history of the charta see MacGregor, op. cit., pp. 372–7 with Appendix 13.

[96] Durandus, *Rationale* Lib. III xviii 1, 9, 'Albis indumentis utendum est … in Sabbato Sancto, in officio Missae … Et est intelligendum quod in Sabbato Sancto in toto officio, quod agitur ante Missam, utendum est violaceo colore, hoc excepto, quod diaconus qui benedicit cereum dalmatica, et subdiaconus ministrans indutus tunicella, albis utuntur, quia benedictio illa, sicut et Missa, ad resurrectionem pertinet. Sed benedictione cerei expleta, diaconus remota dalmatica assumit planetam violacei coloris, et tenet eam usque dum inchoatur officium Missae; subdiaconus vero non mutat vestes' (Dura, pp. 130–1). The planeta was a type of chasuble worn by a deacon instead of a dalmatic on penitential occasions.

[97] *OR* xiv. XCIV (*PL* 78, 1219).

[98] Pontifical of Durandus, Lib. III, iv. 20 (Andrieu, PRM Vol. III, p. 591).

[99] Jungmann, *MRR* Vol. I, pp. 20, 391–3.

[100] The Book of Pontiffs, transl. R. Davis, Liverpool University Press, 1989, p. 34.

[101] Cantalamessa, op. cit., 20.

[102] Conybeare, op. cit., p. 523. For the tropes in the sixth and twelfth readings see chapter 2, pp. 36–7.

[103] Wilson, HBS, Vol. XLIV, pp. 154–7.

[104] Regardless of whether the readings are given in the Old Latin version or in the Vulgate, the former was retained for the three canticles in all the liturgical books, and remains so until the present day.

[105] Mohlberg, 431–441.

[106] Sacramentary of Angoulême, CC CLIX Vol. C 741–754; Sacramentary of

Rheinau, Schmidt, *HS*, pp. 391; Sacramentary of St Gall, ibid., pp. 409–10; Sacramentary of Gellone, CC CLIX Vol. A 680–701; Sacramentary of Autun, CC CLIX Vol. B 523–536.

107 Chavasse, op. cit., pp. 107–15; cf. also 'Leçons et oraisons des vigiles de Pâques et de la Pentecoste dans le sacramentaire gélasien' (*Eph. Lit.* 69, pp. 209–26).

108 Notably Pentecost and Christmas (Schmidt, *HS*, p. 842).

109 Schmidt, *HS*, p. 843.

110 PRG cap. xxix. 32–39 (Andrieu, *ORM* Vol. 5, pp. 273–5).

111 Schmidt, *HS*, pp. 827–47. For a description of the Pentecost Vigil, prior to its abolition in the 1955 reform, see Appendix 4 to this chapter.

112 *Liber Comicus*; Schmidt, *HS*, pp. 478–9; Lectionary of Luxeuil; ibid., pp. 458–69.

113 Frankish Gelasians; see note 106 above; *Comes* of Murbach and *Comes* Theotinchi: ibid., 464, 466.

114 *OR XXVIII* Appendix (Andrieu, *ORM* Vol. 3, pp. 411–13).

115 The twelve-reading system is found in the Roman Pontifical of the Twelfth Century XXXII. 11–12 (Andrieu, *PRM* Vol. I, p. 241) and all subsequent Roman documents.

116 Roman Pontifical of the Twelfth Century XXXII. 12 (Andrieu, *PRM* Vol. I, p. 241); *OR* xi. 43 (*PL* 78, 1041).

117 *OR* x. 17 (*PL* 78, 1014); Pontifical of the Roman Curia XLIV. 8 (Andrieu, *PRM* Vol II, p. 472); Ordinary of the Papal Chaplains and Roman Missal, III, 9 (Andrieu, id., Appendix ii, p. 566); *OR* xiv, XCIV (*PL* 78, 1219).

118 E.g. *OR* XXIV. 42 (Andrieu, *ORM* Vol. 3, p. 295); *OR* XXVII. 52 (ibid., p. 359); *OR* XXVIII. 64 (ibid., p. 404); *OR* XXIX. 46 (ibid., p. 444); *OR.* XXXI 68 (ibid., p. 500); Amalarius, *De eccl. off.* Lib. I cap. xxi (*PL* 105, 1039); Pseudo-Alcuin xix (*PL* 101, 1217); *Disciplina Farfensis*, cap. IV (*PL* 150, 1203); OEL (Fischer p. 62); PRG cap. xxix. 32 (Andrieu, *ORM* Vol. 5, p. 273); Roman Pontifical of the Twelfth Century XXXII 11 (id., *PRM* Vol. I, p. 241); Pontifical of the Roman Curia XLIV 8 (ibid., Vol. II, p. 472); Pontifical of Durandus IV 12 (ibid., Vol III, p. 589); *OR* xiv 29 (*PL* 78, 1218–1219) OR xv 77 (*PL* 78, 1323).

119 Sicardus, *Mitrale* Lib.VI, xiv (*PL* 213, 325); Durandus, *Rationale* Lib. VI. lxxxi, 1 (Dura, p. 546); Honorius, *Gemma animae* III, cii (*PL* 172, 668–669). Cf. Jungmann, *MRR* Vol. I, p. 420.

120 Martène, *DAER* IV, cap. XXIV, col. 417.

121 Sicardus, *Mitrale* Lib. VI, xiv (*PL* 213, 325); Durandus, *Rationale* Lib. VI. lxxxi, 1 (Dura, p. 546).

122 Pseudo-Alcuin, *De divinis officiis* xix (*PL* 101, 1216–1217); *Disciplina Farfensis* cap. iv (*PL* 150, 1203–1204); Cluny, *Consuetudines* cap. xiv (*PL* 149, 663–664). *The Sarum Missal*, Wickham Legg, op. cit., pp. 119–20.

123 Old Gelasian, Mohlberg, 442–443; Sacramentary of Angoulême, CC CLIX Vol C 754; Sacramentary of Gellone, CC CLIX Vol A 701; Sacramentary of Autun, CC CLIX Vol B 536; Sacramentary of St Gall II 98.553, Schmidt, *HS*, p. 410; PRG cap. xxix, 42 (Andrieu, *ORM* Vol. 5, p. 275).

124 The documents which record this practice are the *Ordo Ecclesiae Lateranensis* (Fischer, p. 63), the Pontifical of the Roman Curia XLIV. 15–16 (Andrieu,

PRM, pp. 474–5), and the *Ordines Romani* x.20 (*PL* 78, 1015), xi.43 (id., 1041) and xii.30 (id., 1076), all from the twelfth century. The prayer *Omnipotens sempiterne Deus, respice propitius* is mentioned specifically only in the Pontifical of the Roman Curia but it may be inferred for the other documents.

125 *Missale Romanum* 1474 (HBS, Vol. XVII, p. 190).

126 See Jungmann, MRR Vol. I, pp. 333–46, where the full text of the *deprecatio Gelasii* may be found.

127 'Et incipit clerus litania (*sic*), et procedit sacerdos de sacrario cum ordinibus sacris. Veniunt ante altare stantes inclinato capite usquedum dicent *Agnus Dei, qui tollis peccata mundi, miserere*' (Mohlberg, 425).

128 'Inde procedunt ad fontes cum litania ad baptizandum' (ibid., 443).

129 Postea vero ipse sacerdos revertit cum omnibus ordinibus in sacrario, et post paululum incipiunt tertiam litaniam, et ingrediuntur ad missas' (ibid.). The absence of any reference to a second litany is curious. It is possible that the author of the rubric is counting the opening litany of the Vigil as the first, but perhaps more likely that the original text of the rubric was identical to that in the Sacramentary of Angoulême (see following note), the words 'secundum litaniam et post modicum intervallum cum' being omitted as a result of scribal error, involving in consequence the amendment of the ablative 'tertia litania' to the accusative 'tertiam litaniam' in order to correct the grammar. In any case all three rubrics quoted represent a later stratum in the text of the sacramentary, which originally merely prescribed 'Inde descendis cum litania ad fontem' (ibid., 444. See Chavasse, op. cit., Part 2, Chapter II, pp. 96–7).

130 'et post paululum incipiunt secundum laetaniam et post modicum intervallum cum tercia laetania ingrediuntur ad missas' (CC CLIX Vol. C 730).

131 'Et sic temperent ut in trinitatis numero ipsae litaniae fiant' (Old Gelasian, Mohlberg, 443; Sacramentary of Angoulême, CC CLIX Vol. C 755). The wording of the rubric is however somewhat ambiguous; it is possible that it simply means that three separate litanies are sung, as it seems to mean in *OR* XXXI, 'in nomine et virtute sanctae trinitatis tres laetaniae perficiantur' (*OR* XXXI. 95 [Andrieu *ORM* Vol. 3, p. 504]).

132 CC CLIX Vol. B 537. The response 'Te rogamus, audi nos' may originate in litany-type prayers in pre-Christian Rome (cf. Lactantius, *De mortibus persecutorum* lxvi, 6 [*PL* 7, 264]; Baumstark, op. cit., p. 79).

133 Martène, *DAER* IV. cap. XXIV, col. 437.

134 A. Bugnini, *The Reform of the Liturgy 1948–1975* (Collegeville, MN: Liturgical Press, 1990), p. 329.

135 *OR* XXIII. 23–32 (Andrieu, *ORM* Vol. 3, pp. 272–3); *OR* XXXB. 37–45, 58–62 (ibid., pp. 471–2, 474).

136 *OR* XXIV. 44–45, 51–54 (ibid., pp. 295–6); *OR* XXVII. 54, 61–64 (ibid., pp. 360–1). Similarly *OR* XXVIII. 66–67, 80 (ibid., pp. 405, 408), *OR* XXVIIIA. 2, 17–20 (ibid., pp. 421, 423–4) and XXIX. 57–60 (ibid., p. 445).

137 Fischer, *OEL*, p. 62.

138 Lanfranc, *Decreta* cap. I, iv (*PL* 150, 467).

139 J. Wickham Legg, op. cit., p. 132.

140 Roman Pontifical of the Twelfth Century XXXII. 12, 38 (Andrieu, PRM Vol. I,

pp. 241, 248); Pontifical of the Roman Curia XLIV. 10 (ibid., Vol. II, p. 473).

141 Pontifical of Durandus, Lib. III, iv. 13, 20 (Andrieu, PRM Vol. III, pp. 589, 591).

142 'cantatur letania in medio chori a duobus fratribus utroque choro idem simul respondente' (HBS, Vol. XVII, p. 190–3).

143 'Omnipotens sempiterne Deus respice propitius ad devotionem populi renascentis qui sicut cervus aquarum exspectat fontem, et concede propitius ut fidei ipsius sitis, baptismatis mysterio, animam corpusque sanctificet'. The prayer is first found in the Old Gelasian (Mohlberg, 442) and with only a minor variation in the text ('aquarum tuarum expetit fontem' for 'aquarum exspectat fontem') in the Gregorian Sacramentary (Wilson, HBS, Vol. XLIV, p. 55) and all subsequent Roman liturgical sources.

144 Sacramentary of Reichenau 52.19 (Schmidt, *HS*, p. 412); *OR* XXVIIIA. 4 (Andrieu, *ORM* Vol. 3, p. 421).

145 *Sacramentarium Gregorianum Cameracense* (Cambrai, Codex 164), Ottoboniense (Rome, Vat. lat.313) and Reginense (Rome, Vat. lat.337). Cf. Wilson, HBS, Vol. XLIV, p. 55 notes 8–9.

146 PRG cap. xxiv. 50 (ibid., Vol. 5, p. 278).

147 Roman Pontifical of the Twelfth Century XXXII. 22 (Andrieu, PRM Vol. I, p. 243); Pontifical of the Roman Curia XLIV. 18 (ibid., Vol. II, p. 475); Pontifical of Durandus Lib. III, iv. 15 (ibid., Vol. III, pp. 589–90).

148 Mohlberg, 444–448. For a detailed analysis of the prayer see Schmidt, *HS*, pp. 850–61.

149 Old Gelasian: 'Deus, cuius Spiritus super aquas inter ipsa mundi primordia ferebatur'; St Optatus: 'super quam ante ipsos natales mundi Sanctus Spiritus ferebatur'; Leonine Sacramentary: 'Deus, cuius Spiritus ferebatur super aquas' (Schmidt, *HS*, pp. 847, 850).

150 Compare 'procul ergo hinc, iubente te Domine, omnis spiritus immundus abscedat; procul tota nequitia diabolicae fraudis absistat' with 'procul, o procul este, profani … totoque absistite luco' (Virgil, *Aeneid* VI 258–259). The succeeding words 'non insidiando circumvolet, non latendo subrepat, non inficiendo corrumpat' also sound like a pagan apotropaic formula, though I have not been able to find any exact parallel.

151 Wilson, HBS, Vol. XLIV, pp. 55–7.

152 *OR* XXIII. 29–30 (Andrieu, *ORM* Vol. 3, p. 273); *OR* XXXB. 46–48 (ibid., p. 472).

153 *OR* XXIV. 47 (Andrieu, *ORM* Vol. 3, p 296); *OR* XXVII. 57 (ibid., p. 360); *OR* XXVIII. 70 (ibid., p. 405–6); *OR* XXXI. 80 (ibid., pp. 501–2.)

154 PRG cap. xxix 50 (Andrieu, *ORM* Vol. 5, pp. 278–81).

155 *OR* XXVIIIA. 4 (Andrieu, *ORM* Vol. 3, p. 421–2); *OR* XXXI. 80 (ibid., pp. 501–2).

156 See for example Dom Prosper Guéranger, *The Liturgical Year* (Loreto Publications, 2000), Vol. 6, p. 614.

157 Amalarius, *De ecclesiasticis officiis*, Lib. I cap. xxvi (*PL* 105, 1046).

158 Martène, *DAER* IV, cap. XXIV, col. 435.

159 The direction to touch the water at *Sit haec sancta* occurs in a single manuscript of the Romano-German Pontifical, from which presumably the Pontifical of the Twelfth Century, followed by all later pontificals, took it

(PRG xxix. 50 [Andrieu, *ORM* Vol. 5, p. 279 note 17]; Pontifical of the Twelfth Century xxxii. 22 [id. PRM Vol. I, p. 214]). According to Durandus there is only one triple insufflation at *Tu has simplices aquas* in the form of the letter Ψ, which almost certainly means that he has simply misplaced it from *Totamque huius aquae substantiam.* Unfortunately his error passed into later pontificals as two triple insufflations (Pontifical of Durandus Lib. III, iv. 15 [ibid., Vol. III, p. 590]).

160   *OR* XI. 94–95 (Andrieu, *ORM* Vol. 2, p. 445).

161   Sermo LXIX (*PL* 54, 386–389).

162   *OR* XXIV. 48; *OR* XXVII. 58; *OR* XXVIII. 71–72; *OR* XXVIIIA. 5–6; *OR* XXIX. 54; *OR* XXXI. 81–82 (Andrieu, *ORM* Vol. 3, pp. 296, 360, 406, 422, 445, 502); Sacramentary of Angoulême, CC CLIX Vol. C 758; Sacramentary of Gellone, id., Vol A 705; Sacramentary of Autun, id., Vol B 5391; Bobbio Missal 238 (Lowe, HBS, Vol. LVIII, p. 73); *Missale Gothicum* 259 (Bannister, HBS, Vol. LII, p. 77); *Missale Gallicanum Vetus* XXV (*PL* 72, 367–370).

163   *OR* XXXB. 47 (Andrieu, *ORM* Vol. 3, p. 472).

164   *OR* XXIII. 30 (ibid., p. 273).

165   'subdiaconus sumens vas aureum, unde mitttitur chrisma in fontem, et effundens in id de ampullis utrisque, id est de oleo sancto atque de chrismate, donat diacono, et ille pontifici. Pontifex vero fundit chrisma de vasculo aureo intra fontem super ipsam aquam in modum crucis, dicens lenta voce *Sanctificetur et foecundetur fons iste renascentibus ex eo in vitam aeternam.* Et cum vase aureo miscitat ipsum chrisma cum aqua et spargit cum manu sua per omnem fontem vel super omnem populum circumstantem. Hoc facto, omnis populus qui voluerit accipiat benedictionem, unusquisque in vase suo de ipsa aqua, antequam baptizentur parvuli, ad spargendum in domibus et vineis et campis vel fructibus suis'. The language suggests that the celebrant actually uses the gold vessel as an instrument to mix the oil with the water. (PRG cap. xxix 51–54 [Andrieu, *ORM* Vol. 5, pp. 281–2]).

166   Pontifical of Durandus, Lib. III, iv. 17 (Andrieu, PRM Vol. III, p. 590). In the later Sarum Missal the omission of the rite is mandatory if there is nobody to be baptized (F. E. Warren, op. cit, p. 284).

167   Roman Pontifical of the Twelfth Century XXXII. 23 (Andrieu, PRM Vol. I, p 245); Pontifical of the Roman Curia XLIV. 19 (ibid., Vol. II, p. 470).

168   For a comprehensive account, see E. J. Yarnold, *The Awe-Inspiring Rites of Initiation* (Edinburgh: T. and T. Clark Ltd., 1994).

169   Roman Pontifical of the Twelfth Century XXXII. 24–36 (Andrieu PRM Vol. I, pp. 245–8); cf. Pontifical of the Roman Curia XLIV. 20–26 (ibid., Vol. II, pp. 476–7).

170   'Postea vero ipse sacerdos revertit cum omnibus ordinibus in sacrario, et post paululum incipiunt tertiam litaniam. Et ingrediuntur ad missas in vigilia ut stella in caelo apparuerit' (Mohlberg, 443).

171   The relevant rubric provides that the Vigil should begin 'viii hora die mediante' (Mohlberg, 425). This time would vary somewhat depending on the latitude and the date of Easter.

172   *OR* XVII. 108–9 (Andrieu, *ORM* Vol. 3, p. 191).

173   *OR* XXXA. 13 (ibid., pp. 456–7); *OR* XXXII. 28–29 (ibid., p. 523).

174 PRG cap. xxix. 81–83, 97–98 (Andrieu, *ORM* Vol. 5, pp. 293, 296).

175 Martène, *DAER* IV, cap. XXIV, col. 436. As authority for the belief the pontifical quotes 'Media autem nocte clamor factus est, ecce sponsus venit' (Matt.
25:6).

176 Commentary on Matthew, Lib. IV, cap. xxv (*PL* 26, 184–185).

177 PRG cap. xxx. 1 (Andrieu, *ORM* Vol. 5, p. 297).

178 *OR* XXIII. 32–33 (ibid., Vol. 3, p. 273).

179 *OR* XXIV. 52 (ibid., p. 296); Pontifical of Poitiers (Martène, *DAER* IV. cap.
XXIV cols. 436–7); PRG cap. xxix. 80 (Andrieu, *ORM* Vol. 5, p. 292); Pontifical
of Durandus Lib. III, iv. 21 (id., PRM Vol. III, p. 591). Cf. also *OR* XXVII. 62,
OR XXVIII. 81, *OR* XXVIIIA. 18, *OR* XXIX. 58 and *OR* XXXI. 96 (id., *ORM* Vol.
3, pp. 361, 409, 424, 445 and 504).

180 The Pontifical of the Roman Curia XLIV. 30 says that the litany 'quasi pro
introitu cantatur', in other words it replaces the Introit which on other days
accompanies the procession of ministers from the sacristy to the altar
(Andrieu, PRM Vol. II, p. 478).

181 *OR* XXXI. 98, 'Letania expleta, dicat pontifex *Gloria in excelsis Deo* et
pulsentur signa' (Andrieu, *ORM* Vol. 3, p. 504). A rubric to ring the bells is
found in other ordines, for example in *OR* XXXII. 29 (ibid., p. 523), but in
these it merely seems to be a signal for the commencement of the third litany
which accompanies the procession into church for the start of the Mass, as it
is in the Romano-German Pontifical cap. xxix. 79 (ibid., Vol. 5, p. 292).

182 *Regularis Concordia* (*PL* 137, 494–495); *Disciplina Farfensis* cap. iv (*PL* 150,
1203–1204); Cluny, *Consuetudines* cap. xiv (*PL* 149, 663–664); John of
Avranches, *Lib. de officiis ecclesiasticis* (*PL* 147, 52–53).

183 PRG xxix. 79 (Andrieu, *ORM* Vol. 5, p. 292); Pontifical of Durandus Lib. III,
iv. 23 (id., *PRM* Vol. III, p. 592); *OR* xv, LXXX (*PL* 78, 1325).

184 Chavasse, op. cit., pp. 80–1; Righetti, op. cit., Vol. II.120, p. 200; *OR* XXXB. 64
(Andrieu, *ORM* Vol. 3, p. 473).

185 'Item dicitur *Gloria in excelsis Deo*, si episcopus fuerit, tantummodo die
dominico sive diebus festis, a presbyteris autem minime dicitur, nisi solo in
Pascha' (Jungmann, *MRR* Vol. I, p. 356).

186 *OR* XXXB. 65 (Andrieu, *ORM* Vol. 3, p. 474).

187 *OR* XXIII. 33 however prescribes the singing of the *Agnus Dei*, which must
therefore have been a feature of the papal rite at the time this ordo was
composed (ibid., p. 273). John Beleth, writing towards the end of the twelfth
century, says that some churches sing it and others do not (*Rationale*, cvi (*PL*
202, 111)). The overwhelming majority of the sources prescribe its omission.

188 Durandus, *Rationale*, Lib. VI, lxxxv. 5 (Dura, pp. 567–8).

189 However, the omission of the kiss of peace was probably connected with the
decline in the practice of general communion (Righetti, op. cit, Vol. II.120,
p. 201; Jungmann, *MRR* Vol. II, pp. 322–5). Jungmann also suggested that the
Agnus Dei, introduced into the daily Mass liturgy towards the end of the
seventh century, was omitted at the Easter Vigil Mass because it had already
been sung during the litanies (ibid., p. 333 n.6)

190 The direction to the celebrant to recite the penitential rite seems to occur for
the first time in the Pontifical of the Roman Curia XLIV. 30, from the early

thirteenth century: 'finita laetania, quae quasi pro introitu cantatur, cruce et faculis tunc super altare positis, pontifex ingrediatur ad altare et facit confessionem more solito' (Andrieu, PRM Vol. II, p. 478).

191 *Comes* of Würzburg (Schmidt, *HS*, p. 458); Lectionary of Corbie (ibid., p. 462); Lectionary of Alcuin (ibid., p. 463); *Comes* of Murbach (ibid., p. 464); *Comes* Theotinchi (ibid., p. 466). The Gallican Lectionary of Luxeuil has Romans 6:3–11 as the Epistle (ibid., p. 469).

192 *Evangeliorum Capitulare Romanum* II (ibid., p. 459); A (ibid.); Σ (ibid., p. 460); *Comes* of Murbach (ibid., p. 464); *Comes* Theotinchi (ibid., p. 466). The Gallican Lectionary of Luxeuil has Matt. 28:1–20 (ibid., p. 469).

193 Antiphonaries of Mont Blandin (ibid., p. 483), Rheinau (ibid., p. 485), Gradual of Monza (ibid., p. 488), Antiphonaries of Senlis (ibid., p. 490), Compiègne (ibid., p. 495), Corbie (ibid., p. 498).

194 Mohlberg, 454 & 456, Wilson, HBS, Vol. XLIV, p. 58.

195 Mohlberg, 461–462; Wilson, HBS, Vol. XLIV, p. 59. The Frankish Gelasians also normally contain two Postcommunion prayers, though the second one differs from that in the Old Gelasian. The Sacramentary of Gellone gives all three (CC CLIX Vol. A 724–726).

196 Pontifical of the Twelfth Century XXXIII. 39 (Andrieu, PRM Vol. I, p. 248).

197 Ordinary of the Papal Chaplains and *Missale Romanum* III. 31 (ibid., Vol. II, Appendix ii, pp. 576–7).

198 Pontifical of Durandus Lib.III, iv. 25 (ibid., Vol III, p. 592).

199 Mohlberg, 457–458. Wilson, HBS, Vol. XLIV, p. 59. The Gallican *Missale Gothicum* has a lengthy Preface which repeats some of the thematic material from the *Exsultet* (Bannister, HBS, Vol. LII, p. 79).

200 Sacramentary of Fulda 107.717 (Schmidt, *HS*, p. 426); Sacramentary of St Eligius 141 (ibid., p. 445).

201 CC CLX (*Corpus Orationum*) Vol. I X, nos. 6130a, 6255a (Cf. Mohlberg, 459–460).

202 Sacramentary of San Gall II 99.561 (Schmidt, *HS*, p. 410); Sacramentary of Angoulême, CC CLIX Vol. C 770.

203 CC ibid., no. 6255b. (Cf. Schmidt, *HS*, pp. 872–3).

204 *OR* XXIX. 56 (Andrieu, *ORM* Vol. 3, p. 445); *OR* XXXI. 121 (ibid., p. 508).

205 Where Vespers were sung before the beginning of Mass, it seems likely that the psalms and antiphons would have been those of the Saturday feria. For a comprehensive discussion of the subject see Schmidt, *HS*, pp. 890–900.

206 *OR* XXXII. 32 (Andrieu, *ORM* Vol. 3, p. 524).

207 PRG cap. xxix. 89 (Andrieu, *ORM* Vol. 5, p. 294).

208 *OR* XVI. 38 (ibid., Vol. 3, p. 152); *OR* XXVIII. 58 (ibid., Vol. 3, p. 403).

209 *OR* XXXB. 37 (ibid., Vol. 3, p. 471); PRG cap. xxix. 11 (ibid., Vol. 5, p. 264). *OR* XXIII. 23 and *OR* XXIX. 45 also prescribe the seventh hour as the start time for the Vigil (ibid., Vol. 3, pp. 272, 443).

210 Pontifical of the Roman Curia XLIV. 1 (id., PRM Vol. II, p. 470); Pontifical of Durandus Lib. III, iv 1 (ibid., Vol. III, p. 587); Pontifical of the Twelfth Century XXXII. 1 (ibid., Vol. I, p. 238).

CHAPTER 10

THE 1955 REFORM

As we have seen in earlier chapters, the hours at which the ceremonies of the Triduum were celebrated were gradually advanced
during the course of history until they reached the point when the
Mass of the Lord's Supper on Maundy Thursday, the Solemn
Commemoration of the Passion on Good Friday and the Easter
Vigil on Holy Saturday were all celebrated in the morning of the
respective days, and the Office of Matins and Lauds (Tenebrae) on
the previous afternoon. The celebration of the first Mass of Easter
on the Saturday morning, a day which is properly characterized
as one of mourning and which was therefore regarded from the
beginning, together with Good Friday, as one on which it was not
proper to celebrate the Eucharist, was particularly inappropriate,[1]
but an even more serious consequence was a steady decline in the
numbers of the faithful attending these ceremonies, especially
when, owing to the pressure of social and economic changes,
Urban VIII in his Apostolic Constitution *Universa per orbem* of 24
September 1642 changed the status of the three days to ferias,
thereby removing the obligation of attendance. Eventually it
became the norm in many places for the ceremonies of the
Triduum to be celebrated by the clergy alone in otherwise almost
empty churches.[2] From the point of view of the laity, the liturgical
actions were replaced by popular devotions such as Eucharistic
adoration at the Altar of Repose on Maundy Thursday and the
Stations of the Cross on Good Friday. In their own way these
devotions were highly commendable and they attracted large
numbers of the faithful, but they had no liturgical foundation.

The first move towards rectifying this state of affairs took place
in 1951 and related only to the Easter Vigil. A decree of the Sacred
Congregation of Rites dated 9 February 1951, *Dominicae*

Resurrectionis vigiliam, gave permission for the Vigil to be held in the evening of Holy Saturday. The decree records that a large number of requests for this had been received from 'many Ordinaries, congregations of faithful and men of religion'. The permission related to the year 1951 only, as an experiment. Ordinaries who made use of the permission granted were requested to report to the Sacred Congregation of Rites on the numbers and devotion of the faithful attending and on the success of the experiment.[3]

Some major and important changes were made to the rite, both of the Vigil and of the Mass. These were to be introduced, however, only when the ceremony took place in the evening; where the permission granted by the decree was not taken advantage of, the existing rite was to remain unchanged. For the time being, therefore, there were two different rites in use simultaneously, one for a morning celebration and one for the evening.[4]

The experiment proved successful, and many requests were received by the Sacred Congregation of Rites for its extension. Accordingly it was extended for a further three years, by a decree of 11 January 1952, accompanied by a set of detailed instructions regarding the evening celebration. It was provided that, although normally Mass was not to begin before midnight, in exceptional circumstances it could be anticipated, with the permission of the Ordinary, though in no circumstances was the Vigil itself to begin before eight o'clock in the evening. Strangely perhaps, where Mass was celebrated before midnight, attendance did not fulfil the Sunday obligation. Where Mass began at midnight or later, the Eucharistic fast was enjoined from ten o'clock in the evening; otherwise, from seven o'clock. In places where there was more than one church, the ringing of the bells was to be coordinated; in the cathedral or major church it was to take place at the beginning of the Gloria, and the other churches were to join in simultaneously.[5]

On the expiry of the three-year period, the permission was renewed for a further year by a decree of 15 January 1955. By this time, a thorough revision of the entire Holy Week liturgy by a commission set up by Pope Pius XII was well under way. The commission's proposals were accepted by the Sacred Congregation of Rites on 19 July of the same year and, following approval by the Pope, were published in a decree, *Maxima redemptionis nostra mysteria,* to which was attached a lengthy *instructio,* on 16 November, to come into effect on Palm Sunday, 25 March 1956.[6]

Palm Sunday

The official name of the day was changed from *Dominica in Palmis* (Palm Sunday) to *Dominica II Passionis seu in Palmis* (the Second Sunday in Passiontide, or Palm Sunday).[7] The reason seems to have been to re-emphasize the fact that from the earliest times it was the day on which, in the Roman rite, the Gospel of the Passion according to St Matthew had been read, thereby giving the liturgy of the day a double aspect, of triumph and of mourning.[8]

Major changes were made to the rite of blessing the palms and the subsequent procession. These changes were driven by the desire to transfer the focus of the rite from the former to the latter. As we have seen, the blessing of the palms had, in the course of the Middle Ages, become disproportionately lengthy. In the earliest sources we find a simple blessing of the palms, followed by their distribution to the clergy and congregation. But in the tenth-century Romano-German Pontifical the rite of blessing takes the form of a preliminary *missa sicca,* followed by an exorcism and a large number of prayers of blessing. Some of these were intended as alternatives, depending on whether palms, olives or other species of foliage were to be blessed. Others were incorporated from various sources, in a manner typical of this Pontifical, and may also have been intended as alternatives. In any event as time went by it became the practice to multiply the blessings. Six of the prayers from the Romano-German Pontifical appear in the Roman Missal of 1474, together with three others, and they are all clearly meant to be said. Eight of the prayers from this source found their way into the Missal of Pius V. At the same time the elaborate and frequently highly dramatic ceremonial which accompanied the procession in the later Middle Ages, and in which the entire community took part, gradually went into decline, to the extent that eventually the procession became not much more than an appendage to the blessing, confined to the celebrant and ministers.

A secondary motive which seems to have animated those involved in the 1955 reform was the desire to return to an earlier and simpler form of the rites by removing elements which were seen as the consequence of later development and elaboration, a practice which came to be known, especially by those who did not subscribe to the principle that 'earlier is better', as 'liturgical archaeology'.

The reformed rite accordingly did away altogether with the *missa sicca*, as well as most of the subsequent prayers of blessing. The celebrant is vested in a red cope, and the other ministers are likewise in red. Previously the colour was violet, as for the Mass; the new colour, by contrast with that of the Mass, points more clearly to the festive character of the blessing of palms and procession.[9] There is no preliminary sprinkling with holy water (*Asperges*) of the altar and those present, as was the norm in the previous rite. The faithful may hold their palms in their hands, or they may be placed on a table in the sanctuary, near the altar rails; this table must be easily visible by the people. After the antiphon *Hosanna filio David* the palms are blessed with a single prayer of blessing, *Benedic quaesumus, Domine, hos palmarum ramos* (the seventh prayer in the old missal), then sprinkled three times with holy water, incensed the same number of times, and distributed to the clergy and the congregation. The distribution is accompanied by Psalms 23 and 46, with the antiphons *Pueri Hebraeorum portantes ramos* and *Pueri Hebraeorum vestimenta prosternebant*. The custom of kissing the hand of the celebrant and the palm before taking the latter was abolished. If preferred, the distribution may be dispensed with altogether, in which case the clergy and congregation simply hold their palms in their hands from the outset, and the sprinkling and incensation take place with the celebrant traversing the length of the nave.

The Gospel from St Matthew 21:1–9 is then read, with the usual preliminaries, and the procession follows at once. It is preceded by the thurifer with incense and the cross bearer between two acolytes carrying lighted candles. In contrast to the previous rite, the processional cross is unveiled.[10] Behind them come the clergy and the celebrant, with the deacon and subdeacon, and finally the congregation, carrying their palms. The blessing of the palms may take place in one church and the Mass in another. In any case part of the procession should take place outside the church, wherever possible. During it some or all of the antiphons *Occurrunt turbae, Cum angelis et pueris, Turba multa, Coeperunt omnes, Omnes collaudunt, Fulgentibus palmis* and *Ave Rex noster* are sung, with Psalm 147 and the hymn *Gloria, laus et honor*. Other chants in honour of Christ the King, in particular *Christus vincit*, may be sung. The procession re-enters the church to the antiphon *Ingrediente Domino*. The late medieval ceremony of knocking on the church door with the foot of the processional cross on re-entry was abolished. When the celebrant arrives at the altar, he stands facing the people, and the rite concludes with a prayer, *Domine Jesu Christe, Rex et Redemptor noster*, which, though a new composition, has some verbal similarities with the blessing *Deus qui dispersa congregas* from the old missal. It asks that 'wherever these palms are taken, there the grace of Thy blessing may descend, and may Thy right hand, frustrating every wickedness and delusion of evil spirits, protect those whom it has redeemed'.[11]

Relatively few changes were made to the Palm Sunday Mass itself. The liturgical colour remained violet. The prayers at the foot of the altar were suppressed and the Mass begins directly with the Introit, a return to earlier practice which in this instance attracted little criticism. A more controversial change (and one which was reversed in the 1970 reform) was to shorten the Passion narrative by omitting altogether Matthew 26:1–30, which includes the account of the Last Supper. The main reason for restricting the reading to the account of the Passion proper seems to have been the desire for strict symmetry with the Good Friday narrative, which begins with the entry into the Garden of Gethsemane. It seems a poor reason for depriving the Holy Week liturgy of all the synoptic accounts of the Last Supper (thereby breaking the intimate connection between the institution of the Eucharist and Christ's sacrifice on the Cross), especially since they have been read as part of the Passion narratives on Palm Sunday and Wednesday since the seventh century at the latest, and probably much earlier.[12]

Before the reading begins the deacon requests and receives a blessing in the usual form. *Dominus vobiscum* and *Gloria tibi Domine* are not said, nor does the deacon make the sign of the cross on the book or on himself, but the reading commences simply with *Passio Domini nostri Jesu Christi secundum Matthaeum*.[13] The practice of kneeling and pausing briefly at the words *emisit spiritum* was retained. However, the custom of treating 27:62–66 as effectively the Gospel of the day, separate from the Passion narrative, by singing it in the normal gospel tone, preceded by all the usual preliminaries, was discontinued. For some reason which has never been explained, the final sentence of the narrative, 'Now Mary of Magdala and the other Mary were there, sitting opposite the sepulchre', was expunged. At the end of the reading the book is not kissed or incensed.[14]

The previous practice of the participants holding their palms in their hands during the reading of the Passion was discontinued, deemed inappropriate since that part of the Palm Sunday liturgy which relates to palms has already been concluded, and bears no relation to the reading of the Passion.[15] There were no other changes to the texts of the Mass, except that the Last Gospel was to be said only when the Mass was not preceded by the blessing of palms.[16]

One change of profound significance, however, was made to the manner of celebration during Holy Week generally by the 1955 reform. During the later Middle Ages it had become the standard practice for the celebrant to repeat in a low voice at the altar all the texts which properly belonged to others, whether ministers, choir or congregation. The first mention of this rule seems to be in the *Ordo Ecclesiae Lateranensis* of about 1140, though at this stage it is confined to the Introit, the *Gloria*, the *Credo*, the *Sanctus* and the *Agnus Dei*. In the Dominican ordinarium of 1256 it was prescribed for all the texts sung by the choir, though not yet for the readings.[17] Towards the end of the same century Durandus tells us that when the Pope says or hears Mass his chaplains are in the habit of reading the Introit, *Kyrie, Gloria, Credo, Sanctus* and *Agnus Dei* (but not apparently the Gradual, Alleluia, Offertory or Communion verse), while the choir are singing them.[18] The same practice is found in *Ordo Romanus* xiv from the middle of the fourteenth century.[19] From Rome it seems, like so many other liturgical practices, to have spread outwards, and finally the Pian Missal of 1570 prescribed the duplication by the celebrant of everything. The 1951 ordo revising the Easter Vigil rite however enjoined that the celebrant should simply sit and listen while the lessons were being read. The revised rite of Holy Week restored the original practice whereby those parts of the celebration which were appropriate to a deacon, subdeacon or lector were performed by them alone.[20] It was a change which was to be extended to the liturgy generally in the 1970 reform.

The Intermediate Days

The only major change introduced on these three days was the shortening of the Passion narratives on Tuesday and Wednesday to begin with the entry into the Garden of Gethsemane. As on Palm Sunday, the deacon's request for a blessing was moved from the words *Et iam sero esset factum* (Tuesday) and *Et ecce, vir nomine Joseph* (Wednesday) to the beginning of the narrative. Also as on Palm Sunday, there was no *Dominus vobiscum* or *Gloria tibi Domine*, nor were lights or incense carried or the sign of the cross made by the deacon or celebrant on the book or on himself.

The practice of saying a second Collect, Secret and Postcommunion prayer for the Church or the Pope was prohibited on all three days. On Wednesday, a pause for silent prayer was introduced between *Flectamus genua* and *Levate* before the first Collect.[21]

Tenebrae

The 1955 liturgical reform made only a few relatively minor changes; the silent recitation of the *Pater*, *Ave* and Creed at the beginning of Matins and the repeat of the *Miserere* at the end of Lauds (for which Allegri composed his famous setting) were abolished, as was the *strepitus*, and the final candle is left burning on the hearse until the departure of the participants instead of being hidden behind the altar after the *Benedictus*. The reason given for the abolition of the final *Miserere* was that it was an addition of the twelfth century, the unwritten assumption being that this was in itself a sufficient motive for removing it. The reason given for the abolition of the *strepitus* and the hiding of the final candle was that these were merely practical in origin, designed respectively as a signal to the choir that the office was over, and as a light to enable them to find their way out, and had only later acquired symbolic significance, the former as representing the earthquake which accompanied the death of Christ and the latter his burial and resurrection.[22]

It is true of many liturgical actions (not excluding those surrounding the Paschal Candle) that they had practical origins and acquired their symbolic significance only later. The correct test surely is whether or not the symbolism which they have come

to acquire is still meaningful today. By this standard the conceal-
ment and subsequent disclosure of the final candle should
probably have been retained, though possibly not the *strepitus*. On
this question Thurston rightly remarks,

> The symbolism of any rite depends not upon the fact that it was
> designed with a mystical intention by its first inventors, but only
> upon this, that under the providence of God and with the tacit
> approval of Holy Church, a certain meaning has become attached
> to it in the minds of the faithful ... thus many of our most beautiful
> pieces of symbolism are certainly after-thoughts which never
> entered into the mind of the framers of the ceremony ... but some
> even of the most fanciful interpretations can plead a venerable
> antiquity, and the symbolism is true and deserves respect the
> moment it is generally accepted by the faithful at large.[23]

The principal change however that was made in 1955 was in the
timing of the office; before 1955 it had been sung by anticipation
on the evening preceding the relevant day of the Triduum; the
1955 reform restored it to the morning of the day to which it
belonged. There was one partial exception to this: Tenebrae of
Maundy Thursday was permitted to continue to be sung on the
preceding evening in a church where the Chrism Mass was celebrated on Thursday morning. This change from an evening to a
morning celebration led to a loss in the symbolism and the
dramatic effect of deepening darkness created by the fading of
daylight, accompanied by the gradual extinguishing of the
candles, but it was the necessary consequence of the restoration of
the Holy Thursday and Good Friday liturgies to the evening and
late afternoon respectively of those days.

Maundy Thursday

As we have seen in Chapter 7, there were originally in the Roman
titular churches both a morning Mass, later adapted to include the
reconciliation of penitents, and an evening Mass of the Lord's
Supper. The Pope celebrated a single midday Mass at the Lateran,
at which the chrism and the other oils were blessed. In the
Gelasian tradition there was a third Mass as well, at which the oils
of the sick and of the catechumens for use in the parish were
blessed by the presiding priest. With the decline of the Gelasian

tradition these three Masses went out of use and were replaced by the single Gregorian Mass of the papal liturgy, which in the later Middle Ages came to be celebrated in the morning.

The 1955 reform restored the special Chrism Mass, to be celebrated in the morning, after Terce, at the cathedral or major church of each diocese, in a festive manner, with white vestments. It was the most striking example in the 1955 reform of 'liturgical archaeology', though in the case of the Chrism Mass it took the form of a deliberate revival of a former rite or practice which had long since become obsolete, rather than the simplification of an existing rite.

The Collect, Secret, Preface and Postcommunion prayer of this Mass were taken verbatim from the Old Gelasian Sacramentary.[24] Since no evidence appears to have survived relating to the remaining propers, including the readings, the Introit of the restored Mass was taken from Exodus 30, 25 & 31, the Gradual from Psalm 27:7–8, the Offertory from Psalm 44:7 and the Communion verse from Mark 6:12–13. The Epistle selected was that of James 5:13–16 and the Gospel Mark 6:7–13. Anointing with holy oil is the common thread found in all these texts. The blessing of the oils takes place, as before, during the Canon of the Mass, after the *Nobis quoque peccatoribus*. Only one change was made to the rubrics and texts of the blessing in the existing Pontifical; to avoid duplication, the text of the Preface of the Mass, which had been added to the blessing of the chrism when the old Gelasian Chrism Mass went out of use, was removed. There is no general distribution of Holy Communion. The Mass concludes with the *Ite missa est* and the usual blessing.[25]

Private Masses on this day are proscribed altogether, and priests who are thereby prevented from celebrating Mass should be present in choral dress at the Mass of the Lord's Supper and communicate at that Mass. The original timing of this Mass was restored. It was provided that it should begin at a convenient time, but in any case not earlier than five o'clock and not later than eight. The tabernacle is to be emptied before the start of Mass, with Communion being distributed from a ciborium containing hosts consecrated only at this Mass. White vestments are to be worn, as previously. A brief homily is to be preached after the Gospel, on the themes of the institution of the Eucharist and the priesthood, and the Lord's injunction regarding brotherly love.

Few changes were made to the texts of the existing Mass, but in view of the fact that there was no *Pax* on this day, it was provided that the second repeat of the *Agnus Dei* was to terminate with *miserere nobis* instead of *dona nobis pacem*, and the prayer which immediately follows, *Domine Iesu Christi, qui dixisti*, was to be omitted altogether. The usual confession and absolution before distribution of communion to the sacred ministers, clergy and people are also omitted.[26] Any clergy present receive communion in order of rank, after the ministers, and before the altar servers. All those in the sanctuary are required to approach two by two or four by four, making a genuflection before ascending the altar steps to receive the sacrament. The faithful receive communion at the altar rails, as usual. If the numbers warrant it, other priests than the celebrant may assist with the distribution of communion, and the choir may sing one or more of Psalms 22 (*Dominus regit me*), 71 (*Deus iudicium tuum regi da*), 103 (*Benedic anima mea Domino*) and 150 (*Laudate Dominum in sanctis eius*), repeating the Communion antiphon *Dominus Jesus* between each psalm and at the end. The Mass ends with *Benedicamus Domino* (previously *Ite, Missa est*) and the prayer *Placeat tibi, sancta Trinitas*, with no blessing and no last Gospel.[27]

The *mandatum* had hitherto taken place (if at all) after the stripping of the altars, but it was now recommended that where possible it be carried out immediately after the homily. Any twelve men could be selected to have their feet washed, whether clerics or lay. Otherwise the form of the ceremony remained much as before, except that when it was performed immediately after the homily, the repetition at the beginning of the Gospel of the Mass was, for obvious reasons, to be omitted.[28]

The procession to the Altar of Repose takes place immediately after the end of the evening Mass. The only change of any significance made in the processional rite is that the Blessed Sacrament is now to be conveyed in a ciborium rather than the chalice which had been used since the time of *Ordo Romanus* xv. The hymn *Pange lingua gloriosi* continued to be sung during the procession, as before, with the last two verses reserved until the Altar of Repose was reached. There, after the celebrant has incensed the Sacred Species, the deacon places them in the tabernacle and all remain a few moments on their knees in adoration before departing, in silence, to the sacristy, where the celebrant and deacon lay aside their white vestments and assume a violet stole in preparation for the stripping of the altars. During the latter, which commences with the main altar, Psalm 21 (*Deus meus, respice in me*) is recited by the ministers, with the antiphon *Diviserunt sibi vestimenta mea*, as before.

Vespers, previously recited immediately before the stripping of the altars, are omitted altogether, when (as in normal circumstances) the principal liturgical function is celebrated in the evening. Compline however continued to be said after its conclusion.[29]

Good Friday

The official name of the day was changed from *Feria Sexta in Parasceve* ('Friday of the Preparation') to *Feria Sexta in Passione et Morte Domini* ('Friday of the Passion and Death of the Lord'). The timing of the solemn liturgy of the Passion was moved from the morning to the afternoon, commencing preferably around three o'clock, the hour when Christ died, and in any case not later than six.

In its pre-1955 form the synaxis began with a silent entrance of the priest, deacon and subdeacon, robed in black chasuble, dalmatic and tunicle respectively, without lights or incense. On arriving at the altar all three prostrated themselves in silent prayer, while an acolyte spread a single cloth on the altar. Then the sacred ministers rose and kissed the altar, and a lector began the first reading, without title, while the priest read it in a low voice at the Epistle side. In the reformed rite the priest and deacon simply wear amice, alb and black stole, the subdeacon amice and alb. The altar remains bare throughout the synaxis. After the initial prostration the priest says the Collect *Deus qui peccati veteris*, after which the lector begins the first reading, to which the priest, together with the other ministers, listens.[30]

In the Gelasian tradition there is a Collect before each of the two Old Testament readings, *Deus a quo et Iudas* before the first and *Deus qui peccati veteris* before the second; in the original Gregorian tradition there are no Collects at all. However, during the later eighth century the Collect *Deus a quo et Iudas* was added to the Gregorian system, but before the second reading, not the first. This scheme was followed in almost all the later *Ordines Romani*, the Romano-German Pontifical and in all the subsequent Roman pontificals, and eventually in the Missal of Pius V. Only in *Ordo Romanus* XXXII do we find both *Deus qui peccati veteris* (before the first reading) and *Deus a quo et Iudas* (before the second), and then in only the Paris manuscript of this ordo; the Cambridge manuscript (the only other surviving manuscript) has them in the reverse order, following the Gelasian tradition.[31] The Pontifical of Durandus, however, follows the Paris manuscript of *Ordo* XXIII, and this was evidently the source on which the reformers relied in their revision of the synaxis.[32]

It is prescribed that before the singing or reading of the Passion narrative the celebrant is to give a blessing to the deacon or deacons concerned, though they do not ask for one in the normal manner. Previously this blessing had been neither asked for nor given. Since this had been the practice from time immemorial, the purpose of the change is unclear. The genuflection and pause after *Et inclinato capite tradidit spiritum* was retained, but the practice of saying the *Munda cor meum* after the words *Videbunt in quem transfixerunt* and singing the rest of the narrative in the gospel tone, which began only in the late Middle Ages, was abolished, as on the other days of Holy Week. The practice of having the celebrant simultaneously recite the narrative in a low tone at the Epistle side of the altar, also originating in the later Middle Ages, was abolished too, as during the rest of Holy Week.[33]

After the conclusion of the Passion, the celebrant, deacon and subdeacon vest in a black cope, dalmatic and tunicle respectively, while an acolyte spreads a single cloth on the altar. The celebrant and other ministers then go up to the altar, which they kiss, and the *Orationes Sollemnes* begin. A new prayer for those involved in the government of states was substituted for the old prayer for the Roman Emperor; otherwise there was no change in the text of any of the prayers. However, a brief pause for silent prayer was enjoined between the deacon's *Flectamus genua* and *Levate*.[34]

Significant changes were however made to the Adoration of the Cross.[35] After the conclusion of the *Orationes Sollemnes* the celebrant doffs his cope and the deacon and subdeacon their dalmatic and tunicle. The cross to be solemnly unveiled is brought in procession from the sacristy (previously it had been kept in readiness towards the rear of the Epistle side of the altar, and simply handed to the celebrant by the deacon). The procession is headed by acolytes, followed by the deacon carrying the cross, between two other acolytes with lighted candles. When it enters the sanctuary it is met by the celebrant and subdeacon, and the cross is handed to the former, who takes it to the Epistle side of the altar where, facing the people, he uncovers the upper portion, intoning the antiphon *Ecce lignum Crucis*, which is taken up by the ministers, the choir responding with *Venite adoremus*.[36] The rest of the unveiling takes place as before, though the celebrant is accompanied throughout by the two acolytes with lighted candles, one on each side. The procession with lighted candles was an innovation, without apparent precedent, introduced 'to increase the solemnity of the rite'.[37]

For the veneration, the cross is supported on either side by an acolyte, as in *Ordo Romanus* XXIV and the Romano-German Pontifical, on a footstool in the sanctuary. The two other acolytes place their lighted candles on either side of the cross, and kneel down. It is then venerated by the celebrant and other ministers, in order of rank, each of whom makes a triple genuflection. When they have finished, the cross is taken by the same two acolytes, again accompanied by the two with lighted candles, to the altar rails, where they hold it in the same way while the faithful venerate it one by one, this time with a single genuflection. The rubric provides that the veneration be performed first by the men present, then by the women, a rule which was seldom if ever observed in practice. Meanwhile the *Improperia, Trisagion*, Psalm 66:2 with antiphon *Crucem tuam adoramus* and the hymn *Crux Fidelis* are sung by the choir, but no longer duplicated by the celebrant and ministers. The chants continue as long as required, but must always conclude with the doxology at the end of the *Crux Fidelis, Sempiterna sit beatae Trinitati gloria*. After all present have venerated the cross, it is carried back to the altar, still accompanied by the two acolytes with lighted candles, and installed in a place above the altar, high enough to be seen by all the faithful.

The celebrant, deacon and subdeacon then vest in chasuble, dalmatic and tunicle of violet colour. The deacon places the corporal upon the altar, in the normal way; a bowl of water, with a purificator, is also put on the altar, for washing and drying the ministers' fingers after the distribution of Holy Communion, together with the missal on the Gospel side. The Blessed Sacrament is brought back from the Altar of Repose, but by a deacon, not by the priest. The primitive simplicity of the procession was restored. The deacon, accompanied only by two acolytes and a minister to hold the umbrella, goes to the Altar of Repose. After a simple genuflection he takes the ciborium from the tabernacle and, assuming a white humeral veil, the end of which he wraps around it, carries it back under the umbrella, accompanied by the two acolytes bearing lighted candles, to the main altar, where he places it on the corporal. The acolytes put their candles on the altar. Meanwhile the choir sings three antiphons, *Adoramus te Christe, Per lignum servi facti sumus* and *Salvator mundi salva nos.*[38]

Omitting all the subsequent prayers which were added to the rite in the later Middle Ages, as well as the incensation of the offerings and of the altar, the celebrant immediately pronounces the usual introductory words to the *Pater Noster,* and then all present recite it together. The celebrant says the embolism aloud, and the preparatory prayer for Holy Communion, *Perceptio Corporis tui,* in a low voice, omitting the elevation of the Host and the *fractio* in the former rite, as well as the prayer *Panem caelestem accipiam et nomen Domini invocabo.* He then recites the *Domine, non sum dignus* three times, and receives the Blessed Sacrament, remaining afterwards for a few moments in silent meditation.[39]

Notwithstanding the fact that the Eucharist has never been celebrated on Good Friday, it was usual in the early centuries for all those present, as well as the celebrant, to receive Holy Communion from the reserved Sacrament. This practice declined only gradually, concomitant with the general decline of communion among the laity, though it was not actually forbidden until 1622. The custom was restored in the 1955 reform, in response to numerous requests for its reinstatement.[40] The *Confiteor* is recited and absolution given as usual. Communion is distributed as on Maundy Thursday, except that the priests involved wear a violet stole instead of a white one. During the distribution Psalm 21 *Deus, Deus meus, respice in me* may be sung, or one or more of the responsories from Matins of the day. When it is complete the celebrant washes his hands in silence, and then says three prayers of thanksgiving, *Super populum tuum, Omnipotens et misericors Deus* and *Reminiscere miserationum tuarum Domine.*[41] The first and second of these prayers were taken (with minor verbal changes) from the Leonine Sacramentary, the last is that given in the Old Gelasian as the Collect for Monday in Holy Week.[42] All present stand and repeat *Amen*.

As on the previous day, the recitation of Vespers after the conclusion of the liturgy was suppressed, though Compline continued to be recited, without lights. At a convenient opportunity the Blessed Sacrament is removed to an appropriate place of reservation, and the altar is stripped in silence.[43]

Holy Saturday

The most significant change of the 1955 reform was the return of the Easter Vigil celebration to the evening of Holy Saturday. Over the course of time the most important liturgical function of the entire year had become, so far as the faithful were concerned, merely a series of arcane and largely incomprehensible rites carried out very early in the morning by the clergy in churches empty of all except the odd liturgical enthusiast. It also involved the anomaly of celebrating the first Mass of Easter before the formal conclusion of Lent at midday. It is something of a wonder that this indefensible state of affairs was allowed to continue for so many centuries before the celebration of the Vigil was restored to its proper time.

The Vigil begins with the kindling of the new fire outside the church. The celebrant, clad in a violet cope, blesses it with a single prayer, *Deus qui per Filium tuum, angularem scilicet lapidem*. This represents a return to the earliest practice. In the previous rite there were three prayers of blessing, taken from the Romano-German Pontifical, the compiler of which derived them from various sources and almost certainly intended them to be employed as alternatives.[44] The fire is then sprinkled with holy water and incensed three times, using a thurible lit from the same fire. The blessing of the five grains of incense to be inserted into the Paschal Candle, which followed immediately in the former rite, is deferred till after the blessing of the candle.[45]

The ceremonies surrounding the Paschal Candle were entirely remodelled, with the object of focusing attention more clearly on the candle itself. The blessing of the candle and the insertion of the five grains of incense were detached from the singing of the *Exsultet* and made the subject of a separate rite. The candle is no longer set up inside the sanctuary before the beginning of the ceremony. Instead it is presented at the entrance to the church by an acolyte to the celebrant, who first cuts a cross upon it, saying *Christus heri et hodie* (with the downward stroke) and *Principium et finis* (with the transverse stroke). He then inscribes the Greek letters A and Ω above and below this cross respectively, pronouncing their names as he does so. Finally he inserts the figures making up the current year in the four corners of the cross, saying *Ipsius sunt tempora* (with the figure designating the millenium), *et saecula* (with that of the century), *Ipsi gloria et imperium* (with that of the decade) *per universa aeternitatis saecula* (with that of the current year). He then blesses and incenses the five grains of incense, in silence, and inserts them into the candle, saying *Per sua sancta vulnera* (first) *gloriosa* (second) *custodiat* (third) *et conservet nos* (fourth) *Christus Dominus. Amen* (fifth). The new rite makes explicit, for the first time, the symbolic interpretation of the grains of incense as representing the five wounds of Christ.[46]

The practice of incising a cross on the candle, rather than simply blessing it by making the sign of the cross over it with the hand, seems to be first recorded in the Pontifical of Poitiers of about 900. It recurs in the Romano-German Pontifical of the mid-tenth century (the former adds the current year and indiction, though there is no mention in the latter of any further additions).[47] The inscription of the letters A and Ω and of the current year however both occur in the Sacramentary of Ratoldus (from Corbie, near Amiens), of about 980.[48] The same sacramentary also prescribes the incision of a cross, though this is to be made 'with incense'; this appears to be the first reference we have to the insertion of grains of incense in the shape of a cross on the candle.

It seems to have been around the end of the same century that the ceremonies surrounding the Paschal Candle were adopted, under the influence of the Romano-German Pontifical, in the city of Rome, though they had been practised in the surrounding area since the time of Pope Zosimus. The Roman Pontifical of the Twelfth Century records that according to his prescription a cross is cut with a stylus, and the letters A and Ω and the year are incised on the candle, though this is not done in the city itself. This is not, of course, good evidence for what Zosimus may have prescribed seven hundred years earlier, but it is for the prevailing practice in the dioceses outside the city in the twelfth century.[49] In any event the custom of inserting the Greek letters and the year did not survive for very long and it is not found in the 1474 Missal, the precursor of that of Pius V. The insertion of the five grains of incense was continued, but during the singing of the *Exsultet*, the place which it occupies in the Pontifical of the Twelfth Century. The 1955 rite was revived (in yet another instance of 'liturgical archaeology') from the aforementioned sources. The words which are pronounced by the celebrant during the rite were however entirely new.

After the blessing the candle is lit from the new fire and is then carried in procession to the sanctuary by the deacon, vested in a white stole and dalmatic, preceded by the thurifer and cross bearer and followed by the celebrant, clergy and people. The reason for prescribing the lighting of the candle before the procession is that

> the significance of the candle, as a symbol of the Risen Christ, is fully complete only when it is lit ... The greeting *Lumen Christi* should certainly be directed to the candle, which in the natural order of things takes centre place in the entire sacred action from the blessing of the new fire until the end of the *Laus cerei*.[50]

The procession makes the usual three stations, at each of which the deacon sings *Lumen Christi* in an increasingly higher tone, whereupon the people kneel and reply *Deo gratias*. At the first station the candle carried by the celebrant is lit from the Paschal Candle, at the second those of the clergy and at the third those of the faithful. When the sanctuary is reached the church lights are lit. The deacon requests a blessing in the normal way and then, after incensing the book and the candle, begins the *Exsultet*, during which all present stand and hold their lighted candles. The only change in the text of the *Exsultet* was the substitution of a reference to the civil authorities instead of the emperor at the conclusion.[51]

As we have seen in Chapter 9, the most common practice throughout history was for the Paschal Candle to be set up in the sanctuary beforehand and to be lighted from a candle or candles themselves lit from the new fire and carried in procession through the church. The practice of carrying the Paschal Candle itself (whether lit or unlit) in procession to the sanctuary is found in a number of early documents, for example the *Ordines Romani* XXVIII and XXXI (where it is lighted, though not blessed, before the procession), and in the Sacramentary of Ratoldus and the Romano-German Pontifical (where it is lighted afterwards, during the *Exsultet*).[52] However, in the two ordines the candle is lit in the sacristy and is carried in silence to the sanctuary, and in both the Sacramentary of Ratoldus and the Romano-German Pontifical it remains unlit during the procession. There is therefore no true precedent for the new rite.

One of the most controversial aspects of the 1955 reform was the reduction in the number of Old Testament readings from twelve to four. This seems to have been done for pastoral reasons; one of the major motives for the reform was to encourage the faithful to attend the Easter Vigil in large numbers, and there was a danger that they would be discouraged from doing so if it were to go on for too long.[53] The twelve readings of the Gelasian system undoubtedly took up a good deal of time, especially if they were chanted rather than recited. But, as Adrian Fortescue remarked, 'they form a wonderful account of God's dealings with his people before Christ came', and their reduction to four represents a real impoverishment in the rite.[54] There is, however, an important precedent in the four readings of the old Gregorian Sacramentary, and it was these four readings: Genesis 1:1–31, 2:1–2; Exodus 14:24–31, 15:1; Isaiah 4:1–6; and Deuteronomy 31:22–30, with their accompanying canticles and Collects, which were retained in the new system, with one very minor change – the first verse of Isaiah 4 is omitted and the reading begins with the second.

The deacon or lector, now wearing violet vestments, stands in the centre of the sanctuary, before the Paschal Candle, having the altar on his right and the nave of the church on his left. All present, including the celebrant and ministers, sit and listen to him. The custom of reading the lessons *sine titulo et Deo gratias* was preserved. A brief pause for private prayer was however introduced between the deacon's *Flectamus genua* and *Levate*, after which the celebrant chants the appropriate Collect in a ferial tone.[55]

The blessing of the font and the singing of the litanies represent a synthesis of elements taken from the thirteenth-century Pontifical of Durandus and the 1570 Missal. The litanies are sung in two parts, as in the Pontifical of Durandus. Two cantors begin the first part immediately after the end of the readings and continue down to the end of the invocation of the saints, *Omnes*

sancti et sanctae Dei, intercedite pro nobis. The blessing of the
baptismal water then follows, but in the sanctuary, not at the
baptistery or font, as in the previous rite. After being blessed
the water is carried in procession to the font, while the antiphon
Sicut cervus is sung, as in the 1570 Missal; the prayer *Omnipotens
sempiterne Deus respice propitius* is likewise said after the arrival of
the procession at the font. The second part of the litanies,
commencing with *Propitius esto*, is sung following the return of
the procession to the high altar, as in the Pontifical of Durandus,
though the new rite of the Renewal of Baptismal Promises is
inserted in between. The manner of singing the litany was also
changed. The doubling of the invocations was abolished; hence-
forth the cantors were to sing only the invocation or petition, the
people answering each one with the appropriate response (*Ora
pro nobis, Libera nos Domine*, etc.).[56]

Since the new rubric provides that the vessel containing the
water be blessed, and everything else necessary thereto, should be
set up in the centre of the sanctuary towards the Epistle side in the
sight of the faithful, and that the celebrant should stand facing the
people during the rite, with the vessel in front of him, the Paschal
Candle to his right and a subdeacon carrying the cross to his left,
it seems that the purpose of this change was to involve the people
more closely in the rite than was previously possible in the
confined space in the baptistery or around the font.[57] There is no
change in either the text of the blessing or in the ritual gestures
which accompany it. At the end of the blessing the procession is
formed and the water is solemnly carried to the font, the Paschal
Candle remaining in its place. The procession is headed by the
thurifer, followed by the cross bearer and clergy, then the deacon
carrying the vessel with the baptismal water, and finally the
celebrant. *Sicut cervus* is sung by the choir during this procession.
After the procession has arrived at the font and the baptismal
water has been poured into it, the prayer *Omnipotens sempiterne
Deus respice propitius* is sung in a ferial tone by the celebrant. The
font is incensed and the procession returns to the sanctuary in
silence.

Where the church possesses a separate baptistery, the blessing
of the water may take place, if desired, in that baptistery. In this
case the procession begins immediately after the invocation
Sancta Trinitas, unus Deus, miserere nobis. While the litany

continues in the church, one of the ministers, holding the Paschal Candle, walks at the head of the procession, followed by the cross bearer between two acolytes with lighted candles, the clergy in order of rank, and finally the celebrant and sacred ministers. During the procession *Sicut cervus* is sung and on arrival at the baptistery the prayer *Omnipotens sempiterne Deus respice propitius* is said. The blessing of the water then takes place in the baptistery, after which the procession returns to the sanctuary in silence.

In either case, between the return of the procession and the conclusion of the litany the 1955 reform inserted an entirely new rite, the Renewal of Baptismal Promises. The purpose of this new rite seems to have been twofold, to replace the actual baptisms of children or adults which by this time had fallen into virtually total abeyance, and to involve the faithful more closely in the liturgical action, particularly in its baptismal aspect.[58] To facilitate the latter, it was provided that the rite could be conducted in the vernacular instead of in Latin. The celebrant, having laid aside his violet vestments and assumed a white stole and cope, incenses the Paschal Candle, and then, facing the people, who hold their lighted candles, delivers an address of a didactic character, either from beside the Candle or from the pulpit, beginning,

> On this most sacred night, dearly beloved brethren, Holy Mother Church, recalling the death and burial of Our Lord Jesus Christ, keeps vigil by way of returning His love, and rejoices with a great joy in celebrating His glorious Resurrection. But since, as the Apostle teaches, we are buried together with Christ through baptism into death, in the same way as Christ has risen from the dead, so we too should walk in newness of life.[59]

After the conclusion of this address the same questions which the godparents (or adult neophytes) are required to answer at baptism, since at least the time of St Cyril of Jerusalem, are put to the congregation, who respond accordingly. The rite concludes with the communal recital of the *Pater Noster* and a final prayer 'May Almighty God, the Father of Our Lord Jesus Christ, Who has renewed us through water and the Holy Spirit, and Who has granted us forgiveness of our sins, preserve us by His grace in the same Christ Jesus Our Lord into life everlasting',[60] to which the people reply 'Amen', and are then sprinkled with some of the newly blessed baptismal water.[61]

The new rite provoked the most lively controversy. As an example of those who opposed it we may note the views of the distinguished liturgical scholar Dom Bernard Capelle:

> There is no need for the introduction of this innovation ... To ensure that the task of reforming the liturgy achieves its intended object, it is necessary that it be informed by the desire to return in a wise and discreet manner to its purer origins. It would therefore be highly inopportune to introduce rites which are not only not approved by long tradition, but are entirely novel. It is particularly intolerable when the liturgies into which they are introduced are the most ancient and sacred.[62]

On the other side, the Anglican scholars Roger Greenacre and Jeremy Haselock comment that,

> The Vigil from earliest times has had a strong baptismal reference, but in the conditions of the twentieth century the introduction into the rite of the solemn renewal of baptismal promises makes this unmistakably explicit, and must be counted one of the most brilliant and most profoundly pastoral of all modern liturgical innovations.[63]

After the renewal of baptismal promises, the two cantors resume the litany at *Propitius esto*. Mass begins with the *Kyrie* at the end of the litany, leaving out the psalm *Judica me Deus* and the penitential rite (previously recited in a low tone by the ministers while the choir was singing the *Kyrie*). After the *Kyrie* has been concluded, the celebrant intones the *Gloria*, the bells are rung and the statues and other images in the church, which have been covered since the beginning of Passiontide, are unveiled. Mass then proceeds as in the former rite, except that the prayer *Domine Iesu Christe qui dixisti*, associated with the kiss of peace, was suppressed, a logical change since there has never been a kiss of peace in the Vigil Mass.

In view of the change in the time of celebrating the Vigil, the abbreviated form of Vespers which followed the distribution of communion and the ablutions in the previous rite was replaced with an equally abbreviated form of Lauds. Psalm 150 (*Laudate Dominum in sanctuario eius*) was substituted for Psalm 116, the antiphon remaining *Alleluia, alleluia, alleluia*. The *capitulum*, hymn and verse are omitted, as before, and the *Magnificat* replaced with the *Benedictus*, with the antiphon *Et valde mane una sabbatorum, veniunt ad monumentum, orto iam sole, alleluia*. The concluding prayer remains *Spiritum nobis, Domine, tuae caritatis infunde* and the Vigil ends with *Dominus vobiscum, Ite missa est, alleluia, alleluia*, the silent prayer *Placeat tibi, sancta Trinitas* and the blessing. The last Gospel is no longer to be said.[64]

Notes

[1] Cf. the Decree of the Sacred Congregation of Rites dated 16 November 1955, 'sabbati sancti dies, praecoci paschali gaudio invasus, propriam indolem perdidit luctuosam memoriae dominicae sepulturae' (Schmidt, *HS*, p. 222); Letter of Innocent I to Decentius of Gubbio: 'ut traditio Ecclesiae habeat, isto biduo sacramenta penitus non celebrari' (*PL* 20, 555–556).

[2] A fact recognized in the above-mentioned decree: 'solemnes gravesque has sacri tridui liturgicas actiones a clericis peragi solere, ecclesiarum aulis saepe quasi desertis' (Schmidt, *HS*, p. 223).

[3] Decree of the SCR dated 9 Feb 1951 (ibid., pp. 211–12).

[4] *Comunicazioni intorno alla ripristinata Vigilia Pasquale*, 18 March 1951 (ibid., p. 213).

[5] Decree of the SCR dated 11 January 1952, with appended instructions (ibid., pp. 214–18).

[6] For the text of this decree and instructio, see Schmidt, *HS*, pp. 222–31. The various changes made to the Holy Week ceremonies, both to the rubrics and to the texts, between 1951 and 1955 are described in detail in pp. 3-207 of the same work. There is a very helpful table on pp. 35–56, in which the changes to texts and rubrics are set out in parallel columns.

[7] A comprehensive account of the changes, with the reasoning behind them, is contained in A. Bugnini and C. Braga, 'Ordo Hebdomae Sanctae Instauratus' (*Ephemerides Liturgicae* LXX 1956, pp. 80–222), referred to in subsequent notes as *OHS*.

[8] *OHS*, pp. 87–8.

[9] In introducing this change the commission was also influenced by a mistaken belief that red vestments were used for the procession throughout the Middle Ages (*in tota media aetate*). The sources on which they relied clearly indicate that violet was the colour used in the Roman rite, notwithstanding that red was used in some Gallican churches (*OHS*, p. 109, n.3).

[10] The reason given for this change is that, although it may be appropriate to veil the sacred images at the beginning of Passiontide, it is not proper to keep the cross veiled, since the minds and hearts of the people should be raised to Christ who was crucified for us (*OHS*, p. 113, n.15). The use of an unveiled cross in the Palm Sunday procession however does not fit comfortably with the formal unveiling of the cross on Good Friday.

[11] *OHS*, pp. 108–16.

[12] *OHS*, p. 103. The desire for strict symmetry, so far as possible, in the liturgy

and office between one day and another amounted to something of an obsession with the later post-Vatican II reformers.

13   This is the practice found in the Roman Pontifical of the Twelfth Century XXIX. 19 (Andrieu, PRM Vol. I, p. 214).

14   *OHS*, pp. 103–4, 118–19.

15   *OHS*, p. 116, n.27.

16   *OHS*, p. 120.

17   Jungmann, *MRR* Vol. II, p. 106.

18   *Rationale*, Lib. IV ix. 2.

19   *PL* 78, 1147.

20   *OHS*, pp. 104–6.

21   *OHS*, pp. 121–2.

22   Reasons for the 1955 changes: see *OHS*, pp. 125–6. Origin of the hidden candle and the strepitus: Righetti, op. cit., Vol. II.96, p. 158.

23   Thurston, op. cit., p. 271.

24   Mohlberg, 375, 377, 378 and 394 (the last from the *Missa ad vesperum*).

25   OHS, pp. 131–3, 145–8.

26   This pre-communion confession and absolution were suppressed altogether from the Ordinary of the Mass with effect from 1 January 1961 (decree of the Sacred Congregation of Rites dated 25 July 1960).

27   *OHS*, pp. 135–9, 148–9, 153–5. The reason given for the absence of the final blessing and the substitution of *Benedicamus domino* for *Ite missa est* is that on this day the people should not be dismissed, but invited to continue their devotions (p. 155, n.29).

28   *OHS*, pp. 133–5, 149–53.

29   *OHS*, pp. 139–43, 155–7.

30   *OHS*, pp. 158–9, 170–2.

31   Paris, BN Lat 14088; Cambridge, Corpus Christi Col. Cod. lat. 192 (Andrieu, *ORM* Vol. 2, p. 519). The differences between these two manuscripts are so considerable that they should probably be regarded as two separate ordines rather than different versions of the same ordo.

32   Pontifical of Durandus, Lib. III, iii. 4–7 (Andrieu, PRM Vol III, pp. 582–3).

33   *OHS*, pp. 172–3.

34   *OHS*, pp. 159–61, 173–5.

35   *OHS*, pp. 161–4, 175–9.

36   So says the rubric, though in practice the *Venite adoremus* was normally sung by the whole congregation.

37   *OHS*, p. 164.

38   *OHS*, pp. 179–80.

39   *OHS*, pp. 180–2.

40   *OHS*, p. 168.

41   *OHS*, pp. 182–3.

42   Schmidt, *HS*, p. 806; Mohlberg, 334.

43   *OHS*, p. 183.

44   The three prayers were those numbered A, B1 and C in MacGregor, op. cit., Appendix 4, pp. 457–62. Outside Rome the use of a single prayer of blessing survived in a large number of local rites; for details see Table 15 in MacGregor, op. cit., pp. 158–9.

45   *OHS*, pp. 206–7.
46   *OHS*, pp. 185–8, 208–11.
47   Pontifical of Poitiers: Martène *DAER* III, cap. XXIV, col. 434; PRG cap. xxix, 20 (Andrieu, *ORM* Vol. 5, pp. 264–73).
48   Sacramentary of Ratoldus, *PL* 78, 336. The practice of inscribing a cross and the two Greek letters is also found in the approximately contemporary Mozarabic Antiphonal of Leon (cf. MacGregor, op. cit., pp. 366–8; *OHS*, pp. 185–6).
49   Roman Pontifical of the Twelfth Century XXXII. 10 (Andrieu, *PRM* Vol. I, p. 240).
50   'Ceteroquin cerei significatio, utpote figura Christi a morte resurgentis, tunc tantum omnino plena est cum accenditur ... Salutatio "Lumen Xti" ad cereum certe directa censenda est, qui iuxta naturalem rerum ordinem medium totius actionis sacrae a novi ignis benedictione usque ad laudem cerei completam occupat' (*OHS*, p. 188). However, neither the statement of the authors that the carrying of the Paschal Candle in procession ceased because of the increase in its size, nor that the threefold candle (*trikirion*) originated in the threefold 'Lumen Xti' is correct.
51   *OHS*, pp. 188–92, 211–13.
52   *OR* XXVIII. 59 (Andrieu, *ORM* Vol. 3, p. 403); *OR* XXXI. 63 (ibid., p. 500); Sacramentary of Ratoldus, *PL* 78, 36; PRG cap. xxix 16–20 (Andrieu, *ORM* Vol. 5, pp. 267–8). For the ambiguity in the text of the PRG, see MacGregor pp. 293–5.
53   Bugnini and Braga describe the twelve readings of the Gelasian system as a truly heavy burden, especially for the less learned ('duodecim lectionum numerum vere grave pondus fuisse, praesertim pro rudioribus') (*OHS*, p. 192).
54   Introduction by Fortescue to *Holy Week* (London: Burns Oates and Washbourne, 1951, p. xxviii).
55   *OHS*, pp. 192–6, 214–15.
56   *OHS*, pp. 196, 215–18.
57   'vas aquae baptismalis benedicendae, et cetera omnia quae ad benedictionem requiruntur, praeparantur in medio chori, versus latus epistolae, in conspectu fidelium. In benedicenda aqua baptismali celebrans, stans coram populo, ante se habeat vas aquae baptismalis benedicendae, a dextris cereum benedictum, a sinistris alium subdiaconum, vel clericum, stantem cum cruce' (*OHS*, p. 216). The reason for the change must be inferred from the rubric, because Bugnini and Braga do not supply any reason for it in *OHS*.
58   'now that the principal purpose of the Lenten observance, that of leading the catechumens by means of due instruction to their baptism, is obsolete, another purpose of no less importance remains to be provided for, that of leading the faithful to a spiritual renewal' (*OHS*, p. 197).
59   'Hac sacratissima nocte, fratres carissimi, sancta Mater Ecclesia, recolens Domini nostri Jesu Christi mortem et sepulturam, eum redamando vigilat, et celebrans eiusdem gloriosam resurrectionem, laetabunda gaudet. Quoniam vero, ut docet Apostolus, consepulti sumus cum Christo per baptismum in mortem, quomodo Christus resurrexit a mortuis, ita et nos in novitate vitae oportet ambulare' (Cf. Romans 6:3–11).

60 'Et Deus omnipotens, Pater Domini nostri Jesu Christi, qui nos regeneravit ex aqua et Spiritu Sancto, quique nobis dedit remissionem peccatorum, ipse nos custodiat gratia sua in eodem Christo Jesu Domino nostro in vitam aeternam'.

61 *OHS*, pp. 197–8, 218–20.

62 Quoted in Alcuin Reid, OSB, in *The Organic Development of the Liturgy* (Farnborough: St Michael's Abbey Press, 2003), p. 163, n. 102.

63 R. Greenacre and J. Haselock, *The Sacrament of Easter* (Leominster: Gracewing, 1995), p. 9.

64 *OHS*, pp. 200–1, 220–3.

CHAPTER 11

THE 1970 REFORM

The 1955 reforms, though they introduced some profound changes in the rites, notably in the blessing of the palms on Palm Sunday and the Old Testament readings at the Easter Vigil, made few changes to the texts and rubrics, so that the character of the Holy Week services was hardly affected at all. By contrast, the 1970 changes, and the manner in which they were carried into effect in individual churches, were of such a radical nature that the services as performed today frequently bear little resemblance to the traditional ones.

The principal differences, many of which have affected the liturgy of the Roman Rite generally, are as follows:

- The change in language from Latin to the vernacular. Although the Constitution on the Sacred Liturgy of the Second Vatican Council requires the retention of Latin as the principal liturgical language of the Church,[1] it has in practice been almost entirely replaced by the vernacular in liturgical celebrations since 1970.

- The consequential change in the nature of the musical accompaniment to the rites, from the traditional plainsong and polyphonic settings of the Latin texts to a vernacular repertoire based on nineteenth- and twentieth-century hymnology.[2] Since these hymns have their own words, the result has been to import a whole new series of texts into the liturgy in place of the ancient ones, texts which vary not only from country to country but from parish to parish, depending on the tastes and preferences of the individual clergy and lay people.[3]

- The cessation of the use of the Latin language, and of the plainsong and polyphonic settings to which it had traditionally been sung, together with the growth of a neo-puritanical attitude towards ceremonial, has led to the disappearance of the sensual and dramatic aspects (frequently but erroneously attributed to the influence of the Baroque period) which had been characteristic of the Roman rite generally, and of the Holy Week liturgy in particular, a development which was not entirely unconnected with the twentieth-century vogue for minimalism in ecclesiastical architecture and church furnishings.[4] The effect has been to diminish greatly the capacity of the liturgy to express joy and sorrow, grief and exultation, which was a marked feature of the traditional liturgy, of especial significance during Holy Week and Easter.

- The general simplification of the rites, and the suppression of much of the traditional symbolism. The Constitution provided that the reformed rites should 'shine with a noble simplicity, be concise and clear' and 'should not, as a rule, require any considerable explanation'.[5] However, perhaps not entirely consistently, it also referred to the need for a proper 'liturgical education' of the faithful.[6] In practice, scant attention has been paid to the latter, preference being given to a form of liturgy which makes little or no intellectual demand on the participants.

- The reshaping of the rites in accordance with two of the characteristic guiding principles of the reform, didacticism and activism. The Constitution emphasized very strongly the necessity for active participation (*actuosa participatio*) of the faithful in the celebration of the liturgy.[7] What the authors of the document seem to have had in mind was the restoration of the notion of the Eucharist as a corporate action of the people of God, hieratically assembled, in which each part performed the functions which in history and tradition belonged to it.[8] In practice, it has been interpreted as a direction that as many as possible of the laity must be physically involved in the celebration, and has led to the wholesale transfer of functions traditionally reserved to ordained ministers, such as the reading of scriptural lessons and the distribution of Holy Communion, to the laity.

- The comprehensive revision of the texts, which has left few of the ancient texts in place. Although the Constitution had required a greater use of scripture in the liturgy generally,[9] paradoxically the practical effect of the reform on those attending the whole of the Holy Week liturgy has been to reduce significantly the amount of scripture heard.[10] This is particularly true when, as happens in many churches, the optional shorter versions of the readings are preferred. If we include Tenebrae, which has been replaced by a much shorter Office of Readings and Morning Prayer, the loss of scripture is palpable.

• The relaxation in rubrics, combined with the provision of various alternative rites (for example, in the blessing of the palms and the Veneration of the Cross), as well as a large number of options, which has led not only to considerable variations in the way the rites are celebrated in different parishes and dioceses, but even in many cases to an outburst of 'creative liturgy', in which the rites have been remodelled at a local level to reflect the personal preferences of the members of parish liturgical committees rather than the intentions of the Church.[11] These novelties have generally been defended as being 'within the spirit of Vatican II', but there is no doubt that in fact they represent a wholly unintended consequence of the reform.

Palm Sunday

Palm Sunday has been officially renamed 'Passion Sunday', the name by which the previous Sunday was formerly known. The new name has not caught on, and the day is still generally referred to, even sometimes in official publications, as 'Palm Sunday'. The liturgy begins with the assembly of the congregation, carrying their palms, preferably in a place other than the church where the Mass of the day is to be celebrated. The 1955 reform restored the participation of the faithful in the procession but only permitted the blessing of palms to take place elsewhere; the 1970 reform, rightly, recommends it. After the singing of the antiphon *Hosanna filio David* [12] (or, at option, some other suitable song), the liturgy immediately strikes the didactic note, with an address by the priest to the congregation,

Dear friends in Christ, for five weeks of Lent we have been preparing, by works of charity and self-sacrifice, for the celebration of our Lord's paschal mystery. Today we come together to begin this solemn celebration in union with the whole Church throughout the world. Christ entered in triumph into his own city, to complete his work as our Messiah, to suffer, to die and to rise again. Let us remember with devotion this entry which began his saving work and follow him with a lively faith. United with him in his suffering on the cross, may we share his resurrection and new life.[13]

The palms are then blessed with a very brief prayer (two choices are given), and they (and *ipso facto* those who are carrying them) are sprinkled with holy water, and the Gospel passage relating to Christ's triumphal entry into Jerusalem is read, from one of the three Synoptic Gospels, depending on the cycle of readings for the particular year. Following the Gospel there may be an optional homily.

Priest, ministers and people then go in procession to the church where Mass is to be celebrated. If incense is used (which is optional) the thurifer goes first, followed by the cross, unveiled and appropriately decorated, between two acolytes with candles, then the priest and finally the people, carrying their palms. Any appropriate songs may be sung during the procession and the entry into the church; the missal gives a number of possible choices, including the *Gloria Laus et Honor*, Psalms 23 and 46, and the antiphons *Pueri Hebraeorum* and *Ingrediente Domino*. In practice the *Gloria Laus et Honor*, usually in vernacular translation, seems to have remained a popular choice for the processional hymn. At no point in the rite is the traditional apotropaic function of the blessed palms mentioned.

An alternative rite is provided for cases where a procession cannot be held outside the church. A solemn entrance by the priest and ministers, with a representative group of the faithful, is made into the sanctuary from a suitable place inside the church where the blessing of palms and the reading of the Gospel has taken place. At Masses where no blessing of palms and procession or solemn entrance takes place, the priest and ministers make a simple entrance into the sanctuary while the antiphon *Ante sex dies* and Psalm 23, vv.9–10 (or another song with the same theme) are sung.

At the Mass the Collect remains the prayer *Omnipotens sempiterne Deus qui humano generi ad imitandum*, probably composed by St Leo. The first reading, added to the Mass in accordance with the introduction to the Roman rite of an additional reading taken from the Old Testament on Sundays and solemnities, is from Isaiah 50:4–7 (part of the third song of the Servant of Yahweh), which was read on Monday in the ancient liturgy. The Tract (or Responsorial Psalm as it is now known) consists of a few verses of Psalm 21, which was sung *in extenso* in the old rite. The second reading remains Philippians 2:6–11. The Gospel is the Passion narrative from one of the three Synoptic Gospels, corresponding to that read at the blessing of the palms. The reason for alternating the Synoptic narratives in this way is evidently that, since few people are able to attend Mass on Tuesday and Wednesday, they would otherwise have no opportunity to hear the accounts of Mark and Luke. The narrative of the Last Supper has very properly been restored to the Gospel reading. Unfortunately, however, the benefit of this reform has been somewhat undermined by giving permission to omit the first part of the Gospel entirely, including not only the story of the Last Supper, but also the Agony in the Garden and the trial before the Sanhedrin, and to begin it with the trial before Pilate. It is also permissible, and recommended, though not obligatory, for the Gospel to be sung or recited in the traditional manner by three ministers, one taking the part of Christ, another the part of other individuals and the third acting as the narrator. However the custom of kneeling and pausing for a short while at the point in the narrative recounting the death of Christ, which originated in ninth century Gaul and was retained in the 1955 reform, has been abolished, though it still seems to be quite widely practised.

As on every other day the Offertory verse *Improperium expectavit cor meum et miseriam*, from Psalm 68, has been suppressed and the medieval Offertory prayers replaced with modern compositions in a format based on the ancient Jewish berakah blessings. The Preface of the Holy Cross has been replaced with a new Preface of the Passion, and the prayer over the gifts (formerly the Secret) and the Postcommunion replaced with prayers whose texts are more specifically related to the theme of the Mass. The latter is followed by a blessing in tripartite form.

Tenebrae

In the 1972 reform of the breviary the office of Tenebrae was abolished and replaced with a standardized Office of Readings and Morning Prayer similar to that for other days. The ceremony of the gradual extinguishing of the lights was suppressed at the same time. The Office of Readings for the last three days of Holy Week now consists, as for all the other days of the year, of an invitatory psalm, a hymn, three more psalms, and two readings each followed by a responsory. Morning Prayer (formerly Lauds) has an invitatory psalm, a hymn, two more psalms and a canticle, a short reading followed by a responsory, the *Benedictus*, intercessions and a concluding prayer. The ancient responsories, with the musical settings composed for them, have been banished to the concert hall. The reasons for the change seem to have been twofold: one was a hope (largely unrealized in practice, sadly) that by substantially shortening the offices more of the laity could be persuaded to attend them,[14] the other an obsessive preoccupation with symmetry on the part of the post-conciliar liturgical reformers that also led them to suppress many of the very ancient practices which had survived in the Holy Week liturgy, in order to bring it more closely into line with that obtaining in the rest of the year. With particular reference to Tenebrae, J. D. Crichton (otherwise a strong supporter of the post-conciliar reform) has commented that 'the strait-jacketing of these offices has unfortunately eliminated a considerable number of ancient and important texts through which much of the message of the offices was conveyed'.[15]

However, although it was intended that Tenebrae should be entirely replaced by the new Office, it was never actually proscribed, and continued to be celebrated in a few places after 1972. It is to be hoped that following the issue of the *Motu Proprio* 'Summorum Pontificum' by Benedict XVI on 7 July 2007 this office, which exemplifies in the highest degree that noble simplicity of the Roman rite which the Fathers of the Second Vatican Council especially commended,[16] will secure once again the recognition it deserves and will be celebrated more widely.

Maundy Thursday

The Chrism Mass, which was revived in 1955 from its Gelasian source, has been almost totally rewritten,[17] and a new theme, that of the renewal of priestly commitment, incorporated. As many as possible of the diocesan priests, from different parts of the diocese, are required to assist at the Mass, which is celebrated by the bishop in the cathedral or principal church, either on Maundy Thursday morning or, if the bishop's duties preclude this time, in the morning of an earlier day in Holy Week. The priests concelebrate with their bishop and receive Holy Communion under both kinds. This represents a revival of the ancient custom of the Roman Church, in which the priests of the various *tituli* attended the midday Papal Mass at the Lateran, before returning to their own churches to celebrate the evening Mass. The practice of concelebrating on this day was, it appears, an initiative of Pope Paul VI, influenced by paragraph 41 of the Sacrosanctum Concilium.[18]

Following the homily, the priests present make a formal renewal of their commitment, in a question and answer form, with the bishop. The format appears to have been modelled on the renewal of baptismal promises from the Easter Vigil. Both these rites, as well as the novel informal ceremonies for the renewal of their vows by married couples, reflect the prevailing popularity for repeating at intervals the commitment to the service of God made at baptism, ordination or marriage, which is a development of the second half of the twentieth century. In themselves they are undoubtedly positive and beneficial; the only question is whether they ought to be grafted onto ancient liturgies to which they have hitherto been entirely foreign. It is certainly difficult to see how they can be reconciled with the directive of the Second Vatican Council that care should be taken to ensure that any new forms should grow organically from those already existing.[19] Of the two innovations there is probably a better case to be made for the renewal of baptismal promises at the Easter Vigil, since its introduction as part of the 1955 reform replaced an important feature of the liturgy, namely the baptism of adult converts, which had been lost in the course of time.

The blessing of the oils normally follows the renewal of priestly commitment immediately. Barely a trace of the ancient rite survives. The procession accompanying the oils is combined with the offertory procession. Any suitable hymn may be sung during it. The blessing of the oil of the sick may, if desired, still take place during the Eucharistic Prayer at the traditional place after the *Nobis quoque peccatoribus*, but this rarely happens since the Roman Canon (now known as Eucharistic Prayer I) has largely gone out of use. The blessing of the Oil of Catechumens follows immediately upon that of the Sick; both these oils are blessed by the bishop alone. Then the balsam is mixed with the Chrism and it is blessed by all the priests present in unison. Any vegetable oil may be used instead of olive oil, and in place of balsam any other similar aromatic substance may be employed.[20] There are no exorcisms, and the prayers of blessing are entirely new. The salutation of the oils has been abolished.

At the evening Mass the Introit *Nos autem gloriari oportet* (Gal. 6:14) may be replaced (and usually is) by a congregational hymn. The Collect *A quo et Iudas*, which was probably composed by St Leo the Great,[21] has been replaced by a modern composition of a didactic character,

> God our Father, we are gathered here to share in the supper which your only son left to his Church to reveal his love. He gave it to us when he was about to die and commanded us to celebrate it as the new and eternal sacrifice. We pray that in this Eucharist we may find the fullness of love and life.

The singing of the *Gloria* is still accompanied by the ringing of bells, though the substitution in their place of a clapper from its conclusion until the *Gloria* at the Easter Vigil has been abolished. An Old Testament reading has been added, in accordance with the usual practice on solemnities, by transferring the passage relating to the institution of the Passover (Exodus 12:1–14) from Good Friday. The New Testament reading remains that of the institution of the Eucharist from the First Letter to the Corinthians, though shortened by omitting verses 20–22 and 27–32, which include the sanction 'a person who eats and drinks without recognising the Body is eating and drinking his own condemnation'.[22]

The Gospel remains that of the washing of the feet of the apostles (John 13:1–15). It is followed by an obligatory homily, the subject matter of which should comprise the institution of the

Eucharist and of the priesthood, together with Christ's command of brotherly love. The Creed is omitted, as before.

Although the *mandatum* itself continues to be optional, it has in fact proved popular and is now performed in most churches. The move from after the end of Mass to a position immediately after the homily (permitted but not enjoined in the 1955 reform) seems entirely logical; following the recitation and explanation of Christ's command in the Gospel and the homily respectively it is carried out immediately, rather than, if at all, as something of an afterthought. It is not clear however why the antiphon *Ubi caritas et amor*, traditionally associated with the *mandatum* and particularly appropriate to it, has been transferred to the offertory procession, if there is one (it may in any case be replaced by 'another appropriate song'). The Offertory verse *Dextera Domini fecit virtutem* (Ps. 117:16–17) has been suppressed, in common with Offertory verses generally in the reformed liturgy. As on Palm Sunday, the Preface of the Holy Cross has been replaced with a new Preface specific to the day. The three ancient embolisms are still used when the Roman Canon is chosen as the Eucharistic Prayer of the Mass, which is recommended but not enjoined. The traditional practice of omitting the *Pax* has been abolished, as has the substitution of a third *miserere nobis* in place of *dona nobis pacem* at the Agnus Dei, introduced in the 1955 reform.

In the somewhat unusual circumstances that the solemn liturgy of the Passion is not going to be celebrated in the same church on the following day, no reservation of the Blessed Sacrament may take place, and there is consequently no Altar of Repose. Where, as normal, such a reservation does take place, the processional hymn *Pange lingua* may be replaced by any other suitable hymn, although it seems to be still the practice in most churches to sing it, if not in Latin at least in a vernacular translation. If the *Pange lingua* is employed the final two verses beginning *Tantum ergo* should, as previously, be sung when the procession reaches the Altar of Repose. Watching before the latter is recommended, and may continue beyond midnight, but if so it should be done with no external solemnity. The stripping of the altars which follows the Mass is carried out in silence, a reversal to the most ancient known practice. Crosses should be either removed from the church or, if they are allowed to remain, covered.

Good Friday

The liturgical colour for the day was changed from black to red; the latter colour was deemed more appropriate since this day witnessed the shedding of Christ's blood for our redemption.[23] Apart from the omission of the introductory rite, little remains of the ancient synaxis. The initial prostration has been made optional. With the exception of the Gospel reading all the texts have been changed (though the prayer *Deus qui peccati veteris* has been retained as an optional alternative to the single Collect). Following their pursuit of 'liturgical symmetry' (or 'strait-jacketing'), the reformers have replaced the second Old Testament reading with one taken from the New Testament, suppressed the second Collect, and substituted a psalm for the first responsory and an acclamation in place of the second (incidentally destroying, paradoxically, the ancient internal symmetry of Collect, reading, responsory). The result is that the first part of the Good Friday liturgy, formerly the most ancient Christian service still celebrated in the twentieth century, is now identical in form to that on every other solemnity, except for the absence of the introductory rite.

The first reading is from Isaiah 52:13 to 53:12, transferred from Wednesday, and the second from Hebrews 4:14–16; 5:7–9, which was originally read (in a more extended form) as the seventh lesson at Matins. The ancient custom of omitting the title to each reading and *Deo gratias* at the end has been abolished. A blessing is requested and given before the Gospel is read; otherwise there are no preliminaries. The ancient practice of kneeling and pausing briefly at the words *tradidit spiritum* has also been abolished, as on Palm Sunday, though it appears to continue in many places.

Although the stated intentions of the *orationes sollemnes* remain for the most part the same as before, substantial alterations have been made to the texts, and some of the prayers themselves have been comprehensively rewritten (for the first time in 1,600 years). The changes were said to have been made in the spirit of the Second Vatican Council and 'lest anyone find reason for spiritual discomfort in the prayer of the Church',[24] though some might be forgiven for thinking that they rather reflect the views of the reformers on the diminished role of the Catholic Church in the modern world, and a changed perception of its relationship to other Christian denominations and other religions or indeed to those of no religion at all.

The words *subiciens ei principatus et potestates*, deemed triumphalist, have been removed from Prayer I, notwithstanding that the phrase is taken from St Paul.[25] The references in Prayer III (for clergy and people) to the minor orders and to confessors, virgins and widows has been replaced by one to 'all those who have a special ministry in the Church'. Prayer IV (for those engaged in public affairs) has been moved to penultimate position in the series and the reference in it to 'religious integrity' altered to 'religious liberty'. Prayer VI (for the needs of the faithful) has been moved to the end of the series and shorn of its references to purging the world of its errors. Prayer VII (for the unity of the Church) has been renamed 'For the Unity of Christians' and the reference to 'heretics and schismatics' who have been 'deceived and led astray by the devil' has been changed to a reference to 'our brothers and sisters who share our faith in Christ' and 'are consecrated to you by our common baptism'. Prayers VIII (for the conversion of the Jews) and IX (for the conversion of unbelievers) have been totally rewritten, and the reference in their titles to conversion and in their texts to Our Lord Jesus Christ eliminated.

The short pause for silent prayer between the announcement of the intention of each prayer and the Collect has been retained, though the bidding of the deacon (*Flectamus genua ... Levate*) has been made optional, at the discretion of the local bishops' conference. The people may kneel or stand throughout. Extra petitions may be added to those prescribed, at the discretion of the local bishop, where there is a grave necessity for them. After the conclusion of the *orationes sollemnes* a sermon should be preached (a requirement seldom, it appears, honoured in practice).

The *Adoratio Crucis* may take place in the traditional way, with a covered cross being unveiled at the sanctuary in three stages, to the antiphon *Ecce lignum crucis* (normally in a translation into the local vernacular language); each time the clergy and people respond with a genuflection. As an alternative the celebrant may carry the cross in procession from the door of the church through the nave to the sanctuary, during which he pauses three times, singing the *Ecce lignum crucis* each time. The choice of which method to adopt should be made for pastoral reasons. In either case the cross is then placed at the entrance to the sanctuary for individual veneration by the clergy and faithful. During this time the traditional chants of *Crucem tuam adoramus*, the *Improperia* and *Trisagion* and the hymn *Pange lingua* may be sung, or any other appropriate composition. In practice the ancient chants are now normally replaced by a vernacular hymn from the modern repertory.[26] The rubrics also provide for the veneration by most of the faithful to take place in silence by a genuflection without leaving their seats, after a small number have venerated it in the traditional way; this is supposed to happen only when there is a large number of persons present in the congregation. At the end of the rite the cross is placed on the altar with the lighted candles around it.

There is no formal procession from the place of reservation; the Body of the Lord is brought back simply to the main altar, accompanied by two lighted candles, while the people stand in silence. The Communion rite itself has been reduced, as in the eighth century, to the recitation of the *Pater Noster* and the embolism (in its revised form, which omits the reference in the ancient embolism to the intercession of the saints), followed immediately by the communion of the celebrant and people. Any 'appropriate song' may be sung while the people communicate. Afterwards the liturgy concludes with two short prayers.

Notwithstanding the tendency from early times towards observing Good Friday as a separate commemoration of the Passion and Crucifixion of Christ, the liturgy of the day had never entirely lost its character as part of the celebration of the Paschal Mystery. This could be seen especially in the two Old Testament readings and in the use, as an accompaniment to the Adoration of the Cross, of the hymn *Pange lingua*, whose verses recount the history of our redemption from the fall of Adam to the Resurrection.[27] But the replacement of the readings in question with those from Isaiah and Hebrews, and the general substitution for the *Pange lingua* of modern hymns such as Isaac Watts' 'When I Survey the Wondrous Cross', have effectively deprived the Good Friday liturgy of most of its surviving Paschal character. All that is now left is the reference to the Resurrection in the two new concluding prayers.

The Easter Vigil

The clergy and people assemble in a place outside the church. As on Palm Sunday, the rite now begins with an address by the priest to the people to inform or remind them of the purpose of the celebration. The fire is then blessed, if possible outside the church, with a shortened version of the prayer *Deus qui per Filium tuum, angularem scilicet lapidem*, omitting the reference to Christ as the cornerstone and the production of the fire from stone, since any means of producing the fire is now permitted (in practice safety matches are normally used). As an example of liturgical pedantry this stands comparison with the reformers' similar excision of any reference to bees in the *Exsultet*, on the grounds that modern candles are not always made from beeswax. There is no incensation of the fire or sprinkling with holy water. The Paschal Candle is immediately lit from the new fire. No light other than the Paschal Candle may accompany the clergy and people in the procession from the place where it has been blessed to the altar of the church.

The preliminary blessing of the candle prescribed in the 1955 rite may be omitted entirely if desired, or replaced by some alternative rite if the local bishops' conference so decides. If it does take place, the rite of blessing the five grains of incense and inserting them in the candle is in any case optional.[28] The verse in the *Exsultet* 'O truly blessed night, which saw the ruin of the Egyptians, and the enrichment of the Hebrews, in which heavenly things are joined to earthly ones, and divine to human' has, surprisingly, been excised. It is not obvious what objection the reformers could have had to this verse.[29] Two forms of the canticle are given, a longer and a shorter one. It may be sung by someone other than a deacon, where no deacon is available, in which case the first part of the canticle is omitted, and it begins with the Eucharistic dialogue. Acclamations of the people may be inserted if the local bishops think it desirable, though there is no historical precedent for this, and in practice it seems to be rare.

Seven Old Testament lessons are included in the missal. These consist of two of those from the former rite (Genesis 1:1–2:2 and Exodus 14:15–15:1), four from the pre-1955 rite (Genesis 22:1–18, Isaiah 54:17–55:11, divided and partially expanded to form two readings, and Baruch 3:9–38) and one new to the Vigil (Ezekiel

36:16–28). Of the three canticles, sung at the Roman Vigil from before the time of St Jerome, only *Cantemus Domino* survives. The reading of all seven lessons is encouraged, though seldom realized in practice. It is enjoined that at least three ought to be read, though they may be restricted to two for serious reasons (which in practice seem to be discovered rather more frequently than one imagines was originally intended). In no circumstances, however, should the reading from Exodus 14 be omitted. As on Good Friday, the ancient practice of omitting the titles of the readings has been abolished. Each reading is now followed by a psalm, sung or recited responsorially, and a Collect. Psalm 41 with its antiphon *Sicut cervus* acts as the responsorial psalm to the seventh reading, thus severing its connection with the procession to the font, and reverting to the more ancient tradition in which it formed the conclusion to the Old Testament readings (though it is of course omitted altogether if the seventh reading is not selected).

The custom of not carrying lights at the Gospel, which is in accordance with ancient practice, has been retained. The Gospel reading itself varies according to the standard three-year cycle.

The blessing of the font, which now takes place once more in the baptistery (or at the font where there is no baptistery), together with the baptisms, if there are any, have been moved from their original place following the Old Testament readings, to the position after the Gospel. The principal reason for this innovation, which has no precedent in history or tradition, seems to have been the desire for an uninterrupted Liturgy of the Word from the Old Testament readings through to the Gospel, similar to that on other days of the year. The ancient practice of baptizing the catechumens after the readings from the Old Testament and before those from the New Testament however has an obvious symbolism of its own which the reformers evidently did not think worth retaining. The eucharistic format of the blessing has been suppressed, as have the exorcisms.[30] What remains of the lengthy Gelasian blessing has been significantly shortened, materially rearranged and partly rewritten.[31] The general aversion of the reformers to ritual gestures has led to the abolition of the traditional practices associated with the blessing, the division of the water, scattering a portion to each of the four points of the compass, breathing on the water in the form of a cross and the admixture of the holy oils, though the practice of lowering the Paschal Candle into the water, either once or three times, has been retained as an option.

One of the reasons for the substantial shortening of the blessing seems to have been the desire of the reformers to encourage a revival of the practice of baptisms at the Easter Vigil. The text of the ancient Gelasian blessing in use prior to the 1970 reform envisages that baptisms would immediately follow, and the embolism to the *Hanc igitur* of the Canon of the Mass implies that such baptisms have taken place.[32] However, the practice of baptism at the Easter Vigil had long since largely fallen into decay. Since 1970 it has enjoyed a notable revival, and baptisms, particularly of adult converts, are now common in many parish churches. Although in itself this is unquestionably a gain, one unfortunate result has been the reduction in most parish churches where baptisms take place (and even in many where they do not) of the number of Old Testament readings to only three or even two, a practice which represents a regrettable impoverishment in the Liturgy of the Word.

If there are no baptisms, there is no need to bless the font, in which case an alternative blessing of the water is supplied, and the litany may be omitted. If a litany is said, local saints, or the patron saints of those to be baptized, may be added. The former litany has been drastically shortened by omitting most of the petitions as well as many of the saints previously invoked, though on the positive side the names of some post-medieval saints have been added. The fourfold invocation of the Blessed Trinity was suppressed on the grounds that it represented a duplication of the *Kyrie*. Petitions which were not regarded by the reformers as being 'within the spirit of the Vatican Council', such as that for the humbling of the Church's enemies, were also removed. The triple invocation of Our Lady, 'Holy Mary, pray for us. Holy Mother of God, pray for us. Holy Virgin of virgins, pray for us' has been reduced to a single 'Holy Mary, Mother of God, pray for us', on the grounds that two of the former invocations are duplicates added in the tenth century (though it is not clear why 'Holy Virgin of virgins' should have been regarded as a duplication).[33] The short-lived practice of singing the litany in two parts, before and after the blessing of the font, revived in the 1955 reform, has been abolished.

The new Missal gives a choice of five different Prefaces, of which the first is the traditional one, and the others new compositions.

The embolisms in the Roman Canon, where this is said, have been retained, though another Eucharistic Prayer may be used in its place. The *Pax*, the *Agnus Dei* and a Communion verse have been added to the ancient liturgy, again it appears in consequence of the reformers' apparent aversion to asymmetry, though the Introit and the Creed are still omitted. At the Offertory the bread and wine should be offered by the newly baptized, if there are any such present. The practice of singing a shortened version of Lauds after the communion of the faithful, which constituted a most beautiful and appropriate conclusion to the liturgy of the Easter Vigil, has been abolished.

Appendix

Blessing of the Font – 1970 Missal

Deinde sacerdos benedicit aquam baptismalem, iunctis manibus dicens sequentem orationem:

Deus, qui invisibili potentia per **sacramentorum** signa **mirabilem operaris effectum**, et creaturam aquae multis modis praeparasti, ut baptismi gratiam demonstraret. Deus, **cuius Spiritus super aquas, inter ipsa mundi primordia ferebatur, ut iam tunc virtutem sanctificandi aquarum natura conciperet.** Deus, **qui regenerationis speciem in ipsa diluvione effusione signasti, ut unius eiusdem elementi mysterio et finis esset vitiis et origo virtutum.** Deus, qui Abrahae filios per Mare Rubrum sicco vestigio transire fecisti, ut plebs, a Pharaonis servitute liberata, populum baptizatorum praefiguraret. Deus, cuius Filius, in aqua **Iordanis a Ioanne baptizatus,** Sancto Spiritu est inunctus, et, in cruce pendens, **una cum sanguine** aquam **de latere suo produxit,** ac, post resurrectionem suam, discipulis iussit 'Ite **docete omnes gentes, baptizantes eos in nomine Patris, et Filii, et Spiritus Sancti'. Respice in faciem Ecclesiae tuae,** eique dignare **fontem baptismatis aperire. Sumat** haec aqua **Unigeniti tui gratiam de Spiritu Sancto,** ut homo, **ad imaginem tuam conditus,** sacramento baptismatis a **cunctis squaloribus vetustatis** ablutus, **in novam infantiam** ex aqua et Spiritu Sancto resurgere mereatur.

Et immitens, pro opportunitate, cereum paschalem in aquam semel vel ter, prosequitur: **Descendet,** quaesumus, Domine, **in hanc pleni-tudinem fontis** per Filium tuum **virtus Spiritus Sancti** [*et tenens*

cereum in aqua prosequitur] ut omnes, cum Christo consepulti per baptismum in mortem, ad vitam cum ipso resurgant. **Per Christum Dominum nostrum.**
R. **Amen.**

Then the priest blesses the baptismal water, saying the following prayer with hands joined:

O God, who by means of your invisible power generate a wonderful effect through **sacramental** signs, and have fashioned water, your handiwork, in diverse forms, that it might show forth the grace of baptism; O God, **whose Spirit at the very beginning of the world moved over the waters, so that even then the nature of water might receive the power to sanctify;** O God, **who by unleashing the deluge signified a figure of regeneration, so that the mysterious power of one and the same element might bring about both the end of vice and the beginning of virtue;** O God, who brought the sons of Abraham dry shod through the Red Sea, so that the people, freed from slavery to Pharaoh, might fore-shadow the company of the baptized; O God, whose Son, **baptized by John in** the waters of **the Jordan**, was anointed by the Holy Spirit, and, hanging on the Cross, **poured out** water **together with blood from his side,** and, after his Resurrection, commanded his disciples, **'Go forth and teach all nations, baptising them in the name of the Father, the Son and the Holy Spirit'; look upon the face of your Church**, and condescend to open the fount of baptism to her. **May** this water **receive the grace of your Only-begotten Son from the Holy Spirit,** so that man, **fashioned in your likeness,** cleansed by the sacrament of baptism **from all the filth of yesteryear,** may be worthy of rebirth **into a new infancy** through water and the Holy Spirit.

Then, if he thinks fit, he may dip the Paschal candle into the water once or three times, and proceeds: We pray thee, O Lord, **that the power of the Holy Spirit may descend** through your Son **into every drop of water in this font** [*and holding the candle in the water he proceeds*] that all those buried with Christ into death through baptism may with him rise again into life. **Through Christ our Lord. Amen.**

Note 1. CC CLXI Vol. D, pp. 505–7. Fragments of the Old Gelasian prayer preserved in the new prayer are shown in bold.
Note 2. Scriptural references: Exodus 14:16, 22, 29; Nehemiah 9:11; Romans 6:4; Colossians 2:12.

Notes

1   *SC* 36.§ 1.
2   This has taken place in spite of *SC* 116, according to which plainsong is recognized as the chant which is proper to the Roman liturgy, and which should have the chief place in liturgical functions.
3   For example, at a Chrism Mass which I attended in Westminster Cathedral, the hymn *O Redemptor sume carmen* during the procession with the oils was replaced by 'To be a pilgrim', the text of which is based on Bunyan's 'Pilgrim's Progress'. It is a fine hymn in its own right, no doubt, but its connection with the blessing of the oils on Maundy Thursday is far from obvious.
4   On this point see M. Doorly, *No Place for God, the Denial of the Transcendent in Modern Church Architecture* (San Francisco: Ignatius Press, 2007), passim.
5   *SC* 34.
6   *SC* 14, 19 and 29.
7   See especially *SC* 14.
8   According to *SC* 28, 'each participant, whether minister or simple member of the faithful, in the performance of his office, is to do all that and only that which belongs to him from the nature of things and the rules of liturgy'.
9   *SC* 35 (1).
10 For instance, only two of the four Passion narratives are now read during Holy Week, in the case of the Synoptics often in a shortened form, and although the new Missal provides for a choice of seven Old Testament readings at the Easter Vigil, only two or three are normally read in practice.
11 The aim of some of these committees, consciously or not, seems to have been to put into practice Dom Gregory Dix's dictum that, in liturgical matters, 'the people have a certain right to be vulgar' (*The Shape of the Liturgy*, London: A & C Black, 1945, p. 586).
12 See Appendix to Chapter 4 for the text of this and other antiphons.
13 English translations in this chapter are those of the International Committee on English in the Liturgy (ICEL), which have been approved by the Bishops' Conference of England and Wales and are currently (2010) in general use in the liturgy, though a new translation is due to take their place in the autumn of 2011.
14 'The fact that the Divine Office has been renewed prompts us to ask why it needed renewing. As time went on it had come less and less to fulfil the needs of the vast majority of the ordinary faithful of the Church. It was celebrated in a language they did not understand. It became the preserve of the monastic communities, of the clergy and the religious ... In this document [the Apostolic Constitution *Laudis canticum*] the Holy Father made clear that the first aim of the renewal was to ensure that the Divine Office should once again become the prayer of the *whole* church, not merely the prayer of clergy and religious' (Introduction to *Morning and Evening Prayer*, Glasgow: Collins, 1976). Notwithstanding these admirable sentiments the Divine Office, forty years after the reform, is seldom celebrated outside cathedrals and monastic houses.

15 *A New Dictionary of Liturgy and Worship*, (ed. J. G. Davies, SCM Press, 1986), under 'Tenebrae'.

16 *SC* 34.

17 Only the Secret prayer (prayer over the gifts) survives from the ancient Mass.

18 A. Bugnini, *The Reform of the Liturgy 1948–1975* (Collegeville, MN: Liturgical Press, 1990), p. 117.

19 *SC* 23.

20 Cf. Bugnini, op. cit., p. 798.

21 Though it originally belonged to the morning synaxis on Wednesday of Holy Week (Schmidt, *HS*, p. 707).

22 This omission has been much criticized, and not only by those of a traditionalist inclination. See for example Geenacre and Haselock, op. cit., p. 111.

23 There is a local precedent for this: the Good Friday colour in the Sarum Rite was red.

24 Bugnini, op. cit., p. 119. The 'spirit of Vatican II' is of course an entity which has been much invoked to justify changes for which the actual conciliar documents provide no authority.

25 'et estis in illo repleti, qui est caput omnis principatus et potestatis' (Col. 2:10), 'Et expolians principatus et potestates traduxit confidenter' (id., 2:15); 'cum evacuaverit omnem principatum et potestatem et virtutem' (1 Cor. 15:24); 'constituens ad dexteram suam in caelestibus supra omnem principatum et potestatem et virtutem' (Eph. 1:20–1); 'ut innotescat principatibus et potestatibus in caelestibus per Ecclesiam' (id., 3:10).

26 *The Holy Week Missalette* (Alcester: C. Goodliffe Neale Ltd) has 'When I survey the Wondrous Cross', 'O Sacred Head ill-used', 'O come and mourn with me awhile', 'Soul of my Saviour' and 'Jesus, grant me this I pray' as suggested alternatives to the ancient responsories and the *Pange lingua*.

27 The penultimate verse of the hymn, as it appears in the first printed missal of 1474, was 'Quem totus mundus non capit/ uno saxo clauditur/ atque morte iam perempta/ inferni claustra abigit/ sic deus trinus et unus/ die surgit tertia' (HBS, Vol. XVII, p. 173). Unhappily this verse, with its reference to the Resurrection, was omitted in subsequent missals. It was not restored in either the 1955 or the 1970 reform.

28 It is interesting to note the comment by Bugnini and Braga in connection with the 1955 reform: 'it would by no means have been acceptable to have expunged the grains of incense, in view of their ancient symbolism' ('granorum incensi expunctio, ratione habita eorum antiquae significationis, si facta fuisset, nullimodo comprobata esset') (*OHS*, p. 188). They had evidently changed their minds in the intervening fifteen years.

29 Did they think perhaps that it might be misunderstood as prophetic of the 1967 war between Israel and Egypt, then a recent occurrence?

30 Together with all of the exorcisms in the former missal.

31 See Appendix for the text of the new blessing, and the fragments of the old incorporated within it. The editors of the *Corpus Benedictionum* are strongly supportive of the new prayer, commenting, 'Cette version profondément remaniée revient à la tradition gélasienne primitive, qui ne connaissent qu' une *benedictio seu consecratio fontis*, et non une préface consécratoire, comme

dans l'Hadrianum. Elle a été allégée de ses deux exorcismes (supprimés) enrichie et sensiblement améliorée dans un sens plus clairement baptismal'.

32   'quam tibi offerimus pro his quoque quos regenerare dignatus es ex aqua et Spiritu Sancto, tribuens eis remissionem omnium peccatorum'.

33   Bugnini, op. cit., pp. 327–30.

BIBLIOGRAPHY

PRINCIPAL PRIMARY SOURCES

Sacramentaries

The Old Gelasian Sacramentary: L. C. Mohlberg, *Liber Sacramentorum Romanae Aeclesiae Ordinis Anni Circuli*, Rerum Ecclesiasticarum Documenta, Series Major Fontes iv (Herder, Rome, 1960).

The Gregorian Sacramentary: H. A. Wilson, *The Gregorian Sacramentary under Charles the Great, Edited from Three MSS of the Ninth Century*, HBS Vol. XLIX (London, 1915).

The Sacramentary of Padua: K. Mohlberg and A. Baumstark, *Die älteste erreichbare Gestalt des Liber Sacramentorum anni circuli der Römischen Kirche* (Münster, 1927).

Missale Gallicanum Vetus: *PL* 72, 354–371.

Missale Gothicum: H. Bannister, *Missale Gothicum, a Gallican Sacramentary*, HBS Vol. LII (London, 1916–1919).

Missale Bobbiense: E. A. Lowe, *The Bobbio Missal, a Gallican Massbook*, HBS Vol. LVIII (London, 1920).

The Sacramentary of Angoulême: *CC*, Series Latina Vol. CLIX C (Turnhout, 1987).

The Sacramentary of Gellone: *CC*, Series Latina Vol. CLIX A.

The Sacramentary of Autun: *CC*, Series Latina Vol. CLIX B.

The Sacramentary of St Gall: K. Mohlberg, *Das fränkische Sacramentarium Gelasianum in alamannischer Ueberlieferung*, (Münster, 1939).

The Sacramentary of Reichenau: A. Dold and A. Baumstark, *Das Palimpsestsakramentar im Codex Augiensis CXII* (Beuron-Leipzig, 1925).

The Sacramentary of Rheinau: A. Haenggi and A. Schönherr, *Sacramentarium Rhenaugiense* (Fribourg, 1970).

The Sacramentary of Prague: A. Dold, OSB, and L. Eizenhöfer,

Das Prager Sakramentar der Bibliothek Metropolitankapitels (Beuron im Hohenzollern, 1944, 1949).

The Stowe Missal: G. F. Warner, *The Stowe Missal*, HBS Vols XXXI-XXXII (London, 1906–1915).

The Sacramentary of Ratoldus: *PL* 78, 336.

The Sacramentary of St Eligius: *PL* 78, 25–240.

The Sacramentary of Leofric: F. E. Warren, *The Leofric Missal* (OUP, 1883).

The Sacramentary of Fulda: G. Richter and A. Schönfelder, *Sacramentarium Fuldense saeculi X der K.Universitätsbibliothek zu Göttingen*, HBS Vol. CI (London, 1977).

The Missal of Robert of Jumièges: H. A. Wilson, *The Missal of Robert of Jumièges*, HBS Vol. XI (London, 1896).

The Sacramentary of Ross: J. Brinktrine, *Sacramentarium Rossianum, Cod. Lat. 204* (Freiburg, 1930).

Antiphonals

The Antiphonals of Rheinau, Mont-Blandin, Compiègne, Corbis and Senlis, and the Gradual of Monza: R. Hesbert, OSB: *Antiphonale Missarum Sextuplex d'après le Graduel de Monza et les antiphonaires de Rheinau, du Mont-Blandin, de Compiègne, de Corbis et de Senlis* (Brussels, 1935).

The Antiphonary of Bangor: F. E. Warren, *The Antiphonary of Bangor*, HBS Vols IV and X (London, 1894–1895).

Evangeliaries and Lectionaries

Evangeliorum Capitulare Romanum: Th. Klauser, *Das römische Capitulare evangeliorum* (Münster, 1935).

Evangeliary of St Cuthbert: G. Morin, OSB, *Liber Comicus sive Lectionarius Missae quo Toletana ecclesia ante annos mille et ducentos utebatur* (Maredsous, 1893), pp. 426–35.

Evangeliary of Salzburg: A. Dold, OSB, *Ein Evangelien Perikopen-Fragment des Stiftes St. Peter in Salzburg*, Eph. Lit. 48 (Vatican, 1934), pp. 382–9.

The Lectionary of St Victor of Capua: G. Morin, OSB, *Liber Comicus sive Lectionarius Missae quo Toletana ecclesia ante annos mille et ducentos utebatur* (Maredsous, 1893), pp. 436–44.

The Comes Mozarabicus: J. Perez de Urbel, OSB, A. Gonzalez and

R. Zorrilla, *Liber Comicus, Edicion critica* (Madrid, 1950, 1955).

The Lectionary of Luxeuil: P. Salmon, OSB, *Le Lectionnaire de Luxeuil*, Collectanea Biblica Latina (Rome, 1944, 1953).

The Lectionary of Würzburg: G. Morin, *Le plus ancien comes ou lectionnaire de l'église Romaine*, Revue Bénédictine 27 (1910), pp. 41–74. (Also called the Comes of Würzburg.)

The Lectionary of Corbie: W. Frere, *Studies in Early Roman Liturgy, III. The Roman Epistle-Lectionary* (Alcuin Club Collections No. 32, London, 1935).

The Lectionary of Alcuin: A. Wilmart, OSB, *Le lectionnaire d'Alcuin*, Eph. Lit. LI (Vatican, 1937), pp. 136–97.

The Comes of Murbach: A. Wilmart, OSB, *Le Comes de Murbach*, Revue Bénédictine 30 (1913), pp. 25–69.

The Comes of Theotinchi: *PL* 30, 487–532.

Lectionum Capitulare Ambrosianum: P. Cagin, OSB, *Codex Sacramentorum Bergomensis* (Solesmes, 1900).

Ordines Romani – Early Medieval

Ordines Romani XI, XIII-XVII, XXIII-XXXIII: M. Andrieu, *Les Ordines Romani du Haut Moyen-Age*, Vol. 3 (Louvain, 1948–1961).

Ordines Romani – Late Medieval

Ordo Albini: P. Fabre and L. Duchesne, *Le Liber Censuum de l'Eglise Romaine* (Paris, 1910).

Ordo Ecclesiae Lateranensis (seu Bernardi): L. Fischer, *Bernhardi Cardinalis et Lateranensis Ecclesiae Prioris Ordo Officiorum Ecclesiae Lateranensis* (Munich and Freising, 1916).

Ordo Romanus x: *PL* 78, 1010–1017.

Ordo Romanus xi (seu Benedicti): *PL* 78, 1039–1042.

Ordo Romanus xii (seu Cencii): *PL* 78, 1071–1077.

Ordo Romanus xiii: *PL* 78, 1117–1119.

Ordo Romanus xiv: *PL* 78, 1205–1219.

Ordo Romanus xv: *PL* 78, 1299–1330.

Ordo Romanus xvi: *PL* 78, 1370.

Pontificals

The Pontifical of Egbert: W. Greenwell, *The Pontifical of Egbert, Archbishop of York*, Surtees Society 27 (Durham, 1853).

The Pontifical of Poitiers: Martène, *De Antiquis Ecclesiae Ritibus*, Lib. III, cap. XXIV (Antwerp, 1737).

The Pontifical of Rouen: *PL* 78, 327–331.

The Romano-German Pontifical: M. Andrieu, *Les Ordines Romani du Haut Moyen Age*, Vol. 5 (Louvain 1931).

The Pontifical of Magdalen College: H. A. Wilson, *The Magdalen College Pontifical*, HBS Vol. XXXIX (London, 1910).

The Roman Pontifical of the Twelfth Century: M. Andrieu, *Le Pontifical Romain au Moyen-Age*, Vol. I, Studi e Testi, 86–89 (Vatican, 1938–41).

The Pontifical of the Roman Curia in the Thirteenth Century: M. Andrieu, *Le Pontifical Romain au Moyen-Age*, Vol. II.

The Ordinary of the Papal Chaplains: M. Andrieu, *Le Pontifical Romain au Moyen-Age*, Vol. II, Appendix ii.

The Pontifical of Durand: M. Andrieu, *Le Pontifical Romain au Moyen-Age*, Vol. III.

The Pontificale Romanum (Venice, 1543, 1561, 1572, 1582; Rome, 1595–1596). Modern facsimile edition of the Pontifical of 1595–1596 by M. Sodi and A. M. Triacca (Vatican, 1997).

Missals

The Westminster Missal: J. Wickham Legg, *Missale ad usum Ecclesiae Westmonasteriensis*, HBS Vol. V (London, 1893).

The Sarum Missal: J. Wickham Legg, *The Sarum Missal* (OUP, 1969); F. E. Warren, *The Sarum Missal in English* (Alcuin Club Collections No.11, London, 1911).

The Franciscan Missal: No modern edition; for text, see Bodleian MS Lat. liturg. f. 26.

The Roman Missal of 1474: R. Lippe, HBS Vol. XVII (London, 1899).

Monastic Customaries

Regularis Concordia of St Dunstan: *PL* 137, 489–495.

Disciplina Farfensis et Monasterii Sancti Pauli Romae: *PL* 150, 1195–1204.

Consuetudines of Cluny: *PL* 149, 656–664.
Lanfranc, Decreta pro Ordine S. Benedicti: *PL* 150, 455–468.
Ordinale Gilbertinum: ed. R.M. Wooley, *Ordinale Gilbertinum*, HBS Vol. LIX (London, 1921).

Medieval Commentators

Drepanius Florus, De cereo paschali: *PL* 61, 1087–1088.
St Isidore of Seville, Etymologiarum: *PL* 82, 251; De ecclesiasticis officiis: *PL* 83, 763–766.
Amalarius of Metz, De ecclesiasticis officiis: *PL* 105, 1008–1058; De ordine antiphonarum: *PL* 105, 1291–1294.
Rabanus Maurus, De clericorum institutione: *PL* 107, 347–350.
Walafrid Strabo, Liber de exordiis et incrementis quarundam in observationibus ecclesiasticis rerum: ed. A. Knoepfler (Munich, 1890).
Pseudo-Alcuin, De divinis officiis: *PL* 101, 1200–1222.
John of Avranches, Liber de officiis ecclesiasticis: *PL* 147, 47–52.
Bernoldus of Bregenz, Micrologus: *PL* 151, 1015–1016.
Rupert of Deutz, De divinis officiis, Lib. V: *PL* 170, 129–174.
Honorius of Autun, Gemma animae: *PL* 172, 662–675; Sacramentarium: *PL* 172, 744–751.
Peter Abelard, Epistola x ad Bernadum Abbatem: *PL* 178, 340.
John Beleth, Rationale divinorum officiorum: *PL* 202, 95–117.
Sicardus of Cremona, Mitrale, Lib.VI: *PL* 213, 292–340.
Durandus of Mende, Rationale divinorum officiorum: ed. J. Dura (Naples, 1859).

Miscellaneous

Prudentius, Cathemerinon Liber: ed. M. P. Cunningham, CC Series Latina CXXVI, pp. 23–28.
St Jerome, Epistola xviii ad Praesidium: *PL* 30, 182–183.
St Cyril of Jerusalem, Mystical Catecheses: F. L. Cross, *Catacheses mystagogicae* (London, 1951).
The Peregrinatio Egeriae: Corpus Inscriptionum Christianorum, Vol. 175 (Turnhout, 1953ff.), English translation in *Egeria's Travels* by J. Wilkinson (Jerusalem and Warminster, 1981).
St Augustine, Epistola lv ad Inquistiones Januarii: *PL* 33, 215; Sermo ccxxxii: *PL* 39, 1108.

The Liber Pontificalis: ed. L. Duchesne (Paris, 1955–1957), English translation in *The Book of* Pontiffs by R. Davis (Liverpool University Press, 1989).

Pope Innocent I, Letter to Bishop Decentius of Gubbio: *PL* 20, 555–556.

Pope Zacharias, Epistola xiii ad Bonifacium episcopum: *PL* 89, 951–952.

Pope Leo IV, Homilia: *PL* 115, 681–682.

Ennodius of Pavia, Blessings of the Paschal Candle: *CC*, Series Latina Vol. CLXI, P1646, P1637.

Mozarabic Blessings of the Candle: *CC*, Series Latina Vol. CLXI, P766bis, P499, P1355.

Ambrosian Blessing of the Candle: *CC* Series Latina Vol. CLXI, P1159.

Beneventan Blessing of the Candle: *CC* Series Latina Vol. CLXI, P1094bis.

Oracional Visigotico: *CC*, Series Latina Vol. CLXII, 103.

St Bede, Homilia XXIII: *PL* 94, 120.

Caeremoniale Episcoporum (Rome, 1600).

Secondary Sources

M. Andrieu

   Les Ordines Romani du Haut Moyen-Age, Vols 1–3 (Louvain 1948–1961).

   Le Pontifical Romain au Moyen-Age, Vols I-III (Studi e Testi, 86–89, Vatican, 1938–41).

H. Ashworth, OSB

   Liturgical Prayers of St. Gregory (Traditio, Fordham, 1959).

A. Baumstark

   Liturgie Comparée (Chevetogne-Paris, 1953), translated as *Comparative Liturgy* (Mowbray, London, 1958).

   Der Orient und die Gesänge der Adoratio crucis (Jahrbuch für Liturgiewissenschaft 2, Munster, 1922).

   Orientalisches in den Texten der abendländischen Palmenfeir (Jahrbuch für Liturgiewissenschaft 3, Munster, 1923).

   La solemnité des palmes dans l'ancienne et la nouvelle Rome (Irenikon 13, 1936).

A. Baumstark and O. Casel
Zur Praefation der Palmenweihe (Jahrbuch für Liturgiewissenschaft 2, 1922, pp. 107–10).

G. Benoit-Castelli
Le 'Praeconium Paschale' (*Eph. Lit.* LXVII, Rome, 1953, pp. 309–34).

M. Biddle
The Tomb of Christ (Sutton, Stroud, 1999).

N. M.-D. Boulet
Le Dimanche des Rameaux (La Maison-Dieu, Nr 41, 1955, p. 22).

A. Bugnini
De Reformatione Liturgia Generale, (*Eph. Lit.* LXX, Rome, 1956, pp. 414–29).
The Reform of the Liturgy 1948–1975 (Liturgical Press, Collegeville, Minnesota, 1990).

A. Bugnini and C. Braga
Ordo Hebdomadae Sanctae Instauratus (*Eph. Lit.* LXX, Rome, 1956, pp. 81–222).

R. Cantalamessa
Easter in the Early Church (Liturgical Press, Collegeville, MN, 1993).

A. Capelle
La procession du Lumen Christi au samedi saint (Revue Bénédictine 44, 1932).
Le rite des cinq grains d'encens (Questions liturgiches et paroissales 17, 1932).
La Messe Vespérale In Caena Domini et le Vendredi Saint (*Eph. Lit.* LXX, Rome, 1956, pp. 227–35).
L'Exultet Pascal Oeuvre de Saint Ambroise (Studi e Testi 121, Vatican City, 1946, p. 219).

G. Cavallo
Rotoli Liturgici del Medioevo Meridionale (Istituto Poligrafico e Zecca dello Stato, Rome, 1994).

A. Chavasse
Le Sacramentaire Gélasien (Tournai, 1957).
A Rome, le Jeudi saint, au VIIe siècle, d'après un ancien Ordo (Revue d'histoire ecclésiastique 50, 1955, pp. 61–80).
Leçons et Oraisons des Vigiles de Pâques et de la Pentecôte dans le Sacramentaire Gélasien (*Eph. Lit.* LXIX, Rome, 1955, pp. 209–26).

Congregation for Divine Worship
Celebrating Easter (Catholic Truth Society, London, 1988).

J. D. Crichton
The Liturgy of Holy Week (Dublin, 1983).
The Lord is Risen: the Liturgy from Easter to Pentecost (Kevin Mayhew, Bury St Edmund's, 1992).

F. L. Cross
1 Peter: a Paschal Liturgy (Mowbray, London, 1954).

J. G. Davies
Holy Week: A Short History (Lutterworth, London; John Knox, Richmond, VA, 1963).

S. T. Davis, D. Kendall and G. O'Collins (eds)
The Resurrection (OUP, 1997).

L. Deiss
Early Sources of the Liturgy (G. Chapman, London, 1967).

G. L. Diekman
The Masses of Holy Week and the Easter Vigil (Longmans, Green and Co., London, New York, Toronto, 1957).

G. Dix
The Mass of the Presanctified (Church Literature Association, London, 1933).
The Shape of the Liturgy (A. & C. Black, London, 1945).

F. J. Dölger
"Lumen Christi". Untersuchungen zum abendländischen Lichtsegen (Antike und Christentum 5, Munster, 1936).
Das Karsamstags-Feuer aus der Kristall-Linse (Antike und Christentum 6, Munster, 1950).

M. Doorly
No Place for God, the Denial of the Transcendent in Modern Church Architecture (San Francisco, Ignatius Press, 2007).

B. Fischer
Ambrosius der Verfasser des österlichen Exsultet? (Archiv für Liturgiewissenschaft 2, 1952).

W. H. Frere
Studies in Early Roman Liturgy (Alcuin Club 28, 1930).

J. Gaillard
Holy Week and Easter (Liturgical Press, Collegeville, MN, 1954).

K. Gerlach
The Antenicene Pascha (Peeters, Leuven, 1998).

H. Gräf
Palmenweihe und Palmenprozession in der lateinischen Liturgie (Veröffentlichungen des Misionspriestersem St. Augustin 5, Kaldenkirchen, 1959).

R. Greenacre
The Sacrament of Easter (1st ed., Faith Press, London; Morehouse-Barlow, New York, 1965; 2nd ed. [with J. Haselock], Gracewing, Leominster, 1989).

S. G. Hall
Melito of Sardis: on Pascha and Fragments (OUP, 1979).

D. Hiley
Western Plainchant. A Handbook (OUP, 1993).

M. Huglo
L'auteur de l'Exultet pascal (Vigiliae Christianae 7, 1953, pp. 79–88).

J. A. Jungmann
The Mass of the Roman Rite (Benziger Bros. Inc., 1951).
Public Worship (Challoner, London, 1957).
Die Vorlegung der Ostervigil seit dem Christlichen Altertum (Liturgisches Jahrbuch I, 1951, pp. 48–54).

T. F. Kelly
The Exultet in South Italy (OUP, 1996).

K. Kenyon
Digging Up Jerusalem (Ernest Benn, London, 1974).

T. Klauser
A Short History of the Western Liturgy (OUP, 1979).

R. Kottje
Über die Herkunft der österlichen Feuerweihe (Trierer theologische Zeitschrift 72, 1962).

H. Lausberg
'Exsultet', etc. (Lexikon für Theologie und Kirche 3, 1959).

A. Löhr
Die Heilige Woche (Regensburg, 1957, English translation, 1958).

A. A. McArthur
The Evolution of the Christian Year (SCM Press, 1953).

D. P. McCarthy and A. Breen
The ante-Nicene Christian Pasch, De ratione paschali, The Paschal tract of Anatolius, bishop of Laodicea (Four Courts Press, Dublin, 2003).

A. J. MacGregor
Fire and Light in the Western Triduum (Alcuin Club Collections 71, Liturgical Press, Collegeville, MN, 1992).

A. G. Martimort
The Church at Prayer Vol 4: The Liturgy and Time (2nd ed., Liturgical Press, Collegeville, MN, 1986).

C. Mohrmann
Exsultent divina mysteria (Eph. Lit. LXVI, Rome, 1952, pp. 274–81).
Pascha, Passio, Transitus (Eph. Lit. LXVI, Rome, 1952, pp. 37–52).

J. Monti
The Week of Salvation (Our Sunday Visitor, Inc., Huntington, Indiana, 1993).

Oxford University Press
The Oxford Dictionary of the Christian Church (2nd ed., 1974).

E. Palazzo
A History of Liturgical Books (Liturgical Press, Collegeville, MN,1998).

J. Pinsk
Die Missa Sicca (Jahrbuch für Liturgiewissenschaft 4, 1924, p. 109).

A. Renoux
Le Codex arménien Jérusalem 121 (PO 36), (Brepols, Turnhout, 1971).

M. Righetti
Manuale di Storia Liturgica, Vol. 2 (Editrice Ancora, Milan, 1955, pp. 141– 205).

H. A. P. Schmidt
Hebdomada Sancta (Herder, Rome, 1956–1957).

M. H. Shepherd
The Paschal Liturgy and the Apocalypse (Lutterworth, London, 1960).

K. W. Stevenson
Jerusalem Revisited (Pastoral Press, Washington, DC, 1988).

A. Stewart-Sykes
The Lamb's High Feast (Brill, Leiden, 1998).

R. Taft
The Liturgy of the Hours in East and West (3rd ed., Liturgical Press, Collegeville, MN, 1993).

T. J. Talley
  The Origins of the Liturgical Year (Pueblo Books, New York, 1986).
H. Thurston
  Lent and Holy Week (Longmans Green, London, 1904).
J. W. Tyrer
  Historical Survey of Holy Week (Alcuin Club Collections 29, OUP, 1932).
J. H. Walker
  Early Franciscan Influence on Thirteenth Century Roman Liturgy (Subornost, Series 3, No. 19, 1956).
J. Wilkinson
  Egeria's Travels (1st ed., SPCK, 1971; revised edition, Jerusalem and Warminster, 1981). Latin Text in Corpus Inscriptionum Christianorum Vol. 175 (Turnhout, 1953ff.).
P. Wagner
  Origin and Development of the Forms of Liturgical Chant (London, 1907).
G. G. Willis
  The Solemn Prayers of Good Friday (Essays in Early Roman Liturgy, Alcuin Club Collections 46, SPCK, 1964).
  A History of Early Roman Liturgy (HBS, Subsidia, London, 1994).
E. J. Yarnold
  The Awe-Inspiring Rites of Initiation (St Paul Publications, Slough, 1972).
  Cyril of Jerusalem (Routledge, Abingdon, 2000).
K. Young
  The Drama of the Medieval Church (OUP, 1933).

INDEX

Gallican 50
papal 50, 51, 54
presbyteral 50–1, 52, 128, 207
see also Frankish Gelasian
    sacramentaries; Gregorian
    Sacramentary; Old Gelasian
    Sacramentary
Sacramentary of Angoulême 52,
    67, 103
  and Easter Vigil 232, 263 n.202
  and Good Friday 176, 201 n.91
  and Maundy Thursday 158, 160
    n.23, 162 n.51
Sacramentary of Autun 52, 162
    n.51, 232–3
Sacramentary of Fulda 53
  and Easter Vigil 245, 249, 255
    n.55
  and intermediate days 100, 101,
    103
  and Maundy Thursday 129
  and Palm Sunday 86
Sacramentary of Gellone 52
  and Easter Vigil 242, 263 n.195
  and Good Friday 176
  and Maundy Thursday 158, 160
    n.23, 162 n.51
  and Palm Sunday 67, 70, 72
Sacramentary of Leofric 52
Sacramentary of Padua 52
Sacramentary of Prague 70, 86,
    127, 201 n.91
Sacramentary of Ratoldus
    (Corbie) 219–20, 279, 281
Sacramentary of Reichenau 162
    n.51, 236
Sacramentary of Rheinau 52
Sacramentary of Robert of
    Jumièges *see* Missal of Robert
    of Jumièges
Sacramentary of Ross 53
Sacramentary of St Eligius 52

  and Easter Vigil 245
  and intermediate days 100, 101,
    102, 103
  and Maundy Thursday 144
  and Palm Sunday 98 n.87
Sacramentary of St Gall 52, 162
    n.51, 263 n.202
Sacred Congregation of Rites:
  and Easter Vigil 264–5
  and Maundy Thursday 286
    n.26
Salisbury, Palm Sunday
    procession 79
Sanctorale 49, 50
Sanctus, on Palm Sunday 86–7
Sarum Breviary 118
Sarum Missals:
  and Easter Vigil 210, 231, 234,
    255 n.56, 261 n.166
  and Good Friday 171, 191–2,
    198 n.39, 307 n.23
  and intermediate days 106 n.8
  and Maundy Thursday 155
  and Palm Sunday 76
Schmidt, H. A. P. 50, 62 n.13, 64
    n.50
  and Easter Vigil 228–9
  and Maundy Thursday 148, 157,
    159 n.14, 162 n.65, 166
    n.137, 167 n.148
Second Vatican Council:
  Constitution on the Sacred
    Liturgy 289–91
  liturgical reforms 47, 61 n.7, 62
    n.16, 85–6, 295, 298
  and Triduum 22
  and use of the vernacular 289,
    292, 297
Secret (*Secreta*) 18, 48, 50
  Easter Vigil 244
  Maundy Thursday 134, 272
  Monday in Holy Week 99

Lightning Source UK Ltd.
Milton Keynes UK
UKOW040132060513

210215UK00003B/3/P